The Little Wonder

The Untold Story of Alfred Shrubb
World Champion Runner

DESERT ISLAND FOOTBALL HISTORIES

The Little Wonder

THE UNTOLD STORY OF ALFRED SHRUBB
WORLD CHAMPION RUNNER

Series Editor: Clive Leatherdale

Rob Hadgraft

DESERT ISLAND BOOKS

First published in 2004
by
DESERT ISLAND BOOKS LIMITED
89 Park Street, Westcliff-on-Sea, Essex SS0 7PD
United Kingdom
www.desertislandbooks.com

© 2004 Rob Hadgraft

The right of Rob Hadgraft to be identified as author of this work has been
asserted under The Copyright Designs and Patents Act 1988

British Library Cataloguing-in-Publication Data
A catalogue record for this book is available from the British Library

ISBN 1-874287-81-3

Printed in Great Britain
by
Biddles Ltd, King's Lynn

Contents

On this turf, the remembered of running –
'The Little Wonder' – came by his name,
And now in the calm of the clubhouse
Frowns down from his old-fashioned frame.
His might, it has outlived his moustache,
For photos fade faster than fame.

(adapted from John Arlott's 'Cricket at Swansea,' c.1947)

Author's Note

When runners gather after training for a sociable beer or two, they normally talk about little else but injuries and forthcoming races. This book proves there are exceptions to that rule, for the idea to attempt a biography of Alf Shrubb was born one evening at a certain sports resort in the Canary Islands. And instead of being one of those bar-room schemes that flounders in the cold light of day, this one simply grew and grew.

The further I delved into Shrubb's fascinating life, the more I was convinced it was a tale that should be told in detail. Not only was he the greatest distance runner of his generation, he was a true adventurer, a pioneer with ideas and attitudes ahead of his time. Moreover, his story has never before been told in full. Appropriately it is published in 2004, exactly 100 years after his finest year.

The way Shrubb emerged from humble beginnings in the backwoods of rural England to become famous all over the globe is the stuff of comic books. His story is one of overnight success, heartbreak, clashes with the authorities, and the odd near-death experience for good measure. He won more than a thousand races, too.

Some of the research for this book took place in Canada, where Shrubb spent his final years, and in Australia where the narrative was actually written during a long stay. While in the southern hemisphere it seemed appropriate for me to seek out the legendary Ron Clarke, who had so much in common with Shrubb in relation to their specialist distances, their record-breaking exploits, and their tendency to attack from the front. Ron kindly agreed to write the Foreword, and it was fascinating to discover that even athletes of his calibre are filled with awe at some of Shrubb's achievements.

In Shrubb's day, all athletic performances were hand-timed and seconds broken down into fifths. For the purposes of this book, I have used 0.2 to denote one-fifth of a second, 0.4 to denote two-fifths, etc. The text is inevitably littered with Shrubb's race times and for those not familiar with such statistics, I should explain that '3:16.8', for example, denotes three minutes, sixteen and four-fifths seconds.

The book also features a number of quotes attributed to Shrubb himself. Unless stated otherwise, these are mainly taken from the mini-series of articles he wrote for the magazine *All Sports Weekly* in 1920. Occasionally, when mentioning prize money, I have attempted to give an equivalent value in modern terms. These figures were calculated via the Economic History Services method (EH.net).

Although a full list of acknowledgements and research sources appears elsewhere, I would particularly like to thank the following people for their time and assistance: Norah Allin (Shrubb's daughter), Al Storie (the 'Shrubb 8k' race director), Ron Clarke (multi world record holder), Peter Lovesey (author & athletics historian), Don Taylor (former GB 10,000 metres record holder), Keith May (Horsham Blue Star Harriers), Laurence Chandy and John De'ath (Oxford University Athletics Club), John Stanton and Mike Mendzat (Running Room, Canada), staff at the British Library (Newspaper Library), Horsham Museum, Charles Taws and colleagues (Bowmanville Museum, Ontario), Brian Comber (distant relative of Shrubb), John G Lyng (Longboat Runners, Toronto), Warren Roe (athletics historian & author), Christopher W Osland (Haileybury Heritage Museum, Ontario), P N Heidenstrom (New Zealand athletics historian), Floyd Williston (Winnipeg), Trevor Vincent (Commonwealth Games gold medallist), Tom and Val Worrell (Melbourne) and Ferdie Gilson (South London Harriers).

ROB HADGRAFT
Saffron Walden, Essex,
April 2004

Foreword by Ron Clarke

Because of the modern media's obsession with the Olympic Games, some wonderful feats in Track and Field that occurred during the early 1900s have never been awarded due acclaim, simply because the athlete concerned didn't participate in the Games.

In those early days, the Olympics were regarded more as an upper-class gathering, a rich man's folly only attended by those with the financial means to pay for expensive treks across the world to participate. Gold medallists usually came from the Universities of Oxbridge or the Ivy League in the USA, or from the Officer Corps of the various European Armies. Until the London Games of 1908, they were badly-organised affairs with athletics events sandwiched in as sideshows during World Fairs.

Alf Shrubb could not afford, nor did he have the inclination, to become an Olympian. Yet between 1901 and 1910 he was the world's greatest runner, setting new records in every distance from two miles to the one-hour run.

Rob Hadgraft's biography takes us back to those wonderful times of hansom cabs and good manners. I always had a great affinity with Shrubb from the first time I read about his exploits and his attitudes. He wasn't the world's best miler (although he was no slouch), nor did he enjoy success when he ran his two highly publicised marathons as a professional during the later part of his career. But that didn't deter him.

He delighted in the challenges of racing the best at their best event. And he loved to lead, to throw the gauntlet down and adopt the catch-me-if-you-can type of tactics that I also liked to practice. There's a great satisfaction in taking on the world in this way.

His story is a fascinating one. He was the first great international distance runner to make the long voyage to compete in Australia and New Zealand, where he was often pressed to race a mile, then four miles, and perhaps a two-mile handicap on the same day.

But the chapter I like the most is Rob's recall of the famous marathon and fifteen-mile races he tackled in America at Madison Square Garden and the New York Polo Grounds (a baseball stadium). Would you believe, he ran against the North American marathon champion, Tom Longboat, over a full 26.2 miles (42.212 km) marathon, indoors on a 176 yards, ten-laps-to-the-mile, wooden banked track in a smoke-filled arena packed with 12,000 spectators? Can you imagine this single two-man event, over 262 laps, not only creating the interest to attract a crowd of that size, but then holding every spectator spellbound for just over two and a half hours? Shrubb later commented that the only people not smoking that night were the two contestants.

In 1965 I ran at MSG too, and can testify to the great atmosphere generated by the enthusiastic crowds hanging over the old balconies – but the smoke in there was something else!

Any athlete, any fan of Track and Field, any connoisseur of the grandeur and romance of a long-forgotten society, must read these pages. I felt I was back in my youth, entranced by the adventures of 'Roy of the Rovers' and the other fictional heroes of those golden days.

Yet Alf Shrubb was real. This is a true story. He happened. How I would have loved to have been there.

RON CLARKE*
Australia's Gold Coast,
March 2004

* Born in 1937, Ron Clarke became Australia's greatest distance runner, breaking some 21 world records in a glittering career. Like Alf Shrubb, he reigned supreme at all distances between two and twelve miles and was a bold front-runner. He was the first man to run 10,000 metres in less than 28 minutes.

Note on Athletics in Shrubb's day

If Alf Shrubb were alive today he would be astonished at the changes that have taken place in athletics since his glory days in Edwardian England. In Shrubb's era, shoes were made of stiff unyielding leather, tracks had uneven cinder surfaces, and timing was done by hand. Many top runners only trained a couple of times a week and the Olympic Games was a sideshow of little real interest. And, instead of the drugs issues of today, the authorities fretted over who might be making money from a supposedly amateur sport.

Had Shrubb benefited from the trappings of modern athletics, who knows what times he might have achieved. Basic equipment that we now take for granted was then a lifetime away. Comfortable running shoes with air-cushioned soles, or clothing that wicks away moisture, were never part of Shrubb's world. Neither were running tracks with springy, perfectly level, all-weather surfaces.

Nowadays, training methods take advantage of the very latest in sport science and technology, and corporate contracts and prize money allow the top runners to train full-time. It was all very different when Shrubb first attended a Horsham Blue Star Harriers' training night in 1899, wearing his working boots.

He soon found he needed a pair of track shoes, which might be black or brown and were made of unyielding cowhide. They needed to be broken in with saddle soap and sweat, until, if a runner was lucky, the leather conformed itself to the individual shape of his foot.

A purpose-built lightweight running shoe with a rubber sole had been manufactured for those who could afford it, and this was followed by the widespread arrival of the leather-spiked running shoe. In response to demand from the top English runners, spiked lightweight shoes, allowing good grip on grass or cinders, were introduced in Bolton, Lancashire, by Joseph W Foster, who made them by hand, strictly to order. Based on cycling shoes, they had six spikes, with three grades available, and were cut low below the ankle bone, with leather uppers. These shoes were a great success and Foster's fledgling company soon acquired a distinguished international clientele – Shrubb was one of the first champions on its list of patrons. Years later the company would re-launch as Reebok.

A new product came along – known as 'plimsolls' – boasting rubber soles and canvas uppers. They seemed more comfortable, but turned out to be more suited to croquet and tennis than running. Before long, the first popular 'sneaker' – forerunner of the training shoes of today – was introduced in the USA, under the brand name 'Keds'. Again, these proved more popular among tennis players than runners.

In 1907 comfort was improved for runners by means of stitching a leather strip round the top of running shoes, which formed a collar to help reduce stretching. When a runner found shoes he liked, he preferred to have them re-soled rather than replace them with new ones. Blisters were a major hazard, so it was important that neither stitching nor spikes poked through. In the early modern marathons, runners would often endure huge discomfort, requiring a change of shoes mid-race, as was the case with Shrubb in his famous New York indoor contest of 1909.

Spikes were essential for track or cross-country, but as road marathons became more popular, some runners opted for sturdy ankle-high tennis shoes. Socks might reduce blistering in these longer races, but were rarely seen in track or cross-country. With cushioning in shoes virtually non-existent, Shrubb consistently advocated track and grass running for youngsters coming into the sport: 'Road work leads to shin soreness, to say nothing of other troubles,' he said.

In Shrubb's day, running tracks varied in size and shape, although major meetings would generally take place on a standardised 440 yards (quarter-mile) cinder track laid in an oval shape. Good examples could be found at Stamford Bridge, the home of London AC and the AAA's principal venue, and at Ibrox Park, Glasgow, scene of Shrubb's finest hour in 1904.

Many tracks around the country were of grass, often surrounding cricket pitches. Shrubb loved running on grass but would find that performances on this surface would rarely be ratified for record purposes under the AAA's strict criteria. For sprint races (e.g. the 100-yard 'dash'), lanes would be separated by a waist-high string, but this was not the case for longer races. Occasionally, banking would be found on the indoor circuits and at some outdoor tracks, including Preston Park, Brighton.

Tracks varied in distance. The celebrated Oxford University ground at Iffley Road, for example, was originally three and a bit laps to the mile (533 yards). After an earlier clay track had been prone to flooding, the university leased Iffley Road, levelled the field, and laid nine inches of burnt ballast as a foundation, adding four inches of fine cinders as the top dressing. A talented young student, Roger Bannister, was unimpressed and described it as 'like a cross-country course' and observed how runners seemed to disappear from sight around the bottom bend due to the uneven nature of the surface. Eventually the track was re-laid over 440 yards, and Bannister used it for his famously successful four-minute mile attempt in 1954.

The indoor tracks Shrubb used after turning professional usually offered smooth, even surfaces. However, they were often smaller than 440 yards, with impossibly tight bends, even when banked. In one race in the USA, Shrubb had to run fourteen laps to the mile and negotiate four ninety-degree corners. Even the famous Madison Square Garden track in New York measured just 176 yards, meaning that a marathon required 262 mind-numbing laps in an atmosphere thick with cigarette smoke.

The advantage of running on today's all-weather surfaces, compared to a cinder track, is thought to be worth at least a second per lap, perhaps even more in wet weather. In a 10,000 metres race, that equates to a minimum of 25 seconds. Cinder tracks might be raked between races, but restoring them to pristine condition was difficult, and runners often had to be wary of pot-holes.

On a positive note, most of the tracks of the 1900s were a distinct improvement on those of a few years earlier. For example, Jack White of Gateshead set a world record on a 'wretched apology' of a track at Hackney Wick in May 1863. 'The Shrubbs and Duffeys of today would turn up their noses in disgust and horror if asked to perform on anything similar,' observed one correspondent later.

Hand-held stop-watches were in common use by the time Shrubb entered the sport, but they could divide seconds only into fifths (0.2, 0.4, etc), and relied for their accuracy on the sharp reactions or otherwise of the timekeepers. To ease this problem, bigger championship races would generally call upon three timekeepers, who would put their heads together at the end and come up with a 'consensus' before announcing the 'official' finish time.

To spare the blushes of female spectators, running apparel was unrevealing in Shrubb's era. Guernseys and long drawers were fashionable in the latter part of the nineteenth century, but by Edwardian times long flapping shorts and heavy cotton shirts were permitted. Times were changing, however, and when the Americans appeared in 1903 wearing sleeveless tops, the AAA felt obliged to warn competitors about 'inappropriate' kit.

By the dawn of the twentieth century, the records set by professional runners, or 'pedestrians', were generally faster than those achieved by their amateur counterparts. Pro runners had financial incentives to run hard and their rules were 'looser'. However, as pro running began to die out and amateur athletics prospered, Shrubb led the way in blasting away many of the old marks.

The International Amateur Athletics Federation was formed to administer the sport in 1912 by a group of seventeen nations, and by the year 2000 it oversaw athletics in 207 countries. In 1921 world records were standardised and ratified: Shrubb appears in that very first official list at ten different distances: two, three, four, five, six, seven, eight, nine, ten miles and one-hour – and he was at that time 41 years old!

In Shrubb's days as national champion, the standard AAA championship races for a distance runner were over one, four and ten miles. Three, five and six-mile racing was also fairly popular, but did not carry national titles. Eventually, of course, all these would give way to the metric distances of 1,500, 5,000 and 10,000 metres, with the half-marathon's introduction accompanying the road running boom.

Most track races in Shrubb's day – outside of championship events, that is – involved handicapping. The AAA devised a system of registering performances, which allowed them to give starts to the slower runners. The aim was to create close finishes and give 'an equal chance' to all. Many times Shrubb would find himself running off 'scratch' with all his opponents setting off ahead of him.

One of Shrubb's longest-standing world records would prove to be his one-hour mark, set in 1904. In 1861 the English running scene had been shaken by a professional challenger from America, Louis Bennett, better known as 'Deerfoot'. A native-American, in modern parlance, he was a member of the Eagle tribe of the Seneca nation and his appearance caused a sensation. He ran in a beech-clout (a sort of loin-cloth), with moccasins on his feet, until asked to cover up by the genteel Brits. Deerfoot covered an extraordinary eleven miles and 970 yards in one hour, a record that was not surpassed by an amateur until Shrubb came along. One-hour track runs are rarely attempted nowadays and Ron Hill's 1968 British allcomers' record of twelve miles, 1,268 yards still stood at the time of writing.

Shrubb always believed the emerging American athletes of the 1900s were better organised and had better attitudes to training than their European counterparts: 'The US runner takes the sport more seriously and is more highly strung and sets his mind more determinedly on winning than his British counterpart'.

Shrubb also felt, curiously with hindsight, that a runner, however talented, only had the capacity to run one decent marathon in his lifetime – and even that at peril to his longevity. He would be even more convinced of this after his own failures at the 26.2-mile distance in 1909.

Foodwise, instead of the high carbohydrate and low fat intake recommended by modern nutritionists, Shrubb advocated the following daily diet: Breakfast of two boiled eggs, two cups of coffee and either a little fish or oatmeal porridge; lunch of steak, beef, or mutton with green vegetables, and strictly no potatoes, fruit milk pudding, accompanied by a glass of old ale, or Bovril, or coffee; evening meal similar to breakfast, with the addition of fruit or rhubarb. Pastry, stews or 'made dishes' should be avoided.

Shrubb was a great believer in long walks, but not of swimming or cycling for distance runners. He believed swimming 'made a man slow and stiffens his leg muscles', while cycling 'develops the wrong muscles in the legs and hampers quick movement and encourages pernickety little steps instead of a good stride.'

Bearing in mind all the changes of the past century, it is intriguing to speculate how Shrubb might have fared against the top performers of today. I fancy Shrubb's natural talent, broad-minded approach and willingness to take chances would have made him a superstar in any era.

This then, told for the first time in full, is his story.

Introduction:
Beaten by Kitty M

Alfred Shrubb emerged from the cricket pavilion into pleasant summer evening sunshine amid lusty cheers from his home-town crowd. The champion runner had not performed in Britain for many years and they were delighted to see him again. The women in the crowd clapped excitedly and the men hurled their hats into the air. Just short of his fortieth birthday, Shrubb looked as fit and trim as ever in his all-white kit as he jogged lightly around the outfield of picturesque Horsham cricket ground.

After a few minutes, a burst of polite applause greeted the arrival of his opponent. Kitty M looked in fine fettle as she too completed a gentle warm-up lap with Shrubb and the crowd looking on. Although Shrubb had regularly trounced the world's best runners during his long career, Kitty M had a distinct advantage over him on this August evening. She had four legs.

How on earth had it come to this? Alf Shrubb, for years the finest distance runner in the world, had crossed the Atlantic to perform one last time for his adoring home-town fans – but was pitted against a horse! As the Horsham Town Band struck up in the background, Shrubb must have reflected on the strange path his life had followed since he had first taken the athletics world by storm some twenty years earlier, in 1899. Barely out of his teens, he had sprung from nowhere to win international acclaim with brilliant record-breaking victories over track and country. But nowadays – kicked out of the sport by the authorities and in the twilight of his career – he was reduced to novelty races. Sometimes the opposition was not even human.

Such contests were puerile and demeaning, according to the purists at the Amateur Athletic Association. They espoused healthy competition against one's fellow man, for its own sake, untainted by monetary considerations. But, here in the summer of 1919, what choice did Shrubb now have? He either ran in bizarre sideshows like this, or he did not run at all.

The good folk of West Sussex remembered Shrubb as the classic 'local boy made good'. He was the modest little builder's labourer who had become a sporting champion virtually overnight. Now, exactly twenty years after his first competitive victory on this very field, Shrubb's career as a runner was almost over. The era of Shrubb, champion of the world, had certainly started with a bang – but was it about to end with a whimper and the clatter of hooves?

Kitty M was not Shrubb's first equine opponent. Ten years earlier he had raced trotting horses, harnessed to a buggy, in Canadian exhibition events, in return for big purses and mega-publicity. But that was across the Atlantic, where such contests were more commonplace. Professional racing ('pedestrianism') had been big business across the Atlantic for a spell and there had been little or no unease about the marriage of sport and show-business. But here in humble Horsham – where Shrubb's natural talent first flourished – all this hoop-la seemed a highly inappropriate way to end a unique career.

The omens hadn't been good for the 'homecoming' right from the start. Shrubb's arrival from Canada had been dogged by trouble and his ship, *Empress of Britain*, arrived in Glasgow from Quebec later than scheduled. During the trip, Shrubb's travelling companion Francis Nelson Smith, an experienced Canadian promoter, had called ahead to arrange the runner's activities during this 'homecoming' visit to England.

The original plan had been for Shrubb to be paraded at Horsham's Peace Carnival, celebrating the end of the 1914-1918 War. His estimated arrival time by train was announced by the local newspaper and the Town Band was booked to greet him. Nelson Smith also instigated arrangements for Shrubb to appear in the five-mile race, for which tickets would be put on sale in advance. Frustratingly, the vessel then encountered tricky weather in the Atlantic and the voyage took much longer than planned. It was soon clear that Shrubb would have to miss the Peace Carnival altogether.

A new arrival time was duly announced and the arrangements amended. But these plans also went awry as Shrubb's party eventually arrived at Horsham railway station from London several hours earlier than expected. As a result, not a soul was there to greet them and the famous runner had to make his way unheralded to his hotel, through quiet and near-empty streets. Embarrassingly, communications had 'miscarried', reported *The West Sussex County Times* later that week. The paper tried to make amends for the unfortunate mix-up by giving generous pre-publicity to Shrubb's forthcoming race. The contest would take place, it said, after Shrubb had settled in at his hotel and completed three weeks of special training. Tickets were already selling well for the event.

Shrubb enjoyed the next three weeks, meeting up with old friends and reacquainting himself with all his old familiar running and walking routes. He trained diligently, keen to give his old friends and admirers something to remember him by, for he knew this would probably be his last serious race. Race day, Saturday, August 19th, 1919, duly arrived and the normally tranquil cricket meadow at Horsham, one of the prettiest grounds in all of southern England, was soon abuzz with anticipation.

By early evening, the traditional cricket sounds of leather on willow had been replaced by the excited chatter of 2,300 townsfolk. They had paid one shilling each (8d for children) to see the local-boy-made-good perform one more time. Everyone was happy to see Shrubb back on his old stamping ground and tickets to watch him had sold briskly. Nearly a quarter of the town's population had turned out to see him.

At 7.15pm, Shrubb suddenly emerged from the pavilion into the hazy sunshine. All eyes were on the trim little figure in white as he went through his warm-up routine. Kitty M was manoeuvred to the start-line, where she stood patiently.

Nelson Smith had set up the five-mile contest (25 laps of the cricket field) against the six-year-old trotting horse, who would draw 22 stones (i.e. driver Collins and passenger Blackiston) on a buggy. The rules of the race stated that Kitty M would only be allowed to trot and, if she broke into a gallop, would have to be recalled to cover the distance again at a trot. Driver Collins was forbidden to use his whip and Shrubb would occupy the favoured inside lane. The cricket field was fenced in for the occasion, all spectators having to produce their ticket to gain admission. The proceedings would be recorded 'by a man making moving pictures', said *The West Sussex County Times*, referring to Nelson Smith and his bulky cine-camera equipment.

The weather was ideal and when race officials Juckes, Hancock and Baker had established order, the race was set underway at 7.31pm. Shrubb, as always, shot off from the gun and established an early lead on the first of the 350-yard laps. Kitty M started slowly, but settled into an easy rhythm and by the middle of the second lap had drawn level. Then, steadily, the horse and buggy inched ahead and after a mile Shrubb was labouring forty yards behind and looking uncharacteristically anxious. Kitty M was trotting effortlessly with driver Collins expending little energy. It became clear well before the halfway point that Shrubb's only hope of victory lay in the horse experiencing some sort of trouble.

The runner's first mile had been a respectable 5:05, but he gradually slowed as the race wore on. Kitty M's first two miles were both timed at under five minutes and her pace remained more even than Shrubb's. Just after halfway, the tiring Shrubb had the unfamiliar experience of being lapped and Kitty M continued to increase her lead. This was clearly an embarrassing mis-match, and the sense of disappointment in the crowd was palpable. To muted cheers the horse crossed the finish line in 26:01, with Shrubb still needing to complete almost two laps. At that point the crowd swarmed onto the course, but Shrubb gamely ploughed through them to the finish, crossing the line more than two minutes down in 28:08. Not only had he been well beaten, but his time was disappointing, for he had covered the same distance significantly quicker in Newfoundland just a month earlier.

He received a generous ovation and plenty of hearty back-slapping, but there was no denying the sense of anticlimax that hung in the air. The spectators soon turned their attentions to the nearby dancing ring and coconut shies. Sadly, Shrubb had not been able to give them a farewell victory to remember. Not even a close finish. His spectacular triumphs of the past would have to remain distant memories.

Amid the anticlimax of his last two solo laps on this rural cricket field, a sporting era had come to an end. It is indeed a poignant moment when an elite performer arrives at that defining moment: the point when they know their time is over.

CHAPTER ONE

'Something out of the common'

The 1870s was a tough decade for those working on the land in southern England. The nation was gripped by a major agricultural depression, exacerbated by a succession of wet summers and falling produce prices. There was little Government help for rural communities whose arable farms were hit by bad harvests on account of unusually high rainfall between 1875 and 1879.

Life was not easy for William Shrubb, a West Sussex farm worker and his wife Harriet. The arrival of their fifth child – Alfred, on December 12th, 1879 – meant another mouth to feed and an even greater need for secure employment. Eventually the situation forced William to turn to the building trade in order to feed and clothe his young family. After marrying Harriet Dench, a girl from the neighbouring county of Surrey, William had put down roots in the pretty mediaeval village of Slinfold, but after the birth of Alfred, and then a fourth daughter, Ada, he decided the family must move. They left their tiny home in The Battles, just down the road from the Slinfold village inn, into bigger accommodation in Trafalgar Road in nearby Horsham, where work as a builder's jobber was easier to come by.

Horsham was relatively prosperous, with its brewing, coach-making and milling industries booming. Although dozens working in the tanning trade had recently lost their jobs, it was generally a lively and vibrant market town, whose population was growing fast due to the influx of rural families like the Shrubbs. Around the time of William Shrubb's birth in 1840, Horsham had around 5,000 residents, but that figure had doubled by the time the Shrubb family arrived towards the end of the 1800s.

To cope with its expansion, Horsham was connected to Brighton by railway, a Corn Exchange was constructed, where grain could be bought and sold, a water company provided piped water to those who could pay, and sewers were dug. The first hospital opened in 1892 and all this modernisation was a far cry from the town's early unwelcome reputation for horrors such as wife-selling and 'criminal pressing'.

Half a century earlier, in 1844, a woman by the name of Ann Holland had fetched thirty shillings at Horsham market, when a fellow called Johnson sold his watch for the money to buy her. It was thought to be the last time a wife was openly traded in a British market-place. In the late eighteenth century Horsham had dealt with those refusing to plead at criminal trials by 'pressing' them. Ever greater weights would be placed on a wooden board across the torso to extract a plea. Otherwise, the victim might be pressed to death. But all that was in the past. By the time the Shrubbs arrived, Horsham was a much more welcoming place.

There was work locally for the likes of William Shrubb, particularly when the famous 350-year-old Christ's Hospital School announced plans to move to West Sussex from the City of London. The school purchased 1,027 acres at Stammerham, just south of Horsham, for £47,500 and when building commenced in 1894 vacancies were created for builders and tradesmen of all types. Many locals were involved as the huge school took shape, its tower visible for miles around, ready to cast a shadow over generations of boys beneath, wearing the unique Tudor-style uniform that earned them the nickname The Blue Coat Boys.

Although his older brother, Albert, found a job as a grocer's carman, young Alfred followed his father into the building trade. He started out as an apprentice carpenter at the Christ's Hospital construction site in the mid-1890s. His earnings supplemented the household income and life became a little more comfortable for the Shrubbs, particularly as elder sisters Mary-Ann, Kit and Emily had by now apparently left home to make their way in the world.

On leaving school, Alfred was still a small, thin lad, barely above five feet, but he loved the outdoor life and his lack of height and weight disguised a surprising level of fitness and stamina. As well as learning the skills of a chippie, he ended up doing his fair share of fetching and carrying on the construction site. His wiry frame wasn't ideal for the heavier work, but he coped as well as most of the bigger lads. It could be back-breaking work, as he would recall: 'Carrying bricks up a 30-rung ladder for a labourer's wages, I used to have as many pains in my back and legs as if I had been beaten with staves.' It could be hazardous work, too. A fellow teenage labourer called Seth Evans plunged from scaffolding and died from head and neck injuries.

The school took eight years to construct (1894-1902), for many of which Shrubb was employed there. He would usually run back and forth from his home three miles away. His fellow labourers must have thought him mad, for they had found easier ways to get to work, such as bicycles. There were times – particularly during and after downpours – when the foreman had to lay off young labourers for a day or two. Whenever this happened to Shrubb, he would head into Horsham to earn a few pennies by holding farmers' horses, while their owners went about their business in the town. He loved horses and apparently found this an enjoyable way to spend a day.

Alfred Shrubb was clearly a naturally fit young man, who found hot-footing across the countryside an exhilarating experience. But it had never dawned on him that he had a special talent for running. He had often gone on solo boyhood sorties in pursuit of the Crawley and Horsham Foxhounds. The hunts would meet at Slinfold station or at The Lodge, and he would take off with the pack, often faring better than the hounds over the subsequent couple of hours. A protracted chase came naturally and easily to him. He would go on 'very long draws', many of which would see the hounds exhausted long before he was.

He loved nature and all kinds of animals. He would have enjoyed the occasion when a magnificent stag was chased across the building site where he worked, although the beast was later caught by the Surrey Stag hounds. There was also the strange case of the six-legged cat that became well-known in the area, after being featured in *The West Sussex County Times*. Mr J Miller, of Worthing Road, Horsham, confirmed he'd become the proud possessor of a sandy kitten with four hind legs.

Shrubb felt at home out in the fields. Some years later sportswriters would be enraptured by the sight of him pounding the countryside at speed. *C.B. Fry's Magazine* would eulogise: 'On he plods, never varying his pace, occasionally glancing round – from curiosity, not apprehension – on, on, at the same gait to the end. He is happy even over ploughland. In all the chief cross-country races he has had to travel over ploughed fields, but while his opponents have toiled through the holding earth, Shrubb runs so lightly that he travels over it, skimming it like a bird, and with such grace and ease ...' And Shrubb himself would say: 'Of all the forms of pedestrianism, and indeed, of all branches of athletics, there can be nothing superior to cross-country running for either pleasure or health.'

Shrubb's fondness for chasing foxes, and running to and from his workplace, were not traits picked up from relatives or friends. He would recall: 'No member of my family had shown any ability as a runner and therefore I had to make discoveries for myself. Of course, I had run races at school treats for knives and other prizes that boys value, winning more than my share; but nobody went into raptures over me as a flier – which I never was – and not having run any long races at that time, whatever staying powers I possessed had not made themselves apparent.'

Being something of a restless spirit, Shrubb was easily diverted from his career path in carpentry. He left home for the first time and ultimately spent three of his teenage years working as a 'house-boy' for wealthy Bognor Regis farmer John Harrison. During this period he lodged at High House, Aldwick, with a carter named Finch. One Saturday night, Alf stuck up a conversation outside High House with a local butcher's driver called Charlie Tews, who challenged him to a foot race. The loser was to hand over a 'prize' of two shillings. Shrubb recalled that the cheeky Charlie seemed to fancy himself, but proved to have more bark than bite. They removed their hats and coats, gave them to Finch to hold, and then clattered down a nearby country lane in the pitch black. They reached the agreed turn-round point after a mile and a half, with Shrubb leading by 150 yards, increasing this by another 100 on the return journey. Stunned by the margin of his defeat, Tews is reported to have said: 'You ain't no common runner Alf. If I could run like you it ain't no farmer's boy that I'd be.'

Shrubb had by now passed his eighteenth birthday, and outrunning the butcher's boy gave him his first inkling that he possessed some talent. He had enjoyed the experience, particularly as it had earned him two shillings. This small episode was a hint of things to come, but the night that would prove the real turning point in Shrubb's life would arrive around a year later, after he had left his house-boy job to return to the building trade in Horsham.

The warm evening in question was in June of 1899. The dusky calm was rudely shattered by the clanging of the town fire-bell. Although about to turn in for the night, Shrubb couldn't resist a stroll into the road outside to take a look. As was often the case, the sound of the bell had prompted a few locals to scurry off towards the volunteer fire brigade's HQ to see what was happening. Shrubb recognised one of the passing figures as skinny-framed Fred Spencer, a tailor's cutter a year older than he. Spencer was a near-neighbour and well-known in the town as captain of the local athletics club, the Blue Star Harriers. Spencer yelled over his shoulder that a huge fire was raging in nearby Southwater, and he was off to race the fire-wagon to the scene. Would Shrubb care to join him?

Shrubb was up for the challenge, particularly when he saw an unnatural glow in the night sky, which suggested this was a really spectacular fire. Although it was almost 11pm, this sort of excitement was rare in Horsham. Shrubb, still wearing his heavy working boots, eased his wiry frame into a trot alongside the taller figure of Spencer.

News of the fire had reached the Horsham volunteer firemen by the usual route – delivery of a telegram. The heavy, horse-drawn wagon began its laborious journey through the bumpy lanes towards the red glow in the southern sky. Spencer and Shrubb soon overtook the other youngsters who had joined the chase, some of them on dilapidated bicycles. Picking their own route across moonlit fields, the pair galloped along at a fair clip, and Shrubb, glad to be out in the evening air, noticed he had no trouble keeping up with the celebrated runner alongside him. On they went, over gentle, wooded hills and meadow, past isolated farms and manor houses and down the Pedlar's Way bridlepath.

For Spencer, this was just another training run, but for Shrubb the adrenaline was pumping just like it had when he raced Charlie Tews for two bob. Spencer was surprised to find he was having to work hard to keep pace with the little fellow. Standing 5ft 6in and weighing less than nine stone (126lbs), Shrubb looked barely strong enough to open a barn door, let alone skim across rough terrain in working boots like this. The pair were comfortably keeping pace with the fire wagon, trundling along an adjacent lane, followed by the motley group of young thrill-seekers.

After covering three miles in around twenty minutes, Shrubb, Spencer and the fire-wagon arrived at the scene more or less simultaneously, to find a haystack ablaze on the edge of Southwater village. The flames were quickly damped down to a heap of smouldering hay by Captain Moses Brooks and his brave band of men, a unit that had been set up to protect the Horsham area some fifty years earlier. Captain Brooks was ably assisted by Lieutenant Penfold and former captain Fred Sendall.

This haystack fire was merely the latest in a series of call-outs – 1899 was proving one of their busiest years. In recent weeks they'd dealt with a fire at the Denne Park laundry, farm fires at Faygate, Rusper and Rowhook, a blaze in West Parade in the middle of Horsham, plus a mill fire at Loxwood. Occasionally these enthusiastic part-timers unwittingly created vignettes worthy of the Keystone Cops. On his way to the West Parade incident, for example, fireman Rowland badly hurt his thumb when his helmet unexpectedly fell off and caused him to part company with his bicycle. Nine times in 1899 the full complement of fire-fighters were called into action, complete with wagon, with other smaller fires that year being dealt with by smaller groups.

Tonight's haystack fire proved a disappointing spectacle for the posse of wagon-chasers, but the noisy bunch from Horsham, including Spencer and Shrubb, stayed to socialise with the Southwater locals until about two in the morning. In the dead of night, Shrubb and Spencer then ran back along the same route by which they'd come, jogging easily in the refreshing air. Spencer was enormously impressed by his new-found running partner. He told him he had the makings of a fine athlete and urged him to join the Blue Star Harriers without further ado.

Spencer realised he had found a raw talent who would be a real asset to his club. Before returning to his home in nearby Kempshott Road, he insisted that Alf come along to the Harriers' weekly club night at the Bell Inn, opposite Horsham Park. Shrubb agreed, and by the time they parted his head was full of thoughts about becoming a competitive athlete.

To ensure Shrubb's enthusiasm didn't cool, Spencer returned the next morning. He found his protégé stiff in his legs from the previous night's exertions, a problem Spencer addressed with a quick rub-down. Shrubb recalled: 'Acting on [Spencer's] advice, the Blue Star Harriers next week included me in their pack and in an appearance at a Thursday night road run. I was very nervous and not at all anxious to beat my mates.'

Gathering in their headquarters, The Bell, after this and subsequent group runs, Shrubb's clubmates expressed surprise and delight over his effortless running. Most new-boys would start by jogging along tentatively at the back of group training runs, but greenhorn Shrubb already looked good enough to threaten even Spencer's status as the brightest of the Blue Stars. They puzzled over Shrubb's running style, which didn't seem particularly graceful or sleek. His strides looked unusually small, yet brisk, and he generated surprising speed with an economical shuffle. He presented a slight figure whose upper body appeared to contribute very little to his progress. His new pals were quick to initiate him into the fold by including him in peripheral club events, such as soccer and cricket matches. In one game against a team called CETS, Shrubb was Blue Stars' top performer, taking six wickets for 21 runs and top-scoring with the bat.

Shrubb's first taste of competitive athletics appears to have been at the Horsham Cycling Club's first evening race-meeting that summer of 1899. The opening foot race was a handicap event over 440 yards and novice Shrubb was given a ten-yard start. Wearing the Blue Star colours for the first time, he found the single-lap journey far too short for his stamina-based talents and he finished out of the placings. Next up was a light-hearted event for the womenfolk, in which competitors had to transport an egg and spoon to the finish, while carrying a sun shade *en route*. Later in the evening Shrubb was entered for the 'one mile' and given fifty yards by the handicapper. He raced away hard from the start and did not flag at all, passing the last opponent who'd begun ahead of him on the final lap. It would be the first of countless comprehensive victories over the next twenty years or so. The Harriers mob were jubilant and the rest of the onlookers stunned by what they had witnesed.

The acclaim boosted Shrubb's confidence ahead of a bigger event, a fortnight later. The August Bank Holiday Annual Sports was hosted by Horsham Amateur Athletic Club at the town's picturesque cricket field, and featured running and cycle races. The occasion was the prelude to the town's popular carnival procession. The Band of the 2nd Battalion, the Prince Of Wales' Own West Yorkshire Regiment provided the music and a sizeable crowd relaxed in the sunshine. The 880 yards handicap on this afternoon can be regarded as Shrubb's first major race. He was in a field of nineteen runners and his status as a 'beginner' saw him given a 55-yard start by the handicapper. Again, the distance was too short to demonstrate his staying power and he failed to make an impact. The race was overshadowed by controversy involving Shrubb's mentor, Fred Spencer. Leading the race, Spencer, for reasons best known to himself, suddenly slowed to a gentle lope and appeared to be escorting a runner from Horsham YMCA by the name of Cramp. Spencer pulled up before the finish line, allowing Cramp to win, then marched off the track. Sections of the crowd jeered at what looked like a blatant piece of 'fixing', and it led to the prizes being withheld. The facts were later reported to the Southern Counties AAA officials. It all seemed a poor example for the skipper to be setting a young newcomer like Alfred Shrubb.

Like Horsham, the nearby town of Crawley also staged an annual August sports day, and this set the scene for Shrubb's first taste of victory outside his home town. Although not attuned to two-lap running, Alf swept to the £1 10s first prize in the 880 yards at Crawley off a 26-yard start. Word spread around Sussex that the Blue Star Harriers had uncovered a promising youngster, who had coped well in his first races, despite his talents being clearly suited to longer distances and his need to get to grips with tactical running.

Shrubb's teammates and club officials had enjoyed the sight of their untamed youth tearing away from the opposition, and looked forward to his next appearance – a September half-mile inter-club contest between Blue Star and the local YMCA. Shrubb duly notched an emphatic win in two minutes 13.4 seconds. This was a highly respectable time, considering the conditions and his lack of experience.

With the coming of autumn, the cross-country season commenced, but Shrubb was unable to demonstrate his natural talent for off-road running as Blue Star didn't compete in this branch of athletics at the time. It was frustrating for Shrubb, but he looked forward to the road racing season that would start in January 1900. An influenza epidemic raged across England – fifty people were reportedly dying each day at one point – but Shrubb was fit and well and ready for a crack at his club's three-mile championship handicap. He was afforded the respect of being asked to run off scratch, and cruised home in a time of 15:55. The sight of him coming in first, some twenty yards ahead of club captain Spencer, signalled the start of a new era at Blue Star. A novice had trounced the club's star runner: The king is dead, long live the king!

To prove that this was no flash in the pan, Shrubb needed to repeat the outcome the following month, when Spencer defended his title as the club's four-mile champion. This time Shrubb outpaced the holder by a full 35 seconds, and his superb time of 21:30 lowered the all-time club record by an astonishing eighty seconds and won him a gold medal. He'd simply blasted out from the start and never let up. No fuss, no tactical running, no problem. Despite his defeat, Spencer had also broken the old record, but didn't appear to mind being dethroned in this fashion, and took great delight in the performances of the young man he'd 'discovered' and helped train.

Shrubb was in red-hot form and the established runners of Sussex could be grateful that Blue Star and their new discovery wouldn't be participating in the county cross-country championships at Bexhill-on-Sea shortly afterwards. Bexhill, an ancient resort fast gaining a reputation as a playground for the aristocracy, wouldn't have long to wait, however, before the little bricklayer came to town to show his worth to a wider audience. Spring was in the air when the 1900 Sussex four-mile championship was held there, presenting Shrubb with his biggest stage yet. It would prove to be a red-letter day.

After his systematic double-destruction of Spencer in club races, Blue Star gleefully entered Shrubb's name to face the cream of southern England in Bexhill's attractive Egerton Park. Spencer was convinced the new boy would triumph, and assisted his preparations by putting him through a series of evening time-trials along the Sussex lanes at distances between two and four miles. Race-day was a chilly Easter Monday that nevertheless saw crowds of holiday-makers descend on Bexhill for an event billed as 'an athletics meeting, cycle parade and fete', hosted by the local Hare & Hounds Athletic Club. Entry into the park was sixpence and thousands flocked in, despite strong westerly winds and overcast skies. Many came from neighbouring towns and from 'up country', having taken advantage of special cheap rail fares.

Easter presented the opportunity for working folk to get away for some bracing sea air and lively entertainment, but on this day the weather threatened to spoil the fun. At one point a deluge provoked a stampede for shelter. The event was preceded by the Bexhill town band, who marched ahead of a fancy-dress parade on bicycles. Biggest cheers were reserved for Miss Moore, dressed as an Indian, and Mr Godfrey – a patriotic 'Tommy' – who won prizes for their costumes. Despite the angry skies, the park presented a colourful sight as Shrubb, relishing the occasion, wandered around, nervously studying the heavy grass running track. It would be a hectic afternoon, for he was down to compete in three events – the three-mile team race, the Sussex county four miles championship, and a one-mile handicap.

The serious competition commenced with the team race, in which Blue Star quietly fancied their chances against the established big-name South London club, Herne Hill Harriers. The opposition had never heard of young Alf Shrubb, but that was about to change. With Spencer not far behind him, Shrubb shot away at the gun and soon built a substantial lead. Home supporters groaned when Bexhill's star performer, Maples, pulled up with an injury. Shrubb never faltered, and to general astonishment began lapping tail-enders, who found themselves struggling on the tacky surface, and then lapping everyone else too. Horsham supporters in the big crowd led the cheering and Shrubb felt on top of the world as he completed lap after lap in relentless style. He stormed home, having opened a huge lead of almost two laps – remarkable in a three-mile race – to great applause. His time, 15:57.2, saw him way ahead of second-placed Spencer, but their combined efforts ensured a memorable team win for Blue Star.

The crowd buzzed and chattered excitedly about the next big race – the county four-mile championship. Reigning champion A E Hutchings had been teased by Spencer that Blue Star had a new young runner who would depose him, but Hutchings laughed it off as light-hearted banter. He wasn't quite so confident now, after seeing what had happened in the team race. For his part, inspired by the brash confidence and reassuring words of Spencer, Shrubb found his nerves dissipating and didn't seem concerned about the limited recovery time between the two races. The taste of victory banished any fatigue.

Once again Shrubb and Spencer raced off hard from the start and established an early lead. Experienced Hutchings tucked in behind them, but after just one mile suddenly decided he'd had enough. He stepped off the track and conceded his crown, complaining of a stitch. After this dramatic development, the race turned into a procession and the result was never in doubt. Shrubb pulled clear of his teammate and came home alone in seemingly effortless style. Once again the crowd roared its approval. The joy of victory and the adulation from a big crowd were new sensations for Shrubb. He'd found his vocation.

Shrubb allowed himself an easy ride in his third and final race of the day – a one-mile handicap. A 'tea and coffee service' crockery was on offer to the winner, but even with a 120-yard start, he couldn't rise to the occasion for a third time. Nevertheless, it had been an extraordinary day and such was Shrubb's excitement that he probably hardly noticed when the organisers reluctantly announced that the evening fete was abandoned because of the cold weather. He still had one duty left, however, and that was to step forward from the crowd gathered beside a nearby swimming pool to accept the spoils of victory. The glittering prizes stood on a wooden table and were presented by the smartly-dressed Mrs Sinnott, wife of event referee Thomas S Sinnott. She handed Shrubb a splendid silver cup and a gold medal for becoming Sussex County Champion.

Little did Shrubb know it, but the khaki-blazered figure of Mr Sinnott was already making plans for the next vital stage of Shrubb's running career. The well-known official had been astonished by the size of Shrubb's victories and decided that he must capture this young man for his own club, the bigger and more famous South London Harriers (SLH). Sinnott was a resourceful and powerful man on the athletics scene and knew raw talent like this didn't come along too often. Runners were not permitted to transfer to new clubs overnight, so Sinnott was content to bide his time and find out more about little Shrubb. Equally excited about Shrubb's emergence that day was Harry Andrews, a running coach, who was another well-known figure in athletics circles. He would later recall: 'Shrubb was then a little black-nobbed fellow who ran like a startled deer and I told Mr Sinnott, whose club he eventually joined, he was something out of the common.'

For the time being, though, Shrubb remained a proud member of the Horsham club and his teammates showered him with praise and playful attention. Three days after the Bexhill triumphs came the Blue Stars' sixth annual 'smoking concert and prize-giving' at The Bell. This time the club really did have something to celebrate. The amazing triumphs of their newest member dominated proceedings and Shrubb had to step forward to receive a number of trophies, including the club's own one-mile steeplechase cup, an 'alarum clock' for winning its three-mile handicap, a gold medal for winning its four-mile handicap, and a teapot and cruet set for taking the five-mile handicap title (erstwhile champion Spencer had to settle for a biscuit barrel for coming second).

The night turned into a riotous occasion, with lusty renditions of songs like 'Lulu', 'Fred Archer' and 'Soldier and a Man', ringing out into the Park Street night, accompanied by piano. A toast to Shrubb's health was formally proposed, followed by the inevitable 'For He's A Jolly Good Fellow'. Shrubb's moustache bristled with pleasure as the throng was told how the club had staged 23 runs over the past year and new-boy Shrubb seemed to have won them all. They'd found a runner of truly exceptional ability and were all agreed that the future looked bright for the Blue Star Harriers.

CHAPTER TWO

Shrubb and the Legendary Princess

With the approach of summer 1900, the minds of several of Britain's top distance runners turned to the newly revived Olympic Games. After their successful re-introduction in Athens four years earlier, Paris got the vote as the 1900 hosts. The proud Greeks had wanted to stage all future Olympiads, but the impact of the Cretan revolt and subsequent Greek-Turkish war put them out of contention for 1900. The French authorities arranged for the various competitions to be spread across the five-month staging of the World's Fair, gracing the city from May to October. More than 1,200 sportsmen and women took part over this period, but as most returned home as soon as their event was concluded, the intended Olympic spirit of togetherness was conspicuously absent. The impact of these Games worldwide was negligible and the French were later criticised for poor management.

Twenty-year-old Alf Shrubb was not a nationally known runner by the time the Olympics commenced in May, so was never a contender for participation, although later that year he would fare well against at least four British runners who had returned with medals from France. For the moment, he had domestic matters on his mind. Following Shrubb's shock win at Bexhill in April, the vanquished county champion, A E Hutchings, had challenged him to a re-match over one mile in June. Although thirsting for revenge, Hutchings had been magnanimous in his praise when issuing this challenge: 'You have opened the eyes of all Sussex, Shrubb, and I think you will open a good many more eyes before long,' he reportedly told the younger man. 'Nobody ever heard of you before and I think you're the first novice to come out on any ground and run two such fine races. You have beaten me in the Four Miles championship but I am sure I shall beat you in the One Mile.'

And so it proved. At Eastbourne Rovers' race meeting in Devonshire Park, Hutchings summoned up all his experience and, in a dramatic finish, pipped Shrubb by barely a yard in 4:32.6 to become county mile champion.

By now, Shrubb had agreed with South London Harriers (SLH) officials Thomas Sinnott and Gordon Innes that he would join their club, on condition that he could remain on Horsham Blue Stars' books on a 'second claim' basis. This meant he could represent either outfit, as long as they weren't performing in the same competition. Sinnott and Innes had talked up SLH as offering the only way Shrubb could pit himself against England's best, and the only way to taste top cross-country action, two things Shrubb couldn't achieve at the homely but humble Blue Star club. SLH had been formed back in 1871 and its membership largely comprised men from the professional classes, mostly in banking or insurance, but the committee raised no objection to accepting working-class Shrubb because of his outstanding potential. Sinnott and Innes showered praise on him, calling him 'The Little Wonder'. This soubriquet would subsequently stick, and resurface many times in later press reports.

Shrubb was content to continue in Blue Star colours throughout the summer, as he was not scheduled to make his debut for his new club until later in 1900. He recalled this as a pivotal time in his career: 'It now dawned on me that I should have to take on all-comers anywhere and everywhere, as local talent fell short of giving me anything like strenuous struggles. I had hardly yet acquainted myself with the names of great long-distance runners who I was destined to see for the first time, standing there on the scratch mark beside me!'

Despite his lack of big-race experience, Shrubb's name was put forward for the Amateur Athletic Association's (AAA) national championships at Stamford Bridge in July. By now, everyone associated with him concurred that he was more of a distance man than a miler, although Shrubb himself still fancied his chances over the classic mile distance. Blue Star captain Spencer ensured Shrubb was entered for the four-mile race, where he would meet reigning champion Charlie Bennett of Poole, and other experienced men like Jack Rimmer of Liverpool and Sid Robinson of Northampton. A number of competitors from the USA, Canada, India and Australia had converged on Europe for the Paris Olympics, and took the opportunity to cross the Channel and take part in the AAA's 36th championships. Among them were American sprinters Alvin Kraenzlein, Walter Tewkesbury and Stanley Rowley, who would claim no fewer than twelve medals between them in Paris. This influx of foreign stars led *The Sporting Life* to herald the Stamford Bridge event as '… the most important athletic meeting ever held in this country, or anywhere else for that matter.' Guest American athletes would subsequently win eight of the thirteen events.

A bumper crowd of 7,000 gathered for what was Shrubb's first taste of a major championship. Clerk of the course was his new mentor Thomas Sinnott. It proved a chilly and gusty day, with the strong winds preventing any record-breaking, but the international element ensured a fascinating day's athletics. During his nervous preparation for the four miles, Shrubb was advised by more than one associate that he must run carefully in the early stages and stay with his men, saving himself for a fast finish. By inclination a fast starter, Shrubb didn't like the sound of this, but acquiesced in view of his status as a relative novice. It was a serious-looking Shrubb at the start-line, jogging uneasily on the spot, preparing to pit his wits against Rimmer, Bennett and Robinson, the trio who would make a clean sweep of the medals in the 4,000 metres steeplechase at the Paris Olympics. When the race got underway at 4.40pm, the wind had rendered conditions particularly tricky. First to show was Bennett, but Shrubb had forced his way to the front by the end of the first 440-yard lap in a time of 68 seconds. The Horsham 'unknown' still had his nose in front at the end of the second lap (2:21) but – inhibited by the advice he'd been given – kept himself in check and suppressed the urge to open up a bigger lead.

On the third lap, the lean frame of Rimmer, many people's favourite to win, took the lead and Shrubb obediently fell in behind for the next mile or so. The two-mile mark and halfway point was reached in 9:51. Rimmer allowed Shrubb a brief period in the lead around this point but then forced his way past again, quickly opening up a ten-yard gap. The northerner looked strong and never relinquished the lead again. They passed through three miles with Rimmer timed at 16:16 and at this point Shrubb, wishing he'd gone quicker earlier, couldn't prevent Bennett also going past him. The order was unchanged until the finish, with Rimmer winning in 20:11, some 100 yards and thirteen seconds ahead of Bennett, and Shrubb a battling third in 20:29. These three were in a class of their own, leaving in their wake the remaining twelve runners, many of whom were lapped by the leading trio. Shrubb finished 32 seconds ahead of fourth-placed Fred Appleby.

Many were quick to congratulate Shrubb on finishing third in his first national championship, and he was hailed in the press as a highly promising newcomer, but deep down he knew he could have done better. His mistake had been to run too conservatively early on. In future, he vowed to himself, he would run his own race and ignore well-meaning advice that was inappropriate to his particular talents. Failing to forge an early lead in a race, for whatever reason, always filled Shrubb with dread. Leading was the only way he could run freely and with a clear mind. He openly admitted that this hatred of being hemmed in might be attributable to 'nervousness in my composition'. He would later confess: 'The presence of runners near me always worried me. I resented their attentions as if they had no right to get so close. And every opportunity to widen the distance between competitors and myself at any stage of the race was readily taken.'

It had been an awe-inspiring day in south-west London for Shrubb, and most of it had passed in a blur of excitement and colour. After his race he surveyed the Stamford Bridge ground and marvelled at how far he had come in just a few months as a competitive athlete. A year earlier he'd been just another builders' labourer, never dreaming of performing in front of thousands of people. He felt privileged to be here at the headquarters of the London Athletic Club, the capital's biggest and best, with a huge membership and a reputation for high standards. The stadium, opposite Chelsea railway station on the West London Extension, boasted one of the country's best tracks of four laps to the mile, and a well-appointed pavilion and dressing rooms. Although Crystal Palace was then London's top stadium, Stamford Bridge was nevertheless a very special venue and this taste of the big-time made Shrubb hungry for more. He vowed to return to this place and give his friends and supporters a victory to celebrate.

A swift opportunity to return to winning ways presented itself the following weekend, when Shrubb and Spencer took part in the nineteenth annual Essex athletics and cycling championships at Chelmsford cricket ground, widely regarded as one of the most prestigious meetings in the UK. In their sights was the new fifty-guinea Atalanta Cup, which would go to the winner of the three-mile race, in addition to a £10 gold watch. Spencer was realistic about his own chances in this event, but had a fancy that his young colleague could upset the apple cart and win. This confidence was boosted further by the news that Sid Robinson, Olympic medallist and English ten-mile steeplechase champion, had dropped out of the seventeen-strong starting line-up.

The Essex officials certainly knew how to stage a day of sports. The main streets and train station were decorated with flags of all nations and bunting, and the railway arch in New Street was bedecked by a huge 'welcome' banner. Flowers and flags adorned the cricket ground itself and the racing track was lined with Venetian masts, which supported lines of flags. A 'grand illuminated fairy fete' would take place after the races in the Bishop of Colchester's charming adjacent grounds, in addition to a grand fireworks display and a 'Baden Baden' concert. The Countess of Warwick, a native of Essex, was here to present prizes, accompanied by her husband the Earl, and Lord Brooke, the latter having recently returned to Warwick Castle from service in the Boer War. This aristocratic trio were hosted by General Sir William Gatacre KCB, the Essex Athletic Association's president, and arrived by a special train, which departed from Liverpool Street at 2.32pm. They were met by a four-in-hand carriage which processed through Chelmsford to the cricket ground. On the way, the crowds cheered to greet the VIPs and cries of 'bravo Gatacre' were directed at the club president.

There was a vast array of other dignitaries at the ground to watch proceedings, including Spanish grandees Prince Leopold and Princess Marie de Croy-Solre, who belonged to the party hosted by local businessman James Paxman JP. The special guests would be wined and dined at the Shire Hall at the end of the sports, before returning for the concert and fireworks. The fine weather ensured a healthy crowd, many of whom arrived by train, taking advantage of cut-price fares for the day from Colchester, Maldon and Liverpool Street. The gates opened at lunchtime and admission was one shilling, with places in the reserved enclosure, stand and promenades two shillings extra. Despite the counter-attraction of the Olympics in Paris, there was a strong field of athletes, and interest was particularly high in two brand new events – a 100 yards flat race and the three-mile Atalanta Cup.

The top athletics officials from the south of England had been appointed to ensure fair play, and they were soon called upon when the mile event was hit by controversy. Around thirty competitors registered for the race and some, having been informed there would be an interval, left the arena to rest in the athletes changing tent. Unfortunately, nobody had told the race starter, who eagerly fired his pistol to set off those runners still gathered on the start line. The sound of the gun's retort sparked a stampede of angry non-starters to race from the tent. According to the *Essex Weekly News*, they 'grumbled loudly and demanded to be refunded expenses' because they'd missed their race. These complaints were considered by the officials, but no action taken and the result stood. This shambles no doubt helped Shrubb's Horsham teammate J Sturt to finish fifth, with J Henderson of Beccles College winning in 4:25.2.

Shrubb, suffering his usual pre-race nerves, was glad when his three-mile race got underway, and took off very smartly, forging a substantial early lead. He cut such a fast early pace that a world record on grass looked possible. He steadied past the halfway mark, however, and won at a canter, breasting the tape in 15:05.6, with the nearest opponent – R Wellin of Essex Beagles – 150 yards adrift. C Pearce of Birchfield Harriers came in third and Horsham's Spencer sixth. The VIPs were mightily impressed with Shrubb, after Gatacre leaned over to explain to them that he was a comparative novice.

A platform was erected in front of the grandstand to stage the prize-giving and the Countess handed over the spoils of victory. Gatacre said a few words and the Countess responded: 'As on the occasion of the Olympian Games of old, what is called the "superior sex" is in force [laughter] and we women are here to admire you, and look on and stimulate you for fresh exercises for other years. It is only at these gatherings at Chelmsford that we see sport of this kind – which beats all other kinds in the country.' Shrubb proudly stepped up to accept the huge Atalanta trophy and his gold watch, delighted with such a reward for what had been, frankly, a fairly comfortable afternoon's work. It was his first victory outside of his home county and his fame was beginning to spread.

On the train home to Sussex, Shrubb and Spencer marvelled at the huge piece of silverware. As Greek mythology is unlikely to have been on the curriculum in nineteenth century village schools, the two lads probably hadn't the faintest clue over the identity of Princess Atalanta, or why she should have a trophy in her name. According to legend, Atalanta had been the swiftest runner around, and had vowed not to marry unless she found a man who could outrun her. Shrubb's trophy bore a reproduction of a painting representing the legend by English classicist Sir Edward Poynter, President of the Royal Academy. Commissioned years earlier by Lord Wharncliffe to hang in his billiard room at Wortley Hall, near Sheffield, the painting had been lost when the building became dilapidated in the late nineteenth century. The work now enjoyed a new lease of life in the unlikely form of an athletics trophy, put up for the Essex three-mile race as a perpetual prize by the county association's art-loving vice-president J H A Marshall.

Upon his return to Horsham, Shrubb was astonished to be greeted at the railway station by a number of friends and supporters who'd heard news of his victory at Chelmsford. He was carried shoulder high down North Street like a returning hero, all the way to the Blue Star club's headquarters in Park Street. Impromptu speeches were made to the gathered townsfolk, and one official took the opportunity to convey his annoyance that Shrubb had still not received the Sussex championship cup he'd won at Bexhill earlier in the year, nor had the medals won by him and Spencer yet come to hand. Cries of 'shame' greeted this news of the Bexhill people's tardiness.

The weekend following his Chelmsford triumph, Shrubb participated in a novelty race at Horsham Cycling Club, in which competitors had to walk, cycle and run over a pre-determined course. This early incarnation of the sport of triathlon was not something anyone took too seriously, and Shrubb came in second. Enjoying his new status as the town's star sporting performer, he was more interested in preparing himself for the annual jamboree that was the Horsham AAC sports and carnival day. Sadly, wretched Bank Holiday weather greeted the large crowds who arrived in the town by train for this August event. Many decided not to head for the cricket field where the sports would be held, instead seeking out a sheltered vantage point for the carnival procession. The gales and rain represented the worst weather experienced in the 29 years of this Horsham institution.

Very few were in attendance when the sports began at lunchtime, but thereafter spectators arrived in dribs and drabs, shielded by umbrellas and waterproofs. The band of the Royal Military College, Sandhurst, was invited along to perform, but the conditions forced them to spend much of the afternoon sheltering in the refreshment tent, which was efficiently operated by the Willison sisters. The band decided to strike up a tune from inside the tent, but before long a pole snapped in the wind and half the marquee collapsed on their heads. Nobody was seriously hurt and the bandsmen wisely adjourned to the main cricket pavilion and abandoned the greater part of their proposed programme of music. The gale succeeded in overturning the cricket club's sightscreen next to the pavilion, mowing down barriers, and flooding the ground's entrance area. During the cycle races the wind deposited many riders on their backsides. One brave competitor was sympathetically given a special prize after he came crashing down just feet from the finish, when leading his race by a big margin.

In these circumstances, running would be difficult, but Shrubb was determined to put on a show for the friends, family and townsfolk who'd supported him so well in his short career thus far. He battled through the gales to win the mile in 5:52.2, which looks a very modest time on paper, but was achieved in the face of howling winds. At about 4.30pm the sun finally emerged, but by then the sports programme was virtually over. In the 880 yards handicap, a distance Shrubb didn't usually enjoy, he was given the stiffest handicap and had to concede first place to F Austin in a tight finish. *The West Sussex County Times* reported that Shrubb had proved 'highly popular with the spectators and ran in pretty style'.

The summer athletics season drew to its close, and in the same week that a new product called Coca-Cola was launched in the USA, Shrubb officially signed up with SLH, with his home-town club retaining his 'second claim' registration. His new club was based at the Swan and Sugar Loaf Inn in South Croydon, which was run by Mr John Brown, a leading sportsman in the area. Each winter, SLH hosted and took part in many cross-country events, Shrubb's favourite form of running, and this would expose him to the higher level of competition his talent obviously demanded. SLH employed the services of renowned coach Harry Andrews, who immediately began to pay close attention to the new recruit. Plans were made for Andrews to spend a few weeks in Horsham during the winter to give Shrubb an intensive programme of training prior to the big cross-country fixtures in early 1901.

Beforehand, in early September 1900, SLH hosted its autumn meeting at Kennington Oval, a major event on the athletics calendar and one that traditionally drew large crowds. On this day 4,000 turned out, no doubt encouraged by the reduced admission prices of sixpence and balmy weather. This was also the first opportunity that a full complement of SLH officials and members had to see their new colleague, Shrubb, in action at close quarters. He took his place in a strong field for the three-mile invitation handicap, billed as the feature race of the day. The Metropolitan Police band entertained the crowd and guest of honour was Sir Robert Mowbray, MP for Brixton, who presented prizes. The grass track on this fine day would have been a little slower than a well-prepared cinder track, but Shrubb was in the mood to impress and eager to record a time of under fifteen minutes. He shot off keenly and within three-quarters of a mile had passed the runners in front who'd been given more generous starts by the handicapper. He romped home in a fine 14:38.4, breasting the tape sixty yards clear of experienced Fred Appleby of Herne Hill Harriers. The Manchester-based *Athletic News* reacted to Shrubb's victory enthusiastically: 'There can be no doubt whatever that a future champion has been discovered in this Sussex youngster. He has little or no style and as yet runs extremely green, but, as Americans say, he gets there with both feet.'

A week later Shrubb was performing back in Horsham for the local club, winning the mile race in an inter-club affair against the YMCA. His next big date was back at Stamford Bridge on September 29th, when he tackled a two-mile race, but was disappointed to dead-heat for second place, with Appleby winning in 9:23 and gaining some measure of revenge for his recent drubbing at The Oval by Shrubb.

Since the idea of joining SLH had first been mooted, months earlier, Shrubb had looked forward to the cross-country action that Blue Star had been unable to provide. His first attempt at competitive 'paper-chasing' was awaited with interest, and on November 3rd in South Croydon he did not disappoint. Over a five-mile course he captured his club's Gibb Cup and achieved his Honours badge. The cup, named after James Gibb, the man who introduced 'ping-pong' into the UK, represented the start of a long unbeaten run over the 'country' for Shrubb. Talented paper-chasers H P Jones and J H Bessell were startled as he ran clear with great authority and came home in 28:15 to win by about 400 yards. Another leading performer, C E Haydon, was unable to compete that day, but most observers agreed he wouldn't have overhauled the lively Shrubb anyway.

Three weeks later Shrubb lined up against the Oxford University Athletic Club's cross-country team in a challenge match, and showed the posh-spoken students a clean pair of heels to lead his club to an emphatic victory.

Having already claimed possession of the Gibb Cup for twelve months, in December Shrubb switched his attentions to his club's Brown Cup, another five-mile romp over the country. Shrubb duly won by beating celebrated veteran Herbert Heath, having chosen to run in a more even-paced manner than usual. In a few short weeks Shrubb had made a name for himself as an outstanding performer over the country, in addition to his excellent early track exploits. As 1900 drew to a close, his delighted friends at SLH began preparations for their 'Little Wonder' to make an assault on the really big prizes.

CHAPTER THREE

Champion of All England

Young Alfred Shrubb confirmed his dramatic progress as a novice athlete by putting in some impressive cross-country performances during the winter of 1900-01. His new-found admirers loved his buccaneering running on the track, but were now seeing him in an environment where he felt more in tune – running free and battling against Mother Nature's elements.

Cross-country was still a relatively young sport at the time, for it was barely thirty years since official recognition had been granted to administrative bodies to run the event in each of the four home nations. It was a very British pursuit, which began in earnest following the first official race, the English championship in Epping Forest in 1876. The new sport was often referred to as 'paper chasing' because a paper trail would be laid to indicate the direction of the course. It soon caught on in France, and the first international match took place in 1898 when the French challenged the English to an eight-a-side contest near Paris, the visitors filling the first eight places.

Having won the South London Harriers' Gibb and Norton trophies before Christmas, Shrubb now took the early steps towards becoming cross-country's first superstar. Throughout his career he would declare his love for this branch of running: 'Race or road running is apt to grow monotonous, however exciting it may be, but there is nothing monotonous in an open cross country run.'

Shrubb's views reinforced the generally held view among aficionados that cross-country could boast a purity and integrity that was not evident in other sports. Lapping a measured track seemed 'artificial' in comparison. Furthermore, at the English Cross-Country Union dinner in early 1901 the point was forcibly made: 'No sport is cleaner from the professional element than cross-country running.'

SLH craved the prestige of having a national cross-country champion within their ranks and could see they had a serious candidate in Shrubb. Taking no chances, in early 1901 club officials sent renowned coach Harry Andrews to stay in Horsham for three weeks to prepare Shrubb for the prestigious Southern Championships in March and then the Nationals a week later. It was felt that if Andrews could smooth out a few of Shrubb's rough edges and pass on some of his wisdom, then surely Shrubb would carry SLH to honour and glory in his first season.

The coach, who would later write a number of training books, was devoted to his calling. He had been inspired to train others after spending many childhood hours watching his father supervise the Elborough club's 440-yard runners in south-west London. Andrews Junior became an innovative trainer, who would win praise for his work in the developing field of sports massage. Andrews declared: 'Every other aspect of training is of inferior importance to massage – the rubbing, pinching, and stroking of an athlete's flesh and muscle – but of course massage of these tissues on scientific lines.' He insisted that embrocations were of great benefit when rubbing an athlete, and prepared his own concoctions with secret recipes. He preferred oil embrocations in winter, liniment in warm weather, and believed massage by hand was superior to the glove-rubbing often practiced at that time. These gloves were coarse, sometimes covered with horsehair, and Andrews was critical of practitioners who thought the art of massage was simply a good, hard rub down, the harder the better. He also believed, curiously, in an age limit for masseurs – thinking that men over forty would lose their powers 'by beginning to attract rather than radiate vitality'. According to his theory, an older masseur would actually drain energy from the athlete.

Andrews advocated lots of walking, plenty of rest and the avoidance of tobacco and alcohol. He even banned his athletes from eating bacon, potatoes and new bread. He is also reported to have poured champagne over an athlete's head during a twelve-hour race in a bid to revive him. The results of this particular 'treatment' are unknown. His book *Massage and Training* would be published a few years later by Health & Strength of London, part of a series by this publisher that included *The Fresh Air Book*, *Simple Dumb-Bell Exercises* and the Uncle Bob's self-help books on knock-knees and bowed legs, care of hair, and hollow necks.

Andrews described his mission to Horsham to work with Shrubb for the readers of *Athletic Field and Swimming News*: 'The first thing I did was give [Shrubb] a good dose of medicine. I give the same to every athlete when I start training him. First a little salt and senna leaves and then a little ginger and Spanish liquorice. It is the finest medicine I have ever struck and does not purge a man too much. I have known trainers to give a man stuff that has purged his inside out – a great mistake. The first week's work consisted of walking. We used to do 15-20 miles a day. I remember we often used to meet the local doctor, who was interested in running. Once or twice during that first week he called me aside and told me I was killing Shrubb, giving him too much work to do. I did not take much notice of him however and the results proved I was right. In those days Shrubb did his work well. He would do anything I told him to do.'

The good doctor needn't have worried about Shrubb being damaged by Andrews' regime, for the 21-year-old was clearly in great shape, as he proved when he won his club's Nicholson Cup cross-country event at Croydon. He covered a strength-sapping ten-mile course in 62:08 to record another easy win against his clubmates and maintain his 100 per cent record over the country. The race was run in appallingly heavy conditions following a recent thaw. Could he reproduce this fine running against the big guns though?

During the week in which Shrubb began his intensive training under Andrews, Horsham was identified in the local press as a 'very healthy place'. The Medical Officer of Health, Dr Kelly, noted that not a single one of the town's 10,000 residents died from a notifiable disease during 1900. Horsham's death rate of 14.9 per thousand was less than the national average of seventeen. Old age and influenza were responsible for the few deaths that did occur, said the report. No sooner had the locals digested this good news than bulletins arrived from London that Queen Victoria had died on January 22nd after a short illness, at the age of 81. The grim news was posted in the Carfax in the centre of town, leading to the cancellation of a night of variety entertainment at the King's Head. The town band emerged to play the Dead March in Saul, and a muffled peal was heard from the parish church bells. Sports fixtures scheduled for later in the week were also cancelled and the town dutifully adopted an appropriate air of mourning.

Nevertheless, Shrubb's training moved into full swing, and Andrews recalled: 'By the second week I started giving him running exercises round the local football field and the way he ran startled even me. So to get a real idea of how he was running I took him down to the old cinder track at Preston Park, near Brighton. The track was very loose and heavy and there were so many poles at the side that he had to run wide but he ran four miles in eight seconds outside the record time, despite the awful track. That was enough to convince me what I had already thought was true, and I wired up to the SLH that he would beat any man in the world.'

Shrubb and his coach needed to amend their schedules when his first big date, the Southern cross-country championships at Wembley Park, was put back a week to February 23rd, partly because the nation was still mourning the death of the Queen, and partly due to a severe frost that would have made the going hazardous. The decision was taken at short notice after two officials walked the course, one of them being Thomas Sinnott, Shrubb's mentor at SLH, who was also secretary of the Southern Counties Association. The athletics press reported that Shrubb, the young pretender to the crown, was attracting much attention in the build up, some of the speculation being 'of a monetary nature', meaning he was well backed by gamblers. One correspondent declared: 'Shrubb is held in the highest esteem despite his lack of experience. No man has carried off the Southern in his first try, much less in his first season! If he can do it, he's a veritable wonder.'

Around 200 runners lined up at Wembley Park – the cream of southern England's seventeen top clubs. Shrubb's main opposition would surely come from the highly regarded Pearce, Pratt, Clark and Biss. A fellow SLH man – Foreman – had won the very first Southern at Hendon in 1884 and by coincidence his death was announced just 24 hours before this year's event. Today's ten-mile route would take the runners around the back of Wembley's Variety Hall, past the grandstand, round the Park, along the railway line and into open country and back, this circuit to be completed three times. The course was generally in good condition, although heavy in parts.

The race set off at 3.33pm and Shrubb, anxious not to get trapped in a pack of runners, tried to blast his way to the front. It took longer than he'd hoped, not because of any lack of speed or intent, but due to the congestion and difficulty in finding passing places. Eventually an opening or two presented itself, and Shrubb nipped through the gaps like an eel, emerging alongside early leader George Pearce of Essex Beagles. They ran together for a spell, but on arriving at a long stretch of plough a delighted Shrubb knew this was his moment. 'I had been resting a little till then, preparing for a good scamper,' he recalled. 'Much to Pearce's surprise, as he admitted afterwards, I ran that field almost as if it had been a grass path.' From here on in, there was only one winner.

Shrubb had built an emphatic 100 yards lead by the start of the last circuit and finished the race in 56:39.8, looking comparatively fresh and a good 150 yards ahead of runner-up W J Clark of Essex Beagles (57:03). There was another huge gap until third-placed P Biss of Highgate Harriers (57:34) came in. One correspondent suggested the overall standard of competition had been disappointing, describing this, the first title in the first year of the new king's reign, as a 'hollow victory' which Shrubb won 'without turning a hair'. After his struggles to reach the front in the early stages, Shrubb would surely have disagreed with that verdict.

After the finish, Shrubb was given a great ovation as he made his way to the changing rooms. The celebrations capped a fine day out for the SLH mob, who arrived and departed as a group along with John Brown's smart coach and horses from their HQ, the Croydon Swan and Sugar Loaf. They all made a great fuss of Shrubb, and he received a second reception on his return home to Horsham. A large crowd, along with the town band, went to meet him on the 8.40pm train from London and carried him in triumph though the town to the Anchor Hotel, where he'd been staying with coach Andrews. Shrubb gave a brief speech, saying how pleased he was that Horsham people had taken such an interest in the race. Privately he must have been relieved to find his Horsham associates were not losing interest in him, now that his first allegiance was to SLH.

Alf Shrubb was now Champion of the South. The next task, seven days hence, was to try and become Champion of All England. Andrews believed he could do it, the SLH officials believed he could do it, but others weren't so sure. *Athletic News* hedged its bets, saying that for Shrubb to win both Southern and National titles in his first season would be an achievement without parallel.

The 25th National cross-country championships were staged at Leicester racecourse, just outside the town at Oadby. The course again extended just over ten miles, involving three miles of plough with some stiff jumps and obstacles. Spectators could watch from the grandstand and special trains were laid on to arrive at the two stations nearby in good time for the 3.30pm start. The Irish champions, Cork City, had promised to send a strong team and the Northern England champion Jack Rimmer would, like Shrubb, be making his National debut. Title-holder Charles Bennett would not be competing because of a lumbago attack, and Sid Robinson had cried off with a bad cold. *The Sporting Life* had earlier tipped Robinson to win, on account of his superior experience, sensing that Shrubb might be tired from his efforts at Wembley.

The start-line was positioned on the flat opposite the gate leading to the paddock, giving a long straight stretch in front of the traditional wide start. The runners would proceed down the steeplechase one-mile course, reaching open country at a spot called Rabbit Warren, passing Wigston Lane, crossing a field to a water jump, via gates and railings, two fields of stiff plough, uphill and over a brook. This three-mile circuit had to be negotiated three times after the initial straight mile. Red flags marked the many obstacles, including the brook. There had been squally showers in the morning, but the weather turned fine for the afternoon as race time approached. The crowd of 1,500 was disappointingly low, particularly as there was no major soccer on in the area.

The SLH brake, driven by Charlie Rouse, assisted by his son, arrived at the racecourse carrying Shrubb. Coach Andrews decided to lead his nervous young charge into the dressing rooms to show him the man who was expected to be his main rival. Said Andrews: 'I found Rimmer of Liverpool and pointed him out to Shrubb, and said that's the man you have got to beat. Look at the poor thin fellow, he doesn't look as if he has ever had a good meal inside him. Just prick him in the plough on the second lap.' Shrubb listened to this dutifully but must have been thinking that he would be trying to 'prick' his rival as early as possible, instead of waiting for the second lap.

Twelve clubs were represented by 113 runners, spread wide across the start area, making a spectacular sight in the traditional early stampede. After a mile Shrubb was in the leading pack, with James of Northampton just in front. Rimmer was behind in sixth. The northern and midlands runners had never seen Shrubb in action before and must have been startled by his brisk start. The mile was reached in 5:51 and then the field disappeared into the open countryside. The bulk of the spectators had to wait nearly twenty minutes before the runners would return into view. When this happened, there was an excited gasp as a tiny figure, moving smoothly, came into sight, completely alone. After just four miles Shrubb had forged a lead of no less than 200 yards, ahead of a group of seven. There was no sign of the mighty Rimmer. Shrubb seemed to be running within himself and to have the race sewn up already. He was so far in front that some observers thought he was last and about to be lapped. He was running like a deer, simply striding out at leisure while the rest were travelling with considerable trouble over the heavy, cloying mud. Andrews recalled with pride: 'Shrubb did the pricking business all right. At the end of the second lap we were waiting looking up the racecourse and then a little speck came into sight all alone. He had dropped Rimmer by nearly a minute on the plough and run him off his legs.'

Olympic gold medallist Rimmer was devastated at falling so far behind and his performance went to pieces. With several miles still to go, he ground to a miserable halt and retired from the race, shaking his head sadly. Shrubb had extended his lead to an incredible 500 yards after seven miles. The Irish runners from Cork bravely worked through the plough and later said they'd not experienced anything as tough as this back home. Indeed, the going proved so hard that in the case of the Southport club, not a single team member lasted the distance. The Midland region officials had heard of Shrubb, but never seen him in action and were astonished at how he bounded away from the rest as if they were second-raters. 'You've found a runner this time,' said a local official to one of his southern counterparts.

Shrubb finished in splendid isolation, looking fresh and untroubled with the field hugely scattered behind him, giving the officials no trouble with their time-recording and compiling of results. Volley after volley of cheers rang out as he passed the finishing post, his all-white kit hardly muddied at all. *The Daily Telegraph* noted that the manner in which he sprinted the final eighty yards showed how much reserve power he possessed and praised his finish time in view of the strong wind and heaviness of the ploughed land. He'd covered the ten and a half miles in 63:45.8, 350 yards ahead of W Ashton (Salford), who summoned a strong finish but was still 46 seconds adrift. W Clark (Essex Beagles) grabbed third in 64:41, ahead of Cork City's H Sullivan and J Hayes. Said *Athletic News*: 'Shrubb only commenced cross-country this season and must be one of the most blessed runners this sport has ever seen. He sprinted the final 100 yards in approved style. One wonders by how far he could have won had he gone all out like Ashton, who needed assistance at the line, whereas Shrubb simply walked to the dressing room.'

Although Shrubb grabbed the headlines, he wasn't the only hero on Leicester racecourse that day. Veteran runner Tommy Bartlett of Essex Beagles took part despite the sudden death of his young child earlier in the week. He had not wanted to let his team down and put the team's needs ahead of his private grief. His efforts were certainly not in vain, for without his finish of eighteenth – one correspondent called it the race of his life – the Beagles would have lost first place in the team competition to Cork. So the Beagles' yellow and black banner flew high afterwards as all the runners milled around discussing the day's events. Con Phibbs of Cork City told anyone prepared to listen about how he ran four miles with only one shoe to gain 33rd place. Also with a tale to tell was L Z Kuttner, who had the distinction of finishing last – 21 minutes behind Shrubb, his SLH teammate. To shelter from the chilly wind, most spectators huddled in the main stand area; among the onlookers was S T Dodds, the well-known artist.

A big talking point was the eclipse that day of Rimmer, a man who is remembered 100 years later by local aficionados as 'the greatest human running machine ever produced on Merseyside.' This 1900 Olympic 4,000 yards steeplechase champion had set his heart on the national title at Leicester and found his emphatic defeat by Shrubb a bitter pill to swallow. A policeman by occupation, he was lanky and thin to such an extent that people sometimes worried about his well-being in long-distance races. Before one twenty-mile contest in Glasgow, the race doctor at first refused to allow him to run because he considered such an exhaustive test too much for Rimmer's fragile-looking body. The doctor relented after a great deal of persuasion, and watched in astonishment as he promptly won the race by nearly a mile. Rimmer was not a man used to losing and his pasting by Shrubb made him thirsty for revenge. Their next meeting would be at the following month's AAA ten-mile track championships, being hosted by Rimmer's local association at Crewe. Rimmer was glad he would have a chance of revenge on home soil on this upstart from the south.

In the meantime, Shrubb returned triumphantly to Horsham on the Monday evening, and the town band and a big crowd were once again at the station to greet him. Torches were kindled and the band formed up alongside a van decorated with evergreens (labelled 'Shrubbery!'), which had been loaned by a local man called Stedman. The hero of the evening was carried aloft alongside a Horsham Blue Star Harriers banner. A second banner in the rear of the van bore the letters 'SLH'. The procession turned down Park Street and there was a brief halt outside the Bell Inn, the Blue Star headquarters. Here, Gordon Innes, vice-president of SLH, addressed the crowd, proclaiming that Shrubb had won a splendid race and Horsham should be proud of him. The procession moved slowly to the Anchor Inn, temporary home of Shrubb and his coach in Market Square, where more speeches took place. Innes said Shrubb was one of the finest performers ever seen in England. He'd watched the last fifteen championships and had 'never seen a man who could take Shrubb's number down'. Shrubb responded, once the cheers had died down, and said he had tried hard to get to the top of the tree and, now that he'd made it, he wanted to stay there. He was shouldered into the hotel by H C Hunt of Horsham FC and his colleague F Hatchwell.

A boisterous smoking concert in the Anchor got underway, presided over by SLH's Thomas Sinnott. Songs included 'As Your Hair Grows Whiter', 'Running Up and Down Our Stairs', 'Sons of the Empire', 'When Burke Put Up For Mayor', and – to end with – 'A Little Bit Off The Top', in which the accompanists included Sinnott and Innes. At the end of a jovial evening Sinnott proposed a toast to Shrubb who, he said, had already become the greatest runner their club had ever had. He mentioned the two stars who'd missed the National through being unwell – Robinson and Bennett – and cheekily suggested their ailment was in fact 'a touch of Shrubb fever'.

Within a day or two, five cups and medals won by Shrubb were put on display in the centre of Horsham in the Hunt Brothers' shop. In a press interview, Shrubb was again probed about his running style, and explained that a good many runners left everything to the finish and got 'whacked', but he liked to do his work at the beginning to get well ahead. At the SLH annual dinner in March the new champion of England was awarded a gold watch in recognition of his cross-country 'double'.

CHAPTER FOUR

The Man who Ran in his Sleep

After lifting the Southern and National cross-country championships on successive Saturdays in early 1901, Shrubb was on a hat-trick when he made the short journey to Eastbourne for his local county championship. His mission was to collect a third major title in as many weeks.

Towards the end of the nineteenth century the practice of counties staging their own cross-country championships had begun to die out, but Sussex – no doubt encouraged by Shrubb's emergence – was one of those bidding to revive the event. They set up a course of just under six miles at Eastbourne for the first such meeting of the new century. On March 9th, just a week after taking the English title, Shrubb wore Blue Star colours and confidently captured the Sussex prize. He cruised home in 33:28, with a runner called Sewell gamely giving chase late on, but finishing nineteen seconds adrift. The going was mostly good-to-firm and there was a healthy turnout of 44 entrants. Shrubb's tiny frame meant he struggled a little over some of the jumps, but his superior speed compensated and he won by 100 yards. Blue Star took the team prize.

A week later and the remarkable sequence continued. He chalked up his fourth successive Saturday victory by winning South London Harriers' Thornton Challenge Cup over a ten-mile course on the Surrey-London borders. It was the final cross-country race of the season and Shrubb, in his debut campaign, had won every contest he'd entered. He came home in 61:49, and there was a very long wait until runner-up W R Davies arrived, some five minutes adrift.

Four stamina-sapping races on successive weekends might have contributed to Shrubb's heavy cold in the week before Easter 1901, and he had to pull out of a two-mile race at Preston Park, Brighton. He returned to action a week later but clearly wasn't back to his best. In the SLH spring meeting's three-mile handicap at Kennington Oval, he failed to make up ground on runners given starts ahead of him and walked off the track with 600 yards still to run. Northampton's Sid Robinson had been due to take part, but failed to show, so Shrubb's retirement was a second disappointment for the big crowd. Robinson and Shrubb would renew hostilities in late April when the AAA ten-mile crown, which Robinson currently held, was up for grabs at Crewe Alexandra's track in Cheshire.

By now, Shrubb had convinced coach Harry Andrews that he should be allowed to run races his own way, although he was still happy to take the trainer's advice on matters of pre-race preparation and training schedules. In subsequent years Shrubb would coach himself, but for now he made the most of Andrews' company on the long walks designed to maintain condition. Shrubb recalled: 'He walked with me along the roads, engaging in cheerful conversation, cracking jokes and telling funny stories, for no man was a greater believer in the value of cheerfulness to an athlete than Mr Andrews.'

The coach was also a believer in natural remedies, and one of his maxims was 'there's no tonic in a chemist's shop, and still less at a hotel bar'. Shrubb was shrewd enough to pick and choose between Andrews' pearls of wisdom, and memorise which of his training methods might be useful in the future. He undoubtedly learned much from Andrews during the few months they worked together, but ultimately Shrubb would prove more than capable of taking his training into his own hands.

After his recent cross-country heroics, Shrubb was highly fancied to become English ten-mile champion on the track at Crewe, and *The West Sussex County Times* reported that his preparations had gone well, despite some unseasonal hot weather. It reported that he'd run a swift five-mile time trial in Horsham, paced by the bicycle of Blue Star official G Tuffin of West Street. Ten-mile running on a track was new to Shrubb, although he was, of course, familiar with the distance. In fact, he even claimed to be 'in better wind' at the end of a ten-mile run than he had been at the beginning, a claim that seemed to defy logic. Finchley's Olympian runner Charles Bennett was a notable absentee from the list of starters at Crewe, but title-holder Robinson and Liverpool's Jack Rimmer would be there to ensure a three-cornered fight for glory. Shrubb's supporters had high hopes their man would not only win, but would give Walter George's seventeen-year-old world record of 51:20 'a good shaking'.

Shrubb appreciated their confidence but, as usual, his cool and composed exterior concealed his inner turmoil. Years later he would recall with amusement how he often 'ran races in his sleep' during these early years of his career. His bizarre nocturnal behaviour was sometimes disturbing for other members of the Shrubb household: 'We had so many visitors at the house that my brother [Albert] and I sometimes slept together. He told me in the morning that he had scarcely had a wink of sleep because of my restlessness. He sat up in bed and watched my face. Though my eyes were closed, he said I looked just as when engaged in an actual contest.' On one occasion Shrubb apparently climbed out of bed and did some high-speed sleep-walking, tearing round the bedroom in his pyjamas and only waking up after colliding with a bed-post. A grumpy Albert pleaded with his younger brother out loud to give up the running game, for it was clearly beginning to 'turn his brain'. The sound of Albert's voice made the younger Shrubb chuckle before he returned to his restless slumbers.

There were 1,000 spectators inside the ground for the big race at Crewe, a figure reported in the athletics press as disappointingly low. The track was heavy underfoot and there was some breeze. A total of 22 started the race, but several would drop out along the way after Shrubb set a cracking pace and hit the one-mile mark in 4:53. After being pursued in the early stages by a group of five, Shrubb surged in the second mile and opened up a significant lead. Shortly before the halfway mark Rimmer hauled in the white-shirted figure at the front, but reigning champion Robinson decided he'd had enough and retired. According to one correspondent, the shattered Robinson fell to the ground and 'lay stretched out on the grass looking depressed and discomfited'. *Athletic News* reported that the halfway point was reached in 25:55 after Shrubb injected 'one of those series of amusing little sprints he is becoming known for' to leave Rimmer in his wake once more. Shrubb piled on the pressure over the next ten minutes or so and led the Merseyside policeman by forty yards at the seven-mile mark. From here onwards Rimmer was clearly a beaten man and the winning gap had opened up to 150 yards by the time Shrubb breasted the tape.

Another national honour was his, and the winning time of 53:32 was impressive, given the conditions. Rimmer was runner-up in 54:01 and Arthur Barker of Leeds finished a further 34 seconds back in third. After accepting his gold medal, Shrubb told the press the weather had made it a tough race, for even though the rain held off there had been a stiff, cold breeze which hampered the runners. He was full of praise for the track itself, however.

If Shrubb thought the wind hazardous, within a couple of hours he would find himself in far greater peril. Travelling to the train station for the journey home, Shrubb and his trophy were accompanied by three associates, including SLH officials Sinnott and Innes, in a horse-drawn cab. Huddled inside, the group became alarmed when the vehicle began travelling too quickly for the conditions. Shrubb recalled that a worried Sinnott enquired, 'Are you not satisfied with the records you have already broken, Shrubb? Have you told the cabby to break another for you, and all our bones too?' It was dark and the streets poorly lit. Sinnott stuck his head out to reprimand the driver and was horrified to see the passenger beside him on the 'dickey' trying to wrench the reins away. 'The cab went faster than ever now and it was clearly only a matter of moments till we should be somewhere between life and death,' recalled Shrubb.

Weighing up their chances, Shrubb and Sinnott opted to jump for safety from the careering cab, while Innes elected to sit tight and hope for the best. Moments later the vehicle lurched into a grocer's shop, scattering produce in all directions. 'There was a terrific crash as the plate glass window was shivered to atoms and there, with its head, withers and feet in the shop, the horse stood kicking,' recalled Shrubb. 'The cabman still sat on the seat, holding the reins.' Shrubb and Sinnott picked themselves up, finding they had no cuts or serious injuries, and quickly retrieved the cup, which had fallen into the street and sustained a small dent. Innes and the other passenger also escaped unharmed. Somewhat generously, in view of the circumstances, they paid the cabman his fare and left him to settle matters with the grocer. 'We stole away silently and as quickly as possible to the station, laughing at our exploit, which came near to that of the proverbial bull in the china shop.'

Their eventful journey home concluded at Horsham station with the now inevitable reception from Shrubb's supporters and the trusty town band. None the worse for his adventures, the conquering hero was conveyed around the town in a decorated car, in which he stood in the front and waved the battered trophy he'd won at Crewe. As was now the ritual, the procession halted outside the Bell Inn, where Gordon Innes called for three cheers and insisted to the throng that Shrubb would soon emulate the performances of that great athletics pioneer, Walter George. The parade moved on to the Anchor Inn, where a smoking concert had been arranged, one of the guests being Shrubb's proud father, William. The AAA trophy, valued at fifty guineas and first competed for in 1880, looked magnificent on the top table, its new dent discreetly hidden.

Shrubb's status meant he was in increasing demand at social engagements. A few days after Crewe he was guest of honour at the Horsham Football Club annual dinner. Referring to Shrubb's modest demeanour, the main speaker admitted he 'didn't mind talking about this great runner because he didn't talk about himself'. Even before he spoke, Shrubb was given a standing ovation for the recognition he was bringing to small-town Horsham, whereupon he stood up and replied that he would always try his best for the town as long as he had his health and strength.

The next engagement in his burgeoning social diary was an invitation-only, complimentary dinner on May 13th, again at the Anchor Hotel. Overshadowing the splendid feast was a display of Shrubb's seven major trophies. Among the guests were his father William and brother Albert. The speeches acknowledged that all seven trophies had been won in his first year of running, an unprecedented achievement in Great Britain. To great laughter, the audience learned that Shrubb's father had not run in his youth because it wasn't the fashion, so perhaps he'd inherited his talents from his mother? Thomas Sinnott freely confessed on behalf of the SLH that 'the Horsham boys' had taught Shrubb his running and the London club had no intention of trying to steal the credit from the Blue Star club.

Northampton's ace runner Sid Robinson, having lost his ten-mile title to Shrubb at Crewe, travelled to London on Whit Monday, May 27th, bent on revenge. He would race Shrubb in a five-miler at Stamford Bridge. Billed as a Highland Gathering in aid of the Royal Scottish Corporation and Royal Caledonian Asylum, the highlight of the meeting would undoubtedly be the five-mile confrontation, with the winner's spoils being a £10 case of cutlery. Shrubb realised this silverware would make a handsome addition to the parlour of his hardworking mum. He burst clear early, his first mile a swift 4:40 that demoralised Robinson and the rest. Shrubb forged a big lead and could even afford to slow a little, his second mile being 5:05, the third 5:25, the fourth 5:29 and the final one 5:18. He won by a massive 300 yards.

Afterwards Robinson expressed surprise that Shrubb had been so comfortable at this shorter distance, but his own performance had been disappointing. It was becoming clear that Shrubb was not being fully tested in some races, even when established internationals like Robinson were present. In this particular contest, had Shrubb been really pushed, he might have threatened Sid Thomas's five-mile world record. A rematch between Shrubb and Robinson was quickly arranged over the same distance for the August Bank Holiday meeting at Horsham.

Robinson bounced back from his London defeat with a cracking run over one mile in his home town Northampton shortly afterwards, timed at 4:14. Although this was faster than George Tincler's world record of 4:15.2, set four years earlier, it was apparently never ratified by the authorities and therefore is not recognised in most record books. Shrubb's best time for the mile at that point was around the 4:30 mark, and although he never claimed to be a specialist miler, he did enter the occasional race at this distance to sharpen his speed. One such race came shortly afterwards on a warm midweek June evening, and his appearance was heartily welcomed by the Crawley club. He won their mile handicap in 4:40, barely breaking sweat.

On Friday, July 5th, Shrubb headed north by train for Huddersfield, where he would bid for the AAA four-mile title the next day. Along with the ten-mile event, this was one of two standard track races on offer to the long-distance merchants of this era. Much later, of course, the '4' and '10' would be scrapped in favour of the 5,000 and 10,000 metres. At the

Huddersfield cricket and athletic club grounds, Shrubb noted that the varsity entry was stronger than in previous years, but there was only one entry from Scotland. The pale-faced moustachioed French champion Henri de Loge was taking part, while several renowned American athletes had registered for the sprints, including Arthur Duffey, who repeated his 1900 win in the 100 yards. Shrubb and Duffey would soon become close friends – more of which later.

A healthy crowd of about 4,000 endured constant Yorkshire drizzle for the first hour, but the weather improved by the time the four-milers emerged from the clubhouse. Shrubb, sure that this race would not over-extend him, had also signed up for the mile and the two miles steeplechase in a bid to add more national titles to his portfolio.

In his main event, Shrubb led from start to finish, and although pressed by local favourite Arthur Barker (Leeds) for just over a mile, he drew clear and won by 200 yards in 20:01.8. This was the second-fastest winning time in an AAA title race. As his rivals flagged, Shrubb amazed the crowd by accelerating on the final lap. The pressure had been too much for at least one runner, who quit before the end, while brave Barker paid for his early determination to keep pace by being slowly run into the ground. Shrubb's mile splits were 4:43, 4:56, 5:16 and 5.06, and he picked up the impressive challenge cup from the Earl of Jersey.

Shrubb proved to be the best all-rounder of the day at Huddersfield by finishing second in the mile and third in the steeplechase. The mile was won in 4:21.4 by Francis Cockshott of Cambridge University, whose late sprint saw off Shrubb by fifteen yards. Shrubb narrowly pipped Henri de Loge for second. Despite a major effort on the last lap of the steeplechase, victory went to the more experienced Sid Robinson. Shrubb had achieved his main aim of the day, and the shorter races were part of his learning process. Although he did have natural speed in his legs, his extraordinary stamina was his main asset.

By now, the ceremonial 'meet-and-greet' at Horsham station had become a regular local event, and Blue Star and SLH officials were already struggling to make each occasion different from the last. Shrubb was winning so often, the victory parades were becoming almost monotonous. On this occasion Blue Star requisitioned a vehicle and dressed it in banners and flowers, to lead the procession on its usual route via the Bell and Anchor.

During this purple patch, Shrubb was inevitably making national as well as local headlines, and he had become quite a celebrity in Sussex. However, he stayed loyal to his local club and continued to appear in local meetings that were of far less consequence than some of his recent engagements. He was determined not be considered a 'big-time Charlie'. On a Thursday in July, for example, he represented Blue Star in the two-mile flat race at Horsham Cycling and Athletic club's final evening meet of the summer, and also appeared at the annual sports at Crawley at the end of August. At their annual dinner in the autumn, the C & A club expressed its appreciation for his continuing patronage of their fixtures.

Shrubb retained a great affection for the annual Atalanta Cup event in Chelmsford and was keen to return to Essex in 1901 to defend the trophy he'd won in spectacular style the previous summer. On a blazing hot afternoon at the Essex county cricket ground, a 5,000 crowd sweltered through a four-hour meeting. The three-mile race was the highlight and Shrubb sped to a 150-yards victory over the highly rated Fred Appleby of Herne Hill Harriers. This Essex gathering always attracted major VIPs, this year including the Lord Mayor and Lady Mayoress of London.

On August Bank Holiday Monday, Shrubb's home-town supporters had their first opportunity to see their man in action against a truly national figure, as opposed to local runners. Sid Robinson was in town, 1-2 down to Shrubb in their contests so far this year. A bumper crowd estimated at 7,000 turned out for the annual sports at the Horsham cricket ground in glorious weather. This was a record attendance for the sports and around 10,000 assembled for the carnival that evening in Springfield Meadow, another record. The cricket ground was bursting at the seams and some latecomers had to seek vantage points on the edge of nearby Denne Park, or on the railway bridge. Loud cheers greeted the appearance of Shrubb and Robinson for their 3.30pm showdown over five miles.

The pair set off side by side, with Shrubb looking the more smooth and purposeful of the two. He forged ahead in the second lap, allowing Robinson a brief spell in the lead in the third, before regaining the front. He covered the first mile in a fairly swift 4:42, with Robinson on his shoulder before nipping ahead in the seventh lap. Once they'd passed two miles in 10:03, Shrubb was back in front, and keen observers began to suspect he was toying with his rival, allowing him brief sniffs of the front before immediately reimposing himself. Shrubb appeared in full control, and was probably holding back a little to ensure the big crowd got a close race for its money. The Northampton man was labouring by comparison, but grabbed the lead for another few seconds. Shrubb eased back past him to pass three miles in 15:27. Then, slowly but surely, Shrubb opened up a gap from which Robinson could clearly not recover. It had been like watching a cat toy with a mouse. Over the next mile the lead widened to fifty yards and the crowd responded jubilantly. Poor Robinson didn't appear to have a single friend among the 7,000 screaming voices. As Shrubb cruised through four miles and then almost imperceptibly applied even greater pressure, Robinson began showing signs of distress. But he bravely pulled himself together and ensured the gap grew no wider on the last lap. Shrubb, who'd clearly raced against his man and not the clock, finished with a time of 26:10.8 and Robinson 26:18.2.

The throngs of well-wishers clambered over the flimsy ropes intended to keep them back, and Shrubb was swamped. The correspondent for *The West Sussex County Times* expressed indignation at such boisterousness in his report: 'Things got a little out of hand and the press table was completely obscured from view.' Shrubb received another huge ovation when he stepped forward to receive a clock and ornaments valued at ten guineas from Mrs A C Oddie, wife of the town's carnival association president. She presented runner-up Robinson with a canteen of cutlery. Shrubb was pleased with his prize, and no wonder, for ten guineas represented four months' wages for working men in 1901. A few days later the new monarch, Edward VII, was crowned after recovering from an appendix operation, but there remained no doubt who ruled the roost in Horsham.

With Robinson well and truly put in his place, Shrubb now had more 'unfinished business'. He'd comprehensively beaten Jack Rimmer over ten miles (twice) earlier in the year, but the man they called 'Pride of the North' was another who wanted to restore his reputation. Rimmer issued an invitation, via his club Liverpool Pembroke AC, for the 'Little Wonder' from Sussex to travel to Southport in late August to pit their wits over four miles. It was a distance at which Rimmer felt he could match Shrubb. It was billed as a head-to-head duel between the top runners from North and South, and attracted enormous interest in Lancashire.

Although the 1901 census records him as living at home with his parents, Shrubb was still based at the Anchor Hotel at this time, on the advice of coach Andrews. Shrubb was chaperoned on the long trip to Southport by the Anchor's owner, Dwyer. They arrived the day before the race and enjoyed top-notch northern hospitality during their stay. This was Southport's 32nd annual athletics meeting and it enticed a crowd of 10,000. The contrast in the rivals' appearance was almost comical as they shook hands on the start-line in front of the main grandstand. The gangling Rimmer stood well over six feet, towering above Shrubb by more than six inches. The prize for the victor would be a ten-guinea gold watch.

Rimmer allowed Shrubb the courtesy of occupying the inside lane for the start. Shrubb blasted away as usual but found his long-striding rival more difficult to shake off than most opponents. After half a mile, how-ever, he led by ten yards and increased this to a satisfying 25 yards by the time they passed one mile. Both men possessed a fast finish, but Rimmer was unable to sustain the swift start and Shrubb pounded on, increasing his lead all the time. After the third mile, his lead was fully sixty yards. Although the home crowd urged Rimmer on, by the end the gap had lengthened to more than 100 yards as Shrubb came home in 20:17. Rimmer's defeat could hardly have been more emphatic, and he and the crowd acknowledged the outcome sportingly, cheering and congratulat-ing Shrubb at the finish. The contest had attracted much interest from those who liked a flutter and the bookies took a hammering from Shrubb's associates, who had been gleeful when Rimmer was installed as strong favourite. Shrubb had proved that he had the leg speed and tacti-cal acumen to cope with races as short as twenty minutes in addition to his well-known ability as a stayer. Shrubb recalled later that the eighteen-carat gold watch he received at Southport that year was a splendid speci-men, which gave good service for many years afterwards.

The year of 1901 had so far been like a dream for Shrubb. Just about everything he'd touched turned to gold. He'd pushed himself hard in races and in training and so far his body had withstood the test, his health and well-being never giving cause for concern. Suddenly, in September, all that changed.

One morning he cycled the twelve miles to Hayward's Heath, to stay with friends and attend the local horse show. That evening he complained of a sore throat. The next morning he felt worse and remained in bed. The doctor was summoned by his worried hosts and Shrubb was told he was displaying symptoms associated with both scarlet fever and diphthe-ria. A day or two later there was no improvement and the doctor ordered him to be removed to East Grinstead Isolation Hospital. After three days a telegram was sent to Horsham to report that Shrubb was on the mend, but would remain in hospital. Among the events which his illness and recuperation caused him to miss was SLH's big autumn meeting at Kennington Oval. Shrubb was instructed to spend several weeks in the sanatorium, from where he wrote to Blue Star colleague G Tuffin. He announced that he was getting on well and expected to be home by October 26th – seven weeks after his first symptoms appeared.

Shrubb needed time to rebuild his fitness and was nowhere near ready to defend the SLH's Gibb Challenge Cup in Croydon on November 2nd. However, he was heartened to hear that the new holder was his pal Fred Spencer, who had introduced him to running and who now won the race in Shrubb's absence. Shrubb's comeback was pencilled in for the Blue

Star club's four-miler on November 21st, when he ran off scratch and recorded the day's fastest time of 21:24. Although this beat his own event record by six seconds – and proved he was back to full fitness – it was not quite enough to enable him to overtake all those runners given starts in this handicap event.

The old confidence came flooding back and just over a week later he duly won SLH's Brown Challenge Cup, a five-mile cross-country handicap. He recorded the fastest time of the day (28:35), although again the handicapping meant he didn't cross the line first. To emphatically underline his return to form, he performed superbly for SLH in winning the Nicholls Cup event at West Wickham in Kent, when his club took on Blackheath Harriers over six miles. Shrubb came home in 37:59 to win by around 100 yards, but behind him the home club's runners did enough to capture the team prize.

Illness aside, 1901 had been a wonderful year for Alf Shrubb. And it ended as it had begun – with a stunning victory. On a bone-chillingly cold Boxing Day, Shrubb tried his luck for the first time over fifteen miles, a distance some thirty per cent longer than anything he'd raced before. The race was at Worthing on the Sussex coast, and Shrubb saw it as useful preparation ahead of the big fifteen-miler he'd committed himself to in Manchester a few months hence. The Manchester date was at the behest of Jack Rimmer, who was putting a field together for an attempt on the world record. In the meantime, Shrubb was curious to find out how he would cope with '15', and the Worthing Excelsior club's open race would be an ideal test. The track was semi-frozen turf that was greasy and difficult for running. Teammate Spencer made the early pace and Shrubb made a relatively conservative start, but before long appeared to weary of playing a waiting game and took the lead and stayed there. From here on in, the spectators were treated to those repeated surges that Shrubb was apt to suddenly inject into his running. He survived the latter stages without any significant slowing down and came home an easy first in one hour 26:37.4. Local officials were adamant that this was an accurately measured course, and they heaped praise on Shrubb for maintaining such a brisk pace over an unfamiliar distance. The performance left everyone, including Shrubb presumably, wondering exactly what the great runner's best distance actually was.

CHAPTER FIVE

'No medicine in the world like vigorous exercise'

Great sporting achievement needs context in order to evaluate it. So just how good was Alf Shrubb aged 22, after barely two years as a competitive runner?

The simple answer is that he was in a class of his own. As organised athletics was not yet a truly global affair, Shrubb's status as the leading Briton meant he had to be among the world's elite. There was nobody to touch him at distances of between two and ten miles and the vast majority of his many victories had been by substantial margins. True, he had experienced the occasional defeat at one and fifteen miles, but over the wide range of distances in between he'd become virtually unbeatable. At cross-country, his real forté, he boasted a 100 per cent record. More than one sportswriter has, over the years, suggested Shrubb ran in an era when the opposition was largely mediocre. This casts an unfair shadow on the man, for he not only won almost every race he entered, he usually won them emphatically. Furthermore, had Shrubb competed in a truly 'substandard' era, how do we explain his long list of national and world records, or the fact he retained many of them for decades afterwards?

By the start of 1902, Shrubb believed he was close to his best again, in both running and general health. Figures released early in the year by the local health authorities showed that diphtheria – diagnosed in Shrubb some months earlier – had reached near-epidemic proportions in Horsham. Almost fifty cases were reported, of whom eleven victims died. Its high incidence was attributed to the large numbers of children sent from London to holiday in the countryside. They were thought to have spread the disease among local schoolchildren.

Having missed several cross-country races while indisposed, Shrubb relished the chance to compete against the crack Essex Beagles side, national and southern champions, on January 11th at Horsham. This inter-club contest saw Shrubb lead from start to finish, making light of the soggy course and winning by 150 yards in 31:13.8, 32 seconds clear of Blue Star teammate J Sturt. At a dinner afterwards, the Blue Star officials summoned the Beagles skipper and placed a large wreath on his head, explaining that this was to recreate the example of the Grecians in 777BC. The Beagles were congratulated on their champion status, but reminded by their hosts that Horsham could now boast production of 'the finest runner ever to put on a shoe'.

Treating his recuperation with respect, Shrubb was picking and choosing his races, no doubt keen to be in peak form by the spring, when a number of major events were on the calendar. He missed the South London Harriers' Nicholson Cup at Croydon in January, but gave himself a workout in the ten-mile Thornton Cup and won by 400 yards, apparently without over-exerting himself. Next up, in February, would be the chance to defend his title as Southern cross-country champion. Wembley Park had staged the event for eight successive years but in 1902 it moved to Lingfield Park racecourse in Surrey. Special cheap fares were introduced for trains from London and the south coast. Sunshine and a blue sky greeted the spectators and the going looked good. Shrubb complained beforehand of a minor chest infection, but remained hot favourite to successfully defend his title. The course featured a stretch of his favoured plough, softened nicely by a recent thaw.

Shrubb burst away in his usual style, but Albert Aldridge of Kent AC caught him and even led for a short while before Shrubb regained the front. Perhaps he was preoccupied by his recent health problems, but, unusually, Shrubb seemed to lose track of time and distance in the second half of the race. When passing the judges he practically stopped to ask 'That's it, isn't it?', only to be told he still had one more lap to go. According to one report: 'His face was a picture and it must have required pluck to go on again … he admitted later he almost stopped there, but went on looking rather cut up.' This uncharacteristic show of confusion seemed to give Aldridge a new lease of life and he redoubled his efforts to catch up, encouraged loudly by the crowd. By the end Shrubb's lead had been cut to thirty yards, but he held on to win in 59:44.

A fortnight later Shrubb returned to the same venue, this time to defend his status as National cross-country champion. A crowd of over 2,000 assembled on March 8th in favourable conditions for the 4pm race. The spectacular mass start, spread wide, featured 159 runners representing sixteen clubs from throughout England. The signal to depart sparked the usual stampede and a Derby runner enjoyed a few moments of glory before the top men came to the fore. Shrubb had still not completely shrugged off his cold and, accordingly, had told reporters he might 'try a waiting game this time' to conserve energy. He and Albert Aldridge were at the head of the lead pack. Shrubb felt strong over the country sections, but Aldridge seemed to come alive when they passed the mass of spectators around the main stand. On one occasion Aldridge theatrically threw his hands up in acknowledgment of his supporters and sprinted briefly into the lead, presumably intent on recreating the excitement on this course a fortnight earlier. *The Sportsman* decried these shenanigans as 'nothing more than a gallery spurt' but conceded that it did lead to excitement reaching fever pitch. Shrubb wasn't fazed and maintained his position, slowly easing away to win in 56:56, 200 yards and 45 seconds clear. The improved going meant his winning time was three minutes quicker than on the same course in the Southern, despite Shrubb's relatively conservative early running. Sid Robinson had a poor day and finished only fifteenth, while Highgate Harriers won the team prize.

At Shrubb's hearty reception at Horsham station later on, followed by the usual speeches at the Anchor, the champion struggled to make himself heard, such was the croaky state of his voice. His cold had almost gone a week later when a fine day greeted 32 runners from three clubs, contesting the cross-country championship of Sussex at Springfield Meadow, Horsham. The runners faced some tough sections of plough and a big crowd gathered to watch the two 2½-mile laps. Shrubb took an early lead and, followed by his Blue Star and SLH teammate J Sturt, reached halfway in a lightning 11:53. His strength saw off Sturt's challenge and he increased the lead to 250 yards by the end, running the second lap even quicker to come home in 22:55. Blue Star took the team prize by just three points from Brighton and County Harriers.

Shrubb had now chalked up impressive victories despite running with a persistent cold and perhaps not being recovered from his illness of late 1901. This must have been even more disheartening for his opponents. If he couldn't be beaten when half-fit, what chance would they have when he'd recovered?

Perhaps the other runners were tempted to think of him as some sort of freak of nature. That would have been taking things a little far – for there were plenty of genuine 'freaks' in Horsham around that time. Following the revelations about the town's six-legged cat (two at the front, four at the rear), the latest tittle-tattle now centred on a hen which hatched a chick shortly before Easter which had four legs! Its owner, Mrs Aubrey of West Street, proudly declared that the new arrival could run as well as her other poultry and she took a photo of it to exhibit in her front window.

So, if Shrubb wasn't a freak, then perhaps he was just an eccentric, spending all his time walking and running interminable distances along country lanes. This didn't really fit the bill either, for Horsham's true eccentric was one Methuselah Matthews, a wandering rabbit and rat-catcher with a strong liking for alcohol. When Methuselah wasn't wandering around the countryside – often bumping into Shrubb, no doubt –

he was regularly to be found in the local magistrates court, explaining his latest misdemeanours.

Easter 1902 saw Shrubb focus his mind on the upcoming AAA championships at the London Athletic Club track at Stamford Bridge, where he would defend the ten-mile title he'd won in 1901 at Crewe. He revealed later that his preparations for this long and monotonous event (forty laps) would inevitably be based upon walks of between eight and ten miles along the lanes near Horsham, interspersed with hard five-mile track runs three times a week: 'I used to walk in ordinary pants, just as a boxer would do while preparing for a bout,' he told *All Sports Weekly*. 'The country people came to know me quite well and would call out to me "Well Shrubb, how are you going? Do you think you can win the championship?" They all kept a close eye on my career in those days, watching my performance with the keenest interest, not unmixed with pride. Teammates took turns, day after day, in pacing me. I would tell them how to go and nothing was too hard for them in their eagerness to pull me out. A man who wants to win a championship like that must do a lot of severe training and must be very careful about his habits. I went to bed at 10 or 10.30 and stayed there nine hours – not a moment too long for one who did so much energetic dreaming.'

Many of Shrubb's early victories had appeared almost effortless, but he knew that to remain at the top he needed to maintain a heavy training workload and leave nothing to chance when it came to the major championships. His planning was meticulous for a sportsman of his era, and he admitted that some of the pains he went to astonished even him when he looked back. For example, whenever possible he would visit race venues days in advance to seek out and make a mental note of places where he could 'adopt certain tactics' in mid-race to surprise his rivals.

After the severe winter of 1901-02, the spring was proving to be particularly wet, and Stamford Bridge was deluged on the morning of the AAA championships on April 5th. More than 2,000 turned out to watch a full programme of events, however, and around fifteen of the nation's best distance runners toed the line for the ten-mile showdown. With a moderate breeze and heavy rain resuming just before the pistol sounded, a tough battle was on the cards. Shrubb and the one-mile specialist Joe Binks sped straight to the front and Shrubb pulled clear with a very swift opening two laps: 'My first half mile was covered at a rattling pace, with all the others close on my heels,' he said. 'Finding they were not going to be left behind so easily, there was nothing for it but to keep battling on.'

The mile mark was reached in 4:46 and two in 9:51. After passing three in 14:58, he sensed the opposition was flagging and increased his lead by the time he passed four miles in 20:07. It was a fast time considering he'd still not reached halfway, but Shrubb knew he had the race in hand and he could relax and churn out the remaining laps at a steadier pace. He was never troubled again and, although he looked a little weary near the end, came home 140 yards ahead of Arthur Barker (Leeds) to win in 52:25.6. This was considered a superb time in view of the wind and rain. (See Appendix for Shrubb's split times.)

So the champion had retained his crown, and was delighted to do so at the stadium where his championship debut two years earlier had ended in a 'disappointing' third place. Despite the gruelling nature of ten miles on a windy track, he again declared that he'd felt physically stronger at the end of the race than at the start. Reflecting later on these unexpected sensations, he said: 'This always struck me as strange, and many doctors to whom I spoke wondered at it. Several times in my career I had illnesses when doctors advised me to take my choice between running myself to death in a year, or saving my life by resting for several months. Knowing myself better than the doctors knew me, rest was impossible, and a continuation of training – harder still if anything – soon put me right again … there is no medicine in the world like vigorous exercise.'

A fortnight after Stamford Bridge, Shrubb travelled north to the Fallowfield track in Manchester to fulfil the challenge laid down in 1901 by Jack Rimmer and others, to participate in a fifteen-mile world record attempt. Rimmer felt Sid Thomas's ten-year-old amateur record of one hour 22:15 (at Stamford Bridge) was within his reach and felt the presence of Shrubb, Albert Aldridge and Fred Appleby would inspire him to success. Shrubb entered knowing his training and pre-race build-up had not been geared to such a long distance, but he was confident of putting up a good show after his efforts at the 'Worthing 15' at the end of 1901. Shortly before the 3.50pm start at Fallowfield, Shrubb was heard to complain of a strained leg muscle that had first troubled him some two months earlier. Nevertheless, he and Arthur Barker set off at a cracking pace, a typical Shrubb surge taking him through three miles in 15:07, at which point Barker decided to quit.

There was more drama a mile later when Rimmer suddenly followed Barker's example and walked off the track. Shrubb led by 100 yards at five miles in 25:48 and continued at a pace many onlookers considered unwise. He still led by some distance at ten miles in 53:30 and had a 150-yard lead at eleven, completing eleven miles and 210 yards at the hour mark. By now he was in relatively unfamiliar territory and by thirteen miles began to look ill at ease. Aldridge and Appleby jostled in pursuit and the latter overhauled a slowing Shrubb with just over a mile to go.

Appleby had trained himself to cope with races of more than ten miles and reaped the benefit of a more even pace. Shrubb finished in considerable discomfort, moving uncharacteristically slowly. To the dismay of the crowd, Appleby's dramatic late show won him the race, but he missed the old record by six seconds. He came home in 82:21.8 with Aldridge also passing the fading Shrubb to take second in 83:27. Shrubb, ashen faced and apparently dragging one leg, recorded 84:23. All other starters had fallen by the wayside. Although Shrubb told reporters he would now give shorter races his fuller attention, he and Appleby agreed in the changing room to meet again later in the summer for another crack at the '15' world record. Shrubb left Manchester with food for thought, clutching a small trophy won for completing the fastest lap of the race, plus a silver cigarette case for coming third.

The summer of 1902 was non-stop, with Shrubb racing at all distances between one and fifteen miles. On May 12th he won a 1½-mile inter-club affair at Lower Edmonton in London in 7:07.8, with a gap of 25 yards between him and the next man. Five days later came the Essex Beagles meeting at Ilford, postponed from earlier in the month due to a violent thunderstorm. Once again thunder and lightning struck the region, but the event went ahead and Shrubb attacked the world three-mile grass record in dreadful conditions. He put in a brave display in the circumstances but came home in 14:54, way short of the target.

Two days later he was in action at Hastings, where he turned the tables on local hero Albert Aldridge following the fifteen-mile result in Manchester, beating the Kent man over ten miles in 53:39.2 in front of a 1,500 crowd under rainy skies. The next trophy headed for the Shrubb sideboard was the SLH Willis Challenge Cup, awarded for winning his club's mile championship in 4:46.4 at Crystal Palace.

His schedule was hectic – just the way Shrubb liked it. He accepted an invitation to the West of Scotland Harriers meeting in Glasgow in June. It meant another lengthy rail journey and several days away from home, but by now Shrubb had developed a taste for travelling and visiting new places, and welcomed the chance to see Scotland. In strong winds, he raced over three miles at Ibrox Park and clocked 14:36.4, winning by the length of the home straight, with his old adversary Jack Rimmer back in third. Shrubb said later: 'I developed a great liking for Scotland and it can be truly said that the love of long-distance running was a passion with the hardy Scots, who love the element of endurance in field athletics.'

July offered a procession of major fixtures and Shrubb used minor local meets to help him prepare. At a Horsham Cycling Club evening fixture, he hardly broke sweat when winning a two-mile flat race in 9:28.4, toying with the opposition and staying in a group until the closing stages when he powered ahead to win by twelve yards.

It was a cosmopolitan field who gathered for the AAA championship at Stamford Bridge in July, with athletes from the USA, New Zealand and Hungary challenging the cream of the home nations. Although Shrubb won the four-mile event in fine style, for once he found he wasn't the centre of attention. Twenty-seven-year-old Joe Binks of Unity AC ran the race of his life in the Mile, smashing the seven-year-old British record. Shrubb had also entered and was a central figure in a last lap filled with drama. As the leaders hit the home straight, two of the five contenders, Shrubb and E L Gay-Roberts of Oxford University, both found their tank was dry and simply jogged off the track. Lieutenant Henry Hawtrey of London AC held a narrow lead from Binks, who suddenly surged for the line to win in a British record 4:16.8. That time would not be bettered by a Briton for nineteen years, when Henry Stallard's 4:14.2 eclipsed it in 1921. (Stallard was one of the supporting heroes of the Oscar-winning film *Chariots of Fire*.)

Binks, who would subsequently spend fifty years as athletics correspondent for the *News of the World*, later recalled: 'Shrubb was a bit cocky going to the track that day and I said I'd give him a good tousing. And I did.' Binks was a man of few words and Shrubb remembered that they didn't speak after the race. Perhaps Binks felt he'd done his talking on the track. This was his moment to savour, for he would never beat Shrubb again. Binks was well-known around this time for his ultra-light training schedule: his usual regime reportedly involved only one session a week, lasting just half an hour.

The crowd of 8,000 basking in the Stamford Bridge sunshine were entertained throughout by the London Victoria Military band. Shrubb's main event, the four miles, followed an hour after the mile. He was spiked by a fellow athlete in the rush for an early lead, a nasty wound, but Shrubb stayed on his feet and ran on, only feeling real pain afterwards. The event turned into a procession, with Shrubb coming home in 20:01.4, ninety yards ahead of Herne Hill's Fred Appleby, with A F Simpson of New Zealand a long way back in third. Shrubb's leg wound took weeks to heal, but he bandaged it up and didn't miss any events because of it.

The following weekend, July 19th, saw Shrubb and several other leading distance men head for Chelmsford and the annual Essex championships. A bumper 8,000 crowd saw Shrubb win the Atalanta Cup for a third time. He sprinted home alone on the grass track in 14:25, establishing a new world record for the '3' on grass. It beat James Kibblewhite's

1889 time, set at Kennington Oval, and to mark the achievement Shrubb was awarded a gold medal, which he later described as one of his proudest possessions. The huge Atalanta Trophy – which Shrubb reckoned was one of the largest sporting cups in existence – was now his for another year, thanks to a stunning run that exceeded his two previous performances at Chelmsford. He'd simply stormed home, finishing 200 yards ahead of Aldridge, with Appleby third. Shrubb's mile splits were 4:40, 4:59 and 4:46. He obliterated Kibblewhite's thirteen-year-old record by nine seconds, although in years to come it would not be recognised as an official world record because performances on grass were not formally ratified.

Shrubb's schedule took him back to London 48 hours later for the head-to-head with Fred Appleby over fifteen miles at Stamford Bridge. There were no other competitors, allowing the crowd to focus on a sixty-lap duel between two tenacious and diminutive figures. Appleby was more experienced at this distance and made several early attempts to get away from Shrubb, but this proved fruitless. Eventually he settled in behind Shrubb and hung on, the pair carving out lap after lap at around eighty seconds each, phenomenally fast for this sort of distance in 1902. They passed halfway in 39:48 almost side by side. The hour mark saw them reach eleven miles and 452 yards, and by now the lead was swapping hands regularly. Just before the bell signalling the final lap, Shrubb put in a burst and looked round to check on his opponent. With 350 yards left, Appleby kicked again. Shrubb maintained his lead for about forty yards but then appeared to falter. Halfway round the last lap he was passed and Appleby surged home to win, opening a gap of forty yards by the line. The last lap was completed in 71.4 seconds, easily the fastest of the sixty. Shrubb was uncharacteristically exhausted, and no wonder, for both men had smashed the old world record. The winning time was 80:04.6, with Shrubb clocking 80:15.8. Sid Thomas's amateur record of 82:15, which had stood for ten years, was consigned to history and the professional record was also beaten. Shrubb didn't lose many races, and it had taken something very special to beat him this time.

Because so many of Shrubb's victories turned into solo processions, the Stamford Bridge '15' has to go down as one of the most thrilling he took part in. Reflecting later, he described Appleby's performance that night as one of the Herne Hill man's greatest, and also acknowledged the wisdom of his own coach Harry Andrews, who'd helped make it a great race by persuading Shrubb not to burn himself out too early. Without this advice, Shrubb would surely have tried to bury Appleby early on and then come to grief later. Appleby and his coach, Charlie Ottway, chatted with Shrubb afterwards and agreed that both runners – each around 5ft 6in and eight stones (112lbs) – had conjured up a marvellous race, but in Shrubb's case, fifteen miles was simply not his best distance.

At the end of July, Shrubb was still stiff and sore from the fifteen-miler, but raced for SLH in an inter-club match with Racing Club de France at Crystal Palace. Athletics was beginning to blossom on the Continent and the French were leading the way in spreading its popularity. They still had some way to go, however, before they could match the top English clubs, and SLH won the contest by five events to two. In the mile, Shrubb led throughout a slow race, surged 300 yards from home, but was overtaken by France's top miler Henri de Loge on the home straight. The winning time was a pedestrian 4:52. The Englishman had perhaps been a little too casual, but he made up for it later in the three-mile race. He made a series of bids to break the opposition mid-race, but found L de Fleurac, the French cross-country champion, in inspired form and able to respond to all his moves. Then, on the final bend of the last lap, Shrubb kicked hard and pulled clear to win by 25 yards in 15:27.8.

Following his world record on the grass at Chelmsford in July, Shrubb promised the locals at Horsham that he would bid to create a new mark on home turf at the annual August Bank Holiday sports. A strong field was assembled for the three-mile race, but what had promised to be a great day was spoiled by constant heavy showers. Appleby and Aldridge were among the dozen starters, but Shrubb surged ahead from the gun, quickly began lapping tail-enders, and with two laps left was 200 yards clear of Aldridge. Although he looked in fine fettle running alone, despite the wind and rain, someone challenging him might have pushed him nearer to record pace. He dug in on the last lap and won by 23 seconds, but his time of 14:38.8 was thirteen seconds adrift of his own record on grass. *The Sportsman* called it 'a simply grand display in the circumstances'. Shrubb also gave an assured run of 4:25 in the mile handicap, with some runners given 150 yards start on him. He ran that day with a linen bandage around his ankle to protect the wound sustained at Stamford Bridge.

Such was Shrubb's dominance that not a single other runner bothered entering the Sussex championship at four miles. The race was part of the fifth annual Crawley Sports in August, but with only Shrubb's name registered, the organisers had to hastily invite some 'name' runners to take him on. At such short notice, the only positive response was from Albert Aldridge. Blue Star's Fred Spencer was also roped in and the race duly won by Shrubb in 20:21.4, a lap clear of Aldridge. Without another challenger for the county title, he was declared winner by default and took the gold medal.

Three days later a four-mile inter-club race took place at Reigate sports ground, where Shrubb and Aldridge found themselves in opposition again. Shrubb's prize for winning in a fast time of 19:51.8 was a bicycle; Aldridge, 150 yards behind, won an electro-plated tea urn, while third-placed Fred Appleby received an oil painting. Prizes such as these were commonplace, for the strict amateur code governing athletics meant cash prizes were not an option. Shrubb could have equipped a mansion from the collection of household goods earned from his running.

By September, Shrubb's thoughts were turning to the cross-country season, but he nevertheless threw himself wholeheartedly into the three remaining races on his summer schedule, and declared himself determined to crack a world record or two before the paper-chasing season started. First up was the SLH annual meeting on September 13th at Kennington Oval, where he was bidding for the three-mile world record of 14:24, set in 1894. He won the race easily but missed the record by eight seconds. Three miles of 4:47 each would have done the trick, but Shrubb completed the first in 4:38, meaning he probably took too much out of himself. His second, in 4:55, left him needing a 4:51 final mile, but he paid the price for his quick start and could only manage 4:59.

A week later he tackled a four-miler, on the grass track at the Reigate and Redhill Harriers Sports, watched by a noisy crowd of 3,000. He responded to the vibrant atmosphere and went for the grass world record set by T Conneff in Dublin (19:44.8) fifteen years earlier, and also had an eye on the cinder-track record of Charles Willers, set in 1894 (19:33.8) at Paddington. To beat both he needed to average 4:53 per mile. After streaking away even faster than the previous week at the Oval, he clocked 4:36 for the first mile and 4:54 for the second. He maintained this form in the third (4:56) and it became clear a record was in the offing. Amidst a tremendous roar he accelerated over the final mile and came home in 19:26.8, easily inside both existing marks. He received a rapturous ovation as he made his way slowly back to the pavilion through the back-slapping crowd. It had been a great day, but he would have to do it all over again on the cinder track at Stamford Bridge a week later to gain what would be regarded as an 'official' record.

At Stamford Bridge he lined up in a limited handicap race, promoted mainly with him in mind, as part of the autumn meeting of the London AC. Although Shrubb preferred springy grass to the strength-sapping cinder tracks, he felt his form was good enough to achieve the cinder record regardless. He started extremely quickly and *en route* broke the existing 4,000 yards record of Sid Thomas (10:58.2) set on the same track in 1893 by half a second. He powered on, composed and light on his feet, and crossed the line in 19:34. Moments later he was mortified to learn that he was just one-fifth of a second slower than Willers' Paddington record. Had the race been run an hour earlier, he might have succeeded as the humidity was less noticeable then. He had been changed and ready to go at that point, but the organisers chose to slot in a five-mile race first and a frustrated Shrubb had to stand around and wait his turn. A marching contest had also taken place on the track, meaning it was hardly in good condition for a record attempt. Many in the crowd felt for Shrubb, particularly those who had come especially to witness his record attempt.

For his part, Shrubb now felt that winning races and gaining admiration was no longer enough – he wanted to go down as the fastest man in history, and for that he needed official world records against his name.

CHAPTER SIX

Striding into the International Arena

When the autumn leaves start to fall, a competitive runner's thoughts turn to cross-country. And so it was for Shrubb and his fellow paper-chasers as the 1902-03 season dawned. This would prove a particularly significant campaign in the development of this branch of athletics. Plans would be announced for a prototype world championship in Scotland – and the organisers would have their work cut out finding a date convenient to Shrubb, the sport's star performer.

Cross-country maintained a strong hold over Shrubb throughout his career, rooted firmly in those carefree boyhood sorties in pursuit of Sussex foxes. In races he usually ploughed a lone furrow, way out ahead, but for mere mortals it was a crowded, relentless, high-pitched, punishing pursuit. It was nevertheless strangely addictive. Cross-country was a nineteenth century English invention which subsequently matured into a truly international sport, with a distinguished record of egalitarianism, openness and freedom from politics. In the early days, cross-country – unlike track – never fussed about social rank.

Roger Robinson, a former international runner, wrote a history of cross-country for the USA magazine *Running Times* in 1998. He highlighted how nations such as Belgium, France and the UK had considered the event so important that they would defy every hardship to send teams to compete in the world event. He cited the junior race which dodged the bombardments of Paris in 1940, and told how Yugoslavia ducked under the Iron Curtain to provide a world champion (Franco Mihalic) during the Cold War days of 1953. North African runners would get their first international chance in France's teams, notably Alain Mimoun and Rhadi ben Abdesselem, in the 1950s. The impoverished, beleaguered Ethiopia would reign as world champion nation between 1981 and 1985.

Robinson felt the spirit of cross-country was summed up by two incidents involving his own participation in world championships. He recalled the moment in 1966 when he impulsively took the arm of a Moroccan who staggered off a jump alongside him, a gesture that won him applause from the Rabat crowd. He also recalled his experience at Düsseldorf in 1977, when he was supported semi-conscious on the shoulders of a Sudanese and a Soviet as they all crossed the finish line at the same gasping moment. The three had just spent forty minutes trying to destroy each other.

Championship cross-country had begun life with a washout. At the first event for London clubs in 1876, a storm swamped the paper trail, and competitors were left paddling haplessly for hours around Epping Forest. One of them recalled how officials revived them by rubbing their muscles with brandy: 'Personally I thought internal application would be better and snatched the glass. The next thing I remember is waking up in the Old Pavilion Music Hall,' he added.

England, Scotland, Wales and Ireland set up their own organising bodies in the latter years of the nineteenth century and then, early in 1903, formed a union (the ICCU) and set about promoting the first 'International Championship' at Hamilton in Scotland. When the English officials heard that the exciting new event would be on March 21st, 1903 they were horrified to find their top runner, Shrubb, was already committed that weekend to an event in Paris, which couldn't be put off. England were so desperate to win the first staging of the new event that they applied for a postponement. The ICCU agreed without fuss, and so it came to pass that the sport's very first 'world championship' was rearranged to suit the diary of one special competitor. One wonders what the reaction would be in modern times.

The build-up to this momentous season of cross-country had, for Shrubb in particular, been busy and triumphant. For one thing, he'd finally captured the world record he craved on a brisk autumn day in Preston Park, on the outskirts of Brighton. The October 25th meeting attracted 3,000, most looking forward to the main event, a four-mile invitation handicap in which Shrubb promised another attack on the record. A month earlier, he had achieved the required time, but on grass at Reigate, and had then failed by the narrowest of margins (one-fifth of a second equates to about one yard for a distance runner) on the properly measured cinder-track at Stamford Bridge. Preston Park's track had official approval, so a record here would be worth more than at Reigate. It was the end of the 1902 track season and represented Shrubb's last chance that year to earn a place in the record books.

Charles Willers had covered four miles at Paddington in 19:33.8 in June 1893 and only Shrubb had come really close since. Albert Aldridge was given a 150-yard start under the handicapping system and his was the figure Shrubb would chase when the pistol sounded. The first mile was a fast 4:36 and the halfway point reached in 9:32.8, well inside record pace. He passed Aldridge soon afterwards, and a third mile completed in 5:01 meant the record was still very much within reach. The final mile saw Shrubb battle hard to dip just under five minutes, clocking 19:31.6, a margin of 2.2 seconds inside the nine-year-old record. He won by half a lap, an extraordinary achievement considering the handicapping – third-placed J S Lyon of host club Brighton and County Harriers had received a 280-yard start. The good folk of Horsham were delighted to have another reason to parade their champion, but this time on Shrubb's triumphant return to the town things didn't quite go according to plan. An administrative bungle meant that the proposed smoking concert to celebrate Shrubb's record had not been booked, and the Anchor Hotel was unable to accommodate the happy throng when it showed up at the door that evening.

This slip-up was inconsequential, however, compared to the problems behind the scenes at South London Harriers at this time. Thomas Sinnott's time as club treasurer had expired, but he had refused to return the accounts ledgers, claiming he hadn't been reimbursed for his outlay on Shrubb's training and race expenses. Sinnott insisted he had paid these monies from his own pocket – the club being low on funds – but Shrubb's success had subsequently 'pulled them around'. His message was clear: he had taken the decision to invest in Shrubb and his gamble was paying off, to the financial benefit of the club.

However, given the strict amateur code of the AAA, SLH did not wish to be seen endorsing anything that might be construed as illegal. They simply denied all knowledge of such payments and said they had no intention of reimbursing Sinnott, who had not acted with fellow officials' backing. They subsequently sued Sinnott for the return of the books, upon which he instructed his lawyer to counter-sue for the £40 5s 11d, which he said he was owed. The whole sorry saga would eventually be settled out of court.

This bitter dispute at SLH was, of course, noted by officials at the AAA, who were keen to strictly enforce the amateur code. AAA ears collectively pricked when the matter of 'expenses' and 'training costs' were mentioned in connection with Alfred Shrubb. It was also noted in high places that Shrubb had by this time turned his back on carpentry and labouring to become proprietor of a small tobacconist shop in West Street, Horsham. His associates at SLH, most prominently the controversial Sinnott, had apparently been instrumental in arranging the finance to allow Shrubb to take over this shop during 1902.

Becoming a small businessman held two major benefits for Shrubb: firstly, he could exploit his well-known name to help build the business and earn enough to cover his costs when travelling around the UK; and secondly, the nature of the work would be less demanding physically than his previous occupation, thus aiding his training and preparation for races. His shop was one of seven tobacco emporiums vying for business in Horsham at the time, and was centrally situated at 61 West Street, between Timothy White's the chemist, and Hart's footwear shop.

The patronage of Sinnott and others from SLH had been crucial in allowing this working-class runner to further his career during an era when sponsorship and prize money simply didn't exist. However, the AAA was becoming concerned that Shrubb and his associates might be sailing close to the wind regarding their rules concerning amateurism. This is hardly surprising, for only a completely naïve onlooker could believe that Shrubb, a young working-class man of limited means, was paying all his travel and hotel expenses as he competed here, there and everywhere, often racing more than once a week. This whole issue would come to a dramatic head in 1905.

Meanwhile, as the winter of 1902-03 set in, Shrubb kicked off the new cross-country campaign by winning his club's Croydon Challenge Cup. This five-mile handicap was won off scratch in 27:46 by a fifty-yard margin. Shortly afterwards he underlined his good form at an inter-club race between Blue Star and Essex Beagles at South Woodford. A severe frost necessitated most of the paper-trail being laid on the road instead of through the trees of Epping Forest. Blue Star were let down by several absentees and only had nine running against thirteen, but Shrubb took an early lead and won by 300 yards in 32:08, with Beagles filling the next four places.

1903 started with a calamitous staging of SLH's Nicholson Cup event at South Croydon. T Blackstaffe, better known locally for his exploits as a rower, was given a generous start of eight minutes and fifteen seconds by the handicapper, and made the most of this by coming home first, clear of any challenger. It later emerged that Shrubb had lost his way after three miles and hadn't completed the course.

This wasn't the only event where several runners found themselves lost mid-race. Reminiscing in *All Sports Weekly*, Shrubb recalled a Croydon race where many of the entrants were shrouded in fog for almost six hours, unable to locate their clubhouse: 'This adventure might have given half the pack pneumonia.' He recalled:

'The occasion was a race between the SLH and a varsity team. I left Horsham by the 10 o'clock train in beautiful sunshine. At Purley the train ran into a fog and I had practically made up my mind that my visit must be in vain, as no race could be run unless the fog lifted. Reaching South Croydon, it was no easy matter to find the Swan and Sugar Loaf hotel, groping along the fronts of the houses and scarcely daring to cross the street for fear of bumping into an omnibus. A meeting was held at the hotel to consider the situation. It was decided to postpone the race unless the air should clear within an hour-and-a-half. About 3pm we decided to run the race, seven miles across the country. Never did weather so cruelly deceive a pack of harriers. The trail-layers were sent out to mark the way we should go. Mean time, the fog was beginning to play its great practical joke with us. We started off in wisps of mist, wondering what was going to happen. I took the lead and got about 300 yards ahead. At three miles the fog fell like a blanket and we couldn't even see the paper on the track.

'It was necessary to keep fairly close together and to call our whereabouts to each other. Beside a wood I stopped to wait for others to come along. Some came, but many didn't. We shouted for our comrades, but alas, they had taken the wrong turning somewhere and lost their bearings. Six of us tried to find our way back and the rain came on with cold wind that smote our thinly-clad bodies like a whip, and a wet whip at that. Our plight was a pitiable one in pitiless circumstances. We came to a small wood and were glad of what little shelter it afforded. Bramble bushes scratched our legs till they bled. Stumbling though the wood we struck a country road, and asked ourselves what to do next, as our teeth chattered and we were all too miserable to laugh at the trick the fog had played us.

'One fellow compared us to a pack of lost hounds and another tried to sing a comic song without getting very far with it. The fog didn't lift until pitch darkness took its place, leaving it still impossible to read directions on the finger-posts. At last we came to a small cottage and were told that instead of going towards South Croydon we were going away from it, being then about eight miles from our HQ. Of course, our miseries had to have an end some time, and it was nearly eight o'clock when we reached the club, to be told that the back-men had not been collected. While we enjoyed the luxury of warm drinks and warm baths, others hired cabs to scour the district for the wanderers. The last of these was brought into the fold, a sorry spectacle of cold and exhaustion, at nine o'clock. That experience, thank Heaven, stood alone in my career as a harrier.'

On St Valentine's Day, the Southern cross-country championships were staged at Lingfield Park and, in perfect conditions, all manner of records were broken. The patronage of nineteen clubs constituted a record, as did the field of 216 starters and the attendance of 4,000. Defending champion Shrubb and Albert Aldridge (Kent AC and Highgate Harriers) were expected to be the men to beat over the ten-mile course. Shrubb and George Pearce (Unity AC) got away quickest, but Aldridge soon overhauled Pearce. At halfway, the tail-ender – G Banbrook of Hampstead – was already seven minutes behind Shrubb.

Arriving back at the grandstand on the second lap, Shrubb appeared to be in control, even though Aldridge was by his side. On the final circuit Shrubb blasted away to win by 250 yards amid hearty cheering in 58:30.4 – Aldridge 52 seconds adrift. The next SLH runner could only manage 23rd and the team prize went to Highgate. It was Shrubb's third Southern title in three attempts, and now he prepared himself to achieve the same statistic at the National.

The 27th National was staged at Haydock Park racecourse, near Manchester. It had once been used for the Northern championships, but was making its debut as a National course. Shrubb was hot favourite, with one of his likely challengers – Aldridge – sidelined by a severe and long standing head-cold. After a wet morning, the skies cleared and a crowd of 4,000 assembled to see 146 runners cover five laps (ten miles). Four of the circuits involved ploughed fields and, although it was clearly a testing course, the going was mainly good. Shrubb assumed command after half a mile, following a combative dash for position, and had matters his own way from thereon in, dipping under the hour mark (59:56.6) to clinch a hat-trick of titles. Shrubb was the only southern runner in the leading pack, Sid Robinson was second, nearly a minute down, followed by W A Mercer of Farnworth. Birchfield Harriers took the team prize. Shrubb was now just one short of the record four titles in a row (1877-1880) won by Percy Stenning of Thames Hare and Hounds.

Shrubb might be forbidden to win cash prizes for his exploits, but that did not stop others gambling on his success. His coach, Harry Andrews, had come across a bookmaker on the course quoting Northern champion J Hosker as favourite, and was consequently offering generous odds of 6-4 against a Shrubb victory. Andrews was confident in his man and placed a hefty bet. To ensure the bookie did not disappear before paying up, Andrews recruited a policeman to 'mind' him, in return for two shillings from any winnings he might collect. After the race, Andrews happily collected his winnings but forgot about the policeman. As he made his way to congratulate Shrubb in the changing tent, he was intercepted by the officer, who made it clear he wanted his two bob.

The magazine *Sport and Play* marvelled at Shrubb's imperious victory: 'The consummate ease with which he strode away from his competitors – making all his own running – and the fact that the farther he went the greater became the distance dividing him from his nearest opponent, compelled the admiration of hardened old sports, who scarce ever see anything so good as something they saw years ago.'

According to the magazine, Shrubb had now confirmed he was the best ever, eclipsing even the great Edward Parry and Percy Stenning: 'The relative value of performances in these cross-country races is difficult to gauge for many reasons; but tested any way and every way, the South London star stands out with conspicuous brilliancy and is undoubtedly looked upon by the best of good judges as the equal of any of his predecessors and by many as the best of them all.'

Shortly after the National, the England selectors announced their team of twelve runners – the three regional champions plus the nine best-placed also-rans from the National – to face the other home countries in the new international championship on March 28th. In the meantime, however, Shrubb had two more races to contend with: the annual cross-country title in his home county Sussex, plus an inter-club race in Paris featuring four European clubs. First up was the domestic affair at Lewes on March 14th. Disappointingly, Blue Star were only able to call on the services of two runners – Shrubb and Jarvis. Over a five-mile course, Shrubb jogged alongside W Baker (Brighton and County) for about a mile and a half before drawing away and cantering home by 300 yards in 27:08 to retain his title.

That week, the new edition of *Cycling* magazine featured a portrait of Shrubb, preparing for his trip to Paris by boat and train, along with fellow Horshamite Jarvis. The town declared itself proud to have two representatives in the ten-mile cross-country, even though both would be wearing the colours of their 'other' club – South London Harriers. Arrangements were made to wire Blue Star official G Tuffin of West Street on the Sunday evening after the race to inform locals of the result.

The event got underway at 10.30am on March 22nd in the wooded Parisian district of Bois de St Cloud. SLH were up against hosts Racing Club de Paris, plus teams from Belgium and Switzerland. Shrubb overcame a couple of worrying moments, when he inadvertently wandered off course after losing sight of the trail, but recovered to win by almost a mile in 62:29, with the French club's Chastini second in 67:42. The course was thought to exceed the stated ten miles, and included a four-mile stretch of road, which didn't endear the organisers to those runners wearing spikes.

Shrubb's impeccable unbeaten record at cross-country meant he went into the following week's inaugural international championship as red-hot favourite. The cream of English, Scottish, Welsh and Irish runners competed against each other as a team for the first time, and each fielded its strongest side. They faced four circuits of a difficult Hamilton Park racecourse, near Glasgow – a shade over eight miles – and in miserable weather the going became increasingly heavy. England – represented by Shrubb, Hosker, Smith, Robinson, Mercer, Lawson, Edwards, Silsby,

Pearce, Aldridge, Thomas and Randles – packed seven runners into the first ten to justify their status as favourites. Although Shrubb got to the front early on, it was not until three miles had gone that he was able to open a significant gap. He won by 200 yards in 46:22.6 from teammate T Edwards (Manchester), with Irishman J J Daly third. England collected 25 points, Ireland 78 with Scotland on 107 and Wales 140 (the fewer the points, the better).

The event was regarded as so successful that plans were implemented to make it an annual affair. Before long, runners from abroad were eligible, and in 1908, for the first time, the race was staged outside the UK, in France. Apart from the war years, it was staged annually in Europe until 1966, when Morocco became the first African hosts. A women's championship was introduced in 1967 and, in 1973, a change of name saw it take on the mantle of the IAAF world championships. Even though that first race in Hamilton Park in 1903 generated plenty of attention, it is unlikely that winner Shrubb and the rest could have predicted exactly how the event would develop and prosper in the years to come.

It had been a hugely rewarding, if highly taxing, cross-country season for Shrubb, and he was careful in his training during the following month. In late April came the AAA '10' 1903 championships, at Northampton, where another of his coveted titles would need to be defended. On arriving at the County Ground, Shrubb was pressured into undertaking a world record attempt. This hadn't been in his thoughts at all; he'd simply come to win. Whatever his private thoughts, to pacify the locals he agreed to have a crack at the record and give them an afternoon to remember. An enthusiastic crowd of 3,000 watched in awe as Shrubb set off, battling against a strong wind and a softish track.

The first two miles passed in 9:45 and well before halfway he'd lapped everyone, meaning this was another solo effort against the clock with nobody ahead of him to chase apart from lapped tail-enders. His time at halfway – 25:13 – was a record for that stage of a ten-mile championship race, but the conditions then took their toll and the chance of a record drifted away into the Northamptonshire breeze. Shrubb finished in splendid isolation, literally winning by a mile, one of the biggest victory margins ever seen in a major race, but was more than 35 seconds outside Walter George's amateur record of 51:20. Runner-up F James of Herne Hill was five minutes adrift. Shrubb's time of 51:55.8 was also well short of the event record (51:31), established by Sid Thomas. Victory by such a huge margin ought to have been the cue for celebrations, but expectations were now so high where Shrubb was concerned that missing the record left an air of anticlimax.

After his superb winter, Shrubb remained in tremendous form as the summer approached, continuing his quest for more records. In early May he took part in a three-mile invitation handicap at Fallowfield, Manchester and, showing scant respect for the heavy going, strode to 14:33, well ahead of Charles Straw of Warrington, but nine seconds short of the cinder-track world record. Nine days later, the battle against the clock continued, with Shrubb's attention switching back to ten miles. On a Thursday evening in Preston Park, Brighton, he set his sights on George's 51:20 mark, but was hampered by a stiff breeze. At halfway things looked promising – as they had at Northampton – but once again he lost time in the gruelling later stages and came home ten seconds short of his target. Poor Albert Aldridge trudged home in second place some four minutes adrift.

Going into his fourth summer as a competitive athlete, 23-year-old Shrubb could reflect on his highly satisfying progress over recent months. Unbeaten in three seasons, he now had more than enough titles to lay claim to the title of world's best cross-country runner: he was National track champion at four and ten miles; he was the World record holder at four miles, and getting ever closer to other records, too. With a little help from his friends, he had become a successful small businessman in his home town and at weekends could combine his new-found love of travel with his sport. Everywhere he raced – from Brighton to Glasgow, from Manchester to Paris – the locals cheered him to the rafters and urged him to come back soon.

CHAPTER SEVEN

Man on a Mission

It's a mild May evening in 1903 at Stamford Bridge stadium in London. Chattering in the stands are specially invited guests, among them an array of retired athletes – the running stars of yesteryear. Out on the track, immaculate in his all-white kit, is 23-year-old Alf Shrubb. He is already a champion several times over, but tonight he is convinced he still has a point to prove. His mission? To make the famous sporting names watching him from up in the stands eat humble pie.

Tonight, Thursday May 21st, is the first gathering of a well-connected bunch of sportsmen known as the Irrepressibles, drawn from prominent athletics supporters and faces from the past. This ground, the headquarters of the London Athletic Club, is buzzing with smartly-dressed and well-spoken folk, here to discuss old times and feast on a memorable night's action down on the cinder track below. Shrubb did not intend to let them down.

Several of those well-known faces had been publicly critical of Shrubb's unconventional front-running style. Tonight he would enjoy settling scores. He had already eclipsed their fame and broken some of their records, yet still they urged him to harness his talents in a different way and curtail that natural desire to always force the pace. Ex-champion Walter 'W G' George was particularly insistent that Shrubb would benefit from a more circumspect attitude. The implication was that Shrubb was a brainless runner. Tonight he would demonstrate that they were talking out of their hats. And what better way than by running a world record for three miles in front of them?

Shrubb burst clear from the gun in characteristic fashion and one by one picked off the useful club runners who had started ahead, several from Essex Beagles, who had been given generous handicaps with the aim of coaxing the best out of Shrubb. He did not appear to slow at all, despite his scorching opening. He blasted through the 4,000 and 5,000-yard marks in what would later be confirmed as new world record times. The opposition was made to look sluggish as he strode smoothly on. At the start of the twelfth and final lap it was clear the three-mile record was his for the taking. Kicking hard off the final bend, he produced a late surge that had the crowd roaring and he crossed the line more than six seconds inside Sid Thomas's world record, set almost nine years earlier to the day.

Shrubb's time of 14:17.6 would be ratified by the IAAF and stand proud as an official world record for 29 years! It would remain unbeaten until successfully challenged by Finland's Olympic gold medallist Lauri Lehtinen in June 1932. The other 'Flying Finn' – Paavo Nurmi – laid claim to the record in September 1922, but the IAAF refused to ratify his effort. Shrubb's time would stand as a British and English native record for well over thirty years. His run that day was flawless and would go down as one of his best ever: the durability of the record and the calibre of the men who eventually broke it provided the measure of its greatness. British athletics fans would have to wait 51 years before another three-mile world record would be broken on UK soil, when the Soviet Vladimir Kuts did so in 1954 at the White City stadium. Shrubb's time was a personal best by almost eight seconds, beating his 14:25 on grass at Chelmsford a year earlier, but on a cinder track he had never before gone under the 14:30 mark.

A few days after the Stamford Bridge drama, Shrubb made a bid at Ilford on May 30th to lower the two-mile world record on grass. The professional mark for this distance was 9:11.5, set by Bill Lang, which had stood unbroken for forty years, and the amateur record 9:17.4 by Walter George in 1884 at Catford Bridge. Shrubb was in peak condition and confident he was in the right shape to beat both times.

Shrubb's plans received huge publicity and a large crowd was drawn to the Essex Beagles' 12th Athletic and Cycling meeting at the Ilford Sports Ground. Stand and reserved enclosure tickets were snapped up for 1s 6d each, and admission on the day was 6d for the grounds. The stadium was hosting the event for the last time: it would then be sold for housing development and be known as Airlie and Warwick Gardens. A large number of entries was received for all the races, including seventy for the 880 yards and 61 for the 100 yards. Fine weather greeted the opening races, but by mid-afternoon the humidity intensified and, ominously, peals of thunder could be heard in the distance. However, the rain held off and a field of eleven runners lined up for the highlight of the day, the two-mile invitation handicap. Shrubb would run off scratch, all alone, while starts of between 100 and 200 yards were given to the remaining ten, representing clubs from the London area.

Shrubb clocked 59 seconds for the first quarter-mile lap and 67 seconds for the second, reining in the men in front with every stride. He steadied to seventy seconds for the next two circuits and passed the halfway mark in 4:26.8, well inside record pace. Two laps of 72 seconds followed before he eased past the last man ahead of him. This left nothing to chase except the clock, and his 1½-mile time was 6:50 (beating

Charles Bennett's 1900 record of 6:51). At that pace, even the forty-year-old professional record would be broken if Shrubb could get round the final two laps in seventy seconds apiece. The penultimate lap was 74.6, which meant he would have to speed up considerably on the last circuit, although the amateur mark looked in the bag. With the crowd cheering wildly, Shrubb accelerated to a 66.2-second final lap, which brought him home in 9:11, half a second inside Lang's ancient record. Scenes of jubilation accompanied Shrubb's second world record in nine days.

The Sporting Life was fulsome in its praise the following Monday: 'The South London Harrier succeeded beyond expectation ... H W King, the club's secretary took the precaution to have the track measured by a local surveyor previous to Saturday's performance, which we must not forget to mention was clocked by four watches, all of which agree, so that the accuracy of the record is beyond doubt.'

This apparent validation of the record proved premature. Shrubb's satisfaction was cut short a few days later when it was decided locally to re-measure the Ilford track. To general dismay, it was found to be ten inches short of 440 yards. That meant Shrubb's eight laps amounted, in total, to eighty inches short of two miles and the performance was therefore rendered invalid. An announcement was made in *The Sporting Life*, signed by Ilford surveyor Ben Bailey: 'We have this day measured the turf ... a distance of 12 inches outside the boundary chalked line and we hereby certify that the lap measures 439 yards, 2 ft, 2ins or in the eight lanes travelled by Shrubb, a distance of 6ft 8ins short of two miles.' The original surveyor had got his measurements wrong. Significantly, Bailey's method of re-measuring had used a 'recently-tested new chain and arrows' to do the job. The news must have deflated Shrubb, but his busy race calendar would surely soon throw up another opportunity.

Shrubb and various South London Harriers colleagues crossed the Channel by ferry for France in early June for a challenge match with Racing Club de Paris. The event would be staged in the Bois de Boulogne, at the Croix-Catelan venue. Shrubb won both the 1,500 metres and the three-mile race, covering the metric mile in 4:17 and the latter in 14:53.6, which was hailed as a French allcomers' record, smashing the previous best by 21 seconds.

In mid-June, Shrubb clocked up yet more miles, heading for Scotland for a two-day meeting hosted by West of Scotland Harriers at Parkhead. On the Saturday, he won the three-mile race in 14:34, covering the first mile in 4:35, slowing in the middle part of the race, and then hammering the final lap in 71 seconds. On the Monday he tackled a four-mile handicap, crossing the line less than a second outside his own world record.

He overhauled the last runner ahead of him half a mile from home and might have cracked the record but for a blustery wind. His two performances reinforced his immense popularity at this venue and *The Glasgow Herald* wrote: 'Many years will pass before another such performance as he accomplished at Parkhead is repeated. In the four he ran 19:32, within a second of his own world record of 19:31.2, and its value can be seen from the drawbacks he had to encounter. Had it been at Powderhall, for instance, he would have sliced at least 11 seconds off the Parkhead time as it is far better sheltered than the Celtic ground and less liable to lifting.'

The display was recognised by locals as a genuine milestone in Scottish athletics history, and they gave Shrubb a generous ovation. It was later estimated that he had passed the 5,000 metres mark in around 15:03, which meant he could claim another, albeit 'unofficial', world record. His mile splits were 4:33, 4:58, 5:02 and 4:59.

Shrubb's relentless programme didn't flag. On a Thursday night in late June he won the mile championship of SLH and lifted the Willis Challenge Cup: his 4:31.6 beat W H Clark by eighty yards at Crystal Palace. Two days later, on June 27th, he raced in the first annual meeting of the Isledon Harriers in the London suburbs in front of a large crowd. In the five-mile invitation handicap he was billed as making an attempt to lower Sid Thomas's record of 24:53.6. In the event, the hot weather took its toll and although winning with ease he was well outside the record in 25:24. Albert Aldridge was runner-up.

Having won the AAA ten-mile title at Northampton earlier in the year, Shrubb entered for the mile and four miles when the AAA championships resumed at the same ground in early July. It would constitute a unique 'treble' if he could pull it off, but many observers felt the mile would again be the stumbling block and Shrubb should stick to the longer distances.

But, having learned from previous defeats at this distance, Shrubb ran a canny mile and didn't fly away at the start in his usual fashion. It was a tense and slow first lap and Shrubb shared the lead with E J Gay-Roberts of Oxford University. Reigning champion Joe Binks adopted the same tactics as before and ran at an even pace. At the bell, excitement reached fever pitch. Shrubb led Binks by a yard and Gay-Roberts was falling back. There was nothing between the leading pair as they entered the home straight. Binks suddenly launched a sprint sixty yards from home, just as he had in 1902. This time Shrubb had judged his own effort perfectly and had plenty of strength in reserve. He responded immediately and surged past the frantic Binks in brilliant style, crossing the line well ahead. The time was 4:24 and Shrubb was English mile champion for the first time.

Winning this 'blue riband' event gave him enormous pleasure and it was a popular victory among the crowd. Now he had to recover in time for the four-mile race, but after such a thriller it was always going to be an anticlimax. He nevertheless successfully defended his title, coming home almost a lap ahead of Salford Harriers' Tom Edwards in 20:06.

Apart from the AAA championships, the most prestigious single event in English athletics at that time was the Essex annual championships, and Shrubb prepared himself by cruising to two victories at the Redhill and Reigate Harriers sports at Redhill a week before. He won an inter-club four-miler in 20:05 and then took the two-mile steeplechase prize by a big margin.

For the first time in its 22 years, the big Essex event at Chelmsford was spoiled by rain. A heavy storm in the morning had officials scurrying around anxiously in advance of the arrival of the VIP guests, and efforts to decorate the town with bunting were only half-finished. A big crowd arrived at the county cricket ground, along with the Earl and Countess of Warwick, only to see the weather play havoc with the early cycling races. There were several fallers and some events were delayed in the hope of an improvement in the weather.

A strong field was assembled for the three-mile invitation handicap, in which Shrubb was bidding to win the Atalanta Cup for a fourth successive year, an achievement that would allow him to keep the huge trophy permanently. Jack Rimmer (Liverpool Police AC) and Arthur Barker (Leeds) were the best-known names on the list of challengers who had travelled from northern England to try and foil Shrubb. A solid silver rose bowl worth £7 was also on offer to the winner, and a prize valued at £5 would reward a world record time.

So the incentive was there for Shrubb to win additional prizes worth £740, if converted to modern values. As the race was the fifteenth on the programme, the sodden grass track was in a wretched state. This proved no problem to Shrubb and he surged through the first half-mile inside record pace. Although he slowed later on, he won in 14:38.4, his second-quickest time in his four wins here. The opposition was beaten well before halfway and looked a sorry bunch as they trudged home in Shrubb's wake.

Afterwards, Shrubb and his old adversary Rimmer bantered about their 25th July meeting to contest the Parry Cup over two miles at Salford Harriers' event at Fallowfield, Manchester. Merseysider Rimmer, the holder, ventured that Shrubb would need to run quicker than 9:20, otherwise it wouldn't be worth making the trip north, and Shrubb countered that Rimmer would need to go sub-9:15 if he expected to win. Shrubb, of course, had already run sub-9:12 on grass, but the world record on cinders remained the 9:17.4 by Walter George. When the talking stopped and the action started, Rimmer experienced a bad day and lost his crown, slipping back to third behind Shaw of Warrington, and Shrubb strode confidently to victory in 9:22.2.

Hordes of day-trippers descended on Shrubb's home town over the August Bank Holiday weekend for Horsham's 32nd annual sports and carnival. For the first time, the event was spread over two days. Having certain sports on the Saturday afternoon angered local tradesmen, who protested that it would hit business. Those who extended their opening hours reaped the reward, however, for in the evening the town centre was swamped by refreshment seekers. The second day, the Monday, saw heavy rains early on, but glorious sunshine later. Record numbers took advantage of cut-price rail fares to the town. The Carfax and bandstand were festooned for the occasion. Shrubb entered the two-mile handicap and, a rarity for him, the half-mile, on the Saturday, and then the mile, 440 yards, and three-mile handicap on the Monday.

In the half-mile, Brighton's national champion, Bert Blunden, led throughout, hotly pursued by Shrubb, and won in 1:59. After a short interval, Shrubb won the two-miler in 9:58.6, passing teammate Fred Spencer – who had been given a 233-yard start – on the final lap. Although passed, Spencer hung on and gave Shrubb something to worry about in the home straight.

Shrubb gave his home crowd more to cheer about on the Monday when he set a new world record on grass for the three miles. The track was five laps to the mile and a prize valued at £10 up for grabs (worth £617 at modern prices). Shrubb steamed through one mile in 4:30 and overtook all five other runners who'd been given starts. He worked hard over the second mile (4:53) and got himself 'time in hand' to beat the record he'd set at Chelmsford a year earlier, duly coming home in 14:22.4.

This excitement had the crowd buzzing for hours, and they cheered Shrubb to another personal best in the 440 yards (54.6), where he finished third after running off scratch.

Unusually, he retired from the mile race after just one lap, apparently believing the handicappers had been a little too generous to the others on this occasion. At the prize-giving, Carnival Society president A C Oddie glowed with pride at the feats of Horshamite Shrubb, and generated hilarity by suggesting that everyone who loved tobacco should show their appreciation by visiting his shop in West Street.

Shrubb's imperious form showed no signs of slacking and he drew up plans to attack the world 1½-mile record at Villa Park, Birmingham, the home of Birchfield Harriers, on August 22nd. His build-up involved a busy eight days' travelling and three races. First up was victory in a two-mile invitation race in 9:30.8 at the Atherton Parish Church House Sports in Lancashire. He followed this with wins in a three-mile handicap at Lewes in 14:25, and then in a two-miler in 9:43.4 at the 35th annual Railway Clearing House AC meeting at Crystal Palace.

At Villa Park, English cross-country champions Birchfield Harriers took on SLH in what was a revival of an annual meeting scrapped 25 years earlier. Boldly billed as 'London-versus-Birmingham', the highlight was Shrubb's much-publicised bid to erase Charles Bennett's name from the record books by beating his 1898 time of 6:51 for the 1½ miles at Stamford Bridge.

Shrubb was making his first appearance in Birmingham, the home city of legendary Walter George, England's previous finest runner. Shrubb caught and passed all his opponents in this handicap race, sprinted for the line, but missed Bennett's record by 2.2 seconds. He chalked up another comfortable win in the three miles, finishing a lap and a half clear of the home club's W Day.

Shrubb told correspondents at Villa Park he was now planning to 'rest' for several months to prepare for even greater things in 1904, but his racing diary remained as busy as ever over the coming weeks. On the last day of August he attended the Brighton Volunteer Fire Brigade's annual sports at Preston Park and won the four miles in 20:11. He also recorded the fastest time (9:31) in a two-mile handicap, although he couldn't quite overhaul Reading's A Lake, who'd been given a massive 240-yard start.

Raging storms on the evening of September 10th and into the following day wreaked havoc across southern and eastern England and parts of the Continent. Lives were lost on land and sea as buildings were demolished and trees uprooted. London was badly hit, but the weather calmed sufficiently for SLH's autumn meeting at Kennington Oval to go ahead on September 12th, even though much of the country was still engaged in mopping-up operations. Shrubb wanted another crack at Walter George's two-mile world amateur record of 9:17.4.

The great man himself was in attendance again, as Shrubb set off with nineteen other runners and soon began passing those given starts. The 12,000 crowd cheered him on, and despite the wet and spongy grass track, Shrubb maintained a pace comfortably inside George's historic effort, which had been on a firmer cinder surface. Even-paced running, 69.5 seconds per lap, was Shrubb's required rate, but, as usual, he did not heed the wisdom of others. His first circuit passed in 58.8, the third was

70.8, and the halfway point reached with a 71.8. He was now seventeen seconds inside record pace. The fifth lap was a 72.8, the sixth and seventh both 74 dead. At the bell, he only needed a 76.2 lap to achieve his aim. It was looking like that early flourish had done the trick again. The handicapper had played his part well, for the last of the opposition – Hulford of Herne Hill Harriers – had gone off a 225-yard start and was now up ahead of Shrubb, giving him a figure to chase. Hulford worked hard to stay with him, but he was soon shaken off and Shrubb won by 25 yards. Two of the four appointed timers clocked him at 9:17.0 and the other two pronounced 9:16.8. Agreement was reached that 9.17 would be the official time, and another record had fallen – this time by just 0.4 of a second.

As well as a place in the record books, Shrubb earned a tea and coffee service, which he said later his mother 'greatly prized', adding that the medals and prizes he had now accumulated was enough to make 'a very respectable jewellers shop'. Shrubb demonstrated exactly what he meant when Horsham Carnival Society president A C Oddie, a photographer, visited the Shrubb household to snap the runner alongside his numerous trophies. They filled an entire room. The resulting picture, with Shrubb modestly squeezed into a corner of the room, would appear in the May 1904 edition of *C.B. Fry's Magazine*.

In late September, Shrubb capitalised on his purple patch to have another crack at Charles Bennett's elusive 1½-mile record. The race was staged especially for Shrubb's benefit as part of the traditional London AC autumn meeting at Stamford Bridge, and with one-mile record holder Joe Binks also in the field, an expectant crowd of 4,000-plus turned out. Conditions were perfect for this handicap race, and Shrubb, going off scratch, flew past the mile mark in 4:28. This left few in doubt that this time the record would fall. The remaining two laps were completed in 2:18.4 and Bennett's old mark was lowered by a chunky 3.4 seconds. *En route*, Shrubb created new records at the minor distances of 2,000 yards (5:07.2) and 1¼ miles (5:40.2). In short, Alf Shrubb was now proud possessor of a quartet of world records, at 1½, two, three, and four miles, not to mention world bests at various minor distances.

It was, Shrubb felt, a good time to take a break from almost incessant racing. For three weeks he did very little training and kept out of the public eye. He re-emerged to make a low-key appearance on October 17th, when he recorded the fastest time (15:00) at a three-mile handicap, promoted by the quaintly-named Tee To Tum club at Stamford Hill in London. He failed to catch three runners given starts, but his prize was 'an elaborate dressing case'. Following another five weeks of rest, he returned to action on November 21st in a 7½-mile match between SLH and Oxford University. He led for the entire race, winning by 450 yards to record 43.37. After hammering the Dark Blues, he secured an even bigger victory against the Lights from Cambridge over a soggy Gog Magog Hills course. The city spires loomed spookily through the mists below them as Shrubb ploughed through the mud, crushing the students' resistance. Cambridge's best runner, second-placed A Churchill, finished 300 yards adrift.

Shrubb enjoyed trouncing the students, but was unhappy over a wasted journey he and two Blue Star teammates made by train from Horsham to Croydon in early December, when fog caused the postponement of the Brown Challenge Cup cross-country. Five days later, in the same week that the Wright brothers made history with mankind's first powered flights, Shrubb got up his own head of steam in the colours of Blue Star Harriers. He won a three-mile road race at Horsham in 15:20, and, two days later, repeated the effort, also on the roads, beating the visitors from Guildford Harriers. On muddy and slippery lanes between Bishopric and Broadbridge Heath, Shrubb won a gold meal for cruising effortlessly round a 4½-mile course in 25:38, winning by more than two minutes. Eight of the first ten home were from Blue Star, but the spirits of the chastened visitors revived after the two sets of runners gathered afterwards for sandwiches, cakes and tea in the Anchor Hotel.

Shrubb had more to celebrate later that weekend when it was confirmed that his three world records of 1903 (three miles in 14:17.6, two miles in 9:17 and 1½ in 6:47.6) had been formally 'passed' by the AAA. Shrubb, a habitual hotel-stayer, will have also noted with interest the general committee's proposal to amend AAA rules regarding hotel expenses. This matter was passed on for further discussion later by a more senior committee.

1904 began for Shrubb with a routine win at the rescheduled SLH five-mile cross-country handicap, postponed earlier on account of fog. The nineteen other runners were all given starts, but *Athletic News* remarked that Shrubb went off at a great pace and worked his way through the field in wonderful style, taking the lead less than a mile from home to win by sixty yards from F A Knott. Shrubb clocked 27.42, winning him the new Croydon Challenge Cup, which replaced the trophy he won for keeps a year earlier.

This season Shrubb was bent on making history by winning the Southern and English National cross-country titles for a fourth year in succession. His preparations continued at Guildford in mid-January over 5½ miles where he won in heavy going – the course was submerged in places – and beat his nearest opponent by 450 yards, despite stopping to remove a shoe after a spike penetrated the sole. He ran the last 300 yards with one bare foot, taking a huge risk with the championships so near.

Spectators and runners alike were reportedly disappointed when Shrubb failed to show up to defend his Thornton Cup at Croydon in February, due to what was described as 'a slight [in]disposition'. At least his absence opened up the field in gale force winds and driving rain. Shrubb surfaced again in mid-February in a field of seventeen at SLH's Nicholson Cup event over ten miles. Lengthy starts were given to all others but Shrubb caught them all except Fred Spencer and posted an excellent time of 65 minutes in the heavy going.

The final warm-up before the Southern championships saw him win a match at Horsham between Blue Star and London big guns Herne Hill Harriers over five miles. He won by a massive 600 yards. Blue Star waived admission charges to Springfield Meadow for this race, although donations to club funds were invited. In fine weather, the meadow's owner Gerald Blunt was invited to start proceedings. South of the Thames champions Herne Hill lost the match after encountering several problems, including Charlie Ottway losing his way completely, and J S Raynor dropping out with an injured foot.

A record entry of 21 clubs was blessed by fine weather at the 21st Southern cross-country championships at Lingfield Park on February 27th, 1904, with 213 runners divided into pens according to the clubs they represented. In the mayhem that followed the 4pm start, the 3,000 crowd cheered loudly when hot favourite Shrubb established a clear lead as the field left the racecourse area. By the time they returned he had consolidated his position. At halfway he was 150 yards clear and doubled this lead to win in 59:05 to take his fourth successive title. Albert Aldridge, runner-up in the previous two years, had been prevented from taking part by the rulebook, as he had recently switched clubs, both of whom were participating. Surprise packet of the day was F C Neaves of Hampton, who came third, 600 yards adrift of Shrubb. *The West Sussex County Times* concluded that Shrubb 'was now demonstrating, race after race, that he is pretty well the finest runner the world has ever seen'. As an aside, Highgate won the team event ahead of SLH.

The Midlands AAA had determined in January that Dunstall Park, Wolverhampton, and the adjacent Staveley Hills estate, would stage the 1904 National cross-country championships on Saturday, March 5th. The original choice had been Derby racecourse, but the course executive had turned down the opportunity, and there were also problems with the second choice, Castle Bromwich. Colwick in Nottinghamshire was rejected, and Northampton was unavailable. This left just Dunstall Park and Oadby Racecourse, both of which were regarded as unsuitable by the ECCU, leaving the matter deadlocked. Following criticism from the other British regions at the hash that the Midlands people were making, they subsequently hurried into agreeing that Dunstall Park would have to play host – but only after assurances that a bridge over a canal could be used by runners.

Shrubb's bid for a record-equalling fourth successive title added to the spice already generated by the participation of foreigners for the first time. France's top clubs – Racing Club de Paris and Societé Athletique de Montrouge – had representatives among the 212 names originally entered, as well as the 114 who actually toed the line on the day. It was by far the biggest athletics event ever seen in the Midlands.

However, the Manchester-based newspaper *Athletics News* said this should not hide the fact that standards were generally on a decline in the Midlands, not because of a lack of keenness by athletes, but because of sub-standard accommodation and poor tracks. 'Wretched surroundings and unclean hovels were being used for changing areas,' warned the paper. It added:

'A man of refined tastes objects to being hustled together with hundreds of other competitors and that too in a sort of hovel or tent which lacks cleanliness and space. One thing should certainly be stopped: the allowing of certain favoured competitors the use of grandstands and other quiet places for undressing while the rest, or common hordes have to go to the usual tent. The idea that athletes are so many rag, tag and bobtails should not be carried too far, even among the gentle folk of the AAA.'

The presence of Shrubb and the French contingent enticed a large crowd, some via special trains from Crewe, Stoke, Shrewsbury, Hereford, Worcester, Droitwich, Kidderminster and other provincial towns. The course was just under ten miles, starting with a loop around the racecourse and then into the country and 600 yards of plough on the Oxley estate, finishing up with another circuit of a course made heavy by recent rain and snow. After the usual spectacular stampede at the start, Weston of Small Heath had his nose in front, but Shrubb soon nipped ahead and by the time they hit the country had a commanding lead. Emerging from the plough he was 200 yards ahead of Aldridge and a spreadeagled field. By now, three of the French competitors had dropped out. Shrubb was never under pressure and equalled the achievement of Percy Stenning (four-times winner, 1877-1890) by coming home in 54:25.4, more than a minute clear of Aldridge. The best-placed Frenchmen were G Ragneneau and L Bouchard, who ended up 33rd and 35th respectively, having faded after promising starts. Highgate beat local club Birchfield to the team prize.

The best-placed runners in the National duly earned places in the England team for the second annual International Championships three weeks later, staged this time at Haydock Park racecourse, near Manchester. *Athletic News* suggested: 'It will be a thunderbolt from the clouds if Shrubb doesn't win … although the Irish team have been issuing noisy warnings.'

Most participants arrived in Manchester a day before the March 26th event, but Shrubb travelled earlier to stay with his friend Edward Parry – the retired Salford Harriers champion – at the Wellington Hotel in Stretford Road. The Lumley Shield, to be presented to the winner, was on show in the local offices of *Athletics News*. A solid silver trophy, it carried the national emblems of the four Home countries in enamel on gilt discs, and had scrolls at the sides for the names of the winners. It cost 65 guineas and was donated by Scotsman F A Lumley.

Shrubb duly ran for King and country, despite a heavy cold and back spasms which inflicted him mid-race. According to *Athletic News*, 'He had a particularly parrotty time of it at about 4 miles and England teammate Aldridge looked like going up to him, but lost the opportunity and the little man recovered and went away to win easily.' J J Daly of Ireland had earlier raised the stakes by bragging about his chances, but he could do no better than fourth. Shrubb finished 75 yards clear in 47:58, around 22 seconds ahead of Aldridge. England were well ahead of Wales for the team prize. Said *Athletic News*:

'The lessons learned are that Shrubb is still superlative, in a class of his own and likely to go on until the sport dies for the want of a fresh champion. Daly was a disappointment although a fine hurdler. The highly-rated Campbell of Darlington only came 15th because he ran against nature and a stitch all the way. The Welsh champion, a frail looking youth, fainted on the second lap and had to be helped away.'

A rival paper suggested that other attractions should be added to the day to help bring in bigger crowds. Perhaps the inevitability of a Shrubb victory had played a part in the low attendance. Nevertheless it was a triumphant conclusion to Shrubb's cross-country season, which featured around a dozen straight victories.

Adapting once again to life on the track proved tougher than Shrubb might have expected. At the Barbers' Sports in Putney, SW London, on Good Friday 1904, he flopped twice in front of a bumper 8,000 crowd. He looked sluggish and dropped out of both the mile and the two-mile handicap, deciding early on that the starts given to others were just too much to haul back. He fared better three days later on Easter Monday at Leatherhead, when the opposition was weak and he won a three-mile invitation race by 200 yards in 15.29, then cantered home a relaxed third in the mile.

Shrubb's utter dominance of British distance running continued, to nobody's surprise, when he won his fourth AAA ten-mile track title at Rochdale on April 9th. However, he fell foul of some observers for displaying arrogance and 'playing monkey tricks' during the race. The incident happened just after the halfway mark when he caught a pack of four runners whom he had already lapped once. According to *Athletic News*, 'he started a series of monkey tricks, which made him no friends at ringside. His object seemed to be to get Charles Straw away from the ruck, but the feat did not come off and he rather bottled up the Warrington youth rather than helped him. After nine miles Shrubb chose to leave this group and go about his business.'

Shrubb could have won by a wider margin but seemed content to play to the gallery on this occasion. He was seen to move outside of the group he had lapped, wave to friends in the stands and 'chat' to other runners for long periods. In spite of these distractions, he won by 500 yards in a time of 54:30.4. He had split up the record field of 26 early on with a fast first lap of 63 seconds, and a mile in 4:40, but a promising newcomer called George Butterfield hung on gamely, resisting several attempts to be shaken off. Shrubb produced a devastating 200-yard sprint just before the two-mile mark and Butterfield had no answer. The challenger was not completely broken, however, and won a close tussle for second place.

Another major title was in the bag. Afterwards Shrubb announced he would attack the world five-mile record at Kennington Oval. The athletics press doubted that he was yet fully recovered from the rigours of the cross-country season and suggested he'd need more flat racing before his speed was sufficiently sharpened for track records. But the Doubting Thomases only helped inspire Shrubb to greater effort and their words certainly didn't discourage the fans, who turned up in huge numbers at the Oval on April 16th to see the race. Around 18,000 – a record for an athletics meeting at this venue – came out in good weather. A fresh nor'-westerly was blowing and the turf track seemed lifeless.

Shrubb faced, in the main, modest opposition in the five miles handicap. One reporter noted that he looked 'more fine drawn than usual, and could not have cut his own throat more ably had he wanted to do so, than on this day.' This was a reference to Shrubb's blazing first mile, which included a first lap of under 58 seconds. Thereafter he lacked his usual spark and ended up with 25:10, well outside the record of Sid Thomas of Ranelagh Harriers. This time the critics appeared justified in knocking his tactics. Perhaps he did indeed need time to throw off what they called the winter's cross-country 'slows'.

Ever the optimist, Shrubb was not disheartened. He announced he would make another attempt on the five-mile record at Stamford Bridge a month later, when he hoped the handicapping would be more favourable to his purposes than it had been at the Oval.

CHAPTER EIGHT

At the Peak of his Powers

When an athlete is at the peak of his powers, confidence is sky high and almost anything seems possible. The year of 1904 would be Shrubb's zenith. At distances of more than a mile he was unbeatable and seemed able to pick and choose which championships to win and which records to break.

His talent knew no bounds in 1904 and – just like a comic-book hero – he even called upon his abilities to help the sick and needy. After an evening fixture in South London one night, rather than catch the late train home, Shrubb accepted the hospitality of a National Sporting Club member. In the middle of the night one of the family was taken ill and the ensuing fuss woke everybody, including house-guest Shrubb. The local doctor was summoned but could do little, saying a specialist would have to be fetched from central London first thing in the morning. Recalled Shrubb: 'I said to my host that it might be dangerous to wait so long, as time was a great matter in such cases, and the patient should not be allowed to suffer any longer than we could help. There was no cab to be had at that time of night, and in any case I knew that I could run just about as fast as a cab.'

To the astonishment of his grateful host, Shrubb offered to run the five miles across sleeping London to Harley Street to wake the specialist and bring him back in a cab. 'Without wasting any more words I set off in the early hours of the morning, when the traffic of London was at its lowest ebb. The only vehicles I passed were market carts going to Covent Garden. It was about half past two but the physician promptly left his warm bed and hurried into the cab I had brought to the door. On arrival an operation was immediately performed. What would have happened had this not been done nobody knows.'

Shrubb's pre-dawn mercy run was hailed an act of heroism and he heard later that the patient had made a full recovery. Around the same time, however, he also received sad news. The death was reported of fellow runner Albert Palmer, skipper of the Welsh cross-country team, who had raced against Shrubb several times. Palmer had been killed in a workplace accident at Newport, Monmouthshire, crushed between a wall and a railway truck carrying eight tons of bricks. He had been captain of Newport Harriers and was Welsh cross-country champion in 1900 and 1901.

By now, Shrubb had become a regular star attraction for athletics fans at the thriving Stamford Bridge venue, and another big crowd turned out on Thursday, May 12th to witness his latest attempt on the world five-mile record. He felt in good shape, it was a calm night, the track was in fine fettle, and everything seemed ripe for a record attempt. The handi-capper awarded starts to the other runners that were just generous enough to give Shrubb men to chase right to the end. This was essential, for there certainly weren't any runners who could give him a real test over the full distance. Hulford of Herne Hill was given 575 yards, and Cleveley of Highgate 430.

Shrubb clocked a fast 4:31.2 for the first mile and followed it with another sub-five mile to reach two in 9:30.6. At this point his pace stead-ied to around 75 seconds per lap, meaning both the twelve-year-old ama-teur record of Sid Thomas (24:53) and the 41-year-old professional record (24.40), set by little Jack White, known as 'the Gateshead clipper', were within reach. The three-mile point was passed in 19:35, just four seconds outside the world record for that distance. Now surely only a dis-aster could stop him. There were a few worrying moments when Shrubb appeared to limp slightly as he chased Hulford and Cleveley up ahead. But to his followers' relief he recovered to come home in a triumphant 24:33.4, shattering both existing records. Hulford and Cleveley both fin-ished ahead of Shrubb, but by less than thirty yards, meaning the handi-capper had got it about right. A measure of this run can be gauged by the fact that Shrubb's record time would stand as a British record for 48 years. 'Sprinter', a columnist for *Athletic News*, wrote that he was inclined to regard Shrubb as 'a physical wonder' in the same way that E M Grace had regarded his younger brother, the cricketer W G.

Still on a high, less than 48 hours later Shrubb was scheduled to run at Redhill for a three-mile inter-club race hosted by Herne Hill Harriers. There were only seven events, but they attracted a total of 450 entrants, such was the popularity of this meeting. Shrubb had little difficulty in winning his race in 14:48.2, forty yards clear of Albert Aldridge, who probably had the misfortune to finish second to Shrubb more than any other runner over the years, and must have been sickened by the rear view of Shrubb's wiry little frame.

Following the success of his first visit to Scotland the previous sum-mer, Shrubb was delighted when South London Harriers entered a team to compete for the Connell Cup at Ibrox Park, Glasgow, in May 1904. As the reigning mile champion of England, Shrubb was obliged to defend his country's honour against Scotland's top miler, the burly postman John McGough of Bellahouston Harriers. The two would also meet at three miles. In the shorter race, the Scot allowed Shrubb to make the pace on the first lap (58 seconds), but then moved alongside his smaller opponent and resolutely stayed there until the final bend of the final lap. This was the type of serious challenge that Shrubb rarely received, and there was a deafening roar as the two hurtled for home together. They were shoulder to shoulder as the tape loomed, but the bigger strides of the Scot proved decisive and he forced himself ahead by two yards amid scenes of wild exultation, clocking 4:26. The postman had delivered. The jubilant home fans were delighted to see the Sassenach champion beaten and McGough was carried shoulder high to the pavilion.

The press had a field day, lambasting Shrubb for being beaten by his own bad judgement and by 'a presumed bad runner' – for McGough had finished nowhere in the AAA half-mile championship in Northampton the previous year. It was a setback for Shrubb, who was clearly doing too much running, they suggested. In truth, the mile was always liable to be too short for Shrubb, and he was always likely to be matched by someone with good basic speed, unless he could play psychological games and 'con' them into defeat. Such was the glee at seeing England's 'Little Wonder' beaten, that his later victory in the three-miler (in 14:59.4) received little attention. Shrubb remained in Scotland for the West of Scotland Harriers gala a few days later and this time dropped out of the three-mile race with four laps left, looking less than happy with life. During his stay, Edinburgh Southern Harriers made overtures about him racing at their track on a future visit, and Shrubb promised he would consider this, for he had heard about the excellent cinder track at Powderhall and was keen to try it out.

During his long journey home, Shrubb stopped off at Bollington in Cheshire, where a two-mile handicap had been put on for his benefit, carrying a first prize valued at £10. The local club had spent £30 on improving their track by raising the corners and banking to make them as safe as any grass course could be. Shrubb found the track to his liking and banished his Ibrox blues by scorching to victory in 9:17.8, less than a second outside his own record. *The Daily Telegraph* noted that had anyone been capable on the night of extending him, little Bollington would have surely witnessed a new world record.

At the end of May, Stamford Bridge hosted a new concept – relay racing. London Athletic Club took on a 'Rest of England' side, and the teams completed the distance by passing a flag between members. The event was not without teething problems. One bewildered runner was knocked over by a clumsy teammate and another had to stop and go back after his teammate with the flag slowed up too early for the change-over.

The idea was generally greeted positively, however, but it would be years before relay-racing reached its modern-day status as one of the most exciting of all track events.

On Saturday June 4th, SLH welcomed old friends Racing Club de Paris back to London for a third meeting between the clubs. Shrubb won the three-mile contest in 14:42.2, failing to lap second-placed De Fleurac by just ten yards. He also won the mile in 4:28 by around 200 yards as the Frenchmen were humbled by six events to one. These results restored Shrubb's equilibrium after the knock to his confidence in Scotland. He made up his mind that his return to Glasgow for the WoSH summer meeting on June 11th would be the ideal opportunity to put matters right and show the enthusiastic locals why he was Britain's No 1.

According to *Athletic News*, Shrubb crossed the border 'with his teeth clenched'. They reported that he made amends in a manner that would live long in the memories of those privileged to be at Ibrox. The meeting gave Shrubb the chance of revenge over McGough in the mile, and for good measure he also entered the two and four-mile events.

On race day, Shrubb was seen to be 'in fine humour' and the ground looked at its best, having been carefully tended by James Wilson. It was sunny with a slight breeze as Shrubb set off in the two-miler at a spanking rate. The approving crowd could now treat him as one of their own, for he had agreed to join WoSH and represent them in meetings when SLH and Blue Star weren't competing. Shrubb clocked the first mile in an excellent 4:27, at which point W Robertson (Clydesdale Harriers), who had looked in good form, suddenly walked off the track. Shrubb didn't even notice and hit 1½ miles in 6:49, well inside world record pace. W P Russell (Bellahouston) made a plucky attempt to gain ground but had no answer to Shrubb's final kick, and he came home in 9:09.6, two seconds quicker than the disallowed world record he had set in Ilford a year earlier. The time also obliterated his own amateur record of 9:17, at Kennington Oval, and also beat the 41-year-old professional record of 9.11.2, set at Manchester back in 1863 by Bill Lang. The watches of the two Scottish AAA timekeepers agreed on Shrubb's lap splits (full details in Appendix).

Unlike Ilford, conditions this day were indisputable and *Athletic News* observed: 'This record will live in Scottish history. He looked fresh as paint after his record as he turned out for the mile.' The world record clearly invigorated Shrubb, for he was soon engaged in the mile, another thriller, and this time he avenged the defeat by McGough. Shrubb came home in 4:23.8 – a fraction outside Hugh Welsh's Scottish record – beating McGough in another tight finish which had the crowd in a frenzy.

The meeting resumed two days later, and there was more excitement in the air as Shrubb declared he would repay Scottish hospitality by going for the four-mile world record. Amazingly, he managed it, starting off scratch and flying home in 19:23.4, eighty yards clear of J S Barrie of Motherwell, who had been given a 380-yard start. Shrubb flashed through the notional 5,000 metres point in an estimated 14:59, meaning he had beaten his own unofficial world record for that distance too. The finish time smashed Shrubb's own four-mile mark set in Brighton eighteen months earlier, and also clipped two seconds off the professional world record of Paddy Cannon, established sixteen years earlier. Both of Shrubb's new Glasgow records were later passed by the AAA and, later still, ratified by the world body, the IAAF. The two-mile mark would stand for 22 years until Swedish Olympian Edvin Wide finally cracked it in 1926.

Shrubb's sensational 'double' naturally had the athletics press in raptures and there was much speculation over whether he could maintain this form into the following month's AAA championships in Rochdale. A number of top American athletes were also planning to compete, preferring the prestigious AAA event to the Olympic Games scheduled for their own country.

As Rochdale loomed, AAA officials made headlines of their own by announcing a clampdown on the 'undesirable' modern clothing that had been appearing at recent events. They demanded 'proper dress' for Rochdale, pointing out that at Northampton in 1903, one or two costumes had been deemed indecent. The rules were set out: 'Every competitor must wear complete clothing from the shoulders to the knees, e.g. sleeved jersey and loose drawers.' *Athletic News* gleefully noted that the Americans at Rochdale might struggle to conform with these orders as they always wore sleeveless jerseys and their top sprinter, Arthur Duffey, 'with his splendid girl-like arms hidden in the folds of a Salford Harriers jersey, say, will look a queer figure.'

The American invasion was greeted by media excitement. They noted that four years earlier there had been a similar influx at the AAA championships at Stamford Bridge. Eight titles had gone to Americans on that memorable day. Shrubb now opted to defend his mile title, as well as the four, at Rochdale, and in the absence of favourite Henry Gregson, was thought likely to prevail. The inconsistent Joe Binks was seen as the only man capable of stopping him. To warm up for the big day, Shrubb won the Willis mile cup at a SLH evening meeting in 4:27.4.

The Rochdale event on July 2nd began just hours after the 1904 Olympics opened in St Louis, USA. The Olympics were not seen as a high priority event at the time and Britain and France both decided not to send teams. This did not prevent the St Louis organisers boldly claiming they were hosting the greatest athletes in the world. The Olympic programme was again a protracted affair lasting several months and the whole thing became a second-rate sideshow to the World's Fair, being staged simultaneously. It would be at least another four years before the world at large began to pay serious attention to the Olympic movement.

Rochdale also coincided with the launch of a new athletics magazine, *W.G.'s Athletic Weekly*. Named after its proprietor and editor, legendary former runner Walter George, it featured Shrubb on the front cover of the first issue. He was named 'Man of the Week' and his style and performances were analysed in detail in the inside pages. 'He is one of the world's marvels, if not absolutely the greatest wonder in the shape of an athlete who has ever lived or donned a running shoe.' The article continued to eulogise: 'Shrubb has, times out of number, astonished athletics circles by his phenomenal running, remarkable powers of endurance, and the consistency of his performances. It is open to doubt if any other athlete has ever won so many championships, local races, road handicaps in the same length of time he has.

'He is not a massive man, but what there is of him is wondrous, shapely, neat, pretty and nice. The leg muscles are well formed and although not large in circumference, are particularly long and we might add, decidedly useful. This wonderful runner is unassuming in manner, he is of dark, inclining to a sallow, complexion and above all things is practically a teetotaller. He is wise enough to take the greatest possible care of himself and trains in his own sweet way, eating and drinking in moderation just exactly what is put before him; or rather what he fancies at the moment, not neglecting good ripe fruit and plenty of vegetables.

'He does a moderate amount of walking and takes a lot of steady running exercise finishing with a sharp burst of 50 to 100 yards and then just one or two sprints of about 100 yards to liven himself up. After a good rub-down he has a quiet walk back to his place of business. His action when running is rather low and gliding, consequently his stride is much longer than is apparent to the ordinary observer. The arms are carried particularly well and low, while the body and head remain nicely poised, leaning slightly forward and beautifully steady. When running even at his best pace, he however invariably gallops the last 100 yards or so – this mode of progress is most effective, and alarmingly demoralising to a tried opponent. Mr Horace Crossley (London AC) was the greatest exponent of this style of going that we remember. He was an excellent sprinter and quarter man in the 1870s and early 80s.

'Altogether he has won about 350 prizes and is the possessor of the following records: 2,000 yards 5:07.6; One-and-a-half miles 6:47.6; Two miles 9:09.6; Three miles 14:17.4; Three-and-three-quarter miles 18:25.4; Four miles 19:23.8; Five miles 24:33.2. The above figures, in our opinion, can be beaten by him and we quite anticipate he will do the mile and four-miler at Rochdale today and probably beat 50 minutes for ten miles at Stamford Bridge in September if he will only be satisfied in running his first mile just outside, as opposed to just inside, five minutes and afterwards run to a prepared schedule.'

France, USA, Scotland and Ireland joined the cream of English athletes at Rochdale, a venue *Athletic News* columnist 'Philistine' described as 'not the prettiest ground in the world, but extremely business-like in its equipment, and the surroundings are a quaint blend of the picturesque and the prosaic.' Athletes reaching the required standards still had to pay a race entry fee of five shillings, unless they were current champions in their events, and admission for spectators was sixpence, or a shilling in the reserved enclosure. The sun shone intermittently and there was a brisk wind down the home straight, but the threat of stormy weather failed to materialise.

In his first race, the mile, Shrubb led from the start, but George Butterfield (Darlington) applied pressure just before the bell. According to Philistine, Shrubb then 'started that horrible practice he has taken to of late in shorter races of looking over his shoulder every other stride.' Butterfield passed him 300 yards from home, but Shrubb rallied and hit the front again. McGough, the Bellahouston postman, suddenly burst alongside and Shrubb looked beaten. In a frantic finish, Shrubb forced himself over the line to win by no more than two yards, collapsing in a heap – an unprecedented experience – looking distressed. McGough had also given everything, but remained on his feet and smiling.

An anxious Philistine reported: 'These strains and shocks upon his constitution must be undermining Shrubb's health, but he is a boy to try and win if there's half a chance.' Walter George again took the chance to ram home his usual criticism of Shrubb: 'In my opinion [he] will never be a miler, but his 4:22 beats anything he has ever accomplished before. At longer distances the Little Wonder is superb, he absolutely revels in them, but if he will be advised by an old hand he will not bother about the one-miles for they don't suit him and his constitution.'

A few minutes after the end of the race George caught up with Shrubb, who had slipped behind the grandstand to recover in peace from the sort of exhaustion he had rarely known. 'He looked even then fagged and tired and complained that the wind bothered him,' recalled George.

The four-mile race was scheduled to start just 75 minutes after the mile, but despite his earlier distress, Shrubb won with little difficulty. He darted away in his usual fashion to triumph in 19:56.8 and capture his fourth successive national title at the distance. The winning time was the best at this event in nine years. He again lifted the impressive four-mile challenge cup, said to be worth sixty guineas.

Aged just 24, Shrubb was reported to have now won thirty championship events and a total of 350 prizes – barely five years since he first set foot on a running track. He had also emulated George's record of ten AAA titles. The crowd enveloped him after the finish, their exuberant congratulations even causing annoyance to one man present – Shrubb's former coach Harry Andrews. 'The public spoil almost every champion,' recalled Andrews. 'The people rushed [at Shrubb] at the finish and put their arms round his neck and started kissing him. I soon pulled him away – rather roughly.'

As well as singing Shrubb's praises in Monday's *Athletic News*, its correspondent 'Philistine' found it necessary to remind readers of the great and glorious works of the AAA: 'It stands as the parent of all disciples of athleticism and it encourages and fosters a love for pure sport and laudable competition. It is the head and foot of all the unoffending athletic festivals in England and it exercises a wise and beneficient jurisdiction over all meetings for the distinct and express purpose of keeping a popular pastime and a delightful mode of exercise free from the sordid taint of professionalism.'

A week after his notable 'double' at Rochdale, Shrubb was back at the Chelmsford cricket ground, winning his fifth successive Atalanta Cup in the Essex three-mile championship. Around 350 invited guests enjoyed a sumptuous marquee lunch in the Bishop of Colchester's adjacent private garden, some of them having their fill and then emerging to see Shrubb and 35 others tackle the one-mile open handicap race. The national champion did not like the way things were going after two laps, however, and retired, which allowed his Horsham pal H Browning to come home first.

In the bill-topping three-miler, however, Shrubb took off fast, opened up a lead of 150 yards, and won in 14:37.2. Essex's genial and popular secretary, Robert Cook, was praised for his work on this gloriously hot day, which helped boost the crowd to nearly 10,000. The Essex County Cycling and Athletic Association, which was instituted in 1883, was second to none in its powers of organisation, reported one paper, adding that Essex's annual event had met with immense support, and had done much to encourage the promotion of athletics generally.

A few days after his return to Horsham, Shrubb vacated his West Street tobacconists to go on his travels. Instead of closing the shop, he was able to call on one of his sisters to do duty behind the counter. On this particular trip Shrubb was northward bound, to defend the Parry Challenge Cup at Belle Vue, Manchester. The event was part of Salford Harriers' (the Turkey Reds) 'coming-of-age' celebrations. There were 850 entries and a mammoth attendance as Shrubb repeated his two-mile success of 1903, winning in 9:22.2, which entitled him to keep the £25 cup for good. July also saw him in action in Bristol, where he won a three-miler in 15:14, and then at the Brighton Fire Brigade Sports in Preston Park, where he won the three-mile handicap in 14:40 by a handsome 150-yard margin.

A runner in top form is inevitably a busy runner, and August 1904 was a hectic month for Shrubb, even by his own hyperactive standards. At the annual Horsham sports on a sweltering day, there were record takings and a 5,000 crowd at the cricket meadow. The Band of the King's Dragoon guards entertained the crowd, who looked forward to the much-hyped highlight of the day at 3.30pm, a head-to-head over two miles between Shrubb and the promising young talent Charles Straw (Northern junior champion). Sadly the confrontation failed to live up to expectations as the northerner didn't give Shrubb much of a race and he won easily in 9:33.2. Straw had been given a 100-yard start but, with his long easy strides, Shrubb overhauled him after six laps and Straw wilted. Shrubb won by about twelve yards and took the prize, valued at £10. The torchlight procession that evening saw Shrubb standing in the Blue Star car, holding aloft the Parry Cup he'd won in Manchester in July.

On August 6th, Shrubb won a two-miler at Hampton Harriers Sports in Middlesex, recording a good time in high winds on a track described in the press as 'unusually-shaped'. A week later he took in the Atherton Parish Church Sports in Lancashire, but was set a stiff task by the handicapper and retired in the last lap, apparently to make his point that catching the rest was impossible. In the same week, *W.G.'s Athletic Weekly* reported that Shrubb had his sights on breaking Binks' national mile record before the end of the season. He had calculated that to do so needed laps of 62, 64, 70 and 60 seconds. Wise old 'W G' confidently predicted that such a feat was beyond Shrubb.

In the meantime, Shrubb's next stop was Stoke-on-Trent on August 16th, where he won a two-miler in 9:31.2 and, remaining in the Potteries, two days later won another 'two' at Stone in 9:57. Maintaining a hectic travel schedule that must have been rare in 1904, Shrubb was back south two days later to race over three miles at the Southend-on-Sea Sports in

Marine Park, where he won in 14:51.2, beating Aldridge by sixty yards. It was back north 48 hours later to Burnden Park, Bolton, where Shrubb had an unexpected rest day after thunderstorms caused a postponement of his race. The next day he called in at Tewkesbury, Gloucestershire, to register victory at 1½ miles. His whistle-stop tour of the provinces continued with a three-mile win in the attractive Worcestershire town of Pershore, before making his debut on Welsh soil on August 27th at Abergavenny.

The Inter-Town Sports in Abergavenny's Bailey Park took place under blue skies, but late-arriving Cardiff athletes meant a thirty-minute delay and all events on the picturesque grass track were put back. There was drama in the two-mile walk when Cardiff's J Leary was disqualified for 'shuffling'. Leary is said to have lost self-control at this decision, and violently abused the officials, which led to his being reported to the AAA of South Wales.

Shrubb ran in the three-mile open handicap, where only three finished from a big field. He completed the first lap in just 57 seconds and found the firm, springy grass to his liking. He roared through his twelve laps in 14:17.2, smashing his own existing world record on grass. He had set a time that would not be beaten for eighteen years, although not being on a cinder track meant it was never ratified by the IAAF. F Webber of the home club was a brave second and Cardiff's R Davies third.

With summer turning to autumn, Shrubb cut down on his travelling. In mid-September he performed in front of an estimated 20,000 at SLH's traditional autumn meeting at Kennington Oval. He won the two-mile handicap in 9:22.8 in what seemed like perfect running weather, but the wind got up towards the end to dispel hopes of breaking his own world record for the distance. Two days later, at the same venue, Shrubb took part in a charity cricket match, arranged between teams of jockeys and athletes in aid of the Robert Abel Testimonial Fund.

The diminutive Abel was a former Surrey and England cricketer, forced to retire aged 46 due to a long-standing eye problem. He would later lose his sight completely. Abel once scored 357 in a single innings at the Oval, and was also the first English batsman to carry his bat throughout a Test innings, scoring an unbeaten 132 in Sydney. Admission to his testimonial was sixpence, and players wore numbers on their backs for this fun event. Shrubb looked a decent medium-pace bowler and a superb fielder and managed to dismiss two of the jockeys. He recalled later how the jockeys held their bats in strange ways in order to protect their hands – but confessed he probably also looked odd when trying to fend the ball off his 'valuable' legs. He opened the batting for the athletes, and hit ten runs before being clean-bowled by W Griggs. Shrubb's fellow opener was W Lotinga, *The People* journalist who often used the pen name Larry Lynx, and who had promoted the match. Lotinga later made his name by launching the popular sports tabloid, *Lotinga's Weekly*. Shrubb recalled his cricketing experiences with fondness: 'I thought I bowled like a streak, but hitting the wicket was another matter. Anyhow, the ball was presented to me as a souvenir, with a nice little silver shield, bearing a dated inscription: Presented by Mr Robert Abel to the best bowler of the match.'

Although it seems to have merited little or no publicity at the time, Shrubb had by now been formally invited to travel to Australia and New Zealand to take part in various local championships in early 1905. The invitation had to pass through the AAA of England, who would consider whether Shrubb was a suitable ambassador for the mother country and would report back later with their decision. Shrubb, fond of travel, was excited by the idea of competing in the newly federated Commonwealth of Australia, a vibrant young nation that was not yet four years old. The fact that it was on the other side of the world and involved a six-week boat trip each way, didn't worry him in the slightest.

For the moment, he prepared for a crack at the ten-mile track world record with long walks and brisk medium-length runs around the lanes of Horsham. Shortly before the record attempt at Stamford Bridge, he fulfilled an engagement in the Midlands which he felt might 'sharpen' his speed. He duly won this three-mile evening race at Rugby Railway Servants Club in 14:49.6, nineteen seconds ahead of anyone else. The track had hastily been re-measured before Shrubb's race, following an earlier event in which the winner's time had been deemed too good to be true. The track had indeed been seven yards short and was re-marked just in time for Shrubb's run.

While Shrubb was concentrating on his ten-mile ambitions, the annual meeting of his second-claim club, Horsham Blue Star Harriers, heard a proposal from senior member Fred Spencer that Shrubb be made club captain. The reasoning was that Blue Star didn't want its captain being beaten by younger runners, and if Shrubb took the role it would solve this problem! This was unanimously agreed, and subs for the year were set at two shillings, a sum even the nationally famous Shrubb would have to pay. Blue Star also decided to affiliate to the AAA, having previously abided by its rules without actually joining up.

Shrubb's hectic schedule saw him take in the final meeting of the 1904 track season at Crystal Palace, winning the three-miles in 14:56.6 by a 160-yard margin on a heavy track and in blustery conditions. There was a big crowd in attendance, largely due to the appearance of legendary cricketer Dr W G Grace. Grace had recently played his last game for the MCC at the age of 56 and was described in one report as 'the life and soul of the meeting'. He helped judge the sprints, took part in a 'bowling at the wicket' event, and arranged the starts for the 100 yards members' handicap. After one heat had gone off, the old cricketer couldn't resist having a run himself. In response to cries from the crowd, he doffed his cap, grinned through his famous beard, and took his mark in the next 100 yards heat. He was given a 22-yard start, the length of cricket pitch. He finished second and, suitably encouraged, changed into cricket flannels for the final. Here, again benefitting from a 22-yard advantage, he won by a yard, in twelve seconds, despite his cricketing attire and some strong crosswinds. The crowd marvelled at his versatility and fitness. Earlier in the week, Grace had also reached the semi-finals of the London County bowling club's singles tournament.

The Stamford Bridge ten-mile record attempt and subsequent events at Ibrox Park, Glasgow, are covered fully in the next chapter. Once his demanding autumn programme was over, Shrubb was able to concentrate his mind on the impending trip to Australasia, which had by now been given the seal of approval by the denizens of the AAA. In the meantime, he accepted an invitation to run as a guest for Warrington Harriers against Winnington Park Harriers. Lancashire sports fans turned out in droves to see the multi-record breaker, and he demonstrated his prowess with victory over local favourite Charles Straw in a six-mile contest. Later in the month Shrubb turned out for Blue Star against newly formed Crawley Harriers, winning a four-mile road race in 20:21, by 94 seconds. The course took the runners from Leggatt's restaurant in Crawley to the Red Lion at Lowfield Heath and back.

SLH's Croydon Cup contest kicked off the cross-country season in early December and, despite relatively little running since his Guy Fawkes' night event in Glasgow, Shrubb was asked to concede liberal starts to his opponents. He came in second, overhauling everybody except L Willcocks, who had been given eight minutes. Shrubb's time of 28:21 was quickest of the day, however. Five days later, in another four-miler for Blue Star against the Crawley boys, Shrubb won again by a big margin, this time in a more modest 21:28.

Christmas saw Shrubb preparing for his trip to the southern hemisphere. Such an adventure was a rare and exciting event in 1904, even for a well-known sportsman. Accompanying him 'on tour' would be the top American sprinter Arthur Duffey, the pair having been invited to share top billing at the various meetings they had been invited to. Duffey was a big name in the States at that time, having for a while held the world record for the 100-yard dash (9.6 seconds). He was also 'famous' for the unfortunate tumble he took in the 100 metres final at the 1900 Paris Olympics. It seems likely that Duffey and Shrubb had first met at the Rochdale AAA event in July. Another SLH man, the sprinter J W Morton, originally planned to join the voyage, but 'business and other reasons' caused him to pull out.

Commenting on Shrubb's forthcoming adventure, *The West Sussex County Times* warned that he might be lost to Britain for five months, 'but he can be depended upon to show the Australians a thing or two.' Shrubb was scheduled to leave Horsham on December 29th 1904, to sail the next day from Tilbury docks in Essex aboard the *SS Ortona*. He wouldn't arrive Down Under until well into February. One newspaper pointed out that Shrubb's absence would be a fillip to the runners left behind, particularly Albert Aldridge, who always seemed to play second fiddle to Shrubb in major races. It was even suggested by some that Shrubb's recent superiority had been damaging athletics by making every big event a 'one-horse race.'

The AAA's traditional end-of-year committee meeting at Birmingham surveyed events of the past twelve months and concluded that 1904 had been an extraordinary year for record-breaking. As well as Shrubb's well-publicised efforts, his contemporaries Larner, Butler and Thompson had also gone into the record books. British athletics could look back on the year and be proud of its achievements.

CHAPTER NINE

Fireworks in Glasgow

Even Doctor Badger winced as Alf Shrubb pulled off his blood-stained shoe at the end of the race. His big toe was a mangled mess, the nail almost completely detached. Twenty-four-year-old Shrubb had just lapped the cinder track at London's Stamford Bridge stadium 44 times in an hour, completing eleven miles in the process. Most athletes back in September 1904 would have been mighty pleased at such a performance – but not the moustachioed perfectionist Shrubb. As his wounds were dressed at trackside, the little man from Sussex fretted about an afternoon's work that, for him, had gone horribly wrong.

Never again, he vowed. Never again shall I run to a schedule, or in a fashion dictated by someone else. Normally a quiet, mild-mannered fellow, Shrubb was fuming at having missed the world's ten-mile record – thanks to the interference of others. He was convinced now, more than ever, that to beat the record, things had to be done his way. The record-holder and revered former champion Walter 'W G' George had prepared a training programme and race schedule, and insisted Shrubb follow it to the letter. Shrubb, who loved to run free, uninhibited by instructions or mid-race targets, argued with the great man, but eventually caved in and agreed to follow orders. The result was disastrous.

Irritated by the race officials constantly yelling out lap-times, and inhibited by the detail he had been forced to memorise, Shrubb ran like a man with pressure on his shoulders and without his usual spark. Instead of flying away from the gun as he usually did, injecting bursts of pace as and when he felt like it, today he attempted an even-paced slog from the start. It cramped his style and he faded in the latter stages, falling 38 seconds short of George's twenty-year-old record (51:20) at the ten-mile point. The huge crowd, who had turned out to see Shrubb star in the London Athletic Club's final meeting at this ground, groaned in disappointment. Shrubb kept running beyond the ten-mile mark, as he still had a chance of creating a new one-hour record, but his annoyance at missing the first objective left him in the wrong frame of mind and he soon quit altogether. He hated disappointing his fans, and although he had actually won the race by the usual huge margin, this victory felt hollow. Walter George, now a respected 46-year-old sportswriter, might be right to insist on even-paced running for most record attempts, but this was a rule of distance-running that did not apply to the unique Alfred Shrubb.

Grim-faced in his trilby and raincoat, the diminutive figure of Shrubb was collared later that evening by a newspaper reporter on Clapham Junction station as he made his way home. Ever the diplomat, Shrubb refused to be publicly critical of George and his 'foolproof' schedules. He also urged the reporter not to cite the painful toe injury as the reason he missed the record. Privately, Shrubb was already making plans for another assault on the twenty-year-old ten-mile mark. This new attempt would definitely be done *his* way. He would cancel all races for a four-week period and undergo intensive training, at the end of which he would head for Scotland and attack the record on his favourite track, on Guy Fawkes' day, November 5th, 1904. Ibrox Park in Glasgow boasted a superb running surface and Shrubb had many friends to look after him in the city. Furthermore, he would be performing at a venue where he had already smashed world records at shorter distances.

Shrubb vowed to put his forthcoming Australian trip out of his mind and give full concentration to taking George's old record. For his part, George admired Shrubb's spirit but was regularly critical of the tactics employed by 'The Little Wonder'. It only made Shrubb all the more determined, particularly when he read that George regarded the ten-mile record as 'a bit soft'. George justified this remark by claiming he himself once beat the record by nearly a minute in a private and unofficial time-trial in Birmingham.

Shrubb drew up a four-week training programme, which was timed to begin a fortnight after the Stamford Bridge debacle and end just before the fixture at Ibrox Park. Years later, this programme would be studied and praised as highly innovative for the times. Although it involved no runs of longer than the race distance of ten miles, it represented an unusually heavy workload averaging nine miles per day for three weeks, and then a tapering off towards race day. At the start of the schedule the 5ft 6in (1.69m) Shrubb weighed in at 8st 10lbs. Already snake-thin, he would shed a further four pounds during the period.

The full training programme appears in Appendix 1 to this book. It shows that Shrubb incorporated three ten-mile time trials to gauge his fitness during the four weeks. The routine involved him undertaking a brisk walk before breakfast, and on most days running in both the morning and afternoon. He rarely ran at all on Sundays, although this was not due to religious reasons. Slow, steady running was not a major part of the programme and many of his spins were at a brisk pace over anything between two and eight miles. The three time-trials produced results he kept secret from the press at the time, but we now know to have been as follows: October 19th: 51:10; October 25th: 51:02; November 1st: 50:55.

All three were quicker than the existing record, showing him to be in great shape.

The omens were good. Earlier that year, of course, Shrubb had twice accepted invitations to compete in Glasgow and had thrilled the crowds and the host club – West of Scotland Harriers (WoSH) – with his bold front-running style. On the second visit, he had smashed world records that had stood for many years at two and four miles. It created huge interest and WoSH couldn't wait to have him back again. For his attempt on the '10', Shrubb was again the house guest of Jack Primrose Brown, a senior WoSH official who would be Clerk of the Course for the big day, and his wife, at their cosy home in Darnley Street, Pollokshields.

Shrubb travelled north alone, taking the train to Glasgow, and once in the city received what he called 'wonderful hospitality and cheer'. He was made to feel like a returning son at the Brown's house, which was handily positioned, three miles from Ibrox. Shrubb, who by now was coaching himself, admitted that Mrs Brown was as good as any trainer to him, preparing good, wholesome food that she deemed to be suitable for an athlete. He arrived on the Monday before the race and soon settled in, thanks to the Browns and the particularly helpful Sid Cornish, another WoSH official, who would be a lap-counter and steward on race day. Cornish acted like a minder for the star runner from England, doing everything he could for him. Shrubb was left with nothing to worry about except Saturday afternoon's upcoming race. As usual he was a bag of nerves as the big day approached.

On the Tuesday afternoon, Shrubb blasted a solo time-trial in under 51 minutes. That would be good enough for the record if he could reproduce it. Weighing himself later on, he found he was now a leaner than ever 8st 6lbs. On the Wednesday he ran two miles fast in the morning and then did five at a steady pace after lunch. Thursday, November 3rd saw him jog eight miles in the morning with a brisk four miles in the afternoon. The preparations were now complete, and he rested completely – apart from a brisk walk – the day before the event.

Speaking to the press during his rest day, Shrubb explained that autumn was the best season for making records. He reiterated that it 'crippled him' to run to a schedule and he had never felt worse than during the futile record attempt at Stamford Bridge. 'I simply went from bad to worse and when, after making me go slowly, my friends began shouting that now I was going too slowly, I told them I couldn't help it and dropped into a sluggishness from which there was no escape.'

On race day, Saturday, November 5th, Shrubb was awake by seven, with the usual butterflies in his stomach, in order to carry out his regular morning pre-race routine, including a brisk walk. He was undaunted by the leaden, rain-filled skies above this austere city. Back in Mrs Brown's parlour, he had to be particular what he ate and took care not to overdo things with Mrs Brown's hearty breakfast offerings.

Over at Ibrox Park in the Govan district, home of Glasgow Rangers FC, conditions seemed far from ideal to the casual observer. The track was very wet and a lively wind was blowing, but Shrubb knew the surface was firm and true and able to withstand punishment from runners and the weather. The way the track banked was also helpful when overtaking. It was a place Shrubb knew and loved and it filled him with confidence. Around lunchtime it was still drizzling, but not the type of rain to worry Shrubb: 'A gentle rain refreshes the long-distance runner as he pegs away at his task.'

For all his amazing achievements and wealth of experience, pre-race nerves was something Shrubb never shook off during a career that would ultimately extend to more than 1,000 races. Jack Brown did his best to dispel the anxiety, boisterously urging Shrubb 'not to look so pale' and reassuring him the record was bound to be his, reminding him that the race arrangements were designed to help him. Unlike the usual handicap races, where other runners started ahead of Shrubb at the same time, this was a 'sealed' handicap, with the opposition receiving between two minutes, thirty seconds and six minutes advantage over him. Everyone would line up and start together, and the handicap times only calculated after the finish. Originally twenty entrants were listed but only thirteen would toe the line – all representing Scottish clubs, including Shrubb who was down as a 'guest' of the host club.

His was 'Event Three' on the programme, billed as 'a special attempt to create new world's records for 10 miles and one hour'. Regulations in those days permitted host clubs to openly declare such record attempts and the whole event was openly stage-managed in order to give the Englishman the best possible chance of achieving his goal. Admission to the stadium cost sixpence and official programmes – featuring a full-page picture of Shrubb on the back – were tuppence. The crowd filed in after lunchtime and the official attendance was later given as 1,400, although the racket they created made it seem far higher.

There were six scheduled events, with Shrubb's feature race preceded at 3pm by the heats and semi-finals of a 100 yards handicap. The second half of the programme would feature wrestling in the centre of the stadium, plus the final of the 100 yards. The athletics judge for the day was Dr J G Kerr and the timekeepers J W Brownrigg, A Ross-Scott, A G Rennie and Jimmy Fowler-Dixon. Sixteen lap-scorers and stewards were in place, including the versatile R G Murray, a well-known high-jumper who also participated in the 100 yards heats. George Cameron was to be starter.

Shrubb's previous best ten-mile time was 51:30.4, established at Preston Park, Brighton, eighteen months earlier. He needed to improve that time by a full ten seconds to beat George's amateur record. Shrubb also had his eye on the world professional record of 51:05.6 set by Harry Watkins in 1899.

When he emerged from the dressing room just before 4pm, the skies were dark and forbidding, but Shrubb was uplifted as the crowd ignored the joyless Glasgow weather and gave him a spine-tingling welcome. 'The cheers almost lifted me off my feet and my hair seemed to go upright with excitement,' he recalled. The sprinters from the first two events withdrew to the sidelines to join the brawny, kilted wrestlers to watch the day's main event. Shrubb had earlier asked Jack Brown to lay on some music during the race and Brown had organised pipers, who stood by for the signal to inflate their bagpipes. Brown also supervised a huge blackboard in the centre of the stadium on which everyone could follow Shrubb's progress by checking mile 'splits' and counting down the laps. Shrubb, as was his way, would only rarely glance at this information during the race.

A hush gripped the crowd as the thirteen runners took up their positions and leaned forward expectantly, Shrubb, in white, positioned at the centre. Starter Cameron raised an apparently recalcitrant pistol two or three times before he was able to fire them on their way. Shrubb surged ahead of the pack within seconds. He said later he had been full of running from the start, happy in mind and free from the worries of figures, schedules and times. His one idea was 'to get there'. He opened up a gap and completed the first 440-yard lap in a speedy 64.8 seconds. It would, by a long way, be his fastest lap of the entire race. Employing his usual economical, if not graceful, style he then settled into a rhythm of laps of 75 or 76 seconds each. This pace was maintained until after the halfway point, and there was no sign of the characteristic surges that Shrubb had become famous for. He was clearly disciplining himself to keep things steady.

Clocking 9:44.2 for the two-mile mark, he was well inside world record pace and the crowd roared him on. He seemed to move without much effort but, as George had written, 'His style is peculiar. He does not appear to run from the thigh, but rather from the knee, and to an onlooker seems to have a short stride, but in reality this is not the case for his feet glide over the ground close to the surface for quite a distance before planting themselves.' Shrubb was certainly a puzzle to purists like George, whose ideas were rooted in the past and who found the new star something of a maverick. Shrubb was going his own sweet way and glided past the three-mile mark with the clock still below fifteen minutes, seemingly a suicidally fast pace.

Four miles was a significant point, for this was a standard championship distance at which Shrubb reigned supreme – he was AAA champion and world record holder at '4'. He reached it in 19:50.6, the sort of pace never before sustained over ten miles. He was showing no signs of difficulty and looked composed, his black hair and moustache glistening in the damp air and his stride as smooth as ever. On he went, and the halfway point arrived in 24:55.8, which was not only comfortably inside record pace, but a mere 22.4 seconds short of his own five-mile world record set six months earlier at Stamford Bridge. The time also represented a Scottish allcomers record for five miles. As some tailenders, lapped by Shrubb for a second time, discreetly dropped out of the race, some observers began to wonder if he had gone too fast, too soon.

Shrubb harboured no such doubts. The pipers were by now in full swing and the skirl of the bagpipes provided a stirring and inspirational backdrop. His skin tingled with excitement as he circled the track with the unstoppable momentum of a second hand on a clock. He was running faster than any man before him. Was that the hint of a smile beneath the neatly-clipped moustache? Wide eyes lit up his normally inscrutable face. The adrenaline was pumping and he was moving with an effortless speed and fluency that surprised even him. Many years later, runners would coin the phrase 'runner's high' to describe the experience when body, mind and external conditions are in perfect harmony, producing maximum performance from minimum effort. Ibrox was now witnessing an elite athlete's 'running high'. Already established as the world's best distance runner, the Little Wonder was producing a level of performance he would never repeat.

After throwing in a fast 22nd lap, Sid Thomas's twelve-year-old world record for six miles came within reach. Shrubb swept imperiously past the lap counters, clocking 29:59.4, 18.4 seconds inside Thomas's famous mark, set at Herne Hill cycle track during a one-hour run. The crowd broke into renewed cheering when the news was chalked up on the board – for even if Shrubb blew up now, they would have seen athletics history made. Shrubb had no intention of settling for one world record, however. Six miles held no special significance at that time, although in later years it would become a standard distance, subsequently evolving into the metric version, 10,000 metres.

Shrubb was averaging under five minutes per mile and showing no signs of fatigue. There were still none of those quirky surges and sprints he normally injected mid-race, partly to dispirit the opposition, partly to entertain the crowd, and partly because he simply enjoyed doing it. Although it could not be detected by the naked eye, he had slowed fractionally after six miles, but still passed seven inside Thomas's old world record of 36:36.8 by a massive 34.2 seconds. Two records down, how many more to go?

Just a hint of worry crept into the minds of Jack Brown and the time-keepers when they noted that Shrubb's eighth mile was clocked at 5:11.4. This was his slowest so far, although still comfortably good enough to create another world best (40:16.0). Into the last two gruelling miles and Shrubb was actually enjoying himself: 'In the last two miles the help I received from those gallant pipers was greater than anybody can understand. It put gladness in my heart and mettle into my heels. Never has music had greater charm for me than at such a time as that.'

Shrubb maintained his pace over the penultimate mile and even accelerated on the 35th lap to pass nine miles in yet another world record time (45:27.6). Now there was only a mile to go: 'On nearing home that glorious sensation came over me of new life returning to wind and limb. Finding I was on the last mile of my journey I said to myself: Now or never! Such a chance cannot be hoped for again.' Although he had expressed his wish not to have too much information yelled at him, the officials could not resist bellowing that his 37th lap had seen him slow to eighty seconds. He responded by casually picking up the pace, and when the bell sounded at 49:25.6, all the remaining runners had been lapped twice. Only a disaster could stop him now.

The ringing of the bell prompted him to push hard and complete the last circuit in 75.2, his quickest lap for more than half an hour: 'When the bell rang for the last quarter of a mile, my friend Brown and the spectators were half demented in their joy at seeing the thing I had come to do well within sight of accomplishment. I sprinted the whole way round the last lap right to the tape.'

To a deafening roar Shrubb breasted the tape in 50:40.6, obliterating George's amateur record by 39.4 seconds and Watkins' professional mark by 25. Shrubb felt a wave of relief and emotion at achieving the record, but knew he could not succumb entirely to the glory of the moment just yet. After what looked like momentary hesitation, he responded to the officials urging him to pick up again and go for the hour record: 'For about 300 yards or so it was necessary to nurse myself a little, in this way recovering from the strain. The old stride came back and with it the determination to smash the old one-hour record. The pipers were playing, louder than ever, Cock of the North!'

Circling the track visibly slower now, he even ran for a spell alongside the second and third-placed runners, Tom Jack and Sam Stevenson, who were side by side about a mile down on him. He had covered eleven miles and 1,137 yards when the retort of the starting pistol denoted the completion of sixty minutes. Although virtually jogging by now, Shrubb had completed the task and created a new one-hour world record. Officials rushed across to mark the spot Shrubb had reached when the gun sounded. Meanwhile, the champion continued to jog round to the finish line, his face lit up.

In one momentous race Shrubb had broken world amateur records for six, seven, eight, nine, ten and eleven miles, and one hour, plus every Scottish allcomers record from five miles upwards. He now possessed every world record from 2,000 yards up to the hour. The IAAF had yet to take the step of ratifying world records and standardising distances, so Shrubb could at this point lay claim to fifteen different world records during his career. His new six-mile mark would stand for seven years, until beaten by Frenchman Jean Bouin, and would not be bettered by a Briton until 1936, 32 years later, by William Eaton. The ten-mile mark stood proud until 'the Flying Finn' Paavo Nurmi beat it in 1928, 24 years later, and as a British record it was untouched until 1936, falling to Eaton again. Shrubb's new one-hour time would be bettered by Bouin nine years later in 1913, but would stand as a British record for almost half a century, Scotsman Ian Binnie finally improving it in 1953 by a couple of hundred yards.

If Shrubb thought he could quietly slip away from Ibrox that evening, he was much mistaken. As he made to leave the arena he was hoisted aloft as jubilant spectators surged forward. A heartfelt rendering of 'Will ye no come back again' struck up as he was borne in triumph to the pavilion. 'They carried me off the ground amidst such a storm of cheering as I never heard before or since anywhere,' he would recall.

Almost ignored in all the fuss, in second place in the '10', in a personal best of 56:30 was Tom Jack, 23, a farmer's son from West Calder, representing Edinburgh Southern Harriers (ESH). Sam Stevenson of Clydesdale Harriers was third in 56:33. After the handicaps were calculated, gold medals were awarded to Shrubb, P C Russell of Bellahouston Harriers and George Arnott of ESH. Several others picked up a bronze for finishing under 65 minutes and went home marvelling at how they had managed to win a medal but had still been lapped many times, due to the phenomenal performance by the winner.

During the evening, as Guy Fawkes' night was celebrated with bon-fires up and down the country, Shrubb was being entertained by delight-ed officials of WoSH, who presented him with a gold watch for breaking the '2' and '4'-mile world records back in June. They promised him a fur-ther reward later on for this day's efforts.

Walter George, with his twenty-year-old world record erased, chose not to echo the superlatives that the national press conferred on Shrubb. He wrote: 'Much as Shrubb has done, he has in my opinion not accom-plished his very best performances at any distance he has run because he has not run to schedule. If [he] would only devote his attentions to find-ing out his own peculiar capabilities and from observations plan out some way to improve on the erratic methods adopted by himself, it is quite pos-sible he would establish new records from two to eight that could not be beaten.'

George wasn't the only expert to adopt a negative attitude. No soon-er had reports of the race reached London than letters to the press ques-tioned both Scottish timekeeping and the measurement of the track. To help squash doubts, journalist Jimmy Fowler-Dixon, a time-keeper at the race, despatched the following letter from his Fleet Street office to D Scott-Duncan of the Scottish AAA:

November 24, 1904

Dear Mr Duncan,

I don't know whether you or the committee of the Scottish AAAs will consider any certificate from me at all necessary, for the passing and acceptance of Alfred Shrubb's splendid record performance at Ibrox Park on the 5th inst; but, if so, I should be glad if you will kindly treat this letter as testifying, from my personal knowledge and observation to the strict accuracy of Mr A G Rennie's official times on that occasion and also to the number of laps run by Shrubb. I struck my watch about 3/5th of a second earlier than Mr Rennie struck his; and another timekeeper was 2/5th earlier than Mr Rennie. This was due to a little fidgeting about at the start of the race, and to Mr Rennie being in a better position for timing. Mile after mile there was, practically, only that difference between us, right up to the pistol fire for the end of an hour, when my watch read 1hr: 0mins 0.6 secs.

Assuming the track to be of the stated measurement (and I see no rea-son to doubt it) there is no question in my mind that Shrubb, on that occasion, did all that was claimed for him. Further, what I saw convinced me that his marvellous two miles and four miles records, on the same track earlier in the year, must have been equally genuine. Certainly, as regards time-keeping, I should have implicit faith in Mr Rennie anywhere; and, if on any future occasion I hear of something remarkable being done, and I hear that Mr Rennie took the time I should be satisfied that, in that department, at all events, everything is alright.

As regards lap scoring on November 5th, that, also, was perfect.

I can scarcely convey to you how glad I am that I went and saw for myself how well things can be managed in Scotland. It was a performance which I shall always remember; and the witnessing of which I would not have missed for worlds. I paid my own travelling expenses to and fro, and would gladly do so again, to see so splendid an achievement of which Shrubb was the hero. The West of Scotland Harriers would have seen that my travelling expenses were paid, had I allowed them to do so; but, although I consider a timekeeper is fairly entitled to his expenses if he cares to accept them (and that without any loss of status) it so happens that I have always paid my own expenses in connection with all my official capacities, and I should be sorry to begin doing differently now that I am in my 55th year.

Whenever I can get to Scotland to see athletics sport I shall certainly do so, for I have found Scotsmen thoroughly good sportsmen and every bit as anxious as we are in England that record-breaking attempts shall be properly supervised and checked by officials fully fitted for the task.

With kind regards, and hoping to see you when next I get across the border believe me,

Yours very sincerely,
J. E. Fowler-Dixon.

Fowler-Dixon, who was a long-time admirer and friend of Shrubb, will have been taken seriously by the senior administrators, for he was a respected and well-liked character. He served his sport enthusiastically in a number of roles at club and regional level, and enjoyed a distinguished career himself as a walker and runner. He and Shrubb were delighted when the new record times and their authenticity were formally confirmed by the authorities a few weeks later and Shrubb's place in the history books assured. Looking back at his Glasgow glory day, Shrubb reckoned: 'Crossing the Tweed to enter the land of cakes brought my reputation forward at a bound. The ground was packed with enthusiastic Scotsmen and this race will stand in my memory as the greatest in the whole history of my running career.

'At the station on my departure, one of the funny things I heard was: Haste ye back to Scotland Shrubb, and we'll confer on ye the freedom of Glasga! Glasgow was Scotland for me – I never ran at Edinburgh.' He also recalled hearing one old Scotsman comment: 'Shrubb disna' break records, he cuts 'em doon like a harvester cuttin' corn with a scythe.' The press loved this particular remark and later a cartoon appeared in *All Sports Weekly* of Shrubb wielding a scythe, watched by an admiring Scotsman in full tartan regalia.

Shrubb headed back south a satisfied man. He knew he could now take a well-earned breather and concentrate on the forthcoming adventure to Australia. He could also reflect on his personal high points of 1904, which certainly made a long and impressive list:

A fourth consecutive Southern cross-country title in February;
A fourth consecutive English National cross-country in March;
A second consecutive International cross-country in March;
A fourth consecutive AAA 10-mile title in April;
A world record for five miles in May;
A world record for two miles in June;
A world record for four miles just two days later in June;
For the second year running, AAA mile and four-mile titles on the same
    day (his fourth consecutive win at four);
A world record for three miles in August;
World records for six miles, 10,000 metres, seven, eight, nine ten and
eleven miles, and for one-hour, all in the same race in November.

A complete list of Shrubb's 1904 victories is, of course, even longer. Dominance of the UK domestic distance-running scene on such a scale was unprecedented, and has never since been repeated.

CHAPTER TEN

'Known from one end of the world to the other'

Foreign holidays were a luxury available to only a privileged few in 1904 Britain. Not surprisingly then, Alf Shrubb's family and friends in rural Sussex were in awe of his forthcoming voyage to the other side of the world. This was an age when country folk worked close to home, found a marriage partner close to home and then settled nearby. Shrubb's horizons were far broader. Twenty-five years old, a bachelor, and in excellent health, he packed his bags for what would be the greatest adventure of his life thus far.

The Amateur Athletic Union of Australia and New Zealand had invited Shrubb to compete in various championships, as a means of testing their best runners and boosting interest in the sport. Shrubb had no second thoughts, commenting later: 'I was pleased to go, knowing the opportunity would not come again. It was the chance of a lifetime for seeing a bit of the world.'

Thursday, December 29th, 1904 was a grey day at London's St Pancras station in London. A small but distinguished group of men in raincoats gathered and drank tea while they waited for Shrubb to appear. They were there to see their young 'ambassador' safely on to the boat train to Tilbury docks, the first leg of his 11,000-mile trip. AAA secretary Charles Herbert, officials Jimmy Fowler-Dixon and George Hogsflesh, plus South London Harriers' men Thomas Sinnott and Gordon Innes, were relieved when the little runner finally arrived, bedecked with baggage. He displayed the rubber shoes he had obtained for training spins on the ship's deck. They chatted about the magnificent 8,000-ton vessel that awaited him – the *SS Ortona* – and the exotic cities that it would visit *en route*.

Fowler-Dixon, the journalist who acted as time-keeper at Shrubb's record-breaking run in Glasgow in November, knew Shrubb well by now. He'd written him a farewell letter, in addition to seeing him off personally from St Pancras. 'You are going among a lot of real good sportsmen over there and the better they do, I'm sure, the more you'll like it. All the Australians I have met are rattling good fellows, I assure you,' he wrote. Shrubb was regarded as something of a pioneer, for although American and French athletes had regularly visited the United Kingdom – birthplace of modern athletics – not too many home-based men had headed away from the British Isles for competition.

After lunch on board the following day, with the *Ortona* steaming out of Tilbury, Shrubb was already out on deck having a gentle run to familiarise himself with his home for the next six weeks. Tea followed at 6pm, after which he put in some brisk walking, circling the deck repeatedly until 8.30pm, after which he retired to bed. Plymouth was reached at 3.30am on the Saturday morning, New Year's Eve.

As previously arranged, Shrubb climbed aboard a tender to go and meet AAA secretary Herbert, who was waiting anxiously harbourside with the ticket for Shrubb's fellow tourist, the American sprinter Arthur Duffey. News had come through that Duffey, arriving from the States on the vessel *St Paul*, would be delayed on account of snowstorms in mid-Atlantic. The captain of the *Ortona* agreed to wait as long as he dared, and Duffey's ship docked just thirty minutes before the *Ortona's* rescheduled departure time. A skiff had to be hastily commandeered to get the American on board. Shrubb recalled his relief at seeing his fellow adventurer arriving in a hurry: 'Tripping across the gangway came the great little American, baggage and all'. The *Ortona* sailed out of Plymouth, heading for Gibraltar, at 4.30pm.

So what of Duffey, Shrubb's touring partner for the next few months? Described as 'a sunny soul', Duffey was a Bostonian who raced in the colours of Georgetown University. He had won the AAA 100 yards title for the past four seasons and broke the world record with a run of 9.6 seconds in New York in 1902. He was the same age as Shrubb and, like him, was a short man with a deceptively long stride, but at ten stones (140lbs) was much heavier. He had collapsed with a thigh injury halfway through the 100 metres Olympics final in Paris in 1900, and did not participate in the 1904 games, preferring to defend his AAA title in England. *Athletic News* profiled him thus: 'Duffey pranced like a proud horse up and down the track and there were those that thought he was a trifle too material, not to say beefy, for flying purposes. He was very springy on his toes and heard flattering remarks about himself without blushing.'

The *Ortona* docked at Gibraltar early on Wednesday, January 4th and the two runners went ashore for a stroll before the voyage was resumed at 11am, next stop Marseilles. By now, daily sprints by Duffey, and runs of longer duration by Shrubb, were sandwiched between cricket and other deck games. One member of the athletics press had been allowed to inspect Shrubb's cabin before the ship left England: he reported that he had been particularly struck by its excellent situation and accessibility to the deck: 'Oddly enough, also, [Shrubb] had the advantage of being

attended by a steward, who happened to be present at the South London
Harriers Sports at Kennington Oval when Shrubb and Duffey ran.'

On Friday, January 6th, after a short stop at Marseilles, the *Ortona* left
French waters, heading for Naples. An intriguing passenger who joined
the ship at Marseilles was 36-year-old Gertrude Bell, a keen traveller who
was heading for the Near East (nowadays known as the Middle East).
Miss Bell had led, and would continue to lead, an extraordinary life. A
decade later her expertise would see her recruited by the British
Government to liaise with Arab leaders during the First World War.
Indeed, soon afterwards, her imperial duties would see her become widely regarded as 'the most powerful woman in the British Empire'. Born in
County Durham, Bell read history at Oxford before turning her back on
a privileged life in Victorian England to travel the world. She had become
enchanted by the Arab language and people, and would return, especially to Mesopotamia (Iraq) many times. Her trip on the *Ortona* was docu-
mented in letters and diaries, which would many years later be transcribed
and catalogued by the University of Newcastle-upon-Tyne. The papers
give an insight into life on the vessel as it headed out of Europe bound
for Australia, via the Suez Canal.

In a letter to her father, Miss Bell writes: 'We left Marseilles with a
wind ... and rolled a bit at first, enough to keep half the passengers away
from dinner. Later it became so mild that I sat on deck reading till 10pm,
when the quartermaster came and said would I mind moving into a corner as the champion runners [Shrubb and Duffey] wished to run up and
down the deck to keep themselves in training. They are going to Australia
to meet other champion runners and I expect they'll be out of training,
in spite of all their running on the deck.' Her letter conveys merely polite
interest in the strange activities of two of her fellow passengers, but her
private diary expresses something more akin to irritation: 'I dined with
Mr Osborne, sat on deck after and read. The prize runners took exercise
across my feet.'

The *Ortona* capitalised on favourable conditions to make good speed
past Corsica and Sardinia towards Naples. Early on Sunday, January 8th,
the ship docked in the Italian port and most of the passengers took
advantage of the fourteen-hour stop to explore the celebrated city. The
Ortona then slipped out of the Golfo di Napoli in the cool midnight air,
heading for Port Said in Egypt, at least three days away.

Shrubb and Duffey were determined to use their time constructively
and the special rubber shoes they had brought along saw plenty of action
on deck. At first, other passengers regarded their training sessions with
fascination and even mild amusement, but eventually the sight of Shrubb

endlessly circling the deck, and Duffey on his little shuttle runs, became routine and people stopped taking notice. Sometimes, whole areas of the ship would be cordoned off for their running, other times Shrubb in particular had to keep his wits about him as he raced round tight corners and blind bends. His cabin was handily positioned next to the main deck and he would undertake sessions of varying difficulty at all times of the day and night. He was a single-minded young man and the smoky confines of the lounge or casino held little appeal.

Between their runs and brisk walks, Shrubb and Duffey became the life and soul of the ship. They were always in the games area, enthusiastically organising and participating in cricket, shuffleboard and other pastimes. The captain and his senior crew knew they had famous runners on board and, although the pair benefited from occasional VIP treatment, they were also happy to mix with the less-privileged passengers from the third-class section. The polite, friendly Shrubb and the more outgoing Duffey became popular figures and their presence helped add colour and interest to a long trip that might otherwise have become tedious.

A degree of colour was also added by the red sashes and turbans of the Lascar crew of the *Ortona*. In common with many steamships of the era, a large number of crew were Lascars, and in the *Ortona's* case, the engine room had a monopoly of them. Under the control of a serang (head man), the Lascars were from a race of sailors drawn from the Gulf of Kutch and from Indian fishing villages around Bombay. Trained from childhood to handle boats in all conditions, entire communities or villages of Lascars would often be hired by ship operators to carry out crewing duties on long trips.

Although Australia was building a reputation as a sporting nation and Shrubb and Duffey had been told to expect some 'rattling good fellows' Down Under, the captain and purser of the *Ortona* were not entirely happy about the way this new nation conducted business. Gertrude Bell's diaries describe the *Ortona's* officers as 'rabid' about the manner in which Australians levied duty on every ounce of provisions used by ships in their waters. They also perceived a negative attitude by Australians towards the employment of Lascars.

On Thursday, January 12th, the *Ortona* reached Port Said, where it docked early in the morning, allowing Shrubb to catch a glimpse of a way of life far removed from anything he had seen before. Duffey, on the other hand, was more worldly, having crossed the Atlantic several times and raced in more countries. Gertrude Bell was among those to disembark at this point; she would head down the Suez Canal in another vessel. She had with her a Letter of Introduction to present to Captain

Melville, the Commandant of the Canal, but was unable to locate him. It was but a minor setback, and she set off towards Beirut anyway, leaving the *Ortona* and her passengers to explore Port Said before heading south for the equator and Australia beyond.

Shrubb and Duffey were naturally excited about what awaited them and studied their itinerary many times. They would be performing at championships in Victoria, New South Wales and New Zealand, against the best runners Australasia could muster. Despite the popular outback image of people Down Under, around ninety per cent of Australians lived in coastal cities and in 1905 almost a third of the nation's five million inhabited Melbourne and Sydney, where the two runners would be based. City streets were clogged with horse-drawn vehicles, for there were very few motor cars around. Horses feeding from chaff bags and with their noses in sidewalk water toughs were part of the street scene. Official communication between Australia and Britain was by means of telegraphic cables employing Morse code, but later in 1905 the introduction of Marconi's wireless radio system would begin to change all this. Although poverty was a fact of life for many, Australians even then loved their sport. In 1901 and 1905 their cricketers won the Ashes from England, and sailing, tennis and Australian Rules football were also taking off in a big way.

Shrubb and Duffey had their sights on setting as many 'allcomers' records as they could. Shrubb trained relentlessly, but after forty days of pounding the *Ortona*'s decks, he couldn't wait to get the feel of grass under his feet. After crossing the huge expanse of the Indian Ocean, the ship docked at Melbourne on Wednesday, February 8th. A conference was arranged to allow local athletics officials to formally welcome the runners and discuss logistics. The Mayor was among the greeting party at Melbourne Cricket Ground and the two runners were fêted and generally fussed over. R H Crowl welcomed the pair on behalf of the AAA of New South Wales and warned them that NSW had chosen a squad of its best men to compete against them. In the sprints they had named six and, to take on Shrubb, eight had been selected. B J Parkinson spoke on behalf of the NZAAA, and Sir John Madden, Chief Justice of Victoria, proposed the health of the visitors. Known to be a big supporter of amateurism in sport, Sir John raised his glass and commended athletics as a means of strengthening men's bodies, minds and morality.

Shrubb and Duffey started training in earnest the very next day – long sea voyages presenting no equivalent of today's 'jet-lag' – and Duffey was able to pal up with Todd, a local professional sprinter. As usual, Shrubb trained alone mostly and struggled somewhat in the heat of Melbourne's summer. He had always been a worrier in the build-up to events, but now he became seriously concerned that the heat was sapping his strength and he would not be able to give his best. He hated the idea of disappointing the locals, who were clearly expecting big things. As the Victorian Championships in Melbourne loomed, Shrubb suffered the athletics equivalent of stage fright.

The championships commenced at Melbourne Cricket Ground on Saturday, February 18th with a 4,000 crowd basking in the sunshine and huge interest centred on the visiting internationals. The 100 yards course was set up in the usual fashion, with string on poles separating the lanes. Duffey looked poised and accomplished as he knelt for the start, but some of the others started from a standing position. Duffey won his heat comfortably in 10.6, but in the final was beaten in thrilling fashion on the line by local favourite Francis Mueller of Bendigo in 10.4. The result caused a sensation. Duffey had been billed the fastest man in the world, and the locals were jubilant their man had toppled him. The American clearly needed a couple of races to find his best form after the long journey and realised he would have ample opportunity to make amends.

Wearing the maroon and buff colours of South London Harriers, Shrubb's big introduction came in the three-mile race. Still fretting about the heat, he set off briskly but not in his usual helter-skelter manner. Once he found himself clear at the front he relaxed and the old confidence flooded back. He even let rip with the occasional surge and cruised to victory in 15:15, 37 seconds ahead of George Blake (Melbourne). Later the same afternoon he tackled a 1½-mile handicap and, full of himself, scorched home from scratch in 7:03.6, beating the Australasian record by eight seconds. He also lined up for the two-mile handicap, but that was a race too many for one day, and he quietly retired after five laps.

Shrubb's overwhelming sensation at the end of this first meeting was one of relief. The summer heat had not affected his running as much as he had feared. He was in a better mood afterwards, unlike the withdrawn figure he'd cut earlier in the day. He had beaten some of Australia's finest at two different distances and now he felt entitled to relax and really enjoy the tour. Proper acclimatisation would need a little longer, but he was now sure that the local people would soon see the best of him. Still in buoyant mood the next day, he sent off a letter to his clubmates in England, at South London Harriers, informing them that on his return he would take a crack at the world three-mile record. The club printed the letter in their newsletter, SLH Gazette.

In midweek, Shrubb won a mile staged in Bendigo, eighty miles northwest of Melbourne, in a time of 4:31. It proved a useful warm-up for the resumption of the Victorian championships the following Saturday. Here the delightful weather enticed a 2,500 crowd and Shrubb duly won the mile at Melbourne Cricket Ground in 4:29.5 – establishing a Victorian record – finishing twenty yards ahead of local runner George Blake. He also rollicked home in a four-mile handicap, his dramatic late sprint earning a time of 20:15, which shattered the Victorian record by 45 seconds. Shrubb had captured all the Victorian records between one and four miles on the same day. Duffey, meanwhile, bounced back from defeat as he'd promised, and won the 100 yards invitation handicap from scratch by inches from G A Widmer of Sydney, who had half a yard start. Victoria's sprint and long-jump champion, Francis Mueller, was given a one-yard start but this time had to be satisfied with third place.

The local press pondered the fact that cycling had recently attracted crowds of up to 30,000 in Melbourne, yet champion runners like Shrubb and Duffey were only pulling in around 3,000: 'Why champions in one branch of athletics should succeed in drawing a crowd, and in another should fail, is a question that is hard to answer,' wrote one correspondent: 'Perhaps the reason is that there are fashions in sport as well as in dress. Our Australasian associations, in arranging visits from champion athletes, may in time accustom greater numbers to attend our meetings and take an interest in amateur athletics generally. But it is evident that it is not to be done in a day.'

After his last engagement in the Melbourne area, Shrubb complained of feeling unwell. What at first appeared to be an attack of flu became steadily worse and was diagnosed as gastric influenza. His doctor forbade him from accompanying Duffey on the ship to New Zealand – the next stage of their tour – until such time as he had recovered. In a letter home to his Horsham friend G Kilvington, Shrubb explained: 'Duffey had to go on without me and here I lay in bed, a stranger to all. But I must say I was looked after well by the Australian people. They put a nurse with me night and day. I really thought that was going to be my last run I was so ill. The climate is much too hot for me out here and that's what's been playing me up.'

He was laid low for almost two weeks, but left his sick bed to accept an invitation to go quail shooting, an experience he thoroughly enjoyed. On hearing of this, the doctor relented and said the sea air might now do him good. So, on Wednesday, March 8th, Shrubb said farewell to Melbourne and boarded the *SS Warrimoo* at 4.30pm, bound for Christchurch, on New Zealand's South Island.

The ship – whose name is Aboriginal for eagle – was operated by the Union SS Company of New Zealand and had a curious history. In 1895 it had carried American author Mark Twain on his world tour. Four years later it made headlines when a 'freak of navigation' saw it arrive at the equator on December 31st, 1899, allowing its passengers to be the first in the world to see the arrival of the 1900s. Many years later, during the 1914-18 War, the ship would collide with the French naval destroyer *Catapulte* off the coast of Algeria. The warship sank, but the sturdy *Warrimoo* continued on its merry way. Now, as Shrubb and 165 other passengers climbed aboard on this warm evening in March 1905, another *Warrimoo* adventure was about to unfold.

Six hours out of Port Melbourne, many of the passengers were asleep or preparing for bed when a serious fire broke out. Shrubb was among those to lose belongings and be lucky to escape with their lives. This is how he related the episode later for *All Sports Weekly*:

'The fates were against me. After finally setting off at about 4.30pm, six hours later we were thinking of turning in. One of the passengers said "look, the new moon is shining" and everybody called out "change your money", so we all turned our cash over to get good luck. I went off to bed and my cabin-mate came in shortly after. We both dropped off to sleep, but about half-an-hour later I suddenly awoke nearly stifled. I thought there was something wrong and I could hear the men on deck rushing about. The steward came running along and told the passengers to get their clothes on as soon as possible and come on deck. There were alarming incidents on board. The fellow on the berth above me was so scared by the shouts of "fire" that he jumped on top of me and nearly broke my neck. The knowledge that there were 200 cans of kerosene oil on board wasn't a nice thing to think about as the fire was doing its best to reach them. Great was our relief when the captain had this inflammable cargo thrown overboard.

'On reaching deck I saw that all the boats were swung clear and lowered to the rails ready for use in case of an explosion. About 200 tons of water were pumped into the hold, which suddenly keeled over to a very awkward angle and remained there, the boats on the one side almost touching the water. Heading back into port again we fired rockets when near the Queenscliff lighthouse, but apparently they thought we were a strange vessel asking for signals.'

The fire blazed for some eight hours before being fully extinguished. The beleaguered captain had fired thirteen distress rockets before receiving any response. A lifeboat from Queenscliff eventually arrived and guided the stricken vessel back to Melbourne, during which time the pumping of water towards the fire's source had to stop, for the ship was listing dangerously. More than 500 cases of cargo were apparently dumped overboard to lighten the vessel. The *Warrimoo* limped back into port and after a couple of days undergoing repairs restarted its voyage with the same passenger list. This time the voyage was uneventful. News reached England of Shrubb's latest adventure and several papers carried sensationalised reports of how the champion runner had recovered from illness only to narrowly escape being consumed by fire.

The episode gave Shrubb a story to dine on for many years. His daughter Norah recalls how he relished telling eye-popping tales of how he had fled his cabin and tied a knot in his nightshirt so the garment would trap air inside and keep him afloat if the boat went down. This was presumably an embellishment designed to impress his young daughter, but nothing can diminish the seriousness of the passengers' plight that night in the Tasman Sea.

So, with two good reasons for being several days late, Shrubb finally sailed into Christchurch. The crowd of onlookers on the wharf waited patiently while customs and health officials did their checks, finally allowing the gangway to be lowered. A seaman signalled to the crowd when Shrubb was on his way, and no sooner did he set foot on Kiwi soil than he was surrounded by well-wishers. Messrs Keane and Gilbertson of Invercargill had been given the task of greeting him on behalf of the NZAAA and escorting him through the crowd to the Golden Age Hotel. Here the reception party awaited the arrival of a 'special' train carrying various delegates from athletic clubs and committees who needed to discuss revised timetables.

Various correspondents were able to collar him at this point, including a scribe from the *Southland Times* who reported that Shrubb had nearly recovered from his illness, but was doubtful whether he would be able to complete his full itinerary. Shrubb told him, sadly, that he missed the cinder tracks of England and that it was hard to expect tracks over here to be of the best quality when they had to be shared with cricket and football. He had found Melbourne's track to be better than that at Bendigo. He also expounded his running tactics: 'I ran pretty green in my early races but I run in the same way now, really. I take the lead the whole way if I can and simply batter it out of them. That is the way that I ran then and have run ever since. In the mile I take them along at 2:03 for the first half and there's not much left in them after that.'

Shrubb added that in Melbourne he was affected by the heat and finishing the four-miler in 100 degrees had seen him ready to drop after breaking the tape. He added that he shouldn't really be competing in Christchurch at all. He would give it a go in the three-mile race but probably leave the mile alone, as this was a distance he rarely took seriously.

In addition to the stress of his sea crossing, Shrubb was still far from fully fit, and he missed at least one scheduled meeting in New Zealand. Not wanting to disappoint his hosts and local fans, he pushed himself into action on March 17th, but it wouldn't be until his arrival back in Australia that he felt back to his normal self.

He missed a meeting at Dunedin, in the south-east of South Island, where Duffey took centre stage, equalling his own fifty yards world record of 5.4 seconds. On March 17th and 18th, the NZAAA championships got underway in Christchurch with Shrubb, despite his earlier misgivings, pencilled in for both the three and one-mile events. Although feeling low on energy, he experienced few problems in the longer race and cruised to a 300-yard victory in 15:07.4, with local man Hector Burk second.

The mile was a different matter. Shrubb ran despite his earlier intimation that he would not, and Burk enjoyed the race of his life. He finished forty yards clear of Shrubb to take the title and create a new national record of 4:27.4. The following day Shrubb won a four-mile handicap in 20:39.2, eighty yards clear of the rest. Duffey, meanwhile won the New Zealand 100 yards title in 10.0 seconds dead.

Although Shrubb was trying to make friends and impress, one particular official didn't like the cut of his jib. In a letter to *The Sydney Morning Herald* on March 18th, Mr C D Jones, secretary of the NSW AAA, took a swipe at the great man: 'In your issue today it appears that A. Shrubb is reported to have stated that the climate and tracks of Sydney are unfavourable for record breaking. I cannot understand how Shrubb could be in a position to express an opinion on our tracks. He refers no doubt to the tracks of Melbourne and Bendigo, the only places where he's competed in Australia. His first appearance in this state will be on April 15, a time of year when weather and other conditions could not be equalled in any part of the world.'

Meanwhile, Shrubb had mixed results in Wellington, North Island, running the mile in a slow 4:36 and finishing fifth. On the same day, however, his three-mile handicap time of 14:55 was the quickest of the day, although he was not able to catch all the runners given concessions.

Defeat by Hector Burk in the Christchurch mile had irked Shrubb. On at least three occasions he challenged Burk to a re-match, but the new champion would have none of it. Shrubb's riposte was to settle the argument by smashing Burk's new record in his absence, at the Auckland international meeting at the city's Domain venue. In the one-mile flat handicap he won in 4:22.0, five seconds inside Burk's effort. Shrubb loved the feel of the Auckland track and the result was better than even he had expected. It was not only a New Zealand allcomers record, but also equalled Shrubb's own personal best. His lap splits were: 59.6, 65.4, 71.0 and 66.0.

Also in Auckland, he produced a handsome late sprint to win a three-mile handicap in 14:57.0. *The New Zealand Herald* suggested he looked tireless with his low, daisy-cutting stride, but that his one-mile exertions had taken the sting out of him. After all, Shrubb's three-mile time was not a national record. Duffey, however, in winning his heat of the 75 yards handicap, ran 7.4 for a new world record. Shrubb told the *Herald* the track at Auckland had been the fastest grass track he'd ever known, and second only to the cinder track at Ibrox as the best of any sort. He again emphasised that the gastric flu attack meant the New Zealand folk had not seen him at his very best.

Shrubb and Duffey headed back to Australia, bound for Sydney, where they stayed at a downtown hotel in George Street. With two weeks between major racing commitments, Shrubb was able to enjoy the hospitality of his New South Wales hosts. He also bought some carefully chosen gifts for a certain young lady in England, who awaited his return – more of her later. On April 12th Shrubb was a special guest at the annual dance of Sydney Harriers at the Masonic Hall.

He was also a guest of the retailer, traveller and keen sportsman, Mark Foy, at his new premises, the Majestic Spa, high in the Blue Mountains at Medlow. Forty-one-year-old Foy had recently opened this health spa, based on one he had visited in Buxton, Derbyshire. Foy was keen to promote his new venture and invited Shrubb and Duffey to relax and enjoy the Blue Mountains scenery. Foy had hired a Swiss expert, Dr George Bauer, to devise and supervise a programme of innovative treatments and diets. Shrubb always placed heavy emphasis on diet and health matters, so would have been interested in the workings of the Majestic, but which of their eccentric treatments he allowed himself to receive remains a matter of speculation.

Foy liked to invite his 'special guests' to travel to Penrith, at the foot of the Blue Mountains, by train from Sydney and would send down a limousine to collect them. He was one of the first to own a motor car in New South Wales and loved showing off his vehicles. Among the VIPs who visited the Majestic in those early years were opera singer Dame Nellie Melba, Olympic swimmer Freddie Lane, the Rajah of Pudacoota and the author of Sherlock Holmes, Sir Arthur Conan Doyle. Australia's first prime minister, Sir Edmund Barton, ominously died while staying there, although his demise was not thought to be connected to Dr Bauer's treatments.

It became apparent that few shared Mark Foy's faith in Dr Bauer's methods and the spa soon hit hard times. The owner then converted it into a resort hotel and it prospers to this day. Many years later, Shrubb's granddaughter, Julia Cattran would follow in his footsteps and be a guest at the Majestic.

The peacefulness and cool air of the Blue Mountains helped Shrubb recover fully from his illness, so that by the time his New South Wales fixtures came along he was back to his prime. Saturday, April 15th was the opening day of the NSW international meeting, featuring several state championship events. Sydney Cricket Ground shimmered under blue skies and a 4,000 crowd assembled. Shrubb and Duffey told reporters they felt in the best shape since first arriving on these shores. In the 100 yards, just three men started – Duffey, Nigel Barker of Sydney University, and Stanley Rowley, an experienced sprinter who had run in England before the turn of the century. Duffey got the best start, but Barker came storming home to the delight of the home fans to win in 10.2. Duffey said he found the grass track heavy for sustained effort and much preferred cinders.

NSW's mile championship was won by Shrubb in 4:26.6 thanks to a late sprint, which took him twenty yards clear of the dogged Greg Wheatley (Essendon Harriers). The lap splits were 59, 67, 70.6 and 69.6. The five-mile handicap turned into anticlimax, with the starts Shrubb was asked to concede condemned as 'extraordinary' by *The Sydney Morning Herald*. Shrubb found the effort 'heartbreaking' and quit when told there were five laps to go and he was still a lap behind the leader. As he came off the track he was heard to remark tetchily: 'A man's not a machine.' It emerged later that Shrubb had thought he was winning, but had received conflicting messages from the officials, who did not seem to know what was happening. Shrubb was so annoyed at their incompetence that he walked off. The race finished in the dark because the schedule had run late, and the under-fire officials were also blamed for allowing non-participants on the in-field. In short, the race was a shambles. Shrubb and Duffey had already complained of being harshly handicapped, but Shrubb's walk-off in the five-miler was the nearest he had come to displaying true dissent. Duffey's 'red mist' moments would come later.

The following day Shrubb wrote an open letter to friends back in Horsham. He mentioned that he and Duffey had been heavily handicapped, both in races and by the climate. He added: 'I have had some awfully good luck. I have won 15 out of 17 races and won their one, two and four-mile records. It was 110 degrees in the shade and down to 60 the following week – also cold on the southern end of New Zealand. The weather is much too trying to run the same way every time. You will be surprised to hear I have met a friend from Horsham, Mr Reed, who kept the Anchor Hotel, and who has taken a hotel out here now.'

On Saturday, April 22nd the NSW sporting gala resumed in perfect conditions, watched by 3,000 at Sydney Cricket Ground. *The Morning Herald* described Shrubb's demonstration on this day of sustained pacy running, followed by sprint finishes, as a revelation. Following the fiasco in the five-miler, this time it was the 100 yards that sparked controversy. Duffey found himself up against NSW sprinters Barker and Rowley. A week earlier the trio had put on a magnificent race but today everything went pear-shaped. In the words of *The Morning Herald*, 'Duffey anticipated Mr Alexander's start pistol and secured an advantage of some yards. Rowley scarcely left his mark and Barker got to ten yards before a recall shout was heard. However, Duffey continued alone and ran 10.2, which equalled Barker's winning time of the previous week. After much conferring, the officials decided to re-run the event about an hour later. Duffey refused to cooperate with this idea and was heard to remark that he'd never heard any recall instruction, and that the starter should have used a whistle. Barker and Rowley felt Duffey's absence would lose the race its international flavour and decided to abandon the run-off too. Duffey still had the heats and final of the 60 yards to come and, to his credit, equalled the world record of 6.4 in these, but on both occasions looked to have "anticipated" the gun again – this time with no recall from the officials!'

In the three-mile invitation handicap, Shrubb passed two miles inside NSW record pace and finished with a 100-yard sprint that saw him home 300 yards clear of Morgan (Marrickville Harriers) in 14:54.6. In the two-mile race he ran 9:44.2 to break the Australian record, winning by 100 yards from Lynch of East Sydney. He now felt in better form than at any time since leaving the UK. It was regarded as the best-ever field of runners to assemble in Sydney, and the cricket ground's green carpet looked immaculate. No Queensland athletes were present, out of respect for recently deceased teammate G E Graham. Every competitor, including Shrubb, wore black armbands. Graham, just twenty, had been running in Sydney a few days earlier and had retired unwell during the 440 yards, having earlier won the long and high jumps and the 120 yards hurdles. He had earlier suffered with dengue fever, but Dr Murray Owen now diagnosed appendicitis. Graham was operated on shortly afterwards, but died the following day.

On the evening of April 22nd, the NSW AAA entertained Shrubb and Duffey at a banquet in Bateman's Hotel, central Sydney, during which prizes were presented. Two days later the pair made their farewell appearance of the tour, at St Luke's Park, Burwood, in Sydney's western suburbs. The event was on a patchy looking track, which in part traversed a hard cricket wicket, but the weather for running was excellent. In the 100 yards, Duffey made up ground and threw himself towards the 'worsted yarn'. Judges Jones, Bruce and Marks conferred before declaring a dead heat between Duffey and Barker. Duffey felt cheated and refused to take part when invited to stage a 'run-off' by referee R Coombes. When Duffey's temper subsided he felt a little more benevolent and was heard to compliment the officials on the excellent feel of the track, which he said had been the best yet on grass during the tour. The races in St Luke's Park that day were on a site that would later be renamed the Concord Oval, and would stage international rugby.

The finish was not so tight in the two-mile invitation handicap. Shrubb had to concede 65-second starts to three runners and did his first two laps especially fast, easing slightly and catching them at the mile mark in 4:33.6. He sprinted home to win by sixty yards in 9:33.6, another Australasian allcomers record. He had now beaten both Australian and New Zealand native records for one, two, three and four miles. Later the same evening, Shrubb and Duffey set off for Melbourne by train, where they were to board the *SS Ophir* for the long journey home.

Overall, the tour had been a success, with Shrubb and Duffey enhancing their reputations and breaking most of the native records. From the hosts' point of view, it was a mostly positive experience, although there was criticism on several fronts. The handicapping was thought to have been far too harsh on the visitors; event organisation sometimes left a little to be desired, with some officials appearing out of their depth; and the size of crowds at the main meetings fell below expectations. Nevertheless, the experience would benefit the Australasian-based athletes and their main championships gained more worldwide publicity than would have been the case without the famous visitors.

It presumably meant a costly outlay for the Amateur Athletic Union, as Shrubb and Duffey must have run up hefty expenses in the form of hotels, meals and travelling costs. Normally an amateur athlete was forbidden to have such items paid for him, but this trip was seen as a special case and the arrangements had been approved beforehand. Taking a retrospective view, many years later, however, the New Zealand athletics historian Peter Heidenstrom believes Shrubb and Duffey 'were playing the money game, almost certainly with the connivance of the NZAAA'. The implication is that the pair were lavishly catered for, and rewarded for their appearances 'in kind', if not in fees. For the five months of the tour, Shrubb and Duffey found themselves in a sort of limbo, enjoying a status intermediate between the contrasting worlds of amateur athletics and professional pedestrianism.

Meanwhile, Shrubb's friends and family looked forward to his return to England, only to learn from *The West Sussex County Times* that his globe-trotting days were not over: 'Shrubb, decorated with imperial honours, is expected to reach England towards the end of May and will then accompany the South London Harriers to Paris in early June.' *Athletic News* reflected: 'How splendidly did Shrubb acquit himself is now a matter of history. He is now on his way back to England where he may rely on heaps of congratulations on his return to form and a hearty hope that it may be maintained.'

The local paper caused much amusement in Horsham when it reproduced part of a *Sydney Daily Telegraph* interview with Shrubb, in which he extolled the virtues of beer as a training aid: 'A man should eat and drink exactly what he feels like taking,' advised Shrubb. 'I think beer is a great aid in training, taken of course in moderation. An athlete should drink it as he feels he wants it. During all the time I have been racing I have found it a great help. Look here, it's no use a man trying to run races on tea and soft stuff. It does him more harm than good. You must have something solid and muscle-giving in you. When training I run about three miles a day, plus light exercise in other ways. I never overtax myself, I think it best to train oneself up to a point just under one's best, then there is always room for an extra burst.'

Shrubb was certainly thinking hard about his long-term future, both domestically and career-wise. A switch to the professional ranks must have been considered, even though the professional scene was no longer thriving as it once had. Racing for money also carried a stigma of seaminess and dishonour. In addition, quitting the amateur game would mean an end to the annual round of enjoyable fixtures that Shrubb had become familiar with. Events later in 1905 would bring all this sharply into focus, but for the moment he was simply keen to get home. He and Duffey set sail from Melbourne on the *SS Ophir* with hearty and sincere farewells from their Australasian hosts ringing in their ears.

The 4,726-ton *Ophir*, carrier of many a royal passenger in its time, was the pride of the Orient-Pacific fleet, and Shrubb and Duffey made full use of the entertainments and privileges open to them. They got to know the captain and senior officers and enjoyed an active but relaxing six-week journey. The ship steamed into Tilbury on Saturday, June 3rd, its passengers tanned, relaxed and happy to be home. Because of the train timetables, the runners spent that evening at the theatre and the night in a central London hotel. Sunday saw them take an early train to Sussex where Shrubb had a very important private visit to make.

Awaiting him in Hayward's Heath was the woman in his life, barmaid Ada Brown, the 26-year-old daughter of the landlord of the Sussex Hotel. Alf and Ada had first met many months earlier, and had exchanged letters during the Australasian trip. In one of these, Shrubb wrote about their plan to be married in the near future. Many years later, Shrubb's daughter Norah recalled seeing this letter, which talks of the wedding plans and sets out Shrubb's wish that Ada should look after all his trophies in his absence. Ada had endured five months without seeing her famous fiancé, and on his return he presented her with two gifts, a gold bracelet, set with five opals, and a fan made of white ostrich feathers and tortoiseshell, both purchased in Australia.

After staying the night in Hayward's Heath, the two runners headed for Shrubb's nearby home town, Horsham, on Monday, June 5th to a rapturous welcome from 300 people. Due to heavy rain, the town band and banners were dispensed with, but this did not spoil the party mood and Shrubb was greeted first on the station platform by his father William and brother Albert. A semi-private dinner took place at the Anchor Hotel, arranged jointly by Horsham AC and the Blue Star club. The toast was 'King Edward, the greatest peacemaker in the world'. Shrubb was publicly praised for putting Horsham 'in the van' (on the map) and for being quiet and gentlemanly even after all his success.

Shrubb stood up to respond, explaining that his only defeat Down Under was the result of the after-effects of illness. When he challenged the victor (Hector Burk) to run again he had refused, so he broke Burk's record anyway! He also revealed that awaiting him in the UK had been a challenge from Albert Aldridge to run a five-miler right away – but he said the Kent man would have to wait. There was laughter when another speaker made great play about the newspaper interview which made it sound like Shrubb trained on beer. Duffey was formally welcomed to Horsham and the American said it had been a delight to travel with Shrubb who, it seemed, was known from one end of the world to the other. Speaker F W Kinneir told the gathering that Shrubb was regarded as the greatest runner of the age by the experts and he was so proud that 'Shrubbie' was a household word in Horsham.

Shrubb decided to enter a couple of races in the Midlands to keep fit during June and then tackle the AAA championships at Stamford Bridge at the beginning of July. For his part, globe-trotter Duffey did not plan to return home to the USA just yet, and agreed to accompany Shrubb.

CHAPTER ELEVEN

'Passage booked – fortune here for you'

Shrubb, still only 25, was full of the joys of spring on his return from Australia, blissfully unaware that within a few weeks his life would be turned upside down. Perhaps a sign of things to come was the undignified tumble he took on his return to major competition on Saturday, July 1st. He crashed to the track at the AAA championships, allowing a virtual unknown to snatch the four-mile crown Shrubb had proudly held for four years.

The incident occurred halfway through the race at the new Stamford Bridge ground, which had recently been created beside the Fulham Road, a short distance from where the old stadium stood. Shrubb had already surrendered his one-mile title by not participating, in order to give his full attention to the four-miler. In front of a 7,500 crowd on a fine afternoon, the track was heavy and uneven after earlier rain. Shrubb sped to a brisk first mile in 4:43, then eased up a little more than usual and after six laps was caught by Joseph Smith (Salford Harriers). On the lumpy track Shrubb twice stumbled badly, on the second occasion falling heavily to the ground. The crowd gasped at the unaccustomed sight of the champion floundering. A shock result was on the cards.

Shrubb gingerly picked himself up and carried on for a further lap before giving up. The unheralded Smith won in 21:08.8. With reigning champion Shrubb watching from the sidelines, George Butterfield of Darlington won an exciting mile duel with Scotsman John McGough, the pair jostling and colliding in a physical race. So, by the end of the day, two more of Shrubb's coveted titles had passed into new hands, adding to the various cross-country crowns that had found new homes while he had been in the southern hemisphere.

The manner of his exit in the four miles, and his surprise decision not to contest the mile, had the press speculating that Shrubb was still suffering the after-effects of an exhausting five-month tour. He told *The Morning Leader*: 'No, it would be ungracious to Smith to say this. I was full of running earlier on at Wolverhampton and Birmingham. It was sheer misfortune. I fell heavily and hurt my elbow badly on the first occasion and the second fall was more serious, for I hurt my right leg. Prior to the second accident I felt the race was in my hands. The track was loose and not to my liking and once or twice great holes appeared and in one I caught my foot. I shall run as well as ever when I get another track.'

The interviewer noted a 'twinkle in his eye' as Shrubb talked, from which we can deduce that he was being diplomatic and perhaps economical with the truth. He would never have conceded his AAA titles lightly, so his absence from the mile and retirement from the longer race suggested a lack of sharpness and a refusal to bear the shame of finishing second. He was also clearly annoyed over the track and knew he had little chance of catching Smith after falling a second time. *C.B. Fry's Magazine* observed:

'By taking matters steadily at the start, Smith found himself running strongly just when Shrubb, from falls and other causes, was weak and Smith agreeably surprised himself by acquiring the title of four miles champion. It is perfectly clear that the men who try to hang on to Shrubb when he cuts out the pace, do so at great risk. Very few men can run a mile in a little over four-and-a-half minutes with any hope of ultimate success. Shrubb can do it, but he is an exception. And even he might do better if he were to take a few seconds longer over the first part of the journey. Smith's success points a moral and adorns a tale.'

There had been no signs of fatigue a week earlier when Shrubb won a three-mile handicap in 15:11.6 at the Wolverhampton Charity Sports in front of 20,000. In the 100 yards, though, his touring partner Arthur Duffey had collapsed with an injury fifteen yards from the line. He was still incapacitated at Stamford Bridge, so he said farewell to Shrubb after more than five months together, to return home to the USA. Two days later Shrubb must have felt strange turning up to race without Duffey by his side, but in Netherton, Birmingham, he won a ten-guinea gold watch for powering to a 14:52 win in a three-mile scratch race.

A week after the AAA flop at Stamford Bridge, Shrubb silenced the doubters by bouncing back over two miles in Widnes, clocking 9:27.4 and winning from scratch by 150 yards.

In a low-key meeting at East Grinstead, Shrubb decided to see if he had learned anything from watching Duffey so often in the 100 yards dash. He sampled serious sprinting for the first time and managed an impressive 11.2 seconds. Hardly pausing for breath, he then won a two-miler in 9:26.0. *C.B. Fry's Magazine* was impressed by this display of versatility: 'Any man who can win a 100 yards level race in 11.2 and two miles, from scratch, in 9:26 on one and the same afternoon is entitled to respect.' Although he had lost many of his titles during and after his sojourn abroad, the correspondent believed Shrubb remained the best runner at all distances from a mile upwards.

Shrubb was glad to be fit and well by mid-July, for it meant he could head for Chelmsford, complete with running kit and morning suit, and

attempt to win the Atalanta Cup for a remarkable sixth successive year.
In addition to the race, he had been invited to join the Earl and Countess
of Warwick for dinner afterwards, in a marquee positioned in the adjacent grounds of the Bishop of Colchester's residence. Shrubb duly captured the cup, winning the three-mile invitation race in 14:38, his 4:32
first mile emphatically seeing off the opposition. A week later he took his
revenge over new four-mile champion Smith, beating the Salford man in
a three-mile invitation at Villa Park, Birmingham. Shrubb clocked
14:51.8, but carried on through the finish line, as previously agreed, so
that he could chase the four-mile event record at this fixture. Hosted by
Birchfield Harriers, the figure to beat was 21:08, and he did so by seventeen seconds.

Afterwards, Shrubb headed north to stay with friends in Glasgow and
compete at Ibrox once more in the West of Scotland Harriers sports at
Ibrox Park. Highlight of the Monday afternoon races was a 1½-miler
between Shrubb, the new English mile champion George Butterfield, and
Scotland's flying postman John McGough. Shrubb led through half a
mile in 2:09, three-quarters in 3:22, a mile in 4:37 and a mile and a quarter in 5:49. But his two main rivals showed superior sprinting power
eighty yards from home and surged past him. McGough edged out
Butterfield to win in 6:52.6. While in Scotland, Shrubb finalised arrangements to return to Glasgow the following month, this time across the city
at Parkhead.

Shrubb gave plenty of thought over the summer of 1905 to his future
in athletics, pondering the direction his career should take after his forthcoming marriage to Ada. His tobacco shop was doing well and he was
also attracted by the possibility of becoming a pub licensee. However, he
was still only 25 and felt he had plenty of running left in him. He wanted to weigh the option of having a crack at the highly insecure but potentially exciting world of professional running.

While mulling these matters over, he received an invitation to visit
Canada, to race the best men that could be mustered in far-off cities like
Toronto, Winnipeg, Montreal and possibly further afield in the USA too.
Shrubb had enjoyed his Australian trip and did not need long to respond
positively to this new opportunity. Cables flew to and fro across the
Atlantic fixing up a six-week tour scheduled to start later that same sum-
mer, on August 17th. Shrubb was pencilled in for guest appearances in
Montreal's jubilee championship event, followed by races at Winnipeg,
Chicago, New York and Columbia.

The only cloud on the horizon was the AAA. Although they had given
a seal of approval to his Australian trip, the Canadian arrangements did

not satisfy them. Their decision was not what Shrubb hoped to hear. The AAA flatly refused to sanction his presence in North America. No reason was publicly given, but the refusal sparked what Shrubb would later call 'a great crisis in my career'. Meanwhile, his South London Harriers teammate J W Morton apparently ignored the need for official permission and travelled across the Atlantic anyway, finding himself a number of races in Canada and the USA in late summer. The Scot later wrote home to deny reports that he had turned his back on the amateur scene in Britain in order to settle in Canada and run professionally. He insisted he was still competing in SLH colours and would soon return.

Inevitably, rumours circulated of friction between Shrubb and the sports administrators. Why should they refuse him permission to run in North America? Where might he go from here? Unsure what the future held, Shrubb continued to race in England during early August, accepting a challenge from long-time rival Albert Aldridge for a head-to-head over five miles at the Horsham annual Bank Holiday sports.

Persistent rain kept away some visitors, although the skies cleared by midday, the track dried quickly, and the sports went ahead in near-perfect conditions. Viscount Edward Turnour, MP, the former Sussex cricketer, was among the crowd of 3,700. Shrubb's was not a handicap race, meaning the runners started side by side. As Robert Cook raised the starting pistol, Shrubb, on the inside, beat the gun. Smiling ruefully, he was called back to the line. Then, making ground like a fleeing deer, he set off to lead by twenty yards at the end of the first lap and by more than fifty after the third. His first mile was 4:36 and the rest a shade over five minutes each. He lapped Aldridge towards the end, whereupon his rival stumbled and fell, but recovered. Shrubb sprinted home to beat his own world record on grass, recording 24:51.2, 'looking as fresh as paint' according to one report. (For mile splits, see Appendix.)

Both runners received a warm ovation after Aldridge came home in 26:03.4. The track was laid out at five laps to the mile, and Shrubb won by more than a lap, his prize a cabinet of cutlery. In a post-race interview, he said he knew he'd had 'an easy thing on' and felt in tip-top form. Had he known he had been inside record schedule he would have gone harder and knocked a few more seconds off! With Shrubb overseas, Aldridge had taken his International, National and Southern cross-country titles, plus his AAA ten-mile crown, but today's beating put him in his place. Shrubb extended sympathy to his rival over his brother's death on the morning of the event which cannot have helped Aldridge's state of mind.

Shrubb returned to Scotland for a two-day event at Glasgow Celtic FC's Parkhead stadium. On Saturday, August 12th his presence helped swell the crowd to 15,000 and in a 1½-mile contest he was beaten by a whisker in a dramatic finish by George Butterfield, who clocked 6:55.4. On the following Monday in a four-mile handicap race Shrubb cruised to victory in 19:36.8, ahead of John McGough, who had beaten him at least twice in the past over shorter distances. It was arranged that McGough, who'd had a 100-yard start, would carry on through the finish line to complete a full four miles in an attempt to create a new Scottish native record.

Back in Sussex, on Monday, August 21st – when Shrubb had hoped to be in Canada – Aldridge failed to show for the Worthing Sports, allowing Shrubb an easy three-mile win in 14:49. That week, the talk of the local athletics scene was the bizarre happenings at the Crawley Sports, where race starter Mr Rothery's pistol exploded in his face as he attempted to start a bicycle race. He collapsed and was rushed to hospital.

On Friday 25th, Shrubb won a two-miler in Windsor in 9:37.8 and the following day coped well with a rough and windswept Eastbourne track to win over three miles in 15:10 6, ahead of Aldridge and Midlands champion Fulford.

Shrubb was now looking as dominant as ever on the track, but off it all was not well. Recalling the events of August 1905 in *All Sport Weekly*, he explained: 'The papers began to hint darkly at a well-known British amateur runner being on the eve of suspension. No names were mentioned, and my friends, in common with myself, commenced wondering who this culprit might be. As the rumour was repeated my friends feared the reference might be to me, and some put the question point blank, while I pleaded utter inability either to confirm or remove their fears. I was quite in the dark. A week passed and the suspense became more intense as the sporting papers kept harrying me on the same string … in the end I wished the AAA would let the cat out of the bag.'

Tongues were wagging that Shrubb was contemplating retiring from the amateur scene anyway, regardless of any pending AAA punishment. Shrubb himself appeared to be waiting to see how events panned out before making a decision. *The West Sussex County Times* stated on Friday September 9th: 'Rumour has it that Alfred Shrubb intends to leave the track shortly. Questioned in regard to same, the famous runner was a little uncertain but it is evident he thinks his running days are nearly numbered. It is quite probable that the present season will be his last both on the flat and cross-country.'

Matters came to the boil one morning when a customer rushed into Shrubb's tobacconist shop brandishing a newspaper: 'If he had brought my death warrant he could hardly have looked more troubled,' recalled

Shrubb. The paper announced that the AAA intended to interview Shrubb at a Fleet Street hotel in connection with trips to the Midlands and Scotland. This, at least, confirmed that he was indeed the man they wanted to carpet. Before his date with destiny, Shrubb carried out what would prove to be his last amateur engagement, at the SLH autumn meeting at Kennington Oval on Saturday, September 9th. Crowds were down due to the rain, and fewer than 5,000 turned out, a quarter of the previous year's bumper gate. Shrubb had no problems with the conditions and on a soggy track won a three-mile invitation by 120 yards, beating Fulford of Birchfield Harriers in the pleasing time of 14:54.4.

Ironically, given the nature of the inquiry, Shrubb travelled to London to meet the men from the AAA upon a motorcycle paid for by race winnings. He had come to an agreement with certain race promoters that prizes valued at £10 each, for a series of four races, would be handed over in the shape of a £40 motorcycle if he won all four events. He had duly done just that, and suddenly had personal transport at his disposal. This deal perfectly illustrated how the top runners could – and did – bend the rules governing amateurs and benefit in a material way from a sport that was supposed to be played purely for enjoyment. A £40 motorcycle in 1905, incidentally, would equate to £2,505 at today's prices.

Leaving his bike at his club HQ, the Swan and Sugar Loaf public house at Croydon, Shrubb headed into central London by train. 'I heard my heart beating more when I entered the room to face the AAA officials than ever I did at the close of a record-breaking long-distance race,' he recalled. 'But my conscience was all right in the matter.'

Senior official Mr Schoffield and his colleagues were waiting to interrogate the runner about his proposed visit to Canada the previous month, and certain other races in the UK. Shrubb admitted his Canadian expenses would have been met by 'friends' over there, feigning ignorance about the necessity of consulting the AAA beforehand. Ignorance of the rules, however, is no defence, and Shrubb later admitted: 'In the end it came forcibly home to me that I had incurred the just censure of the AAA and that I deserved to be suspended. After being requested to leave the room for a few minutes I returned to learn my fate, having in the interval handed to one of the members of the committee the cable I had received from Canada, which I wished the President to see.'

This was the moment that Shrubb's goose was well and truly cooked. The cable he handed over – apparently voluntarily – contained the following incriminating words: 'Passage booked – fortune here for you.'

Shrubb's sentence – permanent suspension, subject to appeal, from all amateur athletics – was solemnly delivered and, as Shrubb recalls, there was an atmosphere of sorrow in the room. The officials were evidently saddened they'd had to impose such a heavy punishment, while, for his part, Shrubb smiled bravely, shook their hands and agreed that under the rules they had little choice.

Whether or not he was retrospectively putting a rosy glow on the matter is not clear, although his apparently deferential manner would soon evaporate. Perhaps after taking counsel from friends and associates his resolve stiffened, for a few days later he slapped in an appeal.

News of Shrubb's ban was announced on Friday, September 29th 1905, but the letter of confirmation did not drop through his letterbox until Tuesday, October 3rd. By then, of course, the newspapers were outdoing each other in their lurid coverage of how the world's finest distance runner had been banned 'for practices detrimental to the cause of pure amateurism'. The AAA statement gave no details, but intimated that Shrubb's offence(s) related to the rule about a competitor not being permitted to ask for, or receive, hotel, travelling or other expenses.

Two days after receiving his letter, Shrubb fired off his appeal. *The West Sussex County Times* said he felt aggrieved at receiving no detailed explanation: 'Much sympathy is felt for Shrubb in Horsham for he had recently announced his possible intention of retiring, but will not want it to end in this way.'

The paper continued: 'The nature of the suspension is not unusual, merely that Shrubb is so famous, making it exceptional. It seems many other runners will have to be banned too.' Events of 1896 were recalled, when a sensation was caused by the wholesale suspension of English champions Downer, Bradley, Bacon, Watkins, Crossland and Blair on the eve of the AAA championships. Blair's ban was later withdrawn after his brother, a barrister, appealed on his behalf. Shrubb would be denied the benefit of legal representation, for by now the AAA had changed their rules to prevent it.

Writing under his pseudonym 'Larry Lynx', W Lotinga of *The People* speculated that AAA's use of the word 'permanently' must mean they had convincing proof of Shrubb's misdemeanours. Yet public sympathy was on his side as he had always proved himself 'a pure and modest gentleman'. Indeed, if he had accepted expenses he was no worse than footballers, cricketers and rowers, who were ruled by different bodies. Lotinga added: 'There is no limit to the irreparable harm such an edict must have upon the marvellous little runner. His dethronement is hard to take on the [possible] eve of retirement. The term "malpractices" conveys much more than what is actually meant. If this case is only the means of quashing the sham amateur and bringing about a ruling of equity, no matter who or what the men and what the branch of sport, Shrubb will have done more for athletics – if that's possible – than in the past. His appeal I consider to be the protest of every athlete, every true-intentioned sportsman in the land; it should not be heard with closed doors.'

On Saturday, October 21st the sad figure of Shrubb, clad in motor-cycling gear after riding over from Horsham, was seen spectating at the Gibb Cup cross-country race at Croydon. He told one reporter he had trained hard and set his heart on recapturing this trophy, which he'd last won in 1903. Now all he could do was look on helplessly as his SLH teammate PA Casserley won in 27:59.

The outcome of Shrubb's appeal would not be known until the New Year, giving plenty of time for the wider implications to be debated at length in the sporting media. It slowly emerged that although the payment of expenses for various UK races had been a major factor, Shrubb had specifically been nailed for 'misleading' the Southern Counties committee about his boat ticket to Canada, dated August 1905. By November it had become clear that Shrubb was not the only figure under the AAA's scrutiny, for his club, SLH – which, ironically, had a number of officers serving on AAA committees – was also under investigation. *The Sporting Life* examined the whole issue and published the following lengthy report on Saturday, November 4th. It extends over the next four pages:

'For a considerable time, the athletic world has been perturbed by vague and ugly rumours of indiscretions on the part of men holding the amateur status, rumours that were not allayed but received a fillip by the suspension of Shrubb. When it was announced, the names of clubs were bandied about freely and the AAA was maligned because it did not take action. *The Sporting Life* is among those who think it should not end with the suspension of Shrubb and we have called – perhaps unnecessarily – upon the AAA to thoroughly investigate the whole unsavoury business. We never did believe there was truth in the suggestion of irresponsible people that the AAA were glossing over the errors of club officials. We believe that the AAA have at their head men whose ideals of purity in athletics inspire thousands with an intense enthusiasm for the pastime. As the journal to which amateur athletes look to champion their cause, we have been making close inquiry into the matter and find that statements are in circulation relating to SLH, which that club may be able to explain when the AAA takes the matter in hand. On May 26, 1900, Thomas S Sinnott, secretary of South London Harriers, was referee at sports at Bexhill and was so impressed by Shrubb that he induced him to join his own club – from that day the star of SLH was in the ascendant.

'The year following that which he discovered Shrubb, Sinnott wrote to the then Hon Sec Mr R E Wright to the effect that he wished to resign, but having been asked to reconsider his resignation he eventually agreed to continue in office as assistant treasurer, being appointed to perform the detail work. This arrangement lasted until October 28, 1902 when Mr C W B King was chosen for the office.

'When asked by *The Sporting Life* to give an account of his actions following this, Sinnott said that he had possession of the books, and as (so he declared) he had to make a number of payments on behalf of the club for Shrubb, he would hand over the books when those sums were repaid. The payments, said Sinnott were made for the purpose of enabling Shrubb to compete at different meetings under the aegis of the SLH. The committee of the SLH would have none of this. They denied that there was any such liability and maintained they knew nothing of any indebtedness in respect of Shrubb. The committee took up an attitude of active resistance to any claim and as Mr Sinnott was equally determined to have his demands met, there was a deadlock and Mr Sinnott informs us, recourse was had to the law courts, the committee and other members of the SLH suing for recovery of the books and papers and claiming damages for their unlawful detention. Mr Sinnott made a counter-claim asserting that with the knowledge and consent of the members of the committee of the club he had paid the sum of £40 5s 11d.

'Asked by *The Sporting Life* as to what sums he had paid and for what purposes, Sinnott informs us of the following:

1901

Training expenses, incl. trainer, for Southern XC	£11		
Ditto for National XC	£6		
Railway fares for the two above events		11s	10d
Training expenses for ten miles, AAA champs, Crewe	£4		
Entrance fee (x1) to above championship		5s	
Return railway fare to Crewe	£1	6s	4d
Hotel expenses etc		15s	
Entrance fee (x3) for AAA champs, Huddersfield		15s	
Return railway fare to Huddersfield	£1	10s	3d
Hotel expenses etc	£1	2s	

1902

Training expenses, incl. trainer for National XC	£4	
Railway fares to Southern and National XC		10s
Entrance fee to ten mile AAA champs		5s

Railway fare to the above (Stamford Bridge)		8s
Entrance fee (x2) to Part 2 of AAA champs		10s
Railway fare to the above (Stamford Bridge)		6s
Paid for two pairs of running shoes	£1	5s
Paid for running clothes and ribbon		16s 6d
Insurance of club and AAA cups, 2-yr premiums	£5	
TOTAL	£40	5s 11d

[£40 5s 11d, converted to current values, amounts to around £2,400]

'The action taken against Sinnott was settled out of court, judgement by consent being entered for the delivery of the books and papers and of the counter claim to be dismissed. "There being an understanding that I was to be paid my out-of-pocket expenses as set forth," said Sinnott, "I was the more ready to meet them in this way because I was anxious not to injure Shrubb and yet so badly have I been treated by the committee that but for the arrangement, the case would have been fought out to the bitter end. He is very indignant over this matter. I paid the money on the club's behalf when they were short of funds and now that Shrubb pulled them round and got a big balance for them they coolly repudiate their liability to me. Their object is perfectly clear. The rules of the AAA had been broken and the repayment to me of the 40 odd expended would have been an acknowledgement on their part of their responsibility for the payments. If the club knew nothing of the money I was spending on Shrubb, why did they now make inquires over who was financing the Horsham man?"

'Even if SLH had admitted payment on their behalf of many items in the claim set forth here, they would not have incriminated themselves. Under AAA rules a club may pay entrance fees/expenses to and from meetings but it may not pay training expenses and it would at once damn a club were the purchase of articles of wearing apparel for an amateur traced to it. One of the points in connection with the aspect of the matter on which the AAA will naturally satisfy itself is the position of the SLH. The athletic world was asking: Who is paying all Shrubb's expenses? People suspected that Shrubb's position was such as prevented him from paying his own expenses and if the SLH satisfied itself on this point it will have a complete answer to the suggestion that it was lax in its care of the members, subject to its rules. On the one side, Mr Sinnott maintains that he was accompanied by members of SLH when he went to Horsham to arrange with the Blue Star Harriers for Shrubb's resignation to be accepted and when he agreed to put up Shrubb as a member of SLH, arranging that Shrubb be not asked to pay any entrance fee or subscription, and that other expenses incidental to training etc should be paid by Sinnott on behalf of the club. On the other side, the members of SLH referred to deny all knowledge of any such arrangement as this, and stoutly assert their innocence to this day and up to the time of this article they have so far adhered to their story that they have not paid a penny to their late treasurer for any of the items.

'Before the AAA, the SLH will make a vigorous defence of their actions which so far as we can see, up to this point were in accord with those men innocent of any deviation from the laws of amateur athleticism.

'When the SLH knew from Mr Sinnott that the payments given above had been made, what did they do to put themselves right with the AAA? Did they read the following paragraph of Law 1 of the AAA?: "That a competitor in athletic competitions (other than AAA championships or bona fide international, inter-club, inter-team, inter-college or inter-school contests) who asks for, or receives, travelling expenses ceases to be an amateur. No club, society or managing body promoting an athletic competition shall either directly or indirectly pay or offer a monetary consideration of the travelling expenses of any competitor in such competition. Clubs, college or schools shall be answerable for any payments made by them and if called upon to do so, shall produce full details of the same and accounts to the AAA (north, south or midlands) committee."

'Did they expel Shrubb for accepting the sums or goods mentioned? And did they report the matter to the AAA? The answer to the first part is apparent for Shrubb continued to run for SLH. Whether or not the club reported the matter to the AAA we have no way of knowing, save by inference, but this is a point to which the AAA will doubtless direct attention. Another question that arises is: After the departure of Sinnott from the club, who paid Shrubb's expenses? The reply might be that Shrubb paid his own and always had, and that Mr Sinnott was making charges against his old club in a spirit of pique. This rejoinder, if made, would be futile for we have in our possession a letter from Shrubb in which the question is conclusively settled and which shows the Horsham runner to be a manly fellow and grateful to the man who helped him to fame. It is a letter that Shrubb need not be ashamed of.

'Apart from this and one or two other incidents in the affair, the story is a most sordid one, and leaves a nasty taste in the mouth. Shrubb was not altogether to blame – he was tempted by those who should have known better. He had no private income and his position in life was such that he could not afford to compete at meetings up and down the country at his own expense. The athletic world knew it. Baits were being dangled before Shrubb's eyes as illustrated by a letter sent to him. The names are suppressed and the SLH are in no way concerned:

"Dear Shrubb,

I hope you are well. I was pleased to read of your good wins. A friend of mine... is getting up a meeting and wants you to go for the record. Select your distance – anything from 4 to 10 miles – and find out which you are likely to beat. They will prepare the track for you. You can get £5 and £1 expenses. You can have the money if you like, instead of a prize, but you must not mention this to anybody. The fare to this place from London is only 1s return. Let me know, yes or no."

'That is the kind of communication with which Shrubb was favoured and is it great wonder if an athlete in his position should deviate from the path of athletic rectitude? The greatest sinners (such as the party who wrote this letter) were those who tempted the man to his undoing. Burglaries would be few and far between if there were no fence shops and scandals in the athletic crowd would be less numerous if those who have control of the purse strings and organisation of meetings would run perfectly straight. The majority do, the minority not, but the latter are capable of inflicting grievous injury upon amateur sport.

'We have discharged our duty to sport in directing the attention of the athletic world and the supreme body in the athletic world to an open sore. We leave the matter now in the hands of the body, certain that an action, immediate and satisfactory will be taken. The AAA must act, the late treasurer of the SLH must tell his story before that body and the reply of the SLH must be heard. The purity of amateur athletics demands a thorough investigation and the information in our possession will be at the disposal of the AAA should they consider that our assistance is necessary in the discharge of their onerous and thankless task.'

And so the great debate rumbled on. Edgar Bredin, a coach and former runner, paid public tribute to Shrubb and expressed sympathy with him: 'Running is essentially the poor man's sport. For a few shillings, a man can purchase a training ticket that enables him to practise on a track. Shoes, vests and running knicks are cheap enough.' When questioned by *The Daily Mail*, Shrubb told them the detailed expenses featured in *The Sporting Life* report were correct but not a penny had passed through his hands, adding that since Thomas Sinnott's resignation from SLH he'd paid his own training expenses. Throughout all the press coverage, there was sympathy towards Shrubb, who was called 'the straightest of runners' and painted as more sinned-against than sinning.

An anonymous letter in *The Sporting Life* from 'The Man in the Street' suggested that without the financial help of a benefactor Shrubb would never have reached the pinnacle of fame on which he now finds himself and the chief loss would then have been the public's. And it was strange that amateur cricketers could accept expenses but not athletes. Another letter to the same paper demanded that SLH explain how an athlete of means so slender that he relied on Sinnott's patronage to supply his running pumps, could then 'blossom' after Sinnott's withdrawal.

The editor of *The Sporting Life* expressed the opinion that some letter-writers had condemned the men at the AAA too freely: 'Expressions like muddy-minded, animal, imbecile and lunatic asylum meant the limits of decency had been reached.' He added that one pleasant aspect of the great debate had been the tributes paid to Shrubb himself. Even the nineteenth century legend Walter George put aside his criticisms of Shrubb's tactics to say he believed him to be one of the most straightforward and honourable athletes who had ever run. George quoted an incident where a 'well-known betting man' had sidled up to him before a certain championship to ask if Shrubb could be induced to lose the race. George replied: 'Certainly not and I hope for your own honour's sake you are not thinking of trying to tempt him.' On race-day the man returned and told George he had been quite right, for when offered £50 not to try, Shrubb went close to physically attacking him.

During the second week of December the AAA Southern Counties committee re-adjourned in central London to inquire, by request of the current SLH committee, into that club's previous relations with Shrubb. The committee declared it was now satisfied that: (1) Shrubb did receive sums of money from prominent members of SLH, (2) Those members had found the monies personally and without any intention of recouping them from SLH, and (3) The repetition of such a state of affairs would be prevented by future legislation.

This outcome was condemned as 'disappointingly brief' by *The Sporting Life*, which suggested blame was being deflected from SLH in recognition of the club's good work over the years. The paper was critical that the 'prominent' SLH members were not named by the AAA, adding its discomfort over the fact that SLH still had a high number of members serving on AAA committees. The AAA did not wish to be seen protecting SLH. In early January a proposition by ex-amateur champion walker R H Venn, seconded by C Val Hunter, saw a resolution passed which censured SLH for its past actions in regard to Shrubb, having known he was in receipt of only a small income, yet was obliged to travel all over the country to race in their colours.

C.B. Fry's Magazine reckoned the censuring of SLH was a verdict of guilty, not only on their colleagues at SLH, but on the AAA themselves. 'It has already been argued that if there devolved on the SLH a moral obligation to spy into Shrubb's affairs it became the bound duty of the AAA to do so. A man may strongly suspect that some of his acquaintances are not quite honest or so candid as they should be in the matter of their returns for income tax. His duty to his country is clear; but what man would care, in that connection, to discharge his moral obligations? He would doubtless consider it a matter for the "authorities". Possibly the SLH took a similar view as regards anything some of their members may have suspected with reference to Alfred Shrubb.'

SLH was furious at being publicly censured. Club secretary W E M Martin condemned through the pages of *The Sporting Life* the idea that there had ever been any sort of 'cover-up', because seven AAA committee members were also SLH officials. He said no present member of SLH, with the possible exception of Shrubb himself, had breached the spirit or the letter of the AAA's rules. He conceded that Sinnott, a previous treasurer, had given or loaned Shrubb monies, but denied this had been done with the knowledge of the SLH committee. Other members made contributions towards Shrubb's training expenses for the National cross-country championships of 1901, 1902 and 1903, but these were of a purely private nature and, in their understanding, perfectly legitimate. This money had gone to the club's trainer (Harry Andrews) and not to Shrubb himself. Martin said the SLH committee considered that Shrubb had sufficient income to meet his own travelling expenses, and it was 'an exaggeration' to claim that he had travelled all 'over the country'. He accused the Southern Counties AAA of showing 'an amazing disregard for the ordinary principles of English justice' in their censuring of SLH. The club was 'untouched and undisturbed' by the decision because it had been delivered in haste with reference to facts and principles of justice.

Far from getting SLH off the hook, this letter met with incredulity. Firstly, to suggest that Shrubb did not travel 'all over the country' for races was plainly ridiculous. The exhaustive number of races itemised in this book proves that. Moreover, the idea that SLH had been a paragon of virtue with regard to Shrubb was also hard to swallow. SLH apparently believed it had done no wrong by collecting cash to help Shrubb, as the money had been passed on indirectly, via his coach. At best, these actions were contrary to the spirit of amateurism. The editor of the magazine *Truth* commented: 'I can only say that if the AAA rules permit a club to run a so-called amateur athlete in this way, the sooner they are altered the better and if the committee of the club and its secretary support such a system, I should be very sorry indeed for any young fellow of my acquaintance to join the SLH.'

SLH hit back. L J Manogue, editor of the SLH Gazette, insisted that contributing to a fund for Shrubb's training for the National had not infringed AAA laws. Manogue, a talented half-miler who would later run in the 1908 Olympics, argued through the pages of *The Sporting Life* that Shrubb was suspended for 'hoodwinking' the AAA committee in con-nection with his proposed visit to Canada, not because he had received money from SLH members. Shrubb had borrowed money to purchase his tobacco shop, and due to his popularity and good sense, this had prospered. Manogue denied that Shrubb had an 'arrangement' with the club that he wouldn't have to pay back annual subs or race entry fees. Although former treasurer Sinnott had supplied Shrubb with money, this was done without the knowledge, let alone approval of the committee. Sinnott was no longer a member or friend of the club. Shrubb himself made personal sacrifices, Manogue added, and reaped no personal rewards except for medals.

Athletic News felt the AAA could have put an end to the controversy by naming the SLH officials who had protested their innocence and those responsible for the club's early dealings with Shrubb. 'The athletic-loving public is disappointed over this omission, to put it mildly,' it added.

On Saturday, January 20th 1906, Shrubb's appeal was heard by the AAA's general committee at Anderton's Hotel in Fleet Street, London. Vice-president Montague Shearman KC, a former sprinter, presided over a gathering of representatives from the northern, southern and midland regions. The committee, behind closed doors, listened to Shrubb's case but heard nothing to make them reconsider, and the lifetime ban remained in force. It hammered the final nail in Shrubb's coffin as far as his running career under AAA laws was concerned.

Without further ado, Shrubb and his associates informed the press he would immediately be turning professional. His first race as a paid per-former would take place 48 hours later at London's Olympia. Having anticipated the futility of his appeal, Shrubb had already struck a provi-sional deal with Olympia's manager-promoter Edward Cleary. Shrubb would run a two-mile race against a relay of two other men. He would also attack W G George's one-mile record on the same night.

The Sporting Life described the verdict 'a foregone conclusion', but noted the omission of a detailed statement from the AAA. Those who had directly or indirectly subsidised Shrubb had been allowed to go Scot free. The paper urged the AAA to pursue the matter or risk 'stultifying' itself. In the same week, the cycling authorities also got tough and imposed a life ban on champion cyclist Jimmy Benyon, who had been caught contravening the amateur code.

The Sporting Life's columnist 'The Expert' demanded radical change to the AAA's rules, for otherwise all its favourite champions would be relegated to the professional ranks where they would 'sink into oblivion like their predecessors'. Change to the expenses rule was needed to permit athletes to accept the generosity of wealthy clubs without imperilling their amateur status, although the true amateur was one who paid for his own sport and sought no outside assistance. As soon as gate money came into question, the basis of amateurism was shaken. The spectator in 99 per cent of cases did not care whether a competitor was professional or amateur, they merely wanted to see good sport. The exhibition side of sport, professionalism, should be not only legalised but actively encouraged. 'There is nothing degrading about it ... we go to country galas and see trick cyclists and tight-rope walkers, and all sorts of exhibitions, yet the present state of the laws taboo pro athletics. Only a few months back, there was an endeavour to form an association for the regulation and encouragement of professional sport, but it fell through from the very reason that amateurism had too strong a hold upon the class who are making a bit out of athletics.'

W Lotinga of *The People* – who, it should be remembered, knew Shrubb personally – was determined to defend the runner and condemn the AAA: 'What has he done? Accepted hospitality from, and had his fares occasionally paid by, his own friends. The AAA must have acted upon facts which have not, but ought to, have been made public, otherwise it would seem that amateurism is defined by the status of the individual. 'Tis truly a thin line, for are not our own not-chosen-yet representatives accepting a huge grant towards expenses for the Athens [1906 Olympics] trip? That a magnificent career should in its very closing days be marred by such a stigma must be a poignant grief to all with the good of athletics at heart. Shrubb, but for his temporary Olympia engagement, has done with running and will never compete again. Despite the stigma of his ban, I am still only too pleased to ask Shrubb to be my guest at the London AC dinner on Wednesday.'

Lotinga's instinct that Shrubb 'was done with running' would, of course, prove unfounded, but his tone echoed the opinions of many inside and outside the sport. Shrubb had been made an example of. There must have been many instances down the years where the country's top runners bent the rules, but the incriminating cable Shrubb received from Canada – promising him a fortune – was the straw that broke the camel's back. The question that remained, however, was whether the administrators would heed the advice to change their rules. By enforcing their outdated laws they had surely done more harm than good. They had banished their champion to possible sporting oblivion, yet he was the man who had done most to enhance their international prestige and who pulled in big crowds wherever he ran.

Coincidentally – or maybe not, given the claim that Shrubb and Arthur Duffey 'played the money game' in New Zealand – Duffey was also embroiled in a row in the USA. The AAU secretary James E Sullivan withdrew all Duffey's amateur track records from the official almanac for alleged misdemeanours regarding expenses. Duffey's attorney threatened legal action if these statistics were not reinstated. Duffey denied 'confessing to acting as a professional for several years', claiming those words appeared in an editorial for which he was not responsible. He also insisted that, under existing USA conditions, an athlete could remain an amateur while still receiving expenses.

After months of claim and counter-claim, athletics fans must have grown weary of 'The Shrubb Affair' filling the sports pages. They needed a diversion, and it duly appeared in *The Sporting Life* on Tuesday January 18th. An official at a cross-country race in Bordeaux had used a starting-pistol which, for some reason, was loaded with a ball cartridge. When fired, he found he had shot the star runner. Although the athlete was not mortally wounded, the official was so overcome with remorse that he collapsed and had to be carried away.

After settling in Canada in 1928, Alf Shrubb (left) went into business
with James Lake Morden

Striking a pose. Two images from Shrubb's self-penned coaching manual (1909).
The captions state (left) Starting for a long-distance race; (right) Looking round at the
field (Always try and avoid doing this)

A chest full of medals. Shrubb in his mid-20s (c.1904)

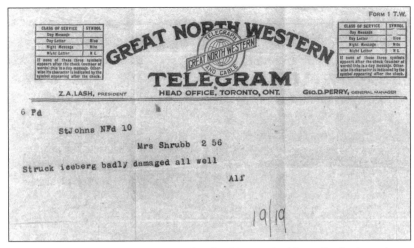

Alf Shrubb despatched this telegram after the ship carrying him to England struck an iceberg head-on off the coast of Newfoundland

And this is the reason why. The *SS Grampian*, which struck an iceberg and limped into port at St John's. It is a mystery how it did not sink. Two crew were killed (July 1919)

Shrubb's daughter, Norah, was delighted when the Mayor of Bowmanville, Ontario, sanctioned a street to be named after her father (July 2003)

After appointing Shrubb (centre row, far right), as their coach, Harvard University's cross-country results improved dramatically (c.1910)

'I returned in time to take a snap of Sherring.'

This is one of the abiding stories attached to Alf Shrubb. He finished so far ahead of the second-placed man that he trotted off to get his camera and returned to photograph him crossing the line

"I returned in time to take a snap of Sherring."

As a youth, Shrubb won a two-shilling bet over a race which he won in his working clothes. Suddenly he was discovering that he had a talent to run

'I was requested to leave the room for a few minutes.' When Shrubb returned, it was to discover that he had been banned from amateur athletics indefinitely

I was requested to leave the room for a few minutes.

MR. AND MRS. SHRUBB LEAVING THE CHURCH AFTER THEIR MARRIAGE.

Wedding bells. Shrubb and Miss Ada Brown tie the knot at Hayward's Heath, Sussex, in February 1906

Villa Park, Saturday, Aug. 22.

At 3 p.m.
BIRMINGHAM v. LONDON.

SHRUBB v. RECORD

WILL HE BEAT IT?

EXTRACT FROM "THE SPORTSMAN," August 12th, 1903.

BIRCHFIELD H. v. SOUTH LONDON H.

A SPORTING MATCH between the National Cross-country Champions and the South London H. has been fixed up for Saturday, August 22, at the Aston Villa Grounds, Birmingham. The events will be run on the Inter-'Varsity principle, and much interest is being taken in sporting centres in the Midlands over the result. It is known that Shrubb will take part in a limit handicap at one mile and a half, and record for this distance will be easy for him to beat. There are also 100 yards, 440 yards, 880 yards, one mile, three miles, and two other inter-club events, with a quarter and one mile open cycle handicaps, a 300 yards open flat handicap, and a 600 yards members' handicap. This programme will give the Birmingham public a chance to see the champion at his best distance, and there is sure to be a large crowd in attendance on the day, for the people of Birmingham have never had a chance of seeing Shrubb con. in any sports in their district. W. G. George, the old Moseley cu. pion, was a great favourite with the Aston crowds, and it was here he put up some of his very best performances; in fact, the name of George and W. Snook, another old Moseley Harrier, would at all times draw large gates at the old Aston Lower Grounds. In those early days of athletic sports, the annual inter-club fixtures of Moseley and South London H. were second to none in the athletic world, and many exciting competitions have taken place between the two clubs. With the Birchfield H. bringing about a revival of these friendly contests, and this being the first appearance of the One, Four, and Ten Miles A.A.A. Champion in Birmingham, there is every pr..... a great Meeting at Aston Villa Park on August 22. Birchfield do not expect to make a big show against the crack London team, for they are a much better club over the country than on the flat, as their performances in the Cross-country Championships will prove. Still, they hope to put up a good race, and, from a sporting view, they will be content with hunting the London men home. Their chief object is to give Birmingham supporters of their club and the public generally the chance of seeing Shrubb cut record, and thereby help to revive the interest in athletics, which will then help to encourage the many young clubs that are springing up in the Midlands, to bring out future champions in every branch of the sport.

The Mile and Half Record is held by C. Bennett, Finchley Harriers, 6min. 51sec., and was made at Stamford Bridge Grounds, in June, 1898.

Everyone should see Shrubb, the greatest Champion since W. G. George, the Birmingham favourite.

ADMISSION - SIXPENCE and ONE SHILLING.

The Sportsman announces Shrubb's Villa Park record attempt (August 1903)

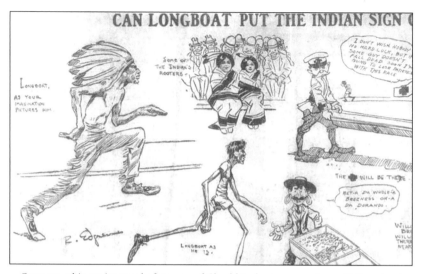

Cartoons whip up interest before one of Shrubb's classic encounters with Longboat

Saturday Feb 18th 1905

Saturday Feb 18th 1905

TIME TABLE OF EVENTS.

No.	Event.			Time.
1.	Three-mile Walk		...	2.30
2.	Putting the Weight		...	2.40
3.	100 Yards Championship, First Heat		...	3.0
4.	,, ,, ,, Second ,,		...	3.5
5.	1 Miles Invitation Scratch		...	3.10
6.	440 Yards Handicap, First Heat		...	3.20
7.	,, ,, ,, Second ,,		...	3.25
8.	,, ,, ,, Third ,,		...	3.30
9.	High Jump		...	3.35
10.	Menagerie Race		...	3.50
11.	100 Yards Championship, Final		...	4.5
12.	120 Yards Hurdles, First Heat		...	4.10
13.	,, ,, ,, Second ,,		...	4.15
14.	440 Yards Handicap, Final		...	4.20
15.	Half Mile Championship		...	4.25
16.	75 Yards Handicap, First Heat		...	4.30
17.	,, ,, ,, Second ,,		...	4.33
18.	,, ,, ,, Third ,,		...	4.36
19.	,, ,, ,, Fourth ,,		...	4.39
20.	,, ,, ,, Fifth ,,		...	4.42
21.	120 Yards Hurdle, Final		...	4.45
22.	Two-Mile Handicap		...	4.48
23.	75 Yards Handicap, Final		...	5.0

Shrubb has arrived in Australia. This is the programme of events for the Victorian Championships in Melbourne, 1905

Four long-distance specialists prepare for battle in New York.
From left: Shrubb, Tom Longboat, Johnny Hayes, and Pietro Dorando (1909)

" Just as we jumped, the horse charged through the window of a grocer's shop."

'Just as we jumped, the horse charged through the window of a grocer's shop.' Shrubb has a narrow escape from a cab, after a race in Crewe

Longboat and Shrubb take a stroll outside their Toronto hotel. Longboat soon turned
professional and was able to take up Shrubb's racing challenge (1908)

" What game is this you are up to, Alf ? "

'What game is this you are up to Alf?'
Shrubb used to sleepwalk, or rather
'sleep-race' in front of his brother at
home in Horsham

As his fame grew, Shrubb left behind the building sites of Horsham and opened a
tobacconist shop in the centre of the town (c.1904)

SHRUBB trains on Beer.
Take McCRACKEN'S for choice.

Four Mile Handicap.

Event No. 24.   At 4.45.

22	**Shrubb, A. R.** (Eng.)	*maroon and gold*	scr.
50	Ferguson, R. A. (E.M.H.)	*blue*	180 yds.
272	Blake, G. (Melb.)	*light blue*	180 ,,
142	Stillwell, J. A. (Ess.)	*black and red*	220 ,.
90	Riddell, J. R. (Carlt.)	*brown and gold*	220 ,.
62	Steele, W. P. (E.M.H.)	*blue and white*	250 ,,
85	Muacvassa, J. (C. and N.)	*light & dark blue*	300 ,.
115	Russell, H. (Ess.)	*black and red*	470 ..
161	Fraser, C. J. (Malv.)	*white*	500 ,.

1....... ....2........   ......3 ....*Time* .. *min*......*secs*.

SHRUBB will in this race attack the following
Victorian Records:

1	Mile, held by H. Sutton	...	4 min. 30 4/5 secs.
2	,,	,, W. Cumming	...	10 min. 5 4/5 secs.
3	,,	,, R. A. Ferguson	..	15 min. 30 secs.
4	,,	,, H. G. Whiting	...	21 min.

'Shrubb trains on beer' says this advertisement. This poster shows him lining up for a four-mile handicap race

On most of his trans-Atlantic boat trips, Shrubb would obtain permission to use the deck for training, and for entertaining fellow-passengers into the bargain

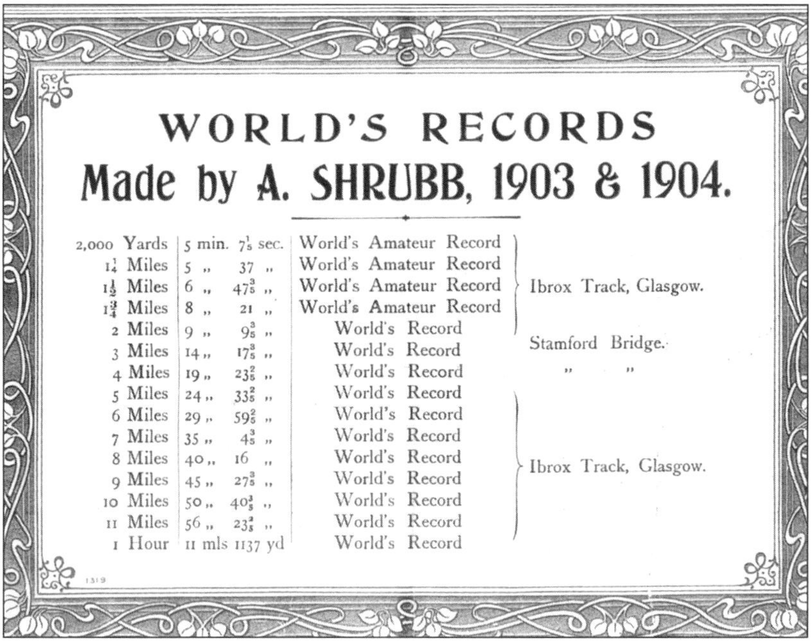

WORLD'S RECORDS

Made by A. SHRUBB, 1903 & 1904.

2,000 Yards	5 min. 7⅕ sec.	World's Amateur Record	
1¼ Miles	5 „ 37 „	World's Amateur Record	
1½ Miles	6 „ 47⅗ „	World's Amateur Record	Ibrox Track, Glasgow.
1¾ Miles	8 „ 21 „	World's Amateur Record	
2 Miles	9 „ 9⅗ „	World's Record	
3 Miles	14 „ 17⅗ „	World's Record	Stamford Bridge.
4 Miles	19 „ 23⅖ „	World's Record	„ „
5 Miles	24 „ 33⅖ „	World's Record	
6 Miles	29 „ 59⅖ „	World's Record	
7 Miles	35 „ 4⅗ „	World's Record	
8 Miles	40 „ 16 „	World's Record	Ibrox Track, Glasgow.
9 Miles	45 „ 27⅗ „	World's Record	
10 Miles	50 „ 40⅗ „	World's Record	
11 Miles	56 „ 23⅖ „	World's Record	
1 Hour	11 mls 1137 yd	World's Record	

1319

Most of Shrubb's record breaking took place in his glory years of 1903 and 1904

Crossing the Atlantic with the Young Turks of Oxbridge, who would be victorious against Harvard and Yale in the Penn Relays, Philadelphia.
Left to right: Shrubb (coach), W R Milligan, E A Montague, W G Tatham, B G B Rudd, Col A M Strade Jackson (manager), W G Stallard (April 1920)

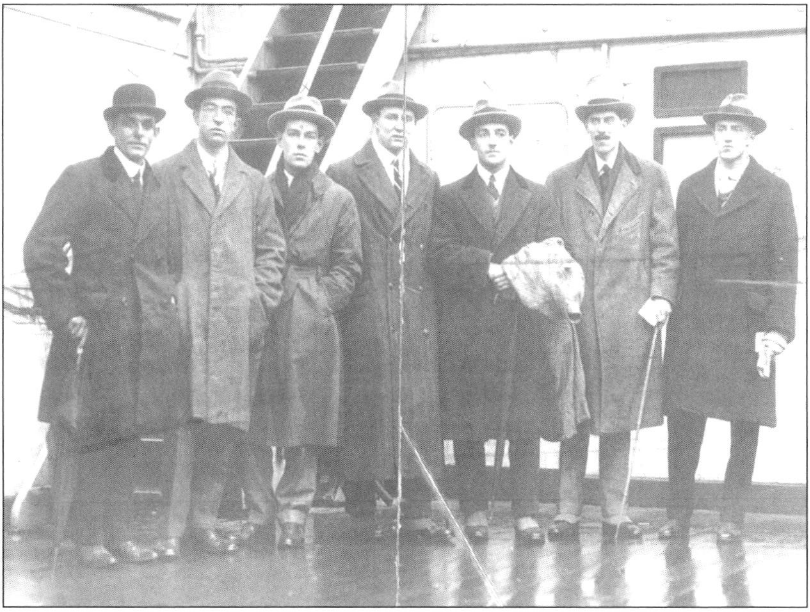

His running days almost over, Shrubb sold his story to a leading UK sports weekly
(March 1920). The cartoons featured here all appeared originally in this magazine

Shrubb stops to change shoes during the 'marathon' duel with Tom Longboat at Madison Square Garden, New York. He was about to lose, after establishing a huge lead (February 1909)

'Well, Shrubb,' Rimmer said, 'You shall have the favour you ask.' Northern Champion Jack Rimmer accepts a Shrubb challenge

A pair of Shrubb's racing pumps, still in excellent condition after 100 years

'The quadruped was a bit too good for me.'

Unable to find humans able to beat him, Shrubb resorted to racing against trotting horses and buggies

The day that man-power beat horse-power in Winnipeg (1907)

Shrubb's bizarre six-mile duel with a trotting horse and buggy gets under way

Shrubb and Longboat go head to head in one of about 10 recorded confrontations as
professionals in Canada and USA. This one was in 1912. Overall, Shrubb won some 7
races to Longboat's 3, but the length of race usually determined the winner. Longboat
generally prevailed at distances of 20 miles or longer, while Shrubb won almost all of
the shorter races. Ambiguity arises because races in which one or both competitors
failed to complete the course were sometimes, but not always, disregarded

The inaugural All Shrubb/Museum 8 kilometre race in 2003 attracted 300 runners and raised 4,000 Canadian dollars (June 2003). Above: Shrubb's daughter Norah (centre) and race organiser Al Storie (second right)

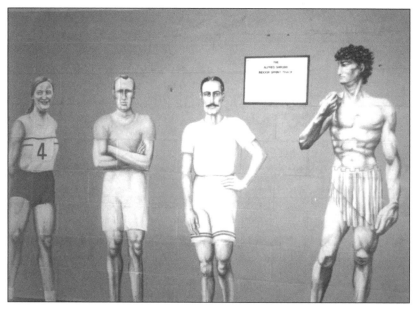

The mural depicting Shrubb (centre) and other athletics greats at the Alfred Shrubb Indoor Sprint Track at Horsham, Sussex (April 2003)

Dedicated to Alfred Shrubb / born in Slinfold on December 12th 1879 /who held every world record for running from 2000 yards to 11 miles / Died on St George's Day 1964 aged 85 years / 'His running was consistent and altogether was a performance that will never be forgotten by those who were privileged to witness it.' / This plaque was unveiled by the daughter of Alfred Shrubb / Mrs N Allin, on January 11th 1990

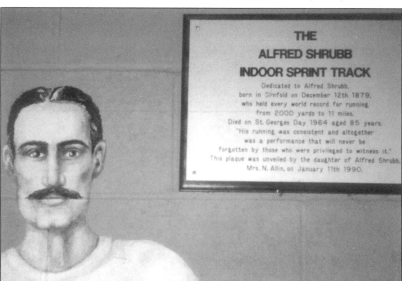

Skipping was just one of many of Shrubb's unconventional training aids (c.1907)

Alfred Shrubb

WORLD CHAMPION RUNNER
1903 - 1912

COACH
HARVARD 4 YEARS
OXFORD 8 YEARS

After going into business, Shrubb had these business cards printed.

"Shrubb disna' break records—he cuts 'em doon like a harvester cuttin' corn wi' a scythe."

The reaction to his 1904 Glasgow heroics: 'Shrubb disna' break records – he cuts 'em doon like a harvester cuttin' corn wi' a scythe.'

The old maestro is tempted into his running shorts one last time, at the age of 78, for a relay at the Bowmanville, Ontario, Centennial celebrations (June 1958)

'Ice-creams were only allowed occasionally, as a reward for good conduct.'

Shrubb explains his working class system of rewards for the dapper students at Oxford

'Turning to me after the race, he said: "I'm not good enough for you, Shrubb, on the cinder track, but my turn will come later".'

N. 178,939   TORONTO, SATURDAY, AUGUST 23, 1930—36 PAGES

HURDLES TO EMPIRE CHA

FINAL SPORTING
AND FINANCIAL

Alf Shrubb Beats Longboat in Exhibition Feature

FAMOUS OLD-TIMERS REVIVE RIVALRY AT EXHIBITION

Memories of a decade ago were recalled at the Exhibition to-day when Alfie Shrubb and Tom Longboat, bitter rivals of the outstanding marathons of twenty years ago, met once again. To-day, in what is probably their last appearance in public, Shrubb, the little Englishman, was the better man. He led Longboat home by 20 yards. On the LEFT is ex-Mayor Sam McBride wishing the two runners good luck before the start. On the RIGHT Shrubb is shown leading the Indian in.

The final race: Shrubb, aged 50, takes on Tom Longboat at the Canadian Exhibition (August 1930)

" He jumped on top of me and nearly broke my neck."

Drama at sea off Australia in 1905: 'He jumped on top of me and nearly broke my ankle.'

A. Shrubb   National Champion

Shrubb with some of the spoils of victory

" Shrubb, the only chance for you now is to take
on two men in relay races."

Advice from an American race promoter: 'Shrubb, the only chance for
you now is to take on two men in
relay races.'

" They carried me shoulder high off the ground."

This happened to Alfred Shrubb many times during the course of his running career

Shrubb (right) prepares to take on Tom Longboat (left, with belt and maple leaf) in a showdown at Haileybury, Ontario (1911)

'My first night in New York was spent at the New Grand Hotel'

Shrubb, athletics coach at Oxford University, shows the students how it's done, leading the way on the famous Iffley Road track (c.1920)

Running for fun: 'Occasionally the fox was good enough to cut across a field as if to give me sporting chance.'

The start of an international 10-mile race in Paris, won by Shrubb (centre),
with runner-up Chastini wearing No 1 (March 1903)

'Aldridge passed me in the last lap from
home.' A rare event

CHAPTER TWELVE

'No prize to compare with Ada'

Shrubb stepped onto the small indoor running track at London's Olympia, near Earl's Court, on the evening of Monday, January 22nd, 1906 to make his debut as a professional athlete and was greeted by a huge ovation from a big crowd. He looked happy enough, but the general perception among the press corps was that he had joined the pro ranks 'in a fit of pique' after being banned from the amateur scene. However, with his wedding just a few days away, the extra cash must have been an influence too.

His bow as a pro, at the age of 26, came just two days after losing his appeal, which certainly made it appear like a gesture of defiance. An editorial in *The People* stated: 'It is a pity that Shrubb, who has never had aspirations out of his class, should immediately become a professional by his own deeds by competing at Olympia, but he accepted the offer out of pique. The receptions given him [by the crowd] are clear evidence of popular favour and there has not been during the past decade any runner whose appearance on the track was a greater assurance of a huge and enthusiastic gate.'

In the first seven days after his ban was confirmed, Shrubb ran in three contests at Olympia, each of them exhibitions whereby he ran alone against a three-man relay team. On the Monday he ran two miles against G Chivers, Sid Thomas (an ex-amateur champion and record-holder) and V Parks, and won by two yards in 9:27. Three days later the race was repeated and this time he won narrowly in 9:23. The latter looked a superb time until the track was measured and found to be a few yards short. Shrubb had to accept that this sort of technical problem was typical in the flighty world of exhibition running. On the Saturday, Parks was replaced by a Grenadier Guardsman called Willis, otherwise the same runners reassembled for a three-miler. Shrubb won in 14:27, a time later declared a world indoor record.

In the wake of these novelty races, *The Times* revealed proposals by retired champion Walter George for Shrubb to run three further matches at Olympia 'for not less than £100 a side'. In 1906 this sort of figure represented a year's wages to a working man. An average tradesman's pay was 35 shillings a week at that time (£91 a year) and many factory workers earned less: A textile worker took home around £70 a year and his female colleagues only around £40. It was, therefore, a fine time for

Shrubb to hit the jackpot, for on Thursday, February 1st he took on new responsibilities. This was the day he would marry his sweetheart from Hayward's Heath, Miss Ada Emily Brown.

On the morning of his wedding, Shrubb visited a friend in Hayward's Heath and was spotted by a *Sporting Life* reporter, sent to the Sussex market town to cover the ceremony. The correspondent dashed across the street to accost Shrubb and pressed him for information about his post-wedding running plans. Shrubb said the 'halfpenny dailies' had got things wrong with their speculation. Once his contract at Olympia had expired, he was finished with running. Anyone who wanted to run against him would have to contact Olympia very quickly or it would be too late. He planned to settle down to married life and become a country pub landlord, and possibly, in time, take over the running of the Sussex Hotel from his father-in-law John Brown.

Although described in the press as a 'relatively quiet' affair, a large crowd of mainly women and girls waited outside St Wilfrid's Church on a grey, wet day for a glimpse of the new Mrs Shrubb. A phalanx of photographers had also gathered. Everyone was astonished to learn that the groom would be racing at Olympia that same evening. His fiancée's views on this are not known, but by now she must have become used to the quirky ways of a runner, having shivered in the cold and rain many a time to cheer her beau to victory. Perhaps the fact that Shrubb was now running for handsome payments tempered her views.

A handful of relatives from each side, plus four or five of Shrubb's personal friends, arrived at the church, scurrying quickly inside to escape the rain. Among them were best man Walter Durrant of Horsham, and the Sussex cricketer T W Tate. The church was nearly full, with local residents turning out in force. The nuptial knot was tied by Rev T G Wyatt, who started the service at 12.15. Facing him was the small figure of Shrubb, smartly attired with a spray of lilies of the valley in his buttonhole. The radiant bride arrived shortly after 12.30, leaning on the arm of her father, John. She wore a dress of cream crèpe de chine, with lace yoke, trimmed with lace and chiffon. Her veil of tulle surmounted a wreath of orange blossoms and she carried a shower bouquet, composed chiefly of lilies of the valley. The bridesmaids – the bride's cousin Rose Sturt and Shrubb's sister, also named Ada – wore pale blue voile dresses with black chiffon hats, trimmed with feathers. Large sprays of roses were worn on the bodices. Accompanying the bridesmaids were two toddlers – Gladys Garman, niece of the groom, and John James, nephew of the bride, the latter in a white suit adorned with one of Shrubb's running medals.

Following the service, the couple were accompanied by a small group into the vestry to sign the register. The church bells rang out as they emerged into the rainy churchyard and the Fleet Street photographers rushed forward to capture the moment. Showers of rice hit the couple as they climbed aboard their carriage to head for the reception, hosted by the Browns at the nearby Sussex Hotel. Here, the centre-table was decked out with dozens of the trophies won by Shrubb, and another side-room also filled with his prizes for guests to inspect. A few days earlier, according to one newspaper, Shrubb had declared: 'Of all the prizes I have won for running, there is none to compare with my promised wife.'

During the reception, a number of telegrams were read out, including from Upton Park FC, South Tottenham Harriers, Warrington Harriers and many well-known sportsmen. The wedding gifts were put on display and included envelopes containing cheques and a handsome table, sent by Worthing Swimming Club. The groom presented the bride with a diamond ring, and she reciprocated with a pair of gold sleeve links. Horsham Blue Star Harriers announced it had sent an invitation to other clubs to contribute to a gift and promised a special presentation to the happy couple later.

In the afternoon the newly-weds left for London, mindful of the need to be at Olympia in good time for Shrubb's race that evening. His bride wore an outfit of grey tweed and a grey hat with pink roses, while Shrubb wore a smart, dark overcoat that hid his running kit underneath. The couple revealed that their short honeymoon – to accommodate Shrubb's running commitments – would be on the Isle of Wight. The couple were taken to the station and caught the 5.30pm train to London.

On arrival at Olympia, the big crowd inside this cavernous, barrel-roofed arena cheered the couple loudly as they made their stage-managed entrance. They were welcomed by the venue's manager, Edward Cleary, who also climbed aboard a shiny black open-topped motor car which slowly circled the running track, covered by a green carpet for the occasion. The couple were clearly touched by the goodwill and Shrubb later recalled these as the greatest of all the events he was involved with at Olympia. Certainly, the twenty-year-old building had seen nothing quite like it before. Built at a cost of £132,000 in 1886, on a four-acre Kensington site, it had originally been intended for agricultural shows.

After the motor car drew to a halt, manager Cleary addressed the hall, welcoming the greatest runner at certain distances the world had ever seen. He presented Ada with a gold watch and Shrubb with a commemorative silver loving cup on behalf of the management and professionals under his charge. The crowd sang 'For he's a jolly good fellow', the car did another circuit, and then Shrubb said a few words, promising the crowd a 'run to remember'.

The management had billed the race as an attempt by Shrubb to beat his world record time for three miles. Once again he would run against a three-man relay team. As no individual could test him over three miles, this was the only way to ensure a good race. Shrubb and Willis set off, with the latter looking stiff and ill at ease. Shrubb finished the first mile mile fifty yards ahead, whereupon Chivers took over from Willis, closed the gap and scooted past Shrubb. The lead then changed again, and by the time Thomas replaced Chivers, Shrubb was twenty yards to the good. Thomas stayed close until the bell approached. Shrubb thundered round the final lap to roars from the crowd and won by 150 yards. His time of 14:23.4 was declared a world indoor record, and almost matched his record on grass four years earlier at Chelmsford. The crowd surged across the track to acclaim Shrubb, and in the mayhem that ensued poor Thomas was unable to even cross the finish line.

The rest of the evening's entertainment featured acts like Dare Devil Schreyer, whose party-piece was 'a marvellous ride and 10 feet dive through space'. Madamoiselle Meteor was also on the bill, performing an act which involved canoeing through space. Not many champion athletes can say they spent their wedding night alongside a French woman who defied gravity.

Before departing for their honeymoon, Shrubb told reporters that anyone harbouring a serious desire to race him over distances between two and ten miles at Olympia had better put their money down. Matching his new pro status with a business-like approach, he said that if there was no proof of money, it would be no use anyone talking of matches, and reiterated his claim of imminent retirement. After a fairly long career, he preferred to quit now, rather than wait for his performances to decline. Hedging his bets, he teased that he might make the occasional appearance in future.

Married life obviously suited Shrubb, for two days after his wedding he returned to Olympia and beat the track record for three miles (21 laps). He outpaced the trio of Willis, Chivers and Thomas again, this time by sixty yards in 14:20.6. Although this was a superb time, it cannot be compared to his three-mile bests on grass and cinder, as doubts remained over the measurements at Olympia. The rest of the world of 'pedestrianism' looked on, disbelieving of Shrubb's exploits, yet it was not long before the first challenges came in. In early February, B R Day put himself forward, offering a 'best-of-three' challenge at 880, 1,000 yards and a mile, with £100-a-side per race, the overall winner to get £600. Shrubb was publicly invited to leave his cash deposit at *The Sporting Life* offices. Shrubb declined the challenge on the grounds that he wasn't a 'sprinter', and one mile was his shortest distance.

Although his days in 'official' athletics were now over, the so-called 'Shrubb Affair' still reverberated at AAA headquarters. Thomas Sinnott, the former SLH treasurer and secretary, was formally suspended, and the committee also accepted the resignation of its own A J Fowden, the SLH vice-chairman. Fowden explained this decision to his clubmates at their annual dinner, a glittering event held in the Adam Chamber of the Gaiety Restaurant in London's Strand. He dismissed the AAA as 'old fools' who had been over-anxious about the whole Shrubb affair. Although he maintained his own innocence, and that of other present-day SLH members, Fowden still felt the time was right to step aside, despite requests from the AAA chairman for him to reconsider. He expressed gratitude for the framed testimonial presented to him by his SLH colleagues. Other speakers made reference to SLH's commendable efforts to strengthen Anglo-French relations by continuing their regular race meetings with runners from Sporting Club de Paris.

Shrubb now belonged to a different world. His proposed 'retirement' was put on ice when he accepted a challenge from Irishman George Blennerhassett Tincler of Edinburgh for a two-mile match at £25 a side. Another came from Alec Nelson to meet over three miles on a date to be fixed. In the meantime, Shrubb turned out at Olympia and easily beat Gibb of Hammersmith over three miles. He followed this with another three-mile win at the same venue on Saturday, February 17th in 14:35, and soon afterwards clocked 14:19, a course record.

February 24th saw him take on George Tincler, who was no mug, having reportedly run 4:08 for the mile in the USA before the turn of the century. If accurate, this would have made him the fastest miler in the world until New Zealander Jack Lovelock, 35 years later. Tincler's mile time of 4:15.2 at Worcester in 1897 also stood as the best championship mile for eighteen years, and was not bettered until 1915 by American Norman Taber. Tincler was an old hand and perhaps past his peak, but he would provide a test. Indeed, he did. The two men could not be separated for four laps, but then Shrubb got the crowd roaring, surging clear and widening the gap to win by half a lap in 9:56.2.

Although he was making good money, Shrubb's thoughts on Saturday March 3rd must have drifted north to Haydock Park, where his amateur pals contested the National cross-country championships without him. It was over a classic Shrubb course, heavy going throughout, and with a 900-yard stretch of thick plough. Charles Straw (Sutton) took the title in

61:12, a time that four-times champion Shrubb could have beaten in his sleep. A week later, Straw also won the international championship in Newport, South Wales, another of Shrubb's favourite races.

In early March, Shrubb completed his final Olympia engagement by beating a three-man team of Chivers, Swann and Smith by a mere three yards, completing the three-mile course in 14:38.2. By now, his money-making opportunities were drying up, and it was not until mid-June that he was presented with another challenge worth taking on. This one constituted his debut as a pro in Scotland and took place at the Partick Police Sports. It was a two-mile contest against a two-man relay team of George Tincler and Stewart Duffus. Shrubb led Duffus by seven yards at halfway, but when Tincler came on fresh he had too much for Shrubb, and Shrubb lost the race and the money.

The Partick result wasn't a real surprise as Shrubb had been largely inactive for three months. This period coincided with the so-called 'intercalated' Olympic Games of 1906 in Athens. Although still not the huge attraction the Olympics would later become, these Games featured one particular race that might well have featured Shrubb, had he not been rendered inactive. It was the five miles, won by 24-year-old Briton Henry Hawtrey, who struck gold with a run of 26:11.8. The time was much slower than Shrubb's average time for that distance.

Following his defeat in Scotland, Shrubb's stated intention to retire appeared to be no idle threat. The professional scene in Britain was no longer thriving as it once had, and no offers came Shrubb's way to tempt him into action. The local press told its readers that summer that Shrubb had turned his back on running altogether. He was a mere spectator at the annual August Bank Holiday sports gala at Horsham, the first time in six years he hadn't been the star of the show. The only Shrubb on active display was his twenty-year-old sister Ada, one of the brightly-dressed maypole dancers.

The weeks went by. On Saturday, November 10th, Shrubb became a father for the first time, wife Ada presenting him with a son they named John Roy Alfred. With another mouth to feed, Shrubb had to take stock of his situation and must have wondered if there was any more money to be made from racing. His only steady income came from his tobacconists and the Sussex Hotel. Restless and naturally fit, he surely missed the buzz of competition. The following month he celebrated his 27th birthday. He was hardly past it, though distance runners of his era tended to peak earlier than they do today. It was more than a year since the aborted tour of Canada and the USA had been proposed – a potential 'fortune' had been missed – and it dawned on Shrubb that perhaps his final chance of racing for riches and glory might lie across the Atlantic Ocean.

Around the same time, Shrubb's old 'partner in crime' Arthur Duffey, the USA sprinter, finally ended his own acrimonious relationship with the American athletics authorities and took the plunge into professional running. If there were opportunities for Duffey in North America, might there not also be some for a multi-world record holder like Shrubb?

CHAPTER THIRTEEN

Never to be an Olympian

Although the termination of his amateur career had been a protracted, messy, five-month affair, Shrubb emerged with head held high and reputation intact. Although he had not denied the charges, few condemned Shrubb or had a bad word to say about him. To a man, the press, public and fellow performers expressed genuine sympathy. A popular champion was widely regarded as a victim of circumstance.

The great debate about amateurism in sport had been brought into sharp focus by 'The Shrubb Affair', but nothing could trigger a change in attitude from the administrators, and the rulebook remained as rigid as ever. Little would change in the subsequent half-century. In British athletics the last of the true amateur champions would be the likes of Bannister, Brasher and Chataway in the glorious 1950s post-1945 revival.

In the modern age, with multi-millionaire sports personalities across the globe, it is easy to forget that in Shrubb's day the idea of the gifted amateur was deeply attractive and entrenched. Olympic double gold medallist Sebastian Coe put it neatly in his 1984 book *The Olympians*: 'The idol who could play the game for the sake of the game, make a century at Lord's and then go back to teach Greek or make a House of Commons speech with his wind-blown hair restored to its Corinthian perfection, was the very model of Edwardian excellence.'

The AAA's message was that sport played by selfless amateurs was a force for good in the world, setting an example to the inhabitants of lesser nations and making a positive contribution to world peace. In the latter part of the nineteenth century and the first half of the twentieth, it was even considered 'rather bad form' for athletes to do too much training, since this could artificially improve performance and give an advantage to the lucky few who had time on their hands and did not have to work for a living. Today, the main problem preoccupying the authorities is how to counter the illegal use of performance-enhancing drugs. One wonders if, in time, the drugs issue will be regarded as quaint in the same way the amateurism debate does now.

Looking back, the life ban imposed on Shrubb – ostensibly for nothing more than accepting payments to cover his basic expenses – seems savage. Had he really committed sins worthy of such a punishment? Why was the purity of amateurism so crucially important in those days? One man with answers is Lincoln Allison, Director of the Warwick Centre for the Study of Sport in Society. In a recent interview on Australian radio, Allison notes that although soccer and rugby league went professional before 1900, other sports, such as tennis and rugby union, did not take the plunge until 1968 and 1995, respectively. And the international athletics and swimming federations did not drop the word 'amateur' from their names until 1982.

Allison explains that, aside from the issue of payment, a major criticism of amateurism was that it encouraged social exclusivity. Attempts were made to exclude the working classes and develop the idea of 'the gentleman amateur'. Rowing, for example, in England and Australia in the nineteenth century simply wasn't open to manual labourers. The amateur/professional distinction was all about class definition, without any qualms or attempts at secrecy. The word 'amateur' – which derives from the Latin amare (to love) – meant doing things for love, not for money. It implied and contained a moral dimension.

Before 1900 it was social status that largely defined the professional and amateur worlds. Professional running – or pedestrianism – developed from contests staged on racecourses or roads and usually involved betting and all sorts of other skulduggery. Although pedestrianism slowly withered and died from 1900 onwards, it would take the better part of a century before the fear that athletes would be tainted by receiving payments become so risible that amateurism's days were numbered. The likes of Avery Brundage, long-time president of the International Olympic Committee, sustained the myth of amateurism by perpetuating the argument that when money and sport mix, gambling and corruption is the outcome. This might have been true in the late eighteenth and early nineteenth centuries, when cricket, pugilism and horse racing were riddled with corrupt practices. Pedestrianism had its unscrupulous characters too, of course, but was certainly not tainted from top to bottom in the same way. Brundage and his ilk were unbending, however, and obstinately reiterated the old strictures, even in the face of a changing world. Thus the ruthless application of ancient rules continued well into the twentieth century and reform and modernisation was a long time coming. One could say that the amateur code was enforced for far too long, with a passion that bordered on fanaticism.

Alfred Shrubb had become merely the latest and most famous in a long line of victims. In 1896, for example, half a dozen top runners had been banned for similar 'crimes' on the very eve of the AAA championships. Payment of appearance money to leading athletes was not uncommon at the turn of the century, it appears, and the AAA clamped down on Alfred Downer after he allegedly tried to negotiate an increase from a Burnley club, only for the outraged club to expose him to the authorities.

Among others suspended were the cream of British distance running: Fred Bacon of Reading was a five-times AAA title-holder and world mile record-holder; Harry Watkins of Walthamstow, the double Southern cross-country champion; and George Crossland of Manchester, the reigning National cross-country champion and world record holder at twenty miles and for the two-hour run. Teenager Alex Blair of Airedale Harriers was also suspended, but reinstated after an appeal spearheaded by his brother, a practising lawyer. Bacon and Watkins both reacted to their bans by turning pro and later established one-hour world records.

In *The Official Centenary History of the AAA*, Peter Lovesey concludes that payments to certain athletes was common, even before 1900. The above-mentioned Downer, for example, admitted in his autobiography that there were few meetings at which he was not paid. The athletes caught generally accepted their fate, but were bitter that little or no action was taken against the clubs making the payments. After the AAA flexed its muscles in such spectacular fashion in 1896, the subsequent two seasons were accompanied by dwindling interest in the sport, shorn of so many household names. Attention switched to pedestrianism for a while, where more famous names now plied their trade. Another noteworthy episode in the 1890s had been the decision by 440 and 880-yards ace Edgar Bredin to voluntarily switch to pro running. Sid Thomas was banned – he was world record holder at three, six and fifteen miles, and five-times AAA champion at four and ten. Following the failure of his appeal, the sport found itself without all the leading British runners from 100 yards up to twenty miles.

Over the years, the authorities' noble efforts to uphold the virtues of amateurism were offset by decisions that seemed crass and petty. They did themselves no favours by rigidly clamping down on minor incidents, when discretion was clearly called for. Sometimes the alleged offences would nowadays be considered unbelievably trivial. Consider the case of Australian's golden girl, swimmer Dawn Fraser, for example. In 1949, at the tender age of twelve, she was reported for accepting a two-shilling Christmas present after swimming at a sports club picnic. The Australian Swimming Union promptly banned her for this 'misdemeanour'. They did not relent until fourteen months later, following bitter protests.

Outposts of the Empire, like Australia, New Zealand and Canada, had, of course, taken their lead from Britain. Another example from the southern hemisphere was the case of Don Chipp, who was rebuffed by the Australian AAA when he hoped to develop his talent for sprinting.

The problem was that he had earlier played a handful of games for professional football club Fitzroy. The authorities accepted he'd never been paid by Fitzroy, but decreed that by simply wearing their kit he had tainted his lily-white amateur status. As a result, Australia lost a potential Olympic athlete, but gained a politician, for Chipp later became founding leader of the Australian Democrats.

As far as Alfred Shrubb was concerned, he had accepted his punishment pragmatically and – although unsuccessfully appealing – with relatively little fuss. The suspension signalled a complete change in lifestyle for the little runner. For more than seven years he had continually trained and raced – often competing more than once a week and mostly in front of large crowds. Suddenly the adrenaline highs were gone. Running had been his life. Had he not married in the midst of all the fuss, and nine months later become a father, one wonders whether he might have lost his sense of purpose completely. Even with his new domestic responsibilities, it must have been a strange and frustrating time for such an active man.

He was philosophical when looking back on the tumultuous events of 1905 and 1906 and appeared to harbour no bitterness towards those who put a stop to his legitimate running. Some years afterwards he said: 'I believe strongly in amateurism. Every young athlete should commence as an amateur and a very large majority would do well to remain such. Amateurism instils the right spirit of sport into a youth, and though it is far from my intention to make any boast, it is still within my rights to say that the love of running for running's sake contributed mainly to my successes [later on] as a professional. In fact I think it is a pity that such a gulf should be fixed between amateurism and professionalism so that men belonging to each class cannot compete together. It is not so in cricket and I think convincing proof of the mutual advantages is afforded in that great English game.'

It is curious that Shrubb should have invoked the example of cricket's place in the great 'pro-am' debate. What became known as 'shamateurism' was rife in cricket. The term was first coined in the late nineteenth century and referred to the hypocrisy and 'turning of a blind eye' regarding illegal payments and other contraventions of the amateur code.

According to the *Oxford English Dictionary*, the term was first coined in 1896 in a magazine. Shamateurism in cricket had been evident many years before that, but during the Shrubb era things improved after some outspoken words from celebrated author R H Lyttleton began to oil the wheels of change. Lyttleton controversially suggested that calling a cricketer a 'professional' was not an insult but honourable. Cricket pros may originate from 'the shop, the factory, the pit and the slum', but they then became prosperous types whose dress and deportment made it hard to tell who was a paid player and who was a so-called 'gentleman amateur', playing for fun and just claiming expenses. The distinction should be dispensed with, he said, and treated as irrelevant. People took note of these wise words. As far as the cricketers themselves were concerned, some amateurs were reluctant to turn pro – not because of the stigma, but because their expenses claims were often higher than a pro's wages. The situation in athletics was a little different, but the issues of class snobbery and greed were broadly similar.

This surreal world of sporting 'shamateurism' attracted the interest of Hollywood. Many years after the Shrubb era, the movie 'On The Edge' starred Bruce Dern as real-life runner Wes Holman, who was banned in the 1970s after exposing clandestine pay-offs to athletes like himself. Holman was no more dishonest than anyone else, but rocked the boat by suggesting that amateurism in athletics was the way the rich kept the poor from competing. As was the case with Shrubb, the world at large thought Holman had been harshly dealt with, and the film features the runner's determined and heroic return to action in the gruelling Cielo Sea Race in the USA.

Competitors who take part in sport simply for love have always been a rarity, one suspects. But examples do exist. One such character was Edgar Kail, born in 1900, who developed into such a feared centre-forward that he was picked three times for the senior England soccer team, despite never playing for a professional club. Kail was determined to remain a true amateur. Between 1919 and 1933 he scored over 400 goals for London non-League side Dulwich Hamlet and turned down many offers to join professional clubs. From Monday to Friday, Kail was a wine and spirits salesman; on Saturdays a dynamic and pacy attacker. That was the way he wanted it to stay. He played for England against France, Belgium and Spain in 1929, but stuck to his Corinthian ideals and would not be lured away from humble Dulwich. He continued to play 'just for fun' and died in obscurity in Scotland in the 1970s, but fans of Dulwich, where he is revered to this day, mounted a campaign which in 2003 resulted in a special blue plaque in Kail's honour being created by Southwark Borough Council.

Shamateurism and snobbery was never more evident than in the sport of rowing. In 1936 the organisers of the Henley Regatta barred the Australian Olympic crew from taking part because they were policemen and therefore not true 'gentleman amateurs'. It was becoming increasingly obvious that this sort of ludicrous decision-making had no place in sport and the barriers slowly began to come down. Athletics resisted change a little longer than most of the other offenders, and by the 1950s British track fans cheered a trio of heroic runners who would prove to be the last of the true 'gentlemen amateurs' to perform at top level. Roger Bannister, Chris Brasher and Chris Chataway ruled the roost during a golden era when all three were embarking on high-profile careers outside of sport, training in their spare time. Despite their relatively low training loads, Bannister was the first to crack the four-minute mile, Brasher struck Olympic gold at Melbourne, and Chataway chalked up a wonderful victory at White City against the seemingly invincible Vladimir Kuts. The Soviet was effectively a full-time athlete, but Chataway – who broke the 5,000 metres world record on that memorable night in 1954 – was a Guinness brewery management trainee.

The distinction between pro and amateur athletics was actually prolonged over the course of the twentieth century by the increasing importance of the Olympic Games, which grew into a money-spinning monster while still purporting to be a celebration of amateur ideals. Television and commercial sponsorship ultimately delivered the death blow to the great divide, firstly ushering in the age of appearance-money in the 1970s, and then the slightly bizarre 'trust fund' idea soon afterwards. The latter saw payments to athletes going into special accounts, instead of directly into their pockets, a measure designed to leave the officials in some sort of control – but all it really did was precipitate the sport's final slither into fully fledged professionalism. By 2003, things had changed to such an extent that the organisers of the Flora London Marathon were more than happy to publish full details of payments to winner Paula Radcliffe (with appearance and prize-money, it exceeded half a million pounds). Nobody batted an eyelid at the fact she was being paid to run, although a few eyebrows were raised over the actual amount.

Apart from ending his 'official' competitive career prematurely, it should not be forgotten that the AAA's 1905 suspension of Shrubb also ensured he would never be an Olympian. In total, five Olympic Games came and went during Shrubb's time as a top runner and he never graced any of them, despite being fêted for most of that time as the world's greatest distance man. He was absent from Paris 1900, St Louis 1904, Athens 1906, London 1908 and Stockholm 1912. So if, hypothetically, he had been able to attend all five, how would he have fared in the medal stakes?

The scheduling and nature of the running events varied at each Games, but over the twelve-year period Shrubb could have chosen from the following: flat races on the track for individuals at five miles, 1,500,

5,000 and 10,000 metres; steeplechases over 2,500, 3,200 and 4,000 metres; cross-country over 12,000 metres; team races over 3,000 and 5,000 metres, three miles and four miles; plus the marathon. A quick survey of the times posted by the medallists in all these events shows that many appear slower than a fit Shrubb is likely to have achieved.

The five Olympiads missed by Shrubb also varied greatly in terms of their appeal and importance to the competitors of the era. The ancient Greek Olympics had been revived in 1896, largely through the efforts of Frenchman Pierre de Coubertin, whose dream was to see the youth of the world meet in peaceful competition, enjoying sport for its own sake. The first of the modern games were duly staged in Athens when Shrubb was still a sixteen-year-old labourer and competitive running had never entered his head. Then, four years later, Paris hosted a largely discredited Games, badly organised and attracting little interest from the world at large. Even so, Britain captured 35 medals and among the winners were athletes Shrubb would soon be beating regularly – men like Charles Bennett, Henri de Loge and Jack Rimmer.

Realistically, the Paris event came too early for Shrubb to be a serious contender, for he had only been on Horsham Blue Star Harriers books a matter of months and, when the Games commenced in May 1900, his talent had yet to blossom beyond rural Sussex. The Games of 1904, in St Louis, Missouri, USA, however, took place at a time when Shrubb was internationally feared and at his peak, smashing world records galore and accumulating championship crowns by the dozen. However, Britain and France, who along with the USA were the world's leading athletics nations, chose not to send teams. Shrubb and others were free to have gone under their own steam, but the idea held little appeal and Shrubb had plenty of important matters occupying him at home. He defended his AAA championship crown at Rochdale on the same weekend the St Louis games opened, and humble Rochdale seemed to him a higher priority than this new-fangled Olympic nonsense. Even certain American athletes – such as champion sprinter Arthur Duffey – chose to compete in Rochdale rather than an Olympics in his own country, such was the lack of interest in de Coubertin's dream at that time.

The St Louis programme of events, as in Paris, was stretched out over several months and the whole thing turned into a second-rate sideshow, absorbed into the World's Fair staged simultaneously. Nevertheless, had he been there, Shrubb would almost certainly have medalled in the 1,500 metres and – barring unforeseen disasters – would have dominated the four-mile team race. The winning time of 21:17.8 was nearly two minutes slower than his best. But it wasn't to be, and by the end of 1904 Shrubb found himself a multi-world record holder with no Olympic medals to his name. This did not trouble him unduly, for at the time there was relatively little kudos attached to victory at an Olympics and the honour of being AAA champion held far greater prestige.

In fact, the future of the Games looked uncertain around this time and the International Olympic Committee defied de Coubertin's wishes when they decided to stage another event just two years after Missouri in 1906. This would return to Athens, in contravention of the Frenchman's wish for a four-year interval between Games. Commentators scoffed at the IOC's optimism, but ultimately their plan saved the Olympics from an early grave. Athens, second time round, provided a much-needed boost to the ailing Olympic movement, even though it was later downgraded to become known as the Intermediate, or Intercalated Games. The Americans sent sixty athletes, while Britain picked a somewhat smaller team, and even approved the grant of £208 from the central committee in Athens towards the cost of sending them. Shrubb, of course, missed out again, for by now his suspension had taken effect. In Athens a total of almost 900 athletes from twenty nations attended and the event was hailed a success. Henry Hawtrey – a British runner who was, frankly, not in Shrubb's class – won the gold medal in the five-mile race in a time of 26:11.8, a massive 98 seconds slower than Shrubb's best time. The marathon was won by Canadian Billy Sherring, a man Shrubb would later beat with almost embarrassing ease over fifteen miles.

The 1908 Olympics came to London – albeit only after Vesuvius's latest eruption forced Italy to withdraw as hosts – by which time Shrubb was 28 and running in very different surroundings. However, had the AAA not rendered him ineligible, this would surely have been the occasion when he would have sealed his place in sporting history. The Games were based at the huge new White City stadium in west London, built earlier in the year for the Franco-British exhibition. There were more than 2,000 participants and a huge squad representing Britain captured 56 of the 110 gold medals available. With his penchant for tackling more than one race in any event, Shrubb would no doubt have taken a crack at the 1,500 metres, five miles, three-mile relay, and maybe even the marathon, too. He might have collected as many as four gold medals, with surely the most comfortable coming in the five-miler where a modest time of 25:11.2 by Manchester's Emil Voight secured gold (38 seconds slower than Shrubb's best).

By the next Olympiad, in Stockholm in 1912, Shrubb was still running well, despite being 32. The Finn, Hannes Kohlemainen, captured a wonderful golden double on the track by winning at 5,000 and 10,000 metres

– but victory at the longer distance was achieved with a time of 31:20.8, over eighteen seconds slower than Shrubb's personal best of 31:02.4. Kohlemainen won a third gold in the cross-country, and although times are not registered in this event, there is little to suggest that Shrubb would not have beaten him.

All this conjecture is, of course, somewhat pointless – Olympic finals are all about the race and not the time – but the fact remains that but for his ban Shrubb would surely have ended his running days with a place on the Olympic roll of honour. At a conservative estimate, it is feasible to suggest he would have won at least *seven* gold medals and a handful of silver or bronze had he attended all five Olympics. To put this into context, Britain's most successful Olympic runners are Douglas Lowe (800 metres, 1924, 1928) and Sebastian Coe (1,500 metres, 1980, 1984) with two golds apiece, and the most successful in any event being the oarsman Steve Redgrave with five.

As it was, eighteen months drifted by after Shrubb's suspension was first announced, in which he was largely inactive. It really began to look as if the athletics world had seen the last of the Little Wonder. The handful of professional races around the time of his wedding looked like being the unsatisfactory swansong to a short but sensational career. Pedestrianism was largely on the decline and, in any case, there were simply too few credible opponents around to give Shrubb a good race. He was willing to listen to challenges, but was simply a class above any other professional on the circuit. Most pro engagements at that time required each side to put up a prize fund in advance, with the winner pocketing the entire kitty. Shrubb's reputation of being virtually unbeatable at distances greater than a mile meant very few were foolish enough to take him on. As the weeks and months of 1906 went by, fewer and fewer opportunities presented themselves for the ex-champion to don his running pumps. Despite this, he remained optimistic, saying: 'My prospects [are] quite rosy if only enough competitors could be found to give me matches.' He was barely 27, still fit and well, and had plenty still to offer.

Early in 1907, just when it looked as if the running world had turned its back on one of its finest champions, Shrubb received a cable from across the Atlantic Ocean. An old friend was making plans for him. This unexpected message would herald some startling developments.

CHAPTER FOURTEEN

A Shock for Spotted Clifford

Before receiving the cable from the USA, Shrubb had more or less resigned himself to the fact that his glory days were over. After dabbling in professional running at London's Olympia and one or two other places, his Foster's running pumps were now gathering dust. But the trans-Atlantic message, delivered to his West Sussex home, changed all that, marking the end of a relatively uneventful period in his life and heralding a whole new set of adventures.

The cable came from his old travelling companion Arthur Duffey, the American sprinter who had also recently been kicked out of the amateur ranks and was now looking for ways to make a living from sport. Duffey suggested Shrubb head out for the States where he would help him fix up some lucrative races. Although the running boom had yet to fully take off Stateside, Shrubb had already picked up promising signals, and the idea of running in the New York, Boston and Toronto areas particularly appealed. He had heard these were hot-beds of interest for runners.

One particular prospect made his mouth water. If Duffey could help set up a contest against Tom Longboat, an Onondagan Indian from the Six Nations reserve near Toronto, he felt sure it would generate massive public interest, not to mention a personal fortune. It would be running's answer to the boxing heavyweight championship of the world.

Shrubb did not take long to respond. Cables flew back and forth, at the end of which Shrubb fired off a final message to confirm he would be sailing from Liverpool to New York during the first week of May 1907. He asked Duffey to meet him. Putting his sister in charge of his tobacconist shop, Shrubb bid a temporary farewell to his wife Ada and four-month-old baby Roy and took a train to Merseyside. Emboldened by his Australian adventure, the prospect of a long sea journey and many weeks away did not give him undue concern. Recalling her father's penchant for long-distance travel, Shrubb's daughter Norah recalls: 'The family used to joke that dad was always "on the run" throughout his life. He was away a lot and always enjoyed sea journeys, even though he could not swim. In all I think he crossed the Atlantic 23 times.'

Although some years later Shrubb told *All Sports Weekly* that he had crossed the Atlantic on the new Cunard luxury liner *Mauretainia*, shipping records show that this particular vessel had yet to make its maiden journey by May 1907. We must therefore assume Shrubb became muddled with his ship names, and that this first trip to the States was on another Cunard liner, the *SS Campania*, which left Liverpool on Saturday, May 4th. His ticket for the six-day journey will have included the train trip from London Euston.

Shrubb had spent five months travelling and racing with Duffey in 1905 and knew he was a man to be trusted. Although no definite race dates awaited him, Shrubb was confident his gregarious and feisty pal knew the ropes and would not have called for him if the prospects were not promising. Nevertheless, Shrubb was only 27, married with a baby, and making such a journey alone with no fixed date to return was unusual and risky, not to mention a source of worry for his wife. Duffey had promised to look after him, though, and was a well-known and respected figure in sporting circles, even though he was by now past his best as a performer. His finest moment had been when breaking the 100 yards dash world record in New York, and he had also been a four-time AAA 100 yards champion and twice the USA inter-collegiate champion.

In later years Duffey would find his niche as a Boston sports writer, but in the meantime fancied his chances as a sporting entrepreneur, particularly after hearing of Shrubb's inactivity. He had quickly assessed the earning potential of pitting Shrubb against Longboat, who had in April 1907 smashed the Boston Marathon record, completing the 26.2 miles in two hours 24:24. Longboat was a superb runner on his day, but a maverick personality who often caused problems with the authorities. Shortly before Shrubb's arrival, Duffey was dismayed to learn that Longboat was determined to remain an amateur, meaning he would not be eligible for matches with Shrubb in the short term. It was a blow, but Duffey felt sure he could find other suitable opponents once the ex-champion from England had arrived.

Shrubb, meanwhile, threw himself wholeheartedly into regaining race fitness in time for this new chapter in his career. He would recall later: 'As I did not intend to waste time upon arriving in New York, I resolved to train as best I could on board the great liner. I travelled second class, and got up early in the morning to make the most of the rather limited space at my disposal. Then I decided to declare myself and make known my wants to the captain, hoping he might permit me to use the first class deck at such times in the morning and evening as might least interfere with the convenience of the saloon passengers. The captain made no bones about granting me the favours I desired. He said the first class passengers were always good sports and would probably enjoy watching me.'

Suitably encouraged, Shrubb performed daily runs up and down the length of the ship, a distance he reckoned was about nine laps to the mile.

He had heard that the track at New York's Madison Square Garden was eight laps to the mile, so considered that the layout of the ship served his purposes well. After his runs he would return to the second class deck to do his other exercises, including long sessions of skipping: 'During rough seas I was occasionally thrown against the deck rails, but on the whole the sea was kind to me.'

After two or three days, fellow passengers inevitably began introducing themselves. Suddenly this solo journey to a big new world didn't seem such a lonely undertaking. Shrubb was urged to give an exhibition of his talents under race conditions, and a three-mile contest was arranged with three young fellow passengers: 'They volunteered to run one mile apiece in relay form, and ran so well that I had my work cut out to beat them. The decks were thoroughly cleared for the race and all the other usual sea-going sports such as the potato race, the needle threading race and "chalking the pig's eye" were postponed that day,' recalled Shrubb.

Shrubb passed an enjoyable six-day journey, excitedly anticipating what lay ahead. The New York of 1907 about to greet him was a vibrant city, a colourful motley of provincials and immigrants in search of refuge and opportunity. It had luxury hotels, slum tenements, unfeasibly tall buildings and cavernous department stores. The streets were more noisy and alive than anything wide-eyed Shrubb would have witnessed before. Electric lights had replaced gas on Broadway, streetcars were now electric, gasoline-powered taxis were replacing the slow battery-powered hansom cabs, and for five cents you could ride the clanking subway trains. The huge Flatiron Building was being dwarfed by skyscrapers under construction and candy stores were full of the new craze, Teddy bears, named after President Theodore Roosevelt. It was a dangerous place, too: recently more than 1,000 people succumbed to typhoid and a similar number died in the East River when a steamboat sank. Not to mention guns and crime. In short, this was not rural Horsham. No wonder Shrubb was a little nervous as the *Campania* sailed into the harbour.

He prepared himself to greet old pal Duffey who, he thought, would be trailing hordes of pressmen at the quay. Within thirty minutes of disembarking, however, Shrubb's brisk and sunny exterior had evaporated. There was no sign of Duffey and the baffled little Englishman, clutching his bags, did not have a clue what to do next.

'Duffey was nowhere to be seen when we drew alongside. Nor was there a line in the New York papers about me. Not a pressman came to interview me. What Duffey was up to I couldn't imagine. On going ashore I felt very much at sea and anything but at home in New York. I wondered whether my cable had miscarried and also whether somebody had impersonated Duffey and played a very bad practical joke on me. Fellow passengers sympathised with me and almost reluctantly left me to make the best of a bad job. One of the most disconsolate mortals alive at that moment, I sat down on a barrow in the dock and viewed my position through anything but rosy spectacles. The world's champion long distance runner friendless in New York and with nowhere to go!'

Later Shrubb would relate his tale of woe upon arriving in the Big Apple to a New York sports editor, and was told that had they known, the paper would not only have collected him and put him in a top hotel, but would have paid for his story, too. This was not what Duffey had in mind. His plan had always been to spring his visitor on an unsuspecting America and make a financial killing before the opposition and bookmakers realised who he was. Shrubb confirmed this later to *All Sports Weekly*: 'My arrival was not to be shouted about. Quite so, for there was sound sense in that. But where was the sense of not coming to meet a stranger in a strange land? Well Shrubb, old boy, I said to myself, it's up to you to say where you are going to go. You can't sit here all day.'

Shrubb was finding the hard way that travel could be a stressful business, and his next problem came in the shape of a burly and aggressive New York cabbie. The fare of nearly three dollars for a half-mile ride to a hotel seemed extortionate to Shrubb, who knew the equivalent trip in London would have cost a shilling at most. He expressed his views to the cabbie, and received an earful in response. After reluctantly paying up, Shrubb had the presence of mind to hand over a 'business card', urging the cabbie to keep it and re-read the name in a few months time. By then, he felt sure, he would be a famous name in this country, and the cabbie would regret his insulting behaviour.

Shrubb allowed himself to be dropped off at the luxurious Grand Hotel in Fifth Avenue, knowing of no alternatives. 'They gave me apartments fit for a millionaire,' he recalled. The following morning he discovered that Duffey's home – 80 Washington Square on the East Side – was less than two miles away. He walked there, to be told by the apartment block's caretaker that Mr Duffey was currently out, searching for a Mr Shrubb from England, as he had been unable to locate him at the docks the previous day.

Mightily relieved, Shrubb sat down to wait in the gardens at the foot of the apartment building. Before long an agitated Duffey strode into view: 'When he passed without noticing me I sneaked up behind and gave him a sound slap on the back,' recalled Shrubb. 'It made him turn sharply and exclaim 'what are you doing?', before he realised who it was. When I told him where I'd stayed the night before he looked alarmed and said I should get out of that swell place as soon as I could, and shouldn't throw away money before I'd even started to make it.'

Duffey confessed that so far he had failed to fix up any races, and that one planned match had fallen through when the opponent realised who, and how good, Shrubb was. They headed for the Grand Hotel, settled the ten-dollar bill for bed, breakfast and lunch, and transferred Shrubb's baggage into the care of the American Transfer Company. Shrubb moved in with Duffey and found himself in the company of a third flatmate, the 'very jolly' Sam Jones, America's top high-jumper. Jones assured Shrubb he would get chances to race in good time and urged him to be patient. When the opening race came along, Jones wanted to be 'in on the haymaking', too. To all intents, Duffey was now 'managing' Shrubb, and the Englishman seemed happy with this arrangement: 'Frankly, he regarded me as a good investment,' recalled Shrubb. 'I was fortunate with my friend Duffey. We pulled together well in all sorts of weather.' In the world of pro running, a manager that could be trusted was a bonus – now all Shrubb needed was some races.

Although the annual Boston Marathon was now immensely popular, the craze for long-distance running had yet to gain real momentum in the USA. Years later, Shrubb would boast that his own arrival had ultimately hastened it: 'The eager Americans eventually became determined to bring out men to beat me. That is the American spirit all over, and it's not a bad spirit either. The will to win goes a long way towards efficiency in sport and everything else. As Sam Jones had predicted I had not long to wait and when the Americans came after me they did so in full cry.'

To set the ball rolling, Shrubb and his 'Mr Fixit' Duffey needed an event big enough to garner maximum publicity and betting, but where he would not be recognised. They discussed whether to enter Shrubb into an event under a false name, but he was anxious not to stoop to such practices. The breakthrough came when Shrubb opened a Philadelphia newspaper and spotted an announcement about a forthcoming Gaelic sports event, scheduled for the end of May at the city's Washington Park. A high number of Scots and Irish had emigrated to the United States and such meetings were immensely popular. The schedule featured 'one and four-mile' foot races. Duffey was delighted, and apologised to Shrubb for completely forgetting about 'these great clan gatherings' where potential fortunes could be made. According to Shrubb, 'This Philadelphia meeting proved, in many respects, the most dramatic in my career as it certainly laid the foundations for whatever fame I won in America and Canada. For that reason Washington Park would always have happy memories for me.'

The pair reached Washington Park on Friday, May 31st two hours
before the start and found a crowd of 20,000 already in place. For Shrubb
this would be his first major race in front of a big crowd in well over a
year. All the old excitement and nervousness returned. 'That crowd does-
n't know what they're going to see today Alf,' said Duffey excitedly.
Shrubb responded: 'I'm going to run in my right name and try to throw
a bombshell into American racing circles right away'.

The pair agreed that honesty was the best policy, and quietly made
their way into the ground, paying the equivalent of half-a-crown at the
gate like the rest of the punters. Shrubb handed over a dollar to 'a brawny
Scotsman' to enter the two races and nobody perked up at his name when
he gave it. Shrubb and Duffey took a stroll around the ground and found
bookies quoting odds of 4-1 against the local favourite, who raced under
the pseudonym 'Spotted Clifford'. Few punters or bookies paid much
heed to the late-entry from England. One assumes at this point Duffey
dug deep into his pockets to back his man.

Just before the scheduled mile race was due to start, the pair bumped
into New York distance runner Bobby Hallen. 'I think I have seen your
fellow somewhere, or seen pictures of him,' exclaimed Hallen to Duffey,
realisation finally dawning. 'If he is not Alf Shrubb of England I am not
Bobby Hallen of New York! No doubt Shrubb will wallop us, but
Spotted Clifford doesn't know he's here. His face will be worth paying to
see.'

Shrubb recalled being curiously studied as he limbered up for the mile.
'Never did any situation tickle me more. I saw the humour of it all. The
instant the gun was fired I shot away as if the race had been 100 yards
and not 1,760 – exactly as I had in my amateur days. At the completion
of a lap I found I was 25 to 30 yards in front. Keeping up the pace for
three laps the distance between me and the rest widened considerably
more and people called out "He'll run himself into the earth – he can't
stick at that pace".'

The track was six laps to the mile and Shrubb led by 100 yards at
halfway without slackening. Unused to the whooping and hollering of an
American crowd, Shrubb recalled that some of the remarks made him
laugh out loud, even though he was travelling virtually flat out. 'Say boy,
have you got wings?' was one of them. With two laps to go he kicked for
home in spectacular fashion, deliberately wanting to put on a show and
finish with a flourish. The crowd loved it. He won by a full lap and was
promptly swamped by well-wishers. 'Men I had never seen before rushed
out to shake hands with me till I was afraid they would mob me. I still
had the four-miler to run and had to keep fit.'

He was quizzed over his identity and only escaped the hullabaloo when a Scots official, who recognised him from runs at Olympia, spirited him away to a quiet corner and massaged his legs in preparation for the next race. The event secretary chased after them and, after confirming who Shrubb was, declared that had they known they would have paid him appearance money and used his name to publicise the event. This was music to the ears of Duffey, of course, and a deal was quickly struck for Shrubb to return there for future fixtures.

His four-mile opponents must have suspected that Shrubb wouldn't be able to repeat his front-running heroics at this longer distance. How wrong they were. Shrubb recalled: 'I smiled quietly to myself and said very little. In contrast to their opinions it was my intention to run the fastest four miles of my life – even though the track was not perfectly adapted to this purpose. I wanted to make as big a name for myself as possible in America.' Spotted Clifford and Bobby Hallen were seen anxiously enquiring of Shrubb about his tactics. They would quickly find out, as he shot away and built a one-lap lead after a mile. 'The applause of the crowd was like the roaring of a tempest – I had never run through such a row,' recalled Shrubb. 'Sceptics who could not trust their eyesight shouted "he'll crack up" as they watched me.'

He came home unchallenged in 20:46 and a stunned Spotted Clifford was first to shake his hand: 'Hallen and I thought we might have carved up the prize money but the lion's share is yours.' Hallen was equally impressed, adding that Shrubb's arrival would stimulate the American running scene, even though he would probably win everything. Hallen issued a challenge for a twelve-miler in New York, and Duffey began negotiations. Shrubb recalled that two clergymen then approached and invited him to take tea nearby. After that, the event secretary took him to dinner, and the next day Shrubb dominated the sports pages of the local press. 'It was left with me to make good, as the Americans say, while fortune's tide was at the flood.'

Memories of his lonely and anxious arrival in New York now seemed an age away, and Shrubb at last had some positive news to write home about. He had left Sussex full of optimism, reassuring his wife and friends that things would work out, but deep down must have harboured the odd misgiving about plunging into the seedy and unscrupulous world of professional sport. Race-fixing and betting scandals were commonplace in pedestrianism – a fact confirmed by an American running enthusiast from that era named Irving Smith. Years later, Smith would say: 'The professional I was acquainted with and who used to watch over my jogging was named T M W Liddecoat … I gathered he was affiliated with a bunch of crooks, who used to fix foot-races all over the place. It was quite prevalent, I have been told, in that period.' Smith remembered the days of Shrubb thrilling US crowds in 1907: 'I remember Shrubb's sort of shuffling dog trot so well.'

Shrubb wrote home to tell Ada he had regained his fitness and felt better than ever. He also referred in his correspondence to negotiations underway for a run in Buffalo against Canadian Billy Sherring, winner of the 1906 'intercalated' Olympic Games marathon in Athens. 'This race will be the greatest of its kind ever seen in the USA,' one paper had trumpeted. 'Sherring startled the world with his marathon win and is more worthy to challenge Shrubb than any other runner in the USA.'

In the meantime, a race with Bobby Hallen over twelve miles was set up at New York's West Side Athletic Club. This small venue, where boxers trained, accommodated about 2,500 around a tight indoor track of nine laps to the mile. Duffey, Hallen and Shrubb promoted the race jointly and Shrubb recalled: 'This was my first venture at race-promoting, but not my last. Often afterwards I did quite well as a promoter with myself as chief attraction. It makes me smile to recall my attempts at drawing up my bills. I am afraid I had lost every grain of modesty when I let myself go like this:

Look! Look!! Look!!!
Alfred Shrubb, the world's champion,
Greatest long-distance runner that ever put on a racing shoe!'

Shrubb trained in New York's Central Park, pounding around the gravel pathway that encircled the reservoir. 'Here I did a lot of running till I learned it was against police regulations to pick holes in the cinder path with spiked shoes. One morning a mounted policeman brought me up sharp, threatening all the pains and penalties of the law. As, however, I was dressed for a run, I set off, noticing that the policeman could not follow on horseback owing to fences in the way. The officer trotted round to the other entrance where he expected to intercept me but I managed to dodge him, darting out towards 63rd Street, thence into Broadway and away.'

By now, Shrubb was practising his idea of putting lead weights into his shoes as a training aid: 'I used to walk long distances in heavy boots with lead inside, like a sock. In this way I walked ten or 12 miles a day, three times a week. The other three days I ran in my light racing shoes. The effect of walking in loaded boots was to impart a feeling of lightness in my feet for running. There are tricks in all trades.'

The evening fixture with Hallen was floodlit and overseen by officials from the Irish-American sports club. Hallen hoped Shrubb would not find the tiny track to his liking, but it posed few problems to a man who had trained on ships' decks, and Shrubb won by two clear laps. In late June, Shrubb tackled his first event in Boston, winning a three-mile race in 14:57 against a three-man relay team at Park Square Coliseum.

At the end of that race an Englishman introduced himself to Shrubb, reminisced for a while about old races in Manchester and invited the runner to dinner. Needing to find the Coliseum's manager to collect his fee, Shrubb accepted the invitation and asked the stranger to mind his bag. Returning fifteen minutes later, he found that man and bag were nowhere to be seen. On being told they had headed towards the subway, Shrubb sprinted off: 'I tried to create another world record, but just got beat to the post as the train was pulling out for Sullivan Square and the gates were closed. Telephoning the next station, I was too late as the majority of passengers had got off. Boston is a city of nearly a million people, so it was like hunting for your brother at a British football final. My bag contained two new shirts and a few collars and a little correspondence and my running suit and shoes. My running shoes had won me many a big race and I had a very hard job to find their equal. I had an idea that the man thought I'd put my money in the bag, but he would find himself mistaken as I'd put it in charge of the office as I did on all occasions.'

This unfortunate theft meant Shrubb henceforth became almost paranoid about caring for his bags. He recalled another incident which happened in New York shortly afterwards: 'Coming out with two bags I met the taxis waiting to take people to their destinations. I dropped my cases and immediately a cabman picked one up and ran off for dear life, leaving me standing. Thinking he had stolen my case I started doing a sprint and he must have had 20 yards lead on me, but I caught him inside of 100. Catching hold of his coat from behind and pulling him over on his back I asked him what his game was. I shall never forget the expression on the poor fellow's face. Wondering what had struck him, and looking up at me, he said 'Sir, didn't you want a cab?' I now understood perfectly that the cabmen must do these things to get a job, as there are so many hundreds of them standing in line. So I gave him the job and he drove me to my destination.'

While spending time in Boston, a city with which he was very taken, Shrubb was invited to inspect the stadium and track at Harvard University. 'It was one of the finest stadiums I ever saw, drawn out as a horseshoe, all built of cement and capable of holding about 80,000 people. While looking around this place, I saw a runner on the track, and was immediately interested to see what this man could do. He stopped just opposite me and we passed the time of day.'

Shrubb yielded to the temptation to join him in a few laps, even though he had no kit with him. He rolled up his trousers and ran two laps, the poor man looking crestfallen that someone wearing everyday clothes could keep pace so easily. The runner was grateful for this stranger's tit-bits of advice, however, and mentioned that he had been receiving coaching advice in recent years by means of letter from the great runner Shrubb in England. Concealing his amazement, Shrubb strung the stranger along for a while but eventually could not help bursting out laughing: 'This is the funniest experience I ever had. I am very proud to know you as I am the man who forwards those letters.' The runner – J W Johnson of Rochester, New York – was left almost speechless. Their friendship blossomed and later Johnson introduced Shrubb to the man in charge of Harvard's athletics section, a meeting that would in time bring about another change of direction in the Englishman's life. Shrubb also agreed to do part-time sales work, between races, for Johnson's company, which manufactured 'Snow White water colour ink'. Shrubb later recalled: 'This is used greatly in the USA for private letter writing on coloured paper, for autograph writing and artists' work. It's not often a runner takes to running ink around, but in this case I ran it so fast that my manufacturer kept supplying it at full speed and I set a number of records as a salesman!'

On Thursday, July 4th, the Cha-na-Gael organisation of Boston staged Gaelic games at Oak Island Grove, including a five-mile race billed as 'the world championship' starring Shrubb, Irish champion Fitzgerald, and local favourite Frank Kanaly. Shrubb maintained his winning ways, finishing a lap ahead of second-placed Tom Williams of Boston. In a mile contest on the same day, American Bart Sullivan pushed Shrubb hard in a dramatic late sprint, but the 13,000 spectators saw the Englishman keep his nose in front. Also on offer was dancing in the casino and a Gaelic football match between Portsmouth, New Hampshire and Garryowens, Boston. The game ended prematurely after the visitors disputed a referee's decision and he abandoned proceedings.

Shrubb may have beaten Frank Kanaly comfortably that day, but there was one occasion against the Massachusetts ace when things didn't go so smoothly: 'Kanaly had made a great reputation as a five-mile champion. He was a fine big, fair-haired fellow, over six feet and a jolly good sportsman. We often ran in matches in my stay in the States and were always keen to beat each other. The only occasion he proved too good was in a handicap at a Caledonian Grove church picnic, when I had to give him

125 yards start in a two-mile race. I gave up the attempt to catch him and later felt rather ashamed of my fit of petulance.'

While Shrubb was staying in the city, *The Boston Post* of Sunday, August 4th, 1907 reported English concern over a perceived shift in their nation's supremacy in athletics (then an umbrella term for many sports, including golf and tennis), which they hoped was just a temporary lapse: 'The decline of British sporting prestige has been a gradual process for the last decade until at present out of the list of principal championships [i.e. world records], England holds but eight out of 32.' These included several in the hands of Shrubb, of course.

On Saturday, August 10th Shrubb defeated Kanaly over three miles. According to *The World*, Shrubb was disappointed with his opponent: 'I expected to have to run my best to win – and fully contemplated establishing a new mark. I am in very good condition but need more opponents to get records.' Shrubb recorded a fast time of 14:46.4, reaching one mile in 4:34 and two in 9:42. Kanaly conceded: 'I'm sure there's no man in the pro ranks to make Shrubb run his best. He is the greatest distance runner in the world.' Still unable to set up a race against Tom Longboat, Shrubb told the press he was now prepared to run against any two American athletes in relay, over five miles, for a purse of 500 dollars.

On Tuesday, September 3rd at the Caledonian Games in New York, Shrubb beat allcomers at one, three and five miles. Back in England, the *Daily Telegraph* reported that his opponents that day had included 'a full-blooded red indian'. Shrubb mowed down six champions as if they were standing still, said the paper, and won by over half a mile. He was carried off the field by two brawny Scots, to the accompaniment of a band of Highland pipers.

Meanwhile, in Canada, *The Montreal Free Press* reported excitedly that marathon champion Billy Sherring was likely to quit the amateur ranks soon and take up the latest challenge from Shrubb. 'It should be one of the most interesting contests of recent times and will be held in either Toronto or Hamilton where the running craze is at its height just now.' Nothing had been agreed by the end of September, however, and Shrubb told the press he was not responsible for the fact that his efforts to meet Sherring had stalled. He would give Sherring almost any terms, within reason, but 'he doesn't want to race me'. He issued a further challenge, this time to run any five men from Canada in relay formation, over two miles upwards, and was anxious that no one should be deterred in expectation of unrealistic financial terms.

The head-to-head with Sherring was finally arranged for the Baseball Grounds in Buffalo. Shrubb agreed the distance of fifteen miles, even though it was rather long for his liking. In the event, he forged an early lead and the Athens gold-medallist never looked like catching him. The result was an anticlimax for local fans, but Shrubb, by now always willing to entertain the crowds, hatched a plan to cause some merriment at the finish line. Breasting the tape a mere six laps to the good, he dashed straight to the changing area, and returned with his camera. He recalled: 'I returned to the track in time to snap a picture of Sherring as he finished second. I wanted a memento of Billy and so helped myself to it. Sherring was an exceedingly good-natured sportsman and he laughed heartily on seeing me snapping him after running my 15 miles. The newspapers made great fun of the incident. It tickled the public to read of a runner winning by such a margin that he had time to go to his tent for his camera.'

Fortunately, for the sake of the spectators, not all Shrubb's victories were by such substantial margins. In Dorchester, Massachusetts, he gave local star Kanaly 100 yards start, Sam Myers 170 yards and Tom Williams 220 yards and just nipped ahead of the latter to win a thriller. He had won over the Boston public by this time, and loved racing in that area: 'Boston captivated me. It's a city unequalled in America and the English flavour of it appealed to me. My training ground was the banks of the Charles River where the Harvard crew row their Varsity races.'

A five-mile race was arranged with Sam Myers at nearby St Lawrence, on a tight, fourteen laps to the mile track, on boards with ninety degree turns. The place was packed to the rafters, forcing the officials to place a row of chairs along the edge of the track to keep the crowds back. The two runners were rightly concerned about how they could run safely in these circumstances. Shrubb jumped into an early lead but lost his footing on a corner and, to avoid crashing into the spectators, caught hold of the back of a chair. He and the chair crashed to the ground, requiring Myers to leapfrog him, both ending in a heap. The officials righted the chairs and the runners scrambled up again, Myers laughing at the farcical scene, and Shrubb eventually winning narrowly. Shrubb wore special-gripped, rubber-soled shoes on the many indoor tracks he encountered in America, most of which had tight bends and some with banking, but they couldn't keep him upright on this occasion.

Back in England, Shrubb's family and friends were hungry for news. He wrote often, but they had to mostly rely on the newspapers for race results. *The West Sussex County Times* carried a report in December that so far he had raced 34 times and won all but one. It also revealed that Shrubb would not be home for Christmas, as hoped, on account of an important new engagement which could only take place in January. This was a ten-mile race in Boston in which Shrubb would take on, single handedly, five of the best American runners available, each running two miles in relay formation. Negotiations had been underway for some time and this was potentially the sort of money-spinner Shrubb could not afford to miss, even if it delayed his return home.

Shortly after New Year's Day 1908, Shrubb tested himself over ten miles at the central Boston venue, The Hub. When first announced, his finish time sounded remarkable, but it soon became clear the course was well short of ten miles. It was nevertheless a good workout prior to the big race scheduled for the night of Thursday, January 16th. What happened that chilly evening in the Park Square Coliseum was little short of sensational. In his definitive *A World History of Long-Distance Running: (1880-2002) Track Events*, Roberto L Quercetani described Shrubb's performance as one of the most remarkable feats in athletics history.

A big crowd turned out, believing the five crack runners representing their country would have enough combined fitness and talent to beat the Englishman, who was running the entire ten miles himself. Sam Myers set off with Shrubb at the gun, the latter speeding to a 4:39.8 for the first mile and forging a one-lap lead. His second mile was also under five minutes (4:59.0) and by the time Myers had handed over to the second runner, the Indian 'Tail Feather', Shrubb had achieved his objective – a big early lead. He was confident the others would not make up the difference. He eased off somewhat, but still increased the overall lead to four laps, with this third and fourth miles timed at 5:19.2 and 5:43.2, respectively. Crook of Fall River took over for the third leg and Shrubb gained another lap after putting in a fifth mile of 5:10.8. When Crook handed over to Scots-born Curran, Shrubb had managed to gain yet another half-lap, meaning that after his sixth mile of 4:56.4 he was almost five laps ahead. Curran dug in, refusing to be lapped, and Shrubb settled on shadowing him. Curran even opened a small gap but, by the end of eight miles, Shrubb remained almost five laps in the lead overall.

In his usual fashion, he was running unevenly, putting in a surge when he felt like it. His seventh mile took him 5:03.0 and the eighth 5:39.6. The Indian 'Black Hawk' was his final opponent, and he took off at great speed, keeping clear of Shrubb for a while before visibly wilting with the Englishman lurking twenty yards behind. With four laps remaining, Shrubb eased past him and sprinted for home, nearly lapping Black Hawk before hitting the tape. His lead at the end was ten yards short of six full laps. His ninth mile had been clocked at 4:59.8 and his tenth 5:02.6. *The Boston Post* described it a wonderful exhibition of running, especially the moment he cut loose and sprinted for home.

Shrubb's winning time of 51:33.4 was extremely fast, considering the lack of corner banking to assist the runners on the flat floor of the Coliseum. Shrubb reflected later: 'When I took this race on, my chances looked very slim to the public, but knowing well if I had the privilege of putting on which man I liked first, I felt the result would never be in doubt. My opponents didn't care for this privilege, but finally agreed. I picked out the slowest man over two miles to go first so that I could force a big lead on him, then the second man would have to run all out to get the lead back. My aim would be to let him fight himself out in his first mile while I took it easy, and then dash for the second mile and get it all back again. It would be the same for the third, fourth and fifth men.'

Alfred Shrubb made it all sound so easy.

CHAPTER FIFTEEN

Horsing around in Canada

Shrubb's first eight months as a touring professional in North America saw him introduced to the charms of Canada, a land which would later play a major role in his life. Although he had grown fond of leafy Boston, it would be the vibrant city of Toronto that would capture Shrubb's heart on a long-term basis.

His relentless search for races in 1907 had inevitably landed him in Toronto, a bustling and fast-growing city of 200,000 people, most of them of British origin. He had come into contact with entrepreneurial types – powerful movers and shakers, along with small-time opportunists. But none would have a greater influence on his affairs than two Irish Canadians, Tom Flanagan and Tim O'Rourke, proprietors of Toronto's Grand Central Hotel in Simcoe Street.

Flanagan was deeply immersed in local sport. In addition to accommodating Shrubb at his hotel, he was also on good terms with local hero Tom Longboat, the Onondagan Indian who was blossoming into one of North America's finest distance runners. Longboat – whose Iroquois name was Cogwagee – was a restless, unpredictable individual who had recently joined Flanagan's Irish-Canadian Athletic Club. Flanagan effectively became Longboat's manager and, from time to time, Shrubb and Longboat, arguably the two best distance runners on the planet, could be found living under the same roof at the Grand Central. Although Shrubb had first laid down the gauntlet to Longboat in June 1907, it would be many months before they would step on a track together. With Flanagan's help, Longboat was discreetly making a living from running while still an amateur, and – to Shrubb's frustration – was not ready to become a fully-fledged pro just yet.

Flanagan was among those who urged Shrubb to be patient on the Longboat issue. One day they would race reach other, he was sure, and if they waited until the optimum moment, it could prove to be a very profitable exercise for all concerned. In the meantime, Longboat was making headlines for the wrong reasons, being arrested at the railway station in Hamilton, Ontario, for being drunk and disorderly. He was said to have given a policeman 'a good shaking' after being warned about his unacceptable behaviour.

Although Shrubb had secured some lucrative races in the New York, Philadelphia, and Boston areas in the latter half of 1907 (covered in the previous chapter), he needed to expand his horizons. He was relentless in his quest to find new markets, and used his temporary Toronto base to branch out and look for action across Canada, in towns and cities that he had barely heard of a few weeks earlier.

The province of Manitoba, another bastion of British influence, would prove to be a particularly happy hunting ground. English-speaking immigrants had flooded to the Red River Valley, and Winnipeg was emerging as a boom town, having grown from a village of 300 in 1870 to a burgeoning town of 125,000 people in less than forty years. Winnipegers loved their sport and with little trouble Shrubb was able to arrange a number of fixtures in the area. *The Manitoba Free Press* of August 21st, 1907, announced: 'Shrubb has been very anxious to visit Winnipeg and give an exhibition of his endurance. He will take part in a relay race, and will also give a novel exhibition when he will run against a horse hitched to a road buggy.'

The shortage of adequately talented humans who could give Shrubb a decent race had meant there had been nothing for it but to turn to four-legged opposition. After his initial misgivings had subsided, Shrubb slowly warmed to the idea of racing a dairy company horse called Patsy, who would be pulling a buggy and driver. He was assured of a big crowd and a good pay-day. It was a far cry from those windswept fields in England's green and pleasant land, when he raced the best cross-country men for honour and glory alone. Now he was in show-business rather than sport – in effect a circus performer – and if ever he needed a stark reminder of his changed circumstances, the sight of Patsy and the buggy provided it. The distance to be raced was ten miles and a bumper crowd of 4,000 curious folk turned out to see the fun at the city's River Park track.

According to one report, Winnipeg was 'seething with Shrubb-mania' on the big day and the prospect of a multi-world record holder from England racing a local carthorse was the talk of the town. The bookies did a roaring trade. Shrubb, not knowing what to expect from his equine opponent, ran a solid race, churning out laps of the track metronomically on a squally day. He clocked 52:20, close to his pre-race target, and for most of the race either led by a short distance or shared the lead with Patsy.

The crowd finally got the excitement they craved in the final stages when a late gallop by the mare was too hot for Shrubb to handle and she crossed the line fifteen yards in front. This did nothing to diminish Shrubb in the eyes of the crowd and press, who marvelled at the sustained bursts he had put in earlier. Mr Roche, the 'jockey' aboard the buggy, said afterwards he had not been obliged to force the animal as it had kept up a good fast clip by itself, but he was truly amazed at how Shrubb had kept going alongside, against a very strong wind.

Many years later, Toronto journalist Jim Coleman proposed a tongue-in-cheek theory over why Patsy had beaten Shrubb on that blustery afternoon. He suggested that because Patsy normally worked for the Crescent Creamery – delivering milk, cream and cottage cheese – she had been used to her solid, predicable, daily routine, only breaking into a gallop when she turned for home off Portage Avenue at the end of her round. The sight of her cosy barn would encourage her to go full pelt over the final yards. On race day, dairy workers had erected a replica of the dairy at the finish-line to ensure that Patsy would come home in fine style and enable them to collect substantial winnings. Coleman backed up his theory with evidence that Patsy's famous 'late gallop' had caused several accidents in the past, adding that the dairy had had to recruit a Mexican mule skinner, with experience in Death Valley, to keep her in check.

Shrubb's defeat did little to diminish the success of the occasion and it was not long before he was at it again, this time against a pair of horses in a ten-mile race. The horses – in this case rather less capable animals than Patsy – had to run five miles each in relay. Shrubb seemed happy to stoop to such circuses, now that it was clear that human opposition was in very short supply.

This particular race came about after he headed west from Winnipeg in search of races, and had ended up in Port de Prairie, which was, he recalled, 'more or less an indian reservation.' He stayed overnight at a small hotel in the main street with his associate, Francis Nelson Smith, and over wine and a cigar they weighed up his prospects. The only way forward seemed to be to visit nearby livery stables to seek out more horses that could be trained up for competition.

The manager of the first stables they visited accepted an advance of 25 dollars to prepare two animals to run five miles each against the visitor from England. Once the event had been publicised, the betting became brisk and a good day's sport was assured the following weekend.

The first horse was tethered to a four-wheeled buggy, complete with driver weighing about 180 pounds, as agreed by both parties. After the start signal, the crowd cheered as the horse trotted into a fifty-yard lead after a mile and a half, but over the next two miles Shrubb made steady inroads as the horse looked increasingly in poor shape. By the time the second animal took over, Shrubb was 120 yards clear in front. He was on course for his personal target of 52:30, but was seen to be constantly checking over his shoulder, as the second horse, fresh and frisky, was closing fast. As the finish line approached, man and beast were virtually neck and neck, although the second horse, like the first, appeared to lack the stamina needed for a strong finish. Shrubb pulled clear and then, to ensure victory, brazenly employed a spot of gamesmanship.

He recalled later: 'I decided there was only one chance for me to win and I jumped deliberately in front of his head, and knowing perfectly well that the driver wouldn't drive over me, I just kept in front of his head all the way to the tape, swerving first to one side of the track and then the other, and just winning on the post.' There had been nothing in the contract to say running had to be in a straight line and Shrubb's tactics worked. He clocked 52:40.6 and his zig-zag finish represented what must have been the oddest climax to a race in all his long career.

Other races with horses would follow, with punters in Philadelphia and Calgary getting their chance to witness the spectacle. Shrubb conceded in later years that the horses he raced were all 'common roadsters' and not animals of any great class.

The flood of European immigrants into North America – thirty million between 1820 and 1920 – threw up occasional chance meetings with people Shrubb knew from the old country. This happened when his travels took him to Fort William in Thunder Bay, on the shores of Lake Superior. Staying at the Avenue Hotel in advance of a race with two local runners, he passed the time after dinner by visiting the billiards room. Here he came across acquaintances he had last seen in London several years earlier. They were quick to push forward one of their number as a suitable billiards opponent for Shrubb. Shrubb was allowed to break, and rattled up a handful of points before his opponent stepped forward with his cue. The mystery man proceeded to clean up the table in a blur of colour and powerful potting. As the dejected Shrubb trooped out to the bar to find his friends, they could hardly stifle their mirth as they enquired whether he had enjoyed his game. 'Yes, but only as a spectator!' he replied, realising he had been set up with the local bar-room hustler.

In the autumn of 1907 Shrubb was persuaded to race John D Marsh, the pride of Manitoba, over fifteen miles in Winnipeg's River Park. This distance was at the upper end of Shrubb's usual repertoire. The local man's strong, steady pace won the day, with Shrubb dominant early on but unable to sustain his performance for more than an hour, and picking up a leg injury into the bargain. It was a rare defeat but, put in a positive light, it gave the home crowd what they wanted, kept their interest alive, and set up the likelihood of a lucrative re-match.

On Monday, November 4th, Shrubb was invited to be guest speaker at a smoking concert given in Winnipeg by the Britannia Football Club. He told the enraptured audience that he wanted a re-match with Marsh and, once he was over his injury, he would even tackle their man at fifteen miles again if necessary. He entertained them with tales about some of his great races of the past and distance running in general.

Shrubb endeared himself to the sporting folk of Winnipeg, and during the last weeks of 1907 was involved in many discussions over potential races, which earned him coverage galore in the local press. There were even rumours that he was planning to buy a hotel and settle in Winnipeg, but he publicly denied this. *The Manitoba Free Press* reported that during a visit to Canada, the veteran distance runner Peter Golden heard about Shrubb and wanted him for a six-day ultra-race planned for Wonderland Park at Revere Beach, just north of Boston. Golden had been unable to persuade Tom Longboat to turn pro and enter this event, but had got agreement from distance runner Billy Davis of Ontario. Shrubb said he would only participate if he was guaranteed 500 dollars. This was rejected, with Golden proposing an arrangement whereby Shrubb could place a bet that would pay up 500 dollars if Shrubb actually won. Golden told the press he had someone in mind to beat Shrubb, but this was one of many potential events tossed in the air which never actually happened.

The subject that dominated all else was the prospect of Shrubb versus Longboat. In mid-November it was announced that *The Montreal Star* had promised Longboat 2,000 dollars if he would change his ways and 'live a clean, temperate life and remain in the field of honest sport for five years'. There was concern over Longboat's drinking and his lack of disciplined training following his 'unedifying conduct' at the Thanksgiving Day events in Hamilton, Ontario. However, shortly after his display of public inebriation, Longboat won a five-miler in Montreal, prompting the press to speculate that 'temperance' was perhaps not a vital quality for a distance runner.

As winter set in, Shrubb's thoughts returned to England. He had made plans to return home in December 1907. Politically, these were turbulent times in Europe and, on the same day that Shrubb lined up for his eagerly anticipated re-match with John D Marsh, Kaiser Wilhelm II, Emperor of Germany and King of Prussia, made a highly publicised visit to London. Dense fog ruined a pageant planned for his arrival, and the Kaiser sparked riotous demonstrations in central London as Socialists disputed his claim to be a man of peace.

Thousands of miles away, Shrubb's performance at the Winnipeg Arena Rink was far more convincing. In front of a highly charged 2,000 crowd, Shrubb took advantage of problems the local runner encountered with his footwear. Marsh had chosen to run in long spikes which, on the rock-hard track, hurt his feet. He was forced to stop and change shoes, losing two laps in the process. He wisely resisted the temptation to try and make up the ground immediately, only to see Shrubb promptly put in one of his famous surges and establish an even bigger lead. Marsh hung in gamely, although the real damage was already done. Shrubb's fastest mile proved to be his second, at 4:40, which came after he had tentatively tested his injured leg on the opening circuit.

The crowd that night was particularly boisterous, with good support for Shrubb from the British expats. Using a small, ten-laps-to-the-mile track, starter Jos Fahey announced the times as the miles were reeled off. After 149 laps timekeeper McIntyre fired a pistol to indicate one to go, and Shrubb roared home two laps clear of Marsh, winning in one hour 21:40. Shrubb had not been his usual confident self beforehand, mentioning his strained leg from the previous race and warning that he might have to quit early. His last five miles were all timed at 5:48 or slower, illustrating the extent to which he had eased up. He overcame a nasty moment after thirteen miles when he visibly flagged and limped for a few paces, but fortunately the moment passed. As he crossed the finish line he was mobbed by the crowd, whose invasion prevented Marsh completing his last two laps. Shrubb was manhandled onto the timekeeper's table and, bowing to pressure, made a short speech. He thanked everyone for their support and the marvellous ovation, and assured them that, but for his leg injury, he would have run two minutes faster.

One Shrubb fan, who happened to be a farm-worker at the nearby village of Napinka, wrote to *The Winnipeg Telegram*. He made great play of Shrubb's name and issued a light-hearted challenge. Now that the threshing was done, the writer was available to take on allcomers in a ten-mile race, especially 'Shrubb, plant, tree, barks, gums, seeds or berries …' He knew of many fine local runners, some of whom trained by running to work at the office, others by running for trains. If his offer was taken up, the stakes would be a keg of beer for the poor or a pot of doughnuts for a church social.

A more serious challenge arrived from John D Marsh, also published in *The Telegram*, when he proposed a third race, this time over a distance of more than fifteen miles for 500 dollars at the Arena Rink. Suggesting a cinder track be placed over the ice, Marsh gave Shrubb the option of putting the track in place himself if he wished. In the usual fashion of the times, Marsh's challenge provided a phone number for Shrubb, or his representative, to call. It seems this particular one was not taken up, probably due to the distance Marsh suggested.

Shrubb was certainly doing his bit to promote distance running generally, with this first stint in North America involving an average of at least one race per week. In his book documenting the history of the Boston Marathon, Tom Derderian points out that more people ran marathons in the fifteen years before the 1914-1918 War than in the fifteen years after it: 'One could consider 1900 to 1909 as the first running boom,' he says. Author Jack Batten also later referred to these years as a time when distance running was 'the king of sports'.

Meanwhile, as Shrubb prepared to return home to England, his desired showdown with Longboat took a step nearer reality. The Onondagan Indian was suspended for transgressing amateur regulations by the Amateur Athletic Union (AAU) of the USA. His offence related to his involvement in a Boston race that did not carry the sanction of AAU president James Sullivan. Longboat's manager, Flanagan, was livid and travelled to New York without an appointment to confront Sullivan, 'who was not pleased to see me'. The episode left many people waiting with bated breath to see if Longboat would now be forced to join Shrubb and the others in the pro ranks.

Having missed Christmas at home due to his commitments, Shrubb sailed from New York on Friday, January 25th 1908 on Cunard's new luxury liner the *SS Mauretainia*. On his arrival, *The West Sussex County Times* revealed that he was likely to return across the Atlantic later in 1908, and would be making a decision soon on whether to settle permanently over there. In the meantime, Shrubb would seek a few races in Britain.

Not long after Shrubb set foot on home soil, the Longboat situation took another twist. The Canadian was now in further trouble for taking part on February 13th in an unsanctioned race in which he had originally been credited with smashing Shrubb's ten-mile world record, but subsequent measurement of the course found it well short of the stated distance. This event was condemned in the American press as farcical and it was felt Longboat had been short-changed: 'Longboat is a wonderful runner, but it's too bad that he is handled by men who are looking out for their own interests rather than his welfare.'

Meanwhile, returning hero Shrubb gave a talk about his American adventures to the Horsham Postmen's annual dinner in March 1908. He speculated that this might be his last season on the track. Amid cries of 'no, no!', he said the Americans had been fine sportsmen who had treated him well and given him rousing receptions. On the subject of his attempts to race Longboat, Shrubb said when it finally happened he would run a pure, sportsmanlike race and do his utmost to win for the honour of his country and Horsham.

A correspondent from *The Sussex Daily News* tracked Shrubb down at his father-in-law's hotel in Hayward's Heath and reported that he looked 'as brown as berry and in the best of health'. Shrubb said his fears on first travelling about regaining fitness had been allayed after just two weeks on USA soil. He judged Frank Kanaly to be the best runner he had met on the tour, and the ten-miler against five men in Boston his best perform- ance. He showed off a gold medal, set with two diamonds, presented to him by the British United Football Club at Providence, Rhode Island. The reporter noted that Shrubb was reluctant to talk about his recent adventures and future hopes, largely because he had plans to 'write some- thing himself'.

This writing project would subsequently surface late in 1908 in the shape of a small book called *Running and Cross-Country Running*, published by Health and Strength Limited, of 12 Burleigh Street, Strand, London. It was not a Shrubb autobiography, rather a coaching manual, packed with homespun tips on how to train and prepare for races of different distances, and how to stay fit and healthy. It may have been down to Shrubb's well-known modesty, or perhaps due to his publishers' specific wishes, but the book contains precious little anecdotal material. Over the years, however, it would come to be looked upon as a gem by those inter- ested in coaching methods and how they developed over the ages. It would also prove an inspiration to more than one quality runner to emerge over the first half of the twentieth century – more of which later.

Stretching to twelve chapters and 85 pages, Shrubb's book sold for half a crown (2s 6d) and featured a 'Brief Word Sketch' of the man him- self, contributed by J Murray. This chapter compensates for Shrubb's modesty by calling him 'probably the most extraordinary athlete the world has ever seen'. Murray was clearly a big admirer: 'He is wondrous- ly beautiful in make. There is not much of him, it is true, but what there is of him is of the finest possible quality.' Read in the modern era, this gushing prose seems almost embarrassing. Murray also manages to get the runner's year of birth wrong, but this aside, he paints a succinct pen picture of the runner and the man. Referring to Shrubb's much-debated 'ugly' running style, he suggests that 'future ages may possibly decide that Shrubb's style is like the Venus of Milo, in that it was not invented in accordance with the canons, but, on the contrary, that it invented them.' Many runners travel in a 'prettier' fashion, but none are so effective. 'No other runner can point to such a career as his,' Murray concludes, 'and it may well be questioned whether his career will ever be equalled. Walter George's alone can be compared with it, and Shrubb has achieved the seemingly impossible by eclipsing even George's fame.'

Shrubb divulged a little more of his plans when a local reporter accosted him spectating at a football match between Horsham and

Helmston. He confirmed he would be returning to North America later in 1908 as he had several engagements unfulfilled, and the list was constantly being added to. Montreal was one of the planned destinations, Shrubb admitting that he had developed a liking for getting around the world. This time he would probably take his wife and son with him, he added, but did not reveal whether they would all settle permanently in the New World.

On Monday, March 9th a 5,000 crowd turned up at London's Stamford Bridge for a benefit meeting for ex-champion runner Sid Thomas. Shrubb won a four-mile scratch race by a full lap in 20:21.4 from H Farrow. Underway simultaneously was an attempt on the 100 miles world record, but the sole contestant, C W Hart, reluctantly gave up the chase after 36 miles of endless circling the track. A few weeks later, 4,000 turned out at Warrington, Lancashire, as Shrubb made a well-publicised attempt on his own four-mile grass record of 19:26.8. George Tincler of Edinburgh had been invited to provide a serious challenge, but failed to show, and although three local men were hastily called in, the lack of serious competition meant Shrubb fell short of the required pace. On May 23rd he headed north again to the scene of some of his greatest races, Ibrox Park in Glasgow, to attack Sid Thomas's twelve-mile amateur record of 62:43. After an hour Shrubb had covered an impressive eleven miles and 380 yards, but ultimately fell short of any records.

With a strange twist of irony, Shrubb was packing his bags to leave the country on the very weekend the British Olympic trials got underway. Following the eruption of Mount Vesuvius, Italy had to withdraw as host of the 1908 Olympic Games and London stepped into the breach at short notice. In consequence, British interest in the Games was higher than ever. Emil Voight of Manchester AC won a place in the Olympic team with a five-mile run that the departing Shrubb would have beaten comfortably. As it was, on Sunday, May 31st Shrubb set sail again for New York, arranging to send for his wife and son to join him, depending on the decision to settle permanently in North America. He sailed this time on the Cunard liner *SS Caronia*, and as usual kept busy with training sessions on deck, supplemented by low-key races with passengers, which he naturally won easily.

The ship docked on Sunday, June 6th and this time Arthur Duffey was there, waiting on the wharf to greet him with the news that long-distance running was booming and that Shrubb's prospects were even brighter. Within a day or two Shrubb was fixed up with a busy afternoon's work in Wednesday Park, on New York's Long Island. Asked to race three times within three hours, Shrubb agreed and won all three events – at one, three, and five miles. It was not long before he recorded an impressive three-mile triumph against Frank Kanaly, at nearby Celtic Park, home of the Irish-American Club. The club staged its events on a Sunday afternoon and Shrubb smashed the American record with 14:46.4. (He passed the half-mile point in 2:06.4 – said to have been the fastest half-mile ever run within a longer distance race – reached one mile in 4:34 and two in 9:42.)

Shrubb would reflect in later years that by the summer of 1908 he was in a position to demand guaranteed appearance money, with an additional sum payable if he won: 'And as I generally won, my gains probably averaged about 250 dollars per meeting, occasionally rising to 500. I never took money bets about myself. In later years in America and Canada my profits per winning race could reach about 1,000 dollars. As my public grew, I was content to run for 30 per cent of the gross receipts, which paid me better than guaranteed appearance fees. But let it be remembered that my expenses were very heavy.'

To put these figures into perspective, in 1908 the sum of 1,000 US dollars was the equivalent, in terms of purchasing power, to roughly 19,400 US dollars today. The average annual salary of a professional worker in the States – for example, a teacher – was around 800 dollars. The popular, ground-breaking motor car, the Model 'T' Ford, was launched that year and a new model cost around 825 dollars. In other words, Shrubb was making very good money during this period – the equivalent of a present-day Premiership footballer, perhaps – so it was hardly surprising that he and the promoters were keen to fix up as many races as possible in order to make hay while the sun was shining.

Shrubb found that American promoters often insisted on him running against relay teams, to ensure maximum excitement. 'This was a serious undertaking and naturally I demurred a little, but Duffey and Alexander McLean, promoters of the Park Square Coliseum, Boston, persuaded me to consent. Running against two men who were in relay was undoubtedly a severe handicap, but not as terrible as people imagined. All the same it tickled the Americans who looked on me as a sort of tireless machine.'

Typical of these contests was a four-mile contest at Boston, in which Shrubb took command when he set off alongside Sam Myers and forced a lead of 100 yards by the time Frank Kanaly took over at halfway. The new man made up some ground in the third mile, but Shrubb pushed hard in the closing stages and won by a big margin. Kanaly told him afterwards that none of them could give him a good race and he would simply have to be content with relays or handicap, a fact that was already clear to Shrubb – unless, of course, he could get Longboat to take up the challenge.

Meanwhile, back in London, a large contingent of foreign athletes arrived for the Olympic Games and warmed up by appearing at the AAA championships at Stamford Bridge. King Edward VII and Queen Alexandra declared the Olympiad underway at the White City stadium in Shepherds Bush on Monday, July 13th. For the first time, the British public and sportswriters were excited about an Olympics. The only regret was that the finest runner that Britain had ever produced was thousands of miles away, running against horses and in smoky exhibition halls.

Shrubb himself had never expected to compete in an Olympics, which only exercised major pulling power in the years after his suspension. But he must have harboured wistful thoughts about what might have been when the excitement in England began to mount. Had he not departed the amateur ranks, he would almost certainly have played a starring role, but at least his commitments in North America meant he would not be confined to watching miserably from the sidelines. In the June 20th issue of *Health and Strength* magazine, he expressed his hopes that Britain would do well, insisting that American athletes were no better than their British counterparts, but merely took the sport more seriously and trained harder.

The only aspect of the Games at White City to really capture Shrubb's attention was the fact that the unpredictable Longboat – still clinging to his amateur status – would be competing in the marathon, which was marked out over a 26-mile course from Windsor Castle to White City and then extended when the Queen insisted the runners finish in front of the royal box. They therefore had to run 26 miles and 385 yards, a distance thereafter retained for all official marathon events. On a muggy, humid day, several runners fell by the wayside and among those failing to finish was Longboat, who quit after twenty miles, close to the Sudbury and Harrow Road railway station. Officials *en route* are said to have administered small amounts of strychnine as a stimulant to the strugglers, but it remains unclear how many received this 'assistance', and whether or not it actually benefited them.

Dramatic scenes accompanied the finish, when Dorando Pietri, an Italian pastry cook, entered the stadium first but repeatedly staggered over, regained his feet and collapsed again in his desperation to reach the finish line. Horrified officials eventually helped him over the line, but this led to his being disqualified. One of those 'helping' Pietri in those fateful moments was Arthur Conan Doyle, creator of Sherlock Holmes, who was an athletics enthusiast and part-time official (and was known to be a great admirer of Shrubb, too). Upon Pietri's disqualification, American Johnny Hayes, who struggled in second, apparently befuddled by strychnine, was promoted to the gold medal position. Afterwards, rumours reached Shrubb and his pals in America that Longboat, Pietri and Hayes would all now be turning professional and would join the pro circus in the United States and Canada.

Shrubb would certainly have welcomed those rumours, for he was still struggling to find men who could give him a credible race. In the summer of 1908 he tackled a six-miler, with three opponents in relay formation – Sam Myers, Tom Williams and Frank Kanaly – at the Fall River Baseball Ground, fifty miles outside Boston. This wool manufacturing town was home to many mill-workers from Britain, and Shrubb received great crowd support as a result. Football and baseball were also on the afternoon's schedule. The weather was cripplingly hot, yet Shrubb was on top form, returning to his base in Boston that night with thirty per cent of the takings in his pocket.

He shortly tackled four relay runners in an eight-miler at Fall River and again won well. 'For a time my races were almost farcical as men were badly wanted to tackle me on level terms,' he recalled. 'But the public were beginning to clamour for races and I wanted business for the usual business reasons. From place to place I went, running and winning relay races exactly as a commercial traveller goes about looking for orders and commissions. In most of the towns I visited there was a large mixture of English and Scottish, who formed themselves into clubs with names like "Sons of the Empire Association". They pressed me to give exhibition races in their towns. Once at Lawrence, in Massachusetts, the Sons of the Empire gave me a concert in my honour and presented me with a three-handled loving cup.'

A group of expats in New Bedford, Massachusetts, calling themselves the Sons of England, invited Shrubb to run in the busy textile centre and whaling port. Shrubb ended up promoting the race himself: 'I took up my quarters in New Bedford ten days before the meeting, very much like a carpet-bagger candidate for Parliament in England,' he recalled. 'I wrote all my own bills and printed my own name in very tall letters, besides engaging the local brass band to blare about the streets as if a circus had come to the town. I sold my own tickets at the box-office while rigged out for running. That was about the end of my race-promoting. It proved a dismal failure.'

On Tuesday, September 8th, Shrubb left the promoting to the experts and stuck to what he did well, cruising to victory in both three and four miles at a Caledonian Games in New York City, pocketing 300 dollars into the bargain. By now, Shrubb was using Toronto's Grand Hotel as his base, but his proximity to its owner, Longboat's manager Flanagan, did not seem to assist getting the runners on the track together. Longboat was said to be concentrating on the upcoming Toronto Ward's Island Marathon, meaning Shrubb would have to wait a while.

With the approach of winter heralding the start of the cross-country season, Shrubb accepted an invitation to coach the Harvard University athletes for their important inter-collegiate championships in late November. He hoped to impress sufficiently to be offered a more permanent position by the university, thus providing the job security that would enable wife Ada and little Roy to come over from England. The pointers were good in this respect, for the Harvard lads responded well to their new coach and their results showed an improvement on previous seasons. Under Shrubb's tutelage, a runner called Herbert Jaques came through the ranks and looked promising.

On Thursday November 26th, the two major figures from the London Olympic marathon – Pietri and Hayes – would make their first big splash as professionals in an indoor event at Madison Square Garden, New York. The promotion, by local man Pat Powers, was a huge success with a bumper 12,000 crowd cheering Pietri to a win by sixty yards.

Even better news, Longboat had finally taken the plunge as a pro. Powers proposed an indoor marathon between Longboat and Shrubb at the MSG. Shrubb did not want to rush into such a commitment, so Powers fixed a meeting between Longboat and Pietri at the same venue on Tuesday, December 15th. The MSG track was so small that 262 laps were needed to cover the marathon distance, which was exhausting both physically and mentally. Pietri collapsed in the final stages – just as he had in London – and an enthralling contest was won by a leg-weary and shattered Longboat.

Delighted with another huge attendance, a great night's racing and massive press coverage, Powers announced that the next stage in this 'Marathon Mania' series would be Shrubb-versus-Longboat in January 1909. The Englishman had never run a marathon before, but he had got his match with Longboat at long last – and it promised to be a real thriller, with riches for all concerned.

CHAPTER SIXTEEN

Marathon Madness

It had been a long time coming, but enthusiastic New Yorkers felt that Shrubb's first race against the maverick native Canadian Tom Longboat was worth the wait. Tickets quickly sold out for their head-to-head indoor marathon at Madison Square Garden, scheduled for late January 1909. An extraordinary level of public interest saw thousands of dollars change hands in pre-race bets, and the authorities laid on special trains to the event.

Longboat had several fine times under his belt, but for Shrubb this was his first attempt at such a distance. Wisely, he insisted on a clause in his contract that he would receive a share of the proceeds, win or lose, and if he lost would be guaranteed re-matches with Longboat over shorter distances. The contract he signed with promoter Pat Powers was shrewdly calculated and virtually guaranteed a pay-day of several thousand dollars, whatever the outcome.

Deals such as this – added to the news that longer-term coaching work was available to him at Harvard University – convinced Shrubb that the time was right for his family to emigrate to North America. He told pressmen he would be making a short visit to England in the early spring of 1909 to sort out a few matters and would then return for good. The prospect of making a good living was much brighter now that the likes of Longboat, Pietri and Hayes had switched to professionalism.

Of immediate concern to Shrubb was the need to increase his training mileage in order to cope with his first marathon. He only had a few weeks to prepare. Plenty of long walks in his lead-filled boots were the order of the day. Plodding along for hours in the cold, wintry weather certainly helped to condition him for the strength-sapping ordeal ahead, even though he knew the big race itself would be played out in a smoky, indoor setting. Running without fresh air was anathema to Shrubb, but he cheered himself with the thought that the financial rewards were far too good to turn down. Further consolation arrived with news that the erratic Longboat's training was not going well.

Between training sessions Shrubb maintained his business acumen by conducting negotiations for future races. He offered both Longboat and Pietri a set of ten, fifteen and twenty mile races each, with a huge 5,000 dollar prize being paid on a 'best of three' basis. Converted to present-day prices, this prize would have a value of around 98,600 US dollars.

Longboat and Pietri both declined, no doubt believing the distances favoured Shrubb.

In the meantime, Shrubb familiarised himself with the small Madison Square Garden track by tackling three of the fastest men around over twelve miles in front of a 5,000 crowd on Saturday, January 9th. Each opponent – Frank Kanaly and Tom Williams from Massachusetts, and Fred Simpson, an Ojibway Indian from the Hiawatha reserve in Ontario – were required to run four miles each. Shrubb and Kanaly shot off at the gun like sprinters. After the first turn Shrubb fell in behind Kanaly and ran on his heels until the next turn. Then Shrubb surged and bustled away to open a 100-yard lead. He covered the first half-mile in 2:17.8 and the mile in 4:53.2. When Simpson relieved Kanaly, he found himself three laps down, with Shrubb recording 21:30 for four miles. Simpson, who had finished sixth in the 1908 Olympic marathon in London, was a big powerful man resembling Longboat. The crowd roared him on his way as he surged after Shrubb, but this only inspired the Englishman to put in a spurt of his own. Shrubb hit eight miles in 43:15. One paper reported that the third runner, Williams, 'dashed away like a frightened fawn amid a tremendous roar.' Williams' early enthusiasm did not frighten Shrubb, who injected yet more bursts before coming home to win nearly four laps in front. Shrubb had blasted out a superb 65:57, more than five minutes faster than Pietri had recently managed against fellow Olympian Hayes in a twelve-miler. *The West Sussex County Times* said this victory proved Shrubb was a 'marvel' and added: 'It is a pity that he has decided to expatriate himself in order to take up a lucrative position at Harvard University as running instructor.'

Promoter Pat Powers was delighted at the hullabaloo attending the big clash between Shrubb and 21-year-old Longboat, even though Shrubb reported inflammation around his left big toe and the event was put back to Friday, February 5th. Longboat also had problems, but they seemed psychological rather than physical. Powers had recently taken over from Tom Flanagan as Longboat's manager, a move which was said to have left the runner unhappy and depressed. He wrote to Flanagan's business partner Tim O'Rourke to say he was not in good shape for the big race and was thinking of pulling out. Longboat even advised against placing bets on him to win and ended, rather desperately: 'I'm good for nothing now.' Although it had been a private letter, O'Rourke apparently handed it to *The Toronto Star*, where it prompted banner headlines, adding to the general frenzy.

Three days prior to the race, Shrubb confirmed to himself that his toe was better by completing a fourteen-mile training run at an average pace of 5:30 a mile. He set off from his Toronto base for his Broadway hotel in New York to meet up with Flanagan, who was playing a pivotal role in staging the race. In his column in *The Toronto Evening Telegram*, Flanagan reported that Shrubb seemed slightly nervous but looked in good shape. Flanagan also visited the Flatiron Building to see Longboat and his veteran trainer Jimmy DeForest, and reckoned the Canadian was not in such good condition as Shrubb, although he still believed the Indian would win. The ten-laps-to-a-mile track at Madison Square Garden was laid by Sparrow Robertson, regarded as the best man in the world at this sort of work. He would be using a layout made of cinder compound on the wooden floor that was similar to the one favoured by Longboat when he had beaten Pietri a few weeks earlier at the same venue.

Two days before the race, Longboat ran a languid eight miles and the day before completed his build-up with an extended walk. His preparations also included an unscheduled sprint down Sixth Avenue in Manhattan, helping a storekeeper pursue a shop-lifter. Shrubb was favoured in the early betting, with odds of 10-7 against him proving popular. But by the Friday morning, the punters were starting to pile money on a Longboat victory, with Flanagan encouraging them, writing in *The Telegram* that Shrubb would not last the distance, irrespective of his instinctive need to uphold the honour of his country. Everyone anticipated that Shrubb's plan would be to go out fast, build a lead and try to hang on. That was his usual way. The unknown factor would be how he coped with a distance six miles longer than he had ever raced before. Longboat's tactics and performance were harder to predict. He had won a handful of marathons in fine style, but occasionally performed erratically and below his potential.

Born on the Six Nations Reserve near Brantford, Ontario in July 1887, Longboat's Onondagan tribe was one of six of the Iroquois confederacy. His first important race had taken place in 1906 when he won the Around the Bay marathon aged nineteen in nearby Hamilton. He topped the world rankings after his 1907 Boston Marathon win, but regularly blotted his copybook with an indisciplined attitude to training and well-documented heavy drinking. He is said to have been a victim of racial discrimination and exploitation, which might partly explain his reputation as a difficult character to manage. Shrubb, modest and canny, who drank little and paid heed to diet and training, could not have presented a more different character.

Around 12,000 squeezed into Madison Square Garden for the big race on the Friday evening, both runners attended by a well-dressed group of assistants. Longboat had additional support from Lauretta Maracle, the young woman he had married six weeks earlier. Both runners expected to earn a minimum of 3,000 dollars from the event, considerably more than a year's salary for most of the audience. The betting saw thousands of dollars change hands in various cities, some bets being as high as 1,400 dollars. W J Little of *The Montreal Star* was appointed judge, Rev J D Morrow from Toronto the scorer, and Francis Nelson Smith of *The Boston Globe* official timer. 'Big' Tim Sullivan was the starter. Thomas Sinnott, Shrubb's former mentor from England was among the other trackside officials assisting the runners.

In the fraught moments before the start the atmosphere was electric. Shrubb nervously bounced around the arena on a warm-up lap and, typically, Longboat simply stood around, waiting for the signal to start. Shrubb noticed an unusually high number of women in the audience. He mentioned this to the starter, the British expat Sullivan, who remarked that the whole scene reminded him of a night at the Covent Garden opera. The arena was thick with tobacco smoke, which did not please Shrubb, and the noise was deafening, with both runners enjoying plenty of support. Shrubb wore a dark top bearing a bold Union Jack on the chest, and the British flag was much in evidence among the crowd. Longboat's fans included excited native Americans who kept up a scream of 'Oyesha!', the Indian battle cry of victory.

The gun went and Shrubb showed his hand, leaping ahead and completing the first lap of 176 yards in thirty seconds, half a mile in 2:25 and a mile in 4:52. It seemed ridiculously fast for a marathon of 262 laps, but Shrubb had his plan and was going to stick to it. In the fourth mile he had a problem with a shoe and stopped to fix it. Longboat set off steadily at an unwavering pace and seemed unfazed by the huge lead that Shrubb had quickly built. At eight miles the watching Flanagan reckoned Shrubb shot him a sarcastic smile, but he felt sure the Englishman would not get the last laugh. Over the first sixteen miles the pattern remained the same, Longboat plodding and Shrubb occasionally surging, finding himself eight laps ahead at one point (1,408 yards). After Shrubb had lapped Longboat yet again, the crowd began to turn on the Canadian and booed him. Consternation spread among Longboat's backers and there was gloom in the telegraph offices in Toronto, where crowds had gathered outside the newspaper offices for 'live' news.

Then, slowly, the tide began to turn. After eighteen miles, a mind-numbing 180 laps, Shrubb no longer had an easy stride and seemed to be labouring. He rallied at nineteen, however, and the lead remained eight clear laps. Although no longer Longboat's manager, Flanagan had a financial stake in his winning and he kept urging Longboat's helpers to stop trying to get their man to speed up. Flanagan could see the way the race was going and was sure that if Longboat maintained his present pace Shrubb would crumble. 'I had figured on Shrubb hitting trouble at 20 miles and I was right,' he wrote later. 'At this point he had to change his shoes, having shown lameness for some time. Longboat gained more than a lap during this operation, closing the gap to six-and-a-half laps.'

At 21 miles Shrubb was clearly limping and showing signs of distress. He was doused on the back of the head with a sponge but continued to wobble. Just before 22 miles Flanagan could contain himself no longer; he threw off his coat and rushed to trackside. He joined Longboat's helpers, taking turns to run alongside their man and chivvy him along. Some of their advice must have been lost amid the general cacophany. Shrubb had slowed badly and the lead was being relentlessly whittled down. Although Longboat looked too heavy-legged to raise any sort of surge, he showed no signs of distress.

At 22 miles Shrubb was forced to walk a few yards, a development that raised the decibels still further. Longboat's job was to recover about 1,100 yards over the remaining four miles. Shrubb again stopped and walked, and the lead was cut further, and almost fell at the 23-mile mark. He was clearly in trouble and every step now looked like the dying effort of a game man. With around three miles left his lead was now reduced to five laps. Shrubb bravely tried to hang on as Longboat passed and gained another lap back, and stayed with his man for two laps before limping painfully again and walking. With less than two miles to go the lead was now down to a single lap. After appearing well beaten earlier, the race was now there for the taking for Longboat. He drew level and then passed Shrubb, a broken man, at 24 miles and 700 yards. The crowd let rip a mighty roar and hats were thrown into the air, one of which hit Longboat. 'The scene beggared description,' recalled Flanagan.

Moments later, Flanagan recalled seeing race judge Mr Little and the walking Shrubb shake hands, and overheard the former say: 'You are the greatest 15-mile runner that ever ran a race. You're beat in this marathon. Don't kill yourself. Give up like a man and the crowd will give you all honour.' Shrubb replied: 'I believe you're right' and in a rare show of emotion threw his arms around a helper's neck and choked a sob of bitter disappointment. Longboat finished alone with Madison Square Garden on its feet and in uproar. Flanagan recalled: 'Not a man there didn't praise Shrubb for his game effort. I'd called Shrubb up in the morning and told him Longboat would surely beat him and this helped a whole lot. There was nothing crooked. It was a true run race. Shrubb was badly advised to set such a clip early.'

While the Longboat camp celebrated loudly at trackside, a distressed Shrubb was carried bodily behind the scenes. His helpers became concerned about his condition and an ambulance was summoned, but physician Dr Henry Coggeshall appeared in the dressing room and took control from the panic-stricken aides. One pressman witnessed the scene: 'Shrubb was breathing strenuously and it was feared his heart had given way. He was put on a platform of boards and his legs lifted so that blood would be sent to his weakened stomach – at this he uttered a cry of mournful protest. His toes were shrivelled like shrimps and he shivered from hips to heels. After midnight he was taken to his hotel wracked of soul and body, beaten in a great and terrible contest, but still in the land of the living.'

The drama of Shrubb's slow and painful collapse, having led by such a huge margin, had made it a thrilling spectacle. Newspapers not just in North America but around the world gave the race major coverage. *The American* wrote: 'It was the old story of the hare and the tortoise, and the tortoise broke the hare's heart. Before a whooping, howling crowd of New York indians, Longboat won a great race from the gamest little man that ever laced a racing shoe. Shrubb had speed, and he had heart but he was playing an Englishman's game and the end was plain from 22 miles.' *The World* decided that 'A woman won this race – sagacious Flanagan led Longboat's wife to the trackside and she said encouraging words to her husband. The result was both physically and sensationally amazing. Longboat knew the smile of his little white wife and he began a desperate plod that wore his brilliant adversary down.'

The Times (London) reported: 'The most stirring and sensational long distance race in a long time and the [12,000] that filled every seat and all available standing room will look back in years to come at one of the great historic contests.' American and Canadian newspapers agreed: 'Shrubb beat himself by a series of spurts intended to run his opponent into the ground. The outcome would seem to prove that Shrubb, invincible for 10 or 15 miles, cannot run the longer route and adopt the same tactics' *(The Tribune)*. 'The power to jog along ceaselessly, that has been bred into the indian for centuries, prevailed' *(The Herald)*. 'The greatest distance runner ever produced in England was beaten in a race that had sensational features and grim, gruelling grit, perhaps never equalled on the cinder track *(Evening Journal)*. 'Shrubb's ambition was his undoing. Had he loafed along in the indian's wake he would have won' *(Evening World)*.

In the Canadian capital, Ottawa, thousands, including cabinet ministers and MPs had followed the progress of the race via bulletin boards,

most of them cheering for Longboat. In Toronto, supporters of both
men had gathered outside *The Telegram*'s offices and at the end crowds
streamed along the streets chanting Longboat's name. *The Telegram* took a
light-hearted view: 'Shrubb will now be botanized, his class will probably
be non-flowering, his order "crow's feet" and his genus "exit" or "has
been".'

Longboat's ex-manager Flanagan earned huge press credit for the victory – which seems unfair on Longboat in retrospect – and the Irishman
was borne shoulder-high by Torontonians after he travelled back from
New York. Presumably they were grateful for his gambling tips.
Longboat was unimpressed: 'Do you think Flanagan could make me run
if I didn't want to?' was his riposte. In the wake of the race Longboat settled down with new wife Lauretta and used his new riches to buy a three-
storey red brick house on Galley Avenue in West Toronto. He quit the
cigar shop he had run while under Flanagan's control.

For his part, Shrubb took his defeat with good grace, admitting only
that the vast amount of tobacco smoke that had built up in the arena had
had a serious effect on him. 'The newspapers had asked spectators to
refrain from smoking while the race lasted,' he recalled, 'but the
Americans are the heaviest smokers in the world and they smoke hardest
of all at their pleasures, lighting each successive cigar with the burning
end of its predecessor. I suppose Longboat and myself were the only two
men in the building that didn't smoke. The indian confessed to me after
the race that tobacco fumes were agreeable to him at any strength. With
me it was very different. As the race proceeded I became dazed and half
suffocated and in the end sickness bowled me over completely. I collapsed in the arms of my trainer, done to danger point, more than half
dead.'

It was later established that Shrubb had broken all existing records
within a marathon, up to 23 miles, but as he had not completed the
course these would not be recorded. Shrubb confirmed he took home a
cheque to the value of 3,400 dollars, similar to the amount won by
Longboat. He added: 'Before the race I met Harry Lauder, the prince of
Scottish comedians. He watched the race after his show at the
Hammerstein Theatre and every now and then I could hear the cheers of
bonny Scotland in that well known ringing voice: "Go on Alfie, you're the
boy for me!" Mr Lauder called to see me at the Empire Hotel on
Broadway the next day and said it was the smoke that beat me, not
Longboat. That was very kind of him, but I'm afraid Longboat had
most to do with it. Never in my running career was I so ill as after
that race. I lay gasping on my back for four hours with two doctors in

constant attendance. They told me afterwards I nearly pegged out. Next day however, I recovered and was able to write my name in hundreds of autograph books.'

This epic race launched a thousand imitators. Quality runners like Longboat, Hayes, Pietri and Simpson were now part of the scene. From Europe, Fred Appleby and Frenchman Henri St Yves were heading over to join the fun. Business was booming in 1909 for the top long-distance men. Their managers and promoters were delighted to cash in, and would stop at nothing to generate publicity. One particular episode in Montreal typified the 'hype' that would often accompany a forthcoming event. This took place while Longboat was still an amateur. Shrubb recalled:

'I'd slipped away to Montreal to see Longboat in a marathon called the Round the Mountain race. In Montreal that week my quest to meet Longboat made me the victim half willingly of an extravagant practical joke which almost ended in a riot. Longboat's [then] manager Flanagan hit upon a bold plan to excite public interest to the utmost in the Montreal marathon and I fell in with it, little imagining how far it would go. Of course, being a professional I was not eligible to run at Montreal, but Flanagan, through the columns of *The Montreal Star* solemnly stated that Shrubb was coming to town to interfere with the amateur marathon. As part of the plan I enlisted the help of *The Montreal Herald* to contradict these allegations as fast as he made them, in this way whipping up public interest to fever heat.

'Special editions of the *Star* came out with all sorts of vamped versions of the bogus controversy till I hardly felt safe to be seen in the streets. The English section of the community took my side and urged me [unsuccessfully] to meet the amateur requirements by running the race one hour after the other runners started, with the object of beating their times. After the race I strolled into a hotel by arrangement with Flanagan and, to his friends' astonishment, he winked at me and then slapped my face in well-feigned rage. I had to take it all in good part, even when the incident was duly reported and exaggerated in the papers. The upshot of this was that before I left, the assurance was given that I would soon have the pleasure of running Longboat as he was about to become professional. Some time later Flanagan called my attention to a cartoon framed and hung on the wall of his office, headed "Flanagan hits Shrubb in the interests of amateur sport". I told him that was going too far, so he promptly pasted two-cent stamps to cover my name – probably removing them again after I'd gone. To give Flanagan his due, he later publicly explained the practical joke in the *Star*, the paper in which he'd perpetrated it.'

During mid-February 1909 Shrubb's old adversary in his amateur days, Fred Appleby, arrived in New York from England to join the pro bandwagon. News also emerged that the success of the Madison Square Garden races had led to a Marathon Derby being fixed, with likely starters to include Shrubb, Longboat, Pietri, Appleby and Hayes. Other significant news was the smashing of the world two-hour record (using a bicycle pacemaker) by a relatively unknown Frenchman, twenty-year-old Henri St Yves, who worked as a chauffeur in London. St Yves had also won a marathon in Edinburgh on New Year's Day. He too was heading for New York.

In the meantime, a re-match between Shrubb and Longboat over fifteen miles had been arranged for Friday, February 26th at the Armouries in Buffalo, upstate New York. Before leaving his Toronto base, Shrubb did a deal with Yonge Street tailors Hobberlin Brothers that saw him provided with a suit and overcoat – in return for endorsements. An advert appeared in *The Toronto Telegram* showing Shrubb wearing their Paletot spring overcoat, with the caption: 'The suit and overcoat made for me by your firm is entirely satisfactory in every way, the fit is perfect.'

Three days before the Buffalo re-match, Longboat mysteriously withdrew. A furious Shrubb wrote to various newspapers urging them to print an appeal, offering all manner of concessions in a bid to get him to turn up. Shrubb was even willing to take a cut in his fee. His efforts failed, however, and the ever-willing Dorando Pietri was hurriedly called upon to take Longboat's place. One paper reported that Longboat had been about to catch his train to Buffalo, but after a long chat with one of the promoters, Charlie Murray, had changed his mind. 'It seems his wife is playing a significant part in his decision making these days and although Longboat is keen for all the money he can earn, he does not like running indoors and has decided to take a rest.' Longboat was also undergoing a managerial upheaval and it emerged that Sol Mintz had taken over from Pat Powers, advising the runner to rest and prepare for the Marathon Derby in April.

The Shrubb-Pietri fifteen-miler at Buffalo was another thriller, described as 'one of the greatest races ever seen in America'. Shrubb looked happy at the start and commented on the excellent state of the track and the fact that the arena was free of tobacco smoke. The first mile was fast and little Pietri stuck close to Shrubb, both runners injecting unexpected mid-race surges. At one point Pietri slowed and complained of feeling sick, but hung on gamely. In the ninth mile he picked up his pace and fortified himself with a goblet of wine offered by his brother at trackside. This stop for his beloved Chianti amused the crowd but cost him forty yards. The wine appeared to have done more harm than good as he lost ground over the next two miles.

Shrubb forged a three-lap lead but Pietri kept going to the bitter end and the outcome was not certain until the final few hundred yards. Shrubb, for some reason not wearing his usual kit with the large Union Jack motif, came home in one hour 24:07 (having passed five miles in 26:43 and ten in 54:50). Pietri came in 84 seconds adrift. At one point Pietri's brother and his trainer Murphy appealed to the race referee Francis Nelson Smith on the grounds that Shrubb had run too close to their man and thus interfered with the swing of his arms, but no action was taken. Flanagan, again reporting the race for *The Toronto Telegram*, confirmed Shrubb had done this in a bid to worry the Italian. He added that it had been a great race, which should do the sport a power of good. A good crowd had roared itself hoarse and the race netted promoters and runners a tidy sum, he added.

As part of the Buffalo event, Shrubb and Pietri were invited by a businessman called Mackay to visit his department store – Sweeney's – in the city centre, to greet customers and dine with store managers. After being presented with gifts, the two runners were asked to perch on a podium by the entrance, where they remained for two hours, shaking hands with shoppers. Shrubb recalled: 'We did as we were asked, but wished halfway through that Mr Mackay had suggested a race around the store instead! Long-distance hand-shaking is hard work. Some of the men gripped so firmly that Pietri and I had to cry out … it's no light matter being a tin god at Sweeney's stores.'

On the same day, Pat Powers reportedly visited the athletics authorities in Ottawa to establish his rights as Longboat's manager. He threatened legal action against anyone who tried to obtain Longboat's services. Later, in March, Montreal marathoner Abbie Wood announced he was turning pro and would be part of a relay team taking on Shrubb. This fixture fell through when the other runners failed to agree a deal.

The shenanigans over Longboat's management raised doubts over his future, but he paid Shrubb a visit in Toronto to apologise for dropping out of the Buffalo race. He promised Shrubb another meeting at fifteen miles and signed an informal agreement to this end. Shrubb was sympathetic about Longboat's off-track difficulties, and even passed on some training tips to the younger man. Longboat was finding training difficult at that time as Toronto's roads were in a poor state after a hard winter.

On Saturday, March 20th, Shrubb had a date to run Fred Simpson, the Hiawatha Ojibway tribesman, over twelve miles in Toronto. The 28-year-old Simpson, from a reserve near Peterborough, Ontario, was five inches taller and twenty pounds heavier than Shrubb and held the world indoor record for ten miles – 56:31 at Buffalo, set in February. However, he was outclassed in this race and Shrubb won by the better part of a mile, causing the press to drool over his performance. Shrubb was compared variously to a hawk, a greyhound and a gazelle who had looked 'perfection in flight'. Simpson had been made to look heavy and resembled an athlete running at a distance greater than he liked. He had recently gone down with a heavy cold, too. Shrubb's winning time of one hour 6:33 featured some wild fluctuations. His ninth mile was a pedestrian 6:06, his tenth a smarter 5:13 and then his eleventh a simple jog at only 7:19. Perhaps he was just showing the watching Longboat that when on top form he could run as he pleased and still win easily.

By now, the line-up had been finalised for the race billed as the greatest professional marathon in history – six men from five nations battling it out in the Marathon Derby at New York's Polo Grounds on Saturday, April 3rd. Shrubb recalled that he entered 'reluctantly' but found the financial rewards too good to turn down. He would be up against Longboat, Pietri, Hayes, St Yves and a newly emerged young American, Matt Maloney. The air was thick with talk of bets and gambling odds. Flanagan wrote in *The Telegram* that Shrubb might win if he used his head, and then joked that the perimeter fence was 35 feet high so Shrubb would not be able to pay him back for that remark by throwing him over it.

Shrubb undertook 'severe training' as he prepared for a race that he did not really want. 'I had always looked forward to years of usefulness when my running days were over – [regular] marathons would have killed me,' he reflected in later years. A huge 5,000 dollar purse was waiting for the winner and 2,500 for the runner-up. After witnessing Shrubb's collapse in New York, most punters favoured Longboat or Pietri. The Frenchman, St Yves, was unfancied and his odds went out as far as 40-1.

The bubbly Pietri had no problem with the pressure of being joint-favourite. Standing just 5ft 3in and hailing from the island of Capri, he was a gutsy runner who had bottles of Chianti standing by for when the going got tough. He had become pally with Shrubb and loved the English generally, never forgetting the ovation he had received in Britain after his heroic 1908 Olympic marathon effort. Queen Alexandra had recognised his bravery that day with a special trophy to compensate for his unlucky disqualification. In later years, after his running days were over, Pietri would settle in Birmingham where he ran a café until after the 1939-45 War. His Olympic efforts inspired a young Tin Pan Alley hack called Izzy Baline to publish his first song ('Dorando') in tribute. The songwriter went on to greater things after changing his name to Irving Berlin.

Despite glowering skies and drizzle, a crowd estimated at between 25,000 and 40,000 'jammed the bleachers to suffocation' for the Marathon Derby. 'Big Tim' Sullivan was again official starter. Longboat opened on Wall Street the day before the race at odds of 12-5 and then closed as 3-2 favourite. Shrubb said he would try his utmost, but tipped Pietri to win. He also tetchily said he was fed up of Fred Appleby crowing about beating him over fifteen miles in the past, and suggested that if Appleby meant business he should put up a thousand dollar deposit as a show of good faith and he would get a race.

The Marathon Derby was a unique race and it got underway to an almost unique start: One runner surged straight to the front, but it was not Shrubb. Frenchman St Yves who, along with Maloney was a rank outsider, cut loose and opened a sixty-yard lead. It was the first time anyone had ever led Shrubb throughout the first mile of a distance race. Attempting to run conservatively, after recent events, Shrubb was clearly anxious about letting St Yves get too far away, and after two miles made a bid to close the gap, dragging Longboat and Pietri with him. Shrubb appeared unhappy at the slow pace and in the fifth mile sailed past the Frenchman. In the sixth mile Shrubb tried to run his opponent into the ground but failed to do so. Bandy-legged, short and stocky, St Yves spun along impressively, if not gracefully. Like Pietri, he was said to refresh himself during training with a drop of wine, preferring light French varieties to Pietri's Chianti.

St Yves re-established his lead towards halfway and Shrubb recalled leaning across to ask Longboat and Pietri: 'What about this fellow, are you going after him or not? They both replied in the negative as if they thought St Yves would oblige by coming back to them.' So Shrubb took on the task alone. The crowd roared as he gave chase. 'My effort put new life in the race, which had become a rather dull affair.' Shrubb took the lead and tried unsuccessfully to ease away from the Frenchman. In the sixteenth mile, St Yves made another bold attempt to shake off Shrubb. Further back, Longboat looked exhausted and lost more ground when stopping to change his shoes. Shrubb led by a whisker at the seventeen-mile point in one hour 38:39, with Pietri two laps behind the leading pair. Longboat was a further four laps down and Maloney and Hayes further back at the rear.

In the eighteenth mile, St Yves made another determined burst and this time Shrubb fell back, looking rather distressed. In the space of four laps the Frenchman stretched half a lap ahead and looked like he had the race in hand. In the twentieth mile a further burst saw Shrubb lapped, with Longboat closing, a mile behind. The Frenchman looked good as he hit twenty miles in one hour 57:24. Dorando pulled back a lap on the struggling Shrubb, who stopped briefly to walk in the 22nd mile, and then dropped out completely in the twenty-fourth.

Shrubb explained later: 'I stopped running, convinced now, for good, that the marathon distance didn't suit me. It is always true of runners that they have their lengths, beyond which it is hopeless and even dangerous to go.' He earned a great ovation from the crowd and was warmly greeted by promoter Powers, pleased with his contribution. Shrubb himself had a guaranteed pay-out coming his way and his dropping out didn't affect that. It had now became a race for second place behind St Yves. Hayes had begun to make ground on the tiring Pietri, with Longboat – wearing spikes for the first time – having quit the race. St Yves breasted the tape five laps ahead of Dorando in two hours 40:50, with the Italian a lap ahead of Hayes and Maloney fourth. Shrubb said afterwards his main aim had been to beat or last longer than Longboat, which he had achieved.

'Waterloo is avenged, Shrubb is drubbed' cried the headlines in Monday's papers. *The Toronto Telegram* included a list of witty quips, some of them politically incorrect by modern standards: 'Dorando, Dorando, shrieked the streets on Saturday, and then the dago slipped on a banana skin; Longboat fell like a piece of toast on its buttered side; France's ancient greatness has returned – St Yves broke the record Napoleon made at Waterloo; Johnny Hayes remarked that everything comes to he who waits, but Hayes waited in vain – had the others all dropped dead he might have been successful; The only good Indian is a dead one, goes the old phrase, and our esteemed fellow countryman appears to have qualified for a pair of wings!'

Some observers suggested a fix, noting that St Yves had won at such long odds, but no convincing evidence was produced. *The Toronto Daily Star* correspondent Lou Marsh, a central figure in the pro running world, was emphatic: 'Get this into your head, Longboat lost fairly. [Promoter] Pat Powers is on the level. That is his reputation from New York to Chicago. The Marathon Derby was won and lost on its merits. Longboat did not lie down.'

It was Shrubb's second and last marathon. Years later he would reflect: 'The marathon is too long for the human runner. Those who do the distance generally finish in a state of total collapse. Athletics was never meant to shorten man's days. The marathon mastered me and I am not sorry. It is also the ruination of young athletes. Putting a boy of 19 or 20 in such long contests means taking about five years off his career as a shorter distance man. Marathon running is only meant for a man who is winding up his career In his last two years, when he may be at the age of 31-35, he is much stronger and better able to take the strain.'

One spectator at the Marathon Derby that afternoon, who had never before seen Shrubb lose, was his father-in-law from England, John Brown. The point of Brown's visit, presumably, had been to escort Shrubb's wife and son from Liverpool to New York. The family was about to make their home in Toronto, where Shrubb planned to build a house.

In the wake of the Marathon Derby, St Yves' manager, Al Copeland, convinced his man that he could beat Shrubb over fifteen miles too, and Shrubb was happy to accept the challenge, scheduled for Saturday, April 24th. The race started after 9pm in the open air at New York Baseball Grounds at Hilltop, floodlit by huge acetylene lamps, and watched by a enthusiastic crowd of 10,000. Shrubb shot into the lead on the glistening grass track, gained two laps in the first five miles and ran superbly throughout. His tactics were crystal clear – he wanted a huge lead over the first ten miles, and would then have time in hand in the last third of the race, when the Frenchman would be stronger. Revenge tasted sweet and he finished with an emphatic solo sprint 200 yards from home, even though he had won by a third of a mile.

Shrubb's time of one hour 26:12 was said to be an American record, but was well adrift of the world best. The crowd had roared its approval at Shrubb's closing sprint and many broke through the barricades to mob him. To everyone's astonishment, the Englishman did not appear at all exhausted, and seeing the advancing hordes, turned on his heel and sprinted 200 yards to the clubhouse – none of his pursuers coming even close to catching him.

CHAPTER SEVENTEEN

Unhappy Scenes at Happyland

Shrubb made Toronto his home in 1909, wife Ada and toddler Roy joining him, the family subsequently having a house built to Shrubb's specifications. He was able to supervise and contribute to the construction work himself, using the skills in carpentry and brick-laying he had acquired as a younger man.

Toronto had a high level of home ownership, thanks to a housing boom that lasted nearly twenty years from the 1890s. Shrubb was proud to build his own home in this clean and well-lit city, where he had become a well-known and popular figure. And, in those early years as an immigrant, his sporting fame helped him develop a number of useful contacts within the Toronto business community, notably the wealthy property magnate and former butcher, Thomas Foster.

Later to become mayor of the city, the ebullient Foster enjoyed Shrubb's company to such an extent that in his will he bequeathed funds to aid local athletics. Foster was something of a maverick, sponsoring offbeat projects, such as rewarding the local woman who had the most children over a ten-year period. His reputation for the unexpected followed him to his grave, for among other things his will also provided funds to feed Toronto's birds in winter, and to improve the lot of the city's newsboys.

Shrubb made other friends in high places, occasionally finding himself awarded non-executive posts, such as a vice-presidency of the Dominion Trunk and Leather Goods Company, who had a store on the corner of Ashdale Avenue and Gerrard Street. He allowed his name to be used for advertising all manner of products, from menswear to foodstuffs. In one newspaper ad for Bovril, for example, he was mistakenly identified as 'Arthur Shrubb' and quoted thus: 'Start on Bovril at once, it is the best preparation you will find for record-breaking.'

He was now 29 and although still arguably the best distance runner in the world, up to a limit of ten miles, was beginning to plan ahead for when his running days were over. He tried to exploit Canada's reputation as a land of enterprise and opportunity. He certainly was not the only one, however, for emigration from Britain around this time reached record levels – almost 500,000 a year were leaving Britain – and well over half this number headed for dominions of the British Empire, as Shrubb had done.

Back in Shrubb's home-town, Horsham, the locals turned out in numbers for presentations such as that at the Albion Hall, which promoted Canada as a fine place to settle. The audience was informed that the Canadian Government would provide free land to any young man over the age of eighteen prepared to pay a £2 registration fee, build a house worth £60 and then cultivate the land commercially. The idea appealed to many, for in 1910 a total of 125,000 Britons headed for a new life in Canada.

Shrubb dabbled in a number of enterprises around this time, including the 1909 publication of his second book – a revamped version of his earlier coaching manual, aimed this time at the Canadian market. *Long-Distance Running* was published by the Imperial News Company of Toronto and did a brisk trade. Instead of J Murray's word sketch, which graced the 1908 London edition, this time Shrubb's ex-South London Harriers mentor Thomas Sinnott penned an introductory chapter. Like Murray, Sinnott found it necessary to paint a picture of Shrubb's physical appearance: 'He is a slim-built, slight and light little fellow. It must not be supposed, however, that Alfred Shrubb is a mere midget. He is neither a Sandow giant in stature nor a Daniel Lambert in build, but he is a mass of whipcord and muscle, stands 5ft 6ins in height and weighs ordinarily when stripped 126lbs. For the benefit of sentimental maidens who may be in danger of losing their hearts to this attractive all-conquering athlete, it may be as well to state that … Mr Shrubb took to himself a wife.'

Notwithstanding the success of some of his off-track ventures, Shrubb still believed there was plenty of running left in those 'whipcord' legs. He was particularly keen to establish superiority over Tom Longboat, the man who had reduced him to a quivering wreck at the Madison Square Garden marathon. On Saturday May 8th, 1909, the pair duelled over fifteen miles in Montreal. Shrubb recalled the occasion:

'For 14 miles Longboat lay labouring hard behind me and I was genuinely surprised, though not really alarmed, at the plucky effort he made to catch me in the last mile. He displayed wonderful speed and stamina. I led by two laps and less than three-quarters of a lap divided us by the finish. I remember Longboat's supporters going into transports as he shot past me in a sudden spurt. The crowd apparently thought he was bent on recovering the laps he had lost and I [could] see his manager running alongside the track regaling him with soda water. With five laps to go, the indian was running faster than at any time in the race. I kept my eyes on him. They signalled three laps to go, and, with victory in sight, I was determined to keep it in my grasp. Pulling myself together and clenching my teeth, I shot away in a fresh burst of speed and Longboat must have known that his great effort had failed – a galling situation when a man has been fast making up ground. I crossed the line an exhausted winner [in one hour 26:08]. Longboat and I never did more than exchange the usual congratulations. The indian was a silent man, without being sullen.'

Seven weeks later the pair raced again over twenty miles at Hanlan's Point stadium in Toronto Bay, on the 600-acre Centre Island. Shrubb built a big lead and lapped Longboat once, but after beginning to fade the Englishman dropped out at the fifteen-mile point. A record 12,000 crowd, including thousands of Brits waving Union Jacks, filled a ground normally home to the Maple Leafs baseball team and named after legendary oarsman Ned Hanlan. Within weeks, fire destroyed the stadium, but it was quickly rebuilt in concrete, with an increased 18,000 capacity.

Not long afterwards, at the Arena Rink in Winnipeg, Longboat and Shrubb renewed acquaintances over sixteen miles and Shrubb won by three laps. It was the same old story, with Shrubb constructing a lead and surging occasionally mid-race, Longboat preferring to plug away at the same pace in the hope Shrubb would come back to him. This time the Indian's ploy failed.

Shrubb continued racing as often as possible as his thirtieth birthday loomed in December 1909. The pro running 'boom' that had gathered momentum with the 1908-09 New York marathon series continued to thrive. Shrubb was still luring packed houses and big fees wherever he ran. He often had to tolerate unruly crowds invading the track and swamp the finish-line after races. But if he thought he had seen everything during his years as a globe-trotting sportsman, he was to be proved wrong. One race – on August 10th, 1909 in Winnipeg – turned into a nightmare that would remain indelibly stamped on his memory.

The occasion was a ten-miler between Shrubb and the Edmonton-based Irishman J F Fitzgerald to be staged at an amusement park called Happyland. Next to the Assiniboine River, the park was a thirteen-hectare site with a central baseball diamond, around which the runners would travel. Rarely can a stadium have had a more inappropriate name than Happyland on that particular night. *The Manitoba Free Press* reported that 'trouble could be felt in the air' at 9pm on race-night, for by then a 2,000-plus crowd was in place, yet Happyland was still in complete darkness and there were no signs of the race starting. The lights would not work because following a local industrial dispute the management had been unable to secure the services of a qualified electrician. The makeshift arrangements had failed at the crucial moment. It emerged later that some of the militant electricians had attended the ground with the objective of sabotaging the lighting anyway, so the event never really stood a chance.

The crowd did not know why they were standing in darkness and became increasingly restless. *The Free Press* reported that venue manager Ernest S Harrison was conspicuous 'in his suit of white duck' and every time he strolled across the ground he provoked jeers and hisses from the bleachers (wooden terracing). Frantic efforts were made to get the lights working and just before 10pm a couple of them spluttered into life, to loud cheers, although one remained very dim. It was announced that if a third could be lit, the race could go ahead. By now, some spectators had given up hope and left for home. Manager Harrison dashed around assuring the two runners and officials that everything would be ready within a few minutes.

Then, suddenly, the two working lights gave a loud 'pop', went out, and sparked mayhem. What can only be described as a riot ensued. Bleachers were pulled out, wire netting torn down and a fire started with the debris. Chairs intended for officials' use were tossed onto the blaze and before long, reported *The Free Press*, the flames were leaping into the sky higher than the grandstand: 'Nobody attempted to hinder the crowd in its work of destruction except a Happyland employee who attached a small rubber hose to a tap in the dressing room. When he reached the fire, however, he found the hose had been cut and the crowd howled in derision. The same man then began carrying pails of water but after he'd thrown the second one on the fire he was set upon by the crowd and kicked and cuffed so much that he did not return.'

Not surprisingly, the two runners – who had been standing around in their running kit – decided to beat a hasty retreat. Shrubb recalls: 'Seeing that the dressing room was going to go too [at the hands of the mob], and it being a very cool evening, we decided the sooner we got our clothes out the better it would be, or we should have to go home without any.' They hurriedly retrieved their clothing and changed on the damp grass. Shrubb then bravely went among the baying masses in an attempt to pacify them. Climbing onto the bandstand and attempting to shout above the racket, he declared that he, Fitzgerald and the local newspapers would see to it that those who had paid would get proper redress. He guaranteed the race would be staged on a new date very soon, and that everybody would all be allowed in free of charge.

Shrubb's words seemed to pacify those within earshot, and for a while it appeared the worst was over. Suddenly, however, flames licked up from under the front row of the bleachers, and had the area not been damp, the entire grandstand would surely have been consumed. This second fire had been blazing for around fifteen minutes when a fire crew and police arrived in numbers. The first fire was quickly extinguished but the crew's hose could not properly reach the second. They had to deal with it by chopping away the blazing section to separate it. 'The crowd stood looking on, groaning and grunting at every blow, but not offering to interfere,' said *The Free Press*.

Once both fires were out and darkness had descended, the rioters resumed, tearing down the park gates and vandalising booths and buildings. They attacked a peanut and cigar booth, whose occupant looked terrified, and its contents were either looted or scattered and trampled. *The Free Press* continued: 'By this time police had arrived and several people felt the weight of the officers "billies" but no-one was seriously hurt.' The main offices were ransacked and windows smashed. The ring-leaders seemed intent on getting their hands on Harrison to demand their money back. There was a dramatic moment when a young woman carrying a cashbox suddenly emerged from the office and was engulfed by the mob. She had presumably banked on the fact that nobody would dare attack a woman, and she was right. The crowd parted like the Red Sea before Moses, and she headed towards the rifle range, no one attempting to molest her.

It emerged later that the cashbox only contained a few dollars, as the gate money had been in the office safe all the time. After this, the crowd's ardour cooled and the young woman received a few cheers before they dispersed from the rifle range, encouraged by the policemen swinging their 'billies'. The trouble wasn't over, however, for a cry of 'free beer' saw the mob turn their frenzy on the refreshment booth. Suddenly the nozzle of a fire hose loomed out of the darkness and a jet of water blasted the ringleaders. *The Free Press* observed: 'Some women in the area, with their escorts, were drinking lemonade at the time and were among those who got a thorough drenching.'

The mob tried to sever the hose and the water momentarily stopped. Thinking they had successfully stemmed the flow, the rioters swarmed around the refreshment booth, only for another jet to douse them. This fuelled their anger even more, and they began toppling lamp standards and ticket booths. A group tried to overturn an obelisk inside the main gates, but it proved too heavy and they had to be content with smashing a sign-board attached to it. By 11pm police reinforcements arrived, at which the crowd slowly dispersed. Mr Harrison was nowhere to be seen, and it was presumed he had left as soon as the trouble flared, fleeing to the safety of his farm beyond Deer Lodge, west of the city in the Headingly area. Amazingly, no arrests were made, mainly due to the lack

of police in the early stages. The damage to Happyland property amounted to many hundreds of dollars.

The two runners jointly wrote to *The Free Press*, pledging to run, with
no admission charge, as soon as possible. The gate money, thought to
have been spirited away when the manager fled, was located in the company safe, which meant the runners could be paid. It was agreed the race
would go ahead later in the week and be free to the public. Work on the
lights would be carried out. Shrubb informed a correspondent:
'Fitzgerald and myself regret very much that the people should be treated in the manner they were last night. We did all in our power to get the
tickets given back but it was utterly impossible as the manager had disappeared. The whole cause of the trouble was through the lights not being
fixed at the proper time. The management were warned time and again
to fix the lights so that they could be tested in good time but they were
not … in my whole racing career of 12 years I have never met with a misfortune like this.'

The race was re-run on August 12th under lights and Shrubb won by
nearly three laps. Dick Roche gave the start signal and Shrubb flew off
and was never headed (his split times were 4:41, 9:57, 15:17, 20:46, 26:21,
31:58, 37:19, 42:57, 48:00 and 54:02). Encouraged by free admission, the
crowd was even bigger than before, and this time a huge police presence
kept a close eye on proceedings. The only moment of concern came
when spectators invaded the field at the end of a baseball game which
preceded the race.

These events were just the latest in a series of troubled episodes at the
three-year-old Happyland. The park had recently been declared bankrupt
and was sold cheaply to new owners, and earlier still a storm had wreaked
havoc on the site, allowing a circus elephant and lion to escape into the
city.

Shrubb remained in Winnipeg a further week to fulfil another hastily
arranged engagement involving Fitzgerald and himself in a three-cornered twelve-mile contest with the Indian Paul Acoose. Much was made
of the fact that the twelve-mile world record was one of the very few to
escape Shrubb, and he confirmed he would have a crack at Sid Thomas's
62:23 mark, set many years earlier at Herne Hill, London. Shrubb said he
was well pleased with the Winnipeg track and felt fit for the attempt on
the evening of Monday, August 16th. *The Free Press* reported that Acoose
'had merely grunted his appreciation at being offered the race'. They said
he and Fitzgerald had struck a side bet over which of the pair would finish furthest ahead – suggesting they had already accepted Shrubb would
be the overall winner. It was announced that a Pitner gasoline system

would be used to light the track in a bid to avoid the farcical scenes of a week earlier.

Instead of breaking the world record, the night proved little short of disastrous for Shrubb. He pulled up just before halfway due to a severe muscle pain in his right leg, which signalled the start of long-term injury troubles which would plague him well into 1910. Earlier in the race Shrubb had entertained the 5,000 crowd with a series of powerful spurts, following a rapid first mile of 4:37. He had passed the five-mile point in 25:53 with a handsome lead but after a further lap suddenly slowed to a walk and stopped in front of the main stand for an attendant to give his leg a rubdown. He looked uneasy and after staggering around the track for another lap he quit altogether. Acoose chose this point to shoot away from Fitzgerald and was never under pressure, going on to win in 68:12, a full lap clear of the Irishman. A grim-faced Shrubb told the press the injury was a nasty one to a tendon, and he would have to cancel a list of forthcoming engagements between Winnipeg and the coast, and several in Vancouver and Seattle, too. 'It looks to be a case of those 25,000 dollar legs having been overworked in the last six to eight months,' commented *The Free Press*.

It was the last time that track fans saw Shrubb in action for a while, but the result boosted the profile of Acoose, who had only turned professional a few months earlier. Born and raised in the village of Grenfell in Saskatchewan's Qu'Appelle Valley, Acoose was a Saulteaux Indian. His father Samuel and his grandfather Qwewitch lived to reach 102 and 105 respectively, and were both legendary runners. By the time of Paul's birth, Indians had been brought under one central administration in Canada and federal policy amounted to 'protection' under the reservation system. Unlike the Ontario Onondagan Longboat, who hated white schooling and religions, Acoose became a devout Roman Catholic. He spent enough of his youth on the Sakimay reserve running with his relatives to develop into a fine athlete, covering vast stretches of open prairie with apparent ease.

Immigration policies of the 1890s and 1900s resulted in tremendous growth in organised sport in Saskatchewan, and Paul Acoose and others caught the tail end of the marathon mania. He turned professional in 1909 after persuasion from promoter Francis Nelson Smith, an associate of Shrubb's. Acoose's pro debut saw him defeat Englishman Fred Appleby in a fifteen-mile race for 500 dollars in a world best time of one hour 22:22. 'He only shakes his head and grunts when asked if he is fit – [his manager] Merrifield does the talking for him,' commented *The Free Press*. Appleby said it was the best race he had been in since his fifteen-mile duel with Shrubb back in 1902. A week later in a re-match with Appleby, Acoose was scandalously defeated by a gambling enthusiast and Appleby supporter, who threw tin-tacks on the track which pierced his moccasins. Appleby and his thickly soled shoes romped to victory.

West Canadians had waited two years for an Acoose-versus-Longboat race, but with both runners preparing Longboat fell ill and pulled out. It would be another three weeks before the so-called 'Redskin Running Championship of the World' took place at Riverdale, a neighbourhood of Toronto. It turned into an anticlimax with Acoose winning the twelve-miler after Longboat dropped out in the tenth mile. Shortly afterwards, Acoose announced he was tired of racing and ready to quit. He had beaten Longboat and now the saskatoons were in bloom and it was time to go home. His professional running career ended with only 500 dollars in the bank, but his mind was made up. He turned to farming, pow-wow celebrations, and service to the community as a councillor. He died in 1978.

Fulfilling his coaching obligations at Harvard University meant Shrubb spent long periods in Boston, far from his Toronto home. During one of these stints in Massachusetts, two friends – William Hammond and Tom Steer – invited him for a day's fishing aboard the pleasure steamer *Mayflower*. Shrubb recalled: 'I have travelled the great oceans many times on the great liners, but after getting 14 miles out on the open water, I began to find I wasn't on a big liner now, for when the boat came to a standstill for the members to throw in their lines, my breakfast began to move on me. But, pulling myself together, and trying to show that I was a real fisherman, I went to the rail and threw out my line the same as the rest, waiting patiently and wishing every moment that fish would catch hold, for it was only a matter of time before I would have to leave in a big hurry.'

Feeling nauseous, Shrubb sprinted for the cabins and stretched out on a bunk, trying to ignore the ship's pitching and rolling. After fifteen minutes his friends found him, reporting a fish on his line, but Shrubb wisely stayed put and asked for something to eat to settle his stomach. His mischievous pals told him the best cure for seasickness was cheese and pickled onions, which he duly ordered and consumed. The food did little good, for he remained firmly indoors for the rest of the trip.

Shrubb pulled on his trusty Foster's spikes on October 25th, 1909 in Kenilworth Park, Buffalo, NY, to take on three runners in a five-miler. Native Canadian Bill Davis, Billy Allen and Jimmy Moynihan of Buffalo were no match for the Englishman, after his first mile of 4:42.8 had left them trailing in his wake. He won in a modest 26:10.6, relieved he had not had to put his tender leg muscle under too much pressure. By early 1910, Shrubb had passed thirty and his body was showing the inevitable signs of wear and tear. His leg continued to trouble him for weeks and reduced his racing considerably. 'Rest works wonders with a crocked leg and it was not long before I was going again as well as ever,' he said later.

During his inactivity he heard news from England that King Edward VII had died after a bout of bronchitis. This was in May of 1910 and Shrubb spent most of that summer in Toronto, unable to compete, but looking forward to returning to Boston in the autumn to continue coaching at Harvard. He arrived back at the university on September 2nd to finalise arrangements with graduate manager W F Garcelon to take charge of the 'crimson cross-country lads' on October 1st. It was agreed that Shrubb would take charge of the team until the inter-collegiate championships in November.

Shrubb's debut as Harvard coach had been back in 1908, when he steered the team to victory in the inter-collegiates, ahead of Massachusetts Institute of Technology (MIT), and his re-appointment for the new 1910 season attracted plenty of publicity. One English paper wrote: 'The good work which Shrubb did for the Harvard team means that professional coaching, by a man who thoroughly knows his game and has the ability to impart the knowledge he possesses, is the right thing in the right place. No man alive knows more about distance running or the hill and dale sport than Shrubb.' Later, Shrubb penned a column for the university's magazine and in one edition he stated: 'Harvard has one of the best men in the country today in the shape of captain, Herbert Jaques. Harvard turned out 28 starters at the start of the year's gatherings and after only one week had just 17 left. Now I feel we should have at least 50 all season. Cornel [University] turned out 250 this year. My advice for the future is to arrange as many inter-team races as possible at a distance of about four miles.'

The following year, 1911, saw Shrubb competing regularly again. Shortly before the June coronation of George V he flew the flag for Britain with a fine win over twelve miles against the Swede Gusta Ljunstrom and Frenchman Henri St Yves. On a tiny thirteen-lap-to-the-mile track, he came home comfortably ahead of Ljunstrom with St Yves well beaten. Later that month Shrubb was beaten by 25 yards in a thrilling ten-miler by American Billy Queal, who clocked 52:15.

Shrubb was still unaccustomed to defeat, particularly at ten miles, and vowed to make amends when he lined up for a twelve-miler in the pretty Northern Ontario hilltop town of Haileybury, on the eastern shores of Lake Timiskaming. Local historian Brian Dobbs recalled: 'The wealth that existed in the town at the time brought some of the best sporting events money could buy. One such memorable contest took place on August 19, 1911 at Farr Park, the oval race track named in honour of the town's founder C C Farr.' The prospect of four of the world's top runners in humble Haileybury, hoping to capture a 1,000 dollars winner-take-all prize, thrilled the townspeople. Shrubb lined up alongside Longboat, South African Charlie Hefferon, and Abbie Wood, the Montreal-based Englishman. Wood was proving to be a major talent at this distance and had the sort of finishing kick that must have worried the other three.

The quartet, arriving separately, checked into the Vendome Hotel, Longboat full of confidence after a recent win over Shrubb at Hanlan's Point, Toronto. Hefferon, complaining of strained stomach muscles, headed for his room and did not reappear until just before the event. He needed extensive treatment from local physician Dr Gordon Jackson. Shrubb and Wood emerged on the Friday for a training spin, but found the oval track in poor shape after recent rain. Shrubb admitted his legs were not what they used to be and the sticky clay would have an effect on the race. Typically, Longboat chose not to train that day, remaining in the town and reminding locals of his easy victory the previous year in a race around nearby Cobalt's Long Lake. Back at the Vendome, a *Cobalt Daily Nugget* reporter landed an interview with Hefferon, who assured him: 'If the indian wins, it will be the fastest 12 miles he ever stepped.'

The crowd began filling the grandstand at Farr Park's south end, while staff of the Haileybury Turf Club, organisers of the event, completed their work on the track. Following a series of afternoon races for local runners, the 1,800 crowd greeted the start of the 5pm main event with loud cheers. Mayor Green welcomed the four runners, beckoned them to the start line and fired the pistol. Shrubb completed the first mile narrowly ahead in 4:59 and over the first five miles little more than ten feet separated the quartet. Shrubb faded, allowing Hefferon a spell at the front; then Shrubb regained his lead but gave way to Wood in the fourth mile. Longboat was happy to conserve energy, and hung back.

Hefferon, troubled by his stomach injury, quit at halfway. Wood lengthened his stride and pulled 100 yards clear of Shrubb who was bothered by his leg in the seventh mile and saw Longboat ease past him. Within a short while Shrubb had called it a day. Wood completed the final mile with a Shrubb-style sprint to finish in 65:45, Longboat labouring in a long way behind. Historian Dobbs points out that although some locals criticised the event, saying runners like these 'ran a racket' from town to town, the fact that sporting champions had set feet on Haileybury soil delighted the majority.

Shrubb and Longboat enjoyed some fascinating battles over the three-year period 1909-12, but perhaps the best was the thriller on America's Labor Day, Monday September 4th, 1911, at Oak Island Grove, Revere, in the Progressive AC Games. Shrubb called this the toughest ten-miler of his career. 'I beat the indian by the hair-line margin of two-fifths of a second – about a couple of strides. The [8,000] spectators whipped themselves into a delirium as we passed and re-passed each other up to the end of the ninth mile. Then I took the lead and held on to it as if for dear life.' Shrubb had overcome difficulties in the third mile, when he'd limped for a spell due to what he called 'a kink in the cords of my right knee', the area that had given him serious problems the previous year.

Sportswriters called it the narrowest victory margin ever achieved in a high-profile ten-mile race. The crowd swarmed over the track at the end, carrying Shrubb off shoulder high. (For a breakdown of the mile splits, see Appendix.) Arthur Duffey, the sprinter who had accompanied Shrubb to Australia, attended the race in his new role as a sportswriter at *The Boston Post*. He wrote that Britain still ruled the roost these days in distance races – noting that Boston's Frank Kanaly had gone there to study British training methods – but in all other athletics events he reckoned the Americans could teach the Brits a thing or two.

With Shrubb's powers on the wane, the younger Longboat enjoyed the most successful period of his colourful career. His three best seasons as a professional (1909-12) earned him an estimated 17,000 dollars, a lifetime's earnings in many jobs of the day. Promoters and handlers took a hefty chunk, but Longboat retained enough to spend freely on family and friends, dress expensively, entertain, and buy a house for his mother. Unlike Shrubb, he lacked business acumen and did not worry too much about the future. When his fortune slowly slipped away he simply sought the old lifestyle he once had.

The newly built Hanlan's Point on Toronto Island was proving a popular venue among runners and sports fans alike, and on one summer's evening a huge crowd saw Shrubb, Longboat, South African Charles Hefferon and the young Briton, Abbie Wood, try to live up to their billing as 'the fastest quartet alive'. Although probably pre-arranged, they each took turns to lead this twelve-mile race, but Longboat had one of his finest runs and stormed home to win in 62:32. It was one of the last occasions Shrubb and Longboat met on a running track. According to Vernon Bale, writing many years later in *World Sport* magazine, Shrubb won the balance of their duels, chalking up at least seven victories in races between ten and sixteen miles, while Longboat was stronger at twenty miles or more.

Publicity surrounding Shrubb's lingering injury generally meant he was no longer expected to win everything he entered. Indeed, he must have accepted that 1912 was the year when his running went into decline – for on business cards he had printed in later years, he described himself as 'world champion runner 1903-1912'.

Shrubb did not formally hang up his Foster's spikes just yet, however, even though races were becoming few and far between. In the early summer of 1912 the Stockholm Olympics saw the stunning emergence of the first of the great Finns, Hannes Kohlemainen. He won triple gold (5,000 and 10,000 metres track and 8,000 metres cross-country), recording times, some of which ought not to have troubled Shrubb in his 1904 pomp. Despite Kohlemainen's heroics, 1912 was seen as the year in which distance running's popularity took a dive. The subsequent 1914-18 War ensured it faded even further as a popular spectacle.

Some of his contemporaries would quickly become forgotten heroes, but in Shrubb's case, his public profile remained high, particularly when his name featured in two works of fiction that would later be regarded as literary classics. Both authors acknowledged that the name 'Shrubb' had by now entered the language as a byword for speed. Arthur Conan Doyle's *The Lost World* – originally serialised in the magazine *The Strand* from April-October 1912 – would later become a novel and then a film. Doyle's tale told of a scientific expedition, headed by the larger-than-life Professor Challenger, which set out to explore a South American plateau that remained frozen in time from the age when dinosaurs roamed the earth. In Chapter Thirteen, Doyle writes: 'These brutes [dinosaurs] could not run as fast as a man in the open. They have short, bandy legs, you see, and heavy bodies. Even Challenger could give a few yards in a hundred to the best of them, and you or I would be a perfect Shrubb.'

Taking a leaf from Doyle, P G Wodehouse also employed Shrubb's name in his novel *Death at the Excelsior*, published in 1914. He wrote: 'Not to invite so old a friend to stay at his home, if he ever happened to be down that way, would, he hinted, be grossly churlish. Mr. Rastall-Retford, impressed, issued the invitation. And now Peter was being punished for his deceit. Nemesis may not be an Alfred Shrubb, but give her time and she gets there.'

In March 1914 the Shrubbs' second child, Norah Ada, was born in Toronto. Two years later a second daughter would follow, Nancy Julia Brown. The family spent the entire 1914-18 War period in Canada, and daughter Norah explained in 2003: 'I think being married with three children and aged 34 were the reasons dad was never called up.' Around 13,000 Torontonians lost their lives in the conflict.

Whatever vestiges of professional racing remained were extinguished by the outbreak of war. Tom Longboat, nine years younger than Shrubb, volunteered in 1916 and served three years in England and France, assigned to various regiments including the 180th Sportsmen's Battalion. He was once given the onerous responsibility of bearing messages from one battlefield post to another in France. He was wounded and wrongly reported as dead, a heart-rending state of affairs which subsequently led to his wife Lauretta remarrying. The shock for both of them when Longboat returned to Canada can only be imagined. Both parties seemed to accept the situation and before long Longboat also remarried, his bride being Martha Silversmith, a woman from his own Six Nations reserve.

Meanwhile, it was rumoured that Shrubb might take up the job of trainer for the Irish Canadian Athletic Club in Toronto, but he maintained his links with Harvard and made it clear he harboured business ambitions. A sports club in Victoria, British Columbia, also tried to tempt him with a job, but was unsuccessful. During the war, Shrubb secured a managerial position at McKay's Cream of Barley Mill at Bowmanville, just outside Toronto, where the famous Cream of Barley cereal was made. His family moved to the town, and 86 years later in 2004 his daughter Norah was still living there.

Soon after the family's move to Bowmanville, slip-shod reporting by *The New York Post* implied that Shrubb had become seriously ill and was not long for this world. The paper repeated ill-founded rumours that the 38-year-old had quit his coaching job at Harvard to spend his last days in Canada. The source of the false story remains a mystery.

Shrubb was very much alive and kicking in 1918 and making headlines in unexpected ways. This was the year he carved a tiny niche for himself in sporting history by becoming the first person to notch a score of 400 in five-pin league bowling. This sport had only been played for around ten years, having been the brainchild of a Torontonian called Terry Ryan. The pins used in ten-pin bowling were lathed down and smaller balls introduced to speed up and popularise the ten-pin game and encourage female players. The modified game became popular and soon leagues were flourishing. In its early days, any player who could maintain a scoring average of 145 was doing extremely well – but in 1918 Shrubb, a mere leisure-time player, set new standards by breaking the 400 mark to create a new record.

As the 1920s approached, Shrubb knew he was reaching a personal crossroads. His years reaping the rewards from running were all but finished, even though coaching opportunities remained open to him. Now that the War was over, the big decision facing him and wife Ada was whether to remain in Canada so he could pursue his new life in business, or to return to a homeland they naturally missed, to bring up their three children.

Having been away from England for ten years, much would have changed. Some friends and family would have moved on or died. Shrubb's close pal Fred Spencer, for example, who had kick-started his running career, was by now a professional soldier in South Africa. Alf and Ada must have pondered long and hard about returning to their beloved Sussex. Although willingly exiled in an outpost of the Empire, the couple clearly felt pangs of homesickness. But Shrubb was fiercely patriotic and the pull of the old country must have been strong.

CHAPTER EIGHTEEN

Drama in the North Atlantic

Ten years after Shrubb and his family first settled in Canada, the early summer of 1919 saw them consider a return to England. Shrubb's impressive credentials as the successful trainer of Harvard athletes had led to his name being linked with Oxford University, which was looking to recruit its first paid athletics coach. It would be quite a wrench to leave Ontario, but the prospect of landing this highly prestigious job was too good to ignore.

Not only was the Oxford vacancy a new and highly coveted position, it was just the type of active outdoor work Shrubb wanted. Despite all his talk of making his way in business, now that he was closing in on middle age, he was still the outdoor type, unsuited to long hours in an office. The ties with Canada were strong, but the opportunity to pass on his knowledge and expertise beneath those quintessentially English dreaming spires was a tempting prospect. The other bonus was the chance to renew contact with relatives and old friends.

So Shrubb made plans to sail 'home' and investigate the Oxford opening further, and to clear the path for a possible return by his family, who could join him later, if and when the situation was clarified. He booked a passage on the Canadian Pacific liner, the *SS Grampian*, which would leave Montreal for Liverpool on Sunday, July 6th. Travelling with him would be Francis Nelson Smith, a promoter who'd been involved in many of Shrubb's races in Canada, and who would help him set up a lucrative 'home-coming' race once they arrived in Shrubb's home town, Horsham.

This trip would give Shrubb the chance to perform in front of his adoring home-town fans one last time. It would be a 'last hurrah' by the old champion in poignant surroundings. He would turn forty in six months' time, and if he wanted to run again on English soil at anything like the standard he used to, it really was a case of now or never.

Shrubb had always enjoyed the week-long crossings of the Atlantic and had done the journey many times. His daughter Norah would recall that he once tallied up these crossings and reckoned he'd done more than twenty over the years. Most of them were relaxing, but this one would prove to be no pleasure cruise. It would turn into perhaps the most eventful and troubled of any of Shrubb's ocean journeys.

Skippered by Captain James Turnbull, the *Grampian* left Montreal at 10am carrying 700 first and second-class passengers, and enjoyed a straightforward trip down the St Lawrence River. The vessel ran into dense fog as it passed Cape Race at the south-east tip of Newfoundland, on the Wednesday morning, July 9th. By the afternoon it was so thick that speed had to be reduced to a minimum. Icebergs were common off Newfoundland even in July, and Captain Turnbull ordered a sharp look-out to be maintained.

Shortly before 6pm, a monster iceberg loomed up, dead ahead, barely fifty yards away. Turnbull instantly knew a collision was inevitable. To change course and attempt to skirt it would probably ensure that the *Grampian*, nearly 500 feet long, would strike the iceberg broadside, and that could rip the side out of ship. The only sensible course was to meet it head on. He ordered the engines to be put into reverse, which slowed the *Grampian's* progress a little, but could not avert a collision of terrifying force. Many passengers were thrown off their feet by the impact, drinks were spilled and card tables up-ended. The iceberg gashed the ship's bows to a depth of thirty feet, thankfully the main impact being above the water line. The *Grampian's* forecastle deck was demolished, the stern flattened in and the sleeping quarters of the stewards and firemen almost completely wrecked.

A dozen men had been in the fo'c'sle at the time and those not asleep fled for their lives, screaming to their shipmates to move. Four of them, however, were unable to escape and of these, two were crushed to death – Thomas Dax, 58, a night watchman, who was in the fireman's quarters, and George Manderson, 54, an assistant steward, had been in the stewards' quarters. Both were natives of Liverpool. David Cormiskey, a fireman, and steward Martin Tobin, also both Liverpudlians, were left trapped in the wreckage. Cormiskey's left arm was pinned beneath a metal plate, and Tobin was trapped by his legs in the debris. It would take nearly an hour to extricate them.

At the time of the collision, which was said later to have happened 45 miles from the port of St John's, Newfoundland, most of the passengers had either been on deck or in the reading, smoking or rest rooms. Although many were thrown off their feet by the impact, none appeared seriously hurt. Most rushed on deck to find out what had happened, but there was little panic and the orders from officers to stay in certain areas were obeyed. When Captain Turnbull had established there had been little or no damage sustained below the ship's waterline, he announced the fact to cheers of delight and relief. Memories were still fresh of the *Titanic* disaster, in which 1,500 had perished seven years earlier in this same stretch of water. Apart from a frantic rescue operation by shipmates to aid the two trapped men, other operations soon resumed as normal and the *Grampian* slowly inched backwards, away from the iceberg. Captain Turnbull had no choice but to put into the nearest major port, which was St John's, where the ship could be examined more closely.

Wireless contact was established with the *Minnedosa*, which had left Montreal on the Monday, and the *Corsican*, plus a number of other vessels. They were informed of what had befallen the *Grampian*, but were told there was no need to come to its aid. The two trapped men were freed and taken into the sick bay, where their wounds would be treated prior to transportation to hospital on arrival at St John's. The two dead men remained imprisoned by the metal plates that had buckled behind them, leaving no chance of escape. The *Grampian* limped towards St John's, fearful of hitting yet more icebergs in the fog. During the night the weather became stormy, but as the ship was not taking water the Captain decided to wait for daylight before making further progress. Shortly after 6am on Thursday, July 10th the passengers strained their eyes to greet the splendid natural harbour, behind which shelters the city of St John's. Once the vessel was safely berthed at Shea and Company's premises, the 700 travellers breathed a collective sigh of relief.

Shocked by the death of the two men, and grateful to be in one piece, some of the passengers took the earliest opportunity to get their feet back on *terra firma*, and headed into town. Others stayed on board that morning to join a thanksgiving service conducted in the *Grampian's* saloon by the Reverend P M Scott from Southampton, who had been on board with his family. He offered a prayer of thanks for having escaped what at first had seemed like 'an awful doom'. The group then sang hymns. After going ashore, Shrubb sent a telegram to his wife, via the Toronto office of the Great North Western Telegraph and Cable company. It read simply: 'Struck iceberg badly damaged all well Alf.'

During the day, hundreds of townsfolk came to the harbourside to inspect the crippled ship. It was front page news in the local press. According to the city's *Evening Telegram*: 'From all sides were heard exclamations of wonder that she had escaped sinking, so deeply had the iceberg penetrated through the steel plates. These were bent and buckled as a matchbox could be crushed. Pieces of blankets and mattresses, which had been on bunks in the fo'c'sle, were sticking out through and testifying to the saddest part of the whole accident. Great pieces of ice, broken from the berg, still remain in the bow.'

Local blacksmith Geoffrey Snow was summoned to perform the gruesome task of releasing the two bodies with his electric welding equipment. According to the St John's *Evening Herald*, one corpse could be seen amid the wreckage by onlookers, its head almost severed. The bodies were removed to the local morgue to be prepared for burial by undertaker Mr Oke. On the Saturday morning, July 12th, the two victims, Dax and Manderson, were buried at the local Church of England cemetery. Union Jacks adorned their oak caskets and the service was attended by Captain Turnbull, officers of the ship and a large number of passengers. Meanwhile, back in the harbour, a Lloyd's surveyor and other officials visited the ship to survey the damage and prepare their report.

Although it had come into port under its own steam, the *Grampian* clearly needed urgent repairs and would be unable to sail again for some time. The 11,000-ton vessel had been built in 1907 in Glasgow by Stephens and Sons, for the Allan Line company, which had recently merged with Canadian Pacific. The ship was 485 feet long and sixty feet wide. Captain Turnbull CBE, a man with an impressive Naval war record, spoke to reporters at harbourside and was full of praise for the 700 passengers and his 300 crew for not panicking and remaining calm at all times. Arrangements had been made, he said, for all passengers to be picked up by another ship, the *Empress of Britain*, which would call at St John's on its journey from Quebec to Glasgow about a week later.

Some passengers donated wreaths for the funeral of the two victims, but Shrubb, enterprisingly, decided to try to raise funds for their widows and orphans by fixing up a race in St John's during the days in hand. The local press and noticeboards were quickly advertising the event. Under the heading 'Charity Sweet Charity', townsfolk were urged to attend an afternoon of sports at St George's Field on Wednesday, July 16th. The main event would be a five-mile foot race, commencing at 4.30pm, between former world champion Alfred Shrubb and a French divisional champion called J Atkins. Proceeds would be split between the local Mount Cashel Orphanage and the *SS Grampian* Casualty Fund. There would also be football and baseball matches. Admission was set at 25 cents, plus a further ten cents for the grandstand.

With a week to pass in St John's, the *Grampian*'s passengers entertained themselves by getting to know the city, one of North American's oldest. Its cobbled streets had a distinct Celtic flavour and there were welcoming taverns, some of which dated back hundreds of years.

The St John's *Daily News* reported that the sports event attracted a record attendance and heralded one of the most interesting occasions of its sort in recent years. A *Grampian* soccer team lost 0-1 to a St John's Select XI, with the most famous person on the field being the senior English referee Alfred J Dodd, one of the stranded passengers. Starring in the *Grampian* team was clergyman A E Minchin from Saskatoon. Talented St John's runner Kavanagh was added to the field for the five-mile race, which proved to be the highlight of the day. Atkins and Kavanagh were given generous starts, but Shrubb cruised to victory by more than half a mile. Locals hoping to see him break the world record for a grass track were disappointed, but his time of 26:05.2 was highly impressive given his lack of racing. He proved he could still run like the champion of old, clocking a first mile of 4:55 and then running consistently for the remaining 28 laps. *The Daily News* said he ran 'easily and without any apparent exertion and many present thought he would have run an even better time with better coaching'. The event was followed that evening by a concert at the nearby College Hall. Money raised at the door was shared between the many *Grampian* stewards who had lost belongings in the incident and the fund for the dependants of those who died.

Shortly before the *Empress of Britain* docked on the morning of Friday, July 18th to collect the waiting passengers, Shrubb received a letter thanking him for his part in the fund-raising sports and for donating an additional 46.17 dollars out of his proportion of the proceeds to the Mount Cashel Orphanage. In addition to Shrubb's donation, 610 dollars had been raised by the event, said the letter. The 700 passengers were taken to their new ship on the tug *John Green*, their baggage conveyed in a barge towed by the Furness Withy company's tug. Captain William Webster, the general superintendent of the Canadian Pacific Line, who arrived on the *Empress*, supervised the transfer, which was complete by 5pm the same day. Webster returned to Montreal the following day.

As they steamed out of St John's, *en route* for Glasgow, Shrubb and his associate Nelson Smith got down to discussing what would happen on arrival in Britain. Shrubb had important matters to discuss at Oxford University of course but, before then, he wanted to spend a couple of weeks preparing for the race they were planning for Horsham, which would have the novelty of being a 'home-coming' and a 'farewell' event rolled into one.

As described in the introductory pages to this book, both Shrubb's arrival in his home town, and the race itself, failed to live up to expectations. Shrubb was easily beaten by a horse called Kitty M and his twenty-year career as a runner ended on a disappointing note. However, 'The Little Wonder' wasn't finished with the sport just yet and remained confident that he had plenty to offer as a coach. Now all he had to do was convince Oxford University that he was the man to fill their vacancy for a full-time athletics trainer.

CHAPTER NINETEEN

The Dreaming Spires of Oxford

A month after his dramatic journey home from Canada, Shrubb agreed terms with the Oxford University Athletic Club (OUAC) to become the first 'outsider' to coach their members, and the first to be paid for his efforts. This ground-breaking appointment was formally announced in *The Times* in September 1919. Shrubb sold his house in Toronto to the city's future mayor, Thomas Foster, and began the search for a new home in Oxford.

It was a strange twist that Shrubb, suspended for life by the AAA of England, should now be welcomed back into the very heart of the sport's 'establishment'. For not only did Oxford University's talented athletes epitomise amateurism and everything it stood for, but this was the place where the world's first organised athletics meeting had been staged, and also the place where the AAA itself was born.

Laurence Chandy of OUAC, with coach Graham Tanner, compiled a record of the club in 2002, uncovering 150 years of sporting history. Chandy agrees that Shrubb's appointment as Oxford's first coach was an extraordinary development, given the circumstances.

Chandy and Tanner believe Oxford University has a powerful claim to be the founder of modern athletics as we now know it. They claim that by the mid-nineteenth century the 'decidedly plebeian' country sports of Britain were being replaced by regular, organised and well-publicised athletics events, with prizes drawing competitors from far afield. This trend started at Oxford in 1850 after a group of high-spirited undergraduates from Exeter College convened in the rooms of one R F Bowles to sip wine and discuss life in general, as students are wont to do. Present was James Aitken, George Russell, Marcus Southwell and Halifax Wyatt. Topic of the day was the difficulty in negotiating the local countryside on the poorly-performing horses at their disposal. 'Sooner than ride such a brute again,' said Wyatt, whose horse had stumbled, 'I'd run across two miles of country on foot.' One of the others responded: 'Well why not? Let's have a college foot grind!' And so it was agreed.

The so-called foot grind – a steeplechase without horses – was set up over two miles of open country, featuring 24 jumps. It cost £1 to enter and on the following afternoon there would be other contests, including flat races over a mile, 440, 300 and 100 yards, plus 140 yards over ten flights of hurdles placed ten yards apart. This series of events would be open only to members of one college (Exeter) and stewards would be appointed to ensure fair play. Twenty-four students started the steeple-chase on marshy farmland at Binsey, near the Severn Bridge Road. Most wore cricket shoes and flannels and about half dropped out after a few hundred yards. Wyatt was first home, beating early leader Aitken. The next day's races were a big success in Port Meadow. And so passed the first organised athletics meeting, not repeated until 1855, when St John's and Emmanuel colleges at Cambridge followed suit.

By 1864 the first inter-varsity contest had taken place and two years later an amateur athletics championships was staged. In 1880 OUAC took things a step further by inaugurating the AAA of England. Prime movers were three OUAC members – tutor Clement Jackson, aged 33, scholar Bernard Wise, 21, and graduate Montague Shearman, 22 – who also host-ed the meeting. Support from Cambridge was lukewarm, but delegates arrived to represent the Northern Counties, the Midlands, and all the main clubs in the south. A draft set of resolutions was drawn up, Bernard Wise elected chairman, and the new AAA was up and running.

Shrubb was made fully aware of OUAC's important role in the histo-ry of athletics, and he soon realised he had a talented bunch of runners to work with. 'The material available at Oxford and Cambridge and in Great Britain in general is second to none,' he commented. He would not start work at Oxford for a few months – until early 1920 – by which time his family would have joined him from Canada. In the meantime, he kept busy by striking a deal with *All Sports Weekly* magazine to publish a series of his reminiscences. So, during the winter of 1919-20 he spent his time painstakingly typing out lengthy articles about his adventures. The maga-zine subsequently published them under the heading '20 Years On Track – My Races and Paces' by Alf Shrubb. Each instalment was illustrated by two or three amusing cartoons.

Shrubb had returned to England a year after the end of the 1914-18 War and there was still unrest in the air. The country was soon afflicted by a wave of industrial conflict, with miners demanding a pay increase and a seven-hour day. The Sankey Commission recommended nationali-sation of the mines but this was rejected by Lloyd George's Government. The 1920s would be a trouble-torn decade, with the slump of 1920 fol-lowed by 'Black Friday' a year later, and the nine-day General Strike of 1926. Having become used to the flourishing enterprise of lively Toronto, Shrubb must have wondered whether he had made the right move.

While working at his magazine memoirs, Shrubb received a letter from a London physician who had a 'rather delicate son' whom he wished to place under a course of training. He wondered if Shrubb could oblige. The doctor said he had more faith in physical training than in medical treatment for ailing young men. 'It was impossible for me to comply with the doctor's wishes, but I undertook to use my influence in finding for his son a first class athletic coach,' recalled Shrubb. 'In due time the young man was running with a pack of harriers in London and doing a little bit of boxing. I have no reason to doubt that beneficial results were soon in evidence. I have known boys who were always ailing to make a complete recovery from this unsatisfactory condition through joining a team of cross-country runners.'

Though no longer running competitively, Shrubb was delighted, on Boxing Day 1919, to turn back the clock and join the Horsham and Crawley Hunt, just as he had in his boyhood. 'A gallop across the fields on foot with the foxhounds still held its old charm,' he said. He was now forty, but had few problems coping with a five-hour session, running with the permission of Master of the Hunt, a man he knew as Dick from the old days. His efforts were much admired by Dick, who recalled: 'You were always the lad that could run with the hounds and no mistake!'

The Boxing Day meeting gathered at Oakendean Gate, near Cowfold, and Shrubb arrived in long running pants with football stockings to combat the rain and strong winds. He had taken the train from Horsham to West Grinstead and then run the two-miles-plus to Oakendean Gate. Shrubb recalled:

'Master Reynard [the fox] lay low for about an hour until the attentions of the hounds rendered him so uncomfortable that he made the desired dash for it. Occasionally the fox was good enough to cut across a field, to give me a sporting chance. We did not have the pleasure of a very long hunt as the fox decided to run to ground, entering 12 or 13 dry drainpipes. The hounds followed up closely but lost the scent. After nosing about for some considerable time, the dogs apparently came to the conclusion that the fox must be in the drainpipe. At once Dick proceeded to dig the fox out with spades and picks from a neighbouring farm.

'The plan of campaign was to dig in a way that would head the fox off so that when he elected to leave the drain the dogs would be in readiness to receive him. We started pulling up the pipes, and it fell to my lot, luckily, to go to work at the spot where Reynard was hiding. Removing a piece of piping I could distinctly see the fox's tail. I called over to Dick and asked if he thought it safe to take hold of the tail – he said yes and I gripped it firmly and pulled with all my might fearing the fox might return and bite me, though the narrowness of the drain made that unlikely. I pulled so hard that the tip of the brush came off in my hand.

Everyone fell about laughing as I yelled that the tail had come off! Most likely nobody present had ever seen anything like this happen before and I'm afraid none of us gave the poor fox much sympathy, for the little fellow must have suffered some pain. Operations were resumed and pipe after pipe dug out till the tail, or what was left of it, came into view and I pulled the fox out – quickly getting out of the way so the hounds could finish the job in a jiffy.'

Now that he was no longer racing, the idea of following hunts on foot once again became a favourite pastime for Shrubb and before long he had become acquainted with the huntsmen of Oxfordshire too. His daughter Norah, just six when they arrived in Oxford, recalled that her father had a number of runs with the dogs around that time and on occasion would reach the fox first and win himself its brush as a 'prize'.

Norah's memory of those childhood years in Oxford remain vivid some eighty years later. She clearly recalled the journey from Canada: 'We came on a Cunard liner, and as I recall we spent a night with friends of dad and mum in Montreal before setting off. As I am only a good sailor in a canoe or a motorboat, the ocean crossing was ghastly, but I do remember the gorgeous dining and drawing rooms and staircases on the ship. For much of the voyage we had dense fog and you couldn't even see your own fingers over the rail, so this meant the engines had to be cut to a near standstill for almost 24 hours – a trip not to be forgotten!' Her father, on the other hand, always relished such trips, fraternising with captain and crew, yet the rest of the family found them an ordeal and suffered from seasickness, especially wife Ada.

Once the family had caught up with him in Oxford, Shrubb moved them into temporary accommodation in Walton Street. Norah remembers on their second day there sparks from a fireplace ignited something to set off a blaze. She recalls the general uproar as efforts were made to put the fire out and save their belongings, people coming in off the street to help.

Once he had begun working with them, Shrubb found most of the Oxford athletes very different in attitude from those he had coached at Harvard. The attitude of the Oxbridge student sportsman was described by Sir Roger Bannister years later in his book *The First Four Minutes*: 'The university athlete is first and foremost a human being who runs his sport and does not allow it to run him. He drinks beer and he listens to coaches when he feels inclined. It has produced men whose personality and determination were sufficient to enable them to achieve balanced lives and at the same time to plan successful athletics careers and to stand the strain of first class competition.'

Shrubb was dealing with talented individuals who were not necessarily determined to fulfil their sporting potential. Athletics was not the be-all and end-all of their lives and this must have occasionally been frustrating for a man who had reached the top thanks to single-minded dedication. At Harvard he had worked his young charges very hard and had not been afraid to make himself unpopular in doing so. He recalled: 'To be sure I put the young Americans through the hoop, submitting them to the severest possible course of training, consistently reaping the best results. At first and for a considerable time they jibbed at my methods, wanting to know, in their plain-speaking democratic way, whether I had come over from England to kill off American athletic stock … but there is always this to be said for the American: the spirit of emulation is strong enough within them to set them trying their utmost to beat competitors in any sphere of athletics excepting perhaps cricket, which is considered by them to be too slow and too purely English. I threw myself heart and soul into the training of these wiry young Americans and in the end they came to see eye to eye with me.'

Bevil Rudd, an all-round sportsman who grew up in South Africa and won three medals at the 1920 Antwerp Olympics, linked up with Shrubb and the others at OUAC after winning a Rhodes scholarship to Oxford. Rudd recalled: 'I belonged primarily to the pre-war era when training at the universities was essentially casual and competition very occasional. We conformed to a traditional training schedule, which while it kept us fit in no way tested our individual abilities or polished our style. A faulty action was regarded as a fascinating idiosyncrasy and misplaced energy regarded a sign of guts.'

The American magazine *Harper's Weekly* sent writer Caspar Whitney to Britain to study the athletics scene. He reported that – before Oxford took on Shrubb as a professional coach – its attitude to sport had been rather casual. Whitney did concede that Clement Jackson worked hard, however, and 'gave the athletics of his alma mater a great deal of personal and valuable attention'. Shrubb had his work cut out to change the *laissez faire* attitude, especially as most of the students were from privileged backgrounds and unused to taking instructions from those of working class. Shrubb had good, sound ideas about coaching and was worth listening to, but he was dealing with people whose main aim was to enjoy their sport as opposed to improving their results. Shrubb was wise enough to modify his approach on occasions, and sensed that a light-hearted attitude was sometimes necessary. His hurdlers, for example, found themselves being asked to clear crystal wine glasses perched on the top corner of each hurdle. This unconventional idea would later be featured in the film *Chariots of Fire*. Shrubb set a good example, under-taking at least as much fitness work as the best of his students, and was often seen running through the streets of Oxford at night to keep him-self in shape.

In addition to his coaching duties, Shrubb subsequently took over the running of the Market Vaults Hotel at 134 High Street, a small premises that was effectively a private club for the students. He went behind the bar and served them personally, happy to promote his personal philoso-phy that 'a good pint induces relaxing sleep'. His family lived upstairs and daughter Norah remembers how she and younger sister Nancy would sneak out of bed and peep down when any party or special event was going on. She particularly remembers one gala occasion when the stu-dents were using the premises to entertain an important royal personage from overseas, who wore a grand turban and spectacular colours. 'We were like a couple of church mice creeping about,' she recalled, 'but as we grew more confident our squeals would get us noticed and sent briskly back to bed.' As always, Shrubb loved to keep busy and he also found the time to enter local government, serving on Oxford City Council, a role that often kept him busy for two or three days a week, said Norah.

Soon after starting work at Oxford, Shrubb was pictured in a local paper demonstrating to his son Roy, then fourteen, how to stand pre-pared at the start of a race. It may have been coincidence, or maybe shy-ness in front of the camera, but young Roy looked ill at ease in his run-ning kit. Norah confirmed that Roy never followed his father's urge to run and was more inclined to academic pursuits. Instead of following in dad's famous footsteps, Roy went on to study chiropractic and specialised in this branch of the medical world. He occasionally played tennis but had no interest in athletics. Roy soon entered Oxford himself, studying for a degree in chemistry. Perhaps it was his younger sister Norah (still trim and active in her 91st year) who inherited the running genes from her dad?

Shrubb's first months as Oxford coach coincided with the return of the Varsity Sports contest against Cambridge, after an interval of six years due to the Great War. The tradition of the Oxford team spending a week in Brighton in training was resurrected, too, and Shrubb super-vised track-work in the town's Preston Park, scene of some of his own great triumphs. In later years the Brighton jaunt would be abandoned for economic reasons. When suspended by the onset of war in 1914, the Varsity Sports score showed 22 victories for Oxford, Cambridge having won 25, and four matches tied. OUAC was keen for Shrubb to help redress the balance.

The 1920 meeting took place at Queen's Club, Barons Court, London in the world's first multi-purpose sports complex. On a four lap-per-mile track, a raucous crowd of nearly 10,000 witnessed a thriller, with Oxford prevailing by five and a half events to four and a half. Rudd clinched victory by winning the 880 yards for the Dark Blues, shortly after dead-heating in the 440 with Guy Butler. It was a fine start as far as Shrubb was concerned. Over the next five years, Cambridge would win only one of these annual contests, with two ending level.

Along with Rudd, another Oxford star in Shrubb's time was the New Zealander Arthur Espie Porritt of Magdalen College. Porritt would go on to win a sprint bronze at the 1924 Paris Olympics and would attend subsequent Games as team captain or team manager. He would leave Oxford in 1926 to become a doctor, becoming an OBE in 1943 and surgeon to King George VI and Queen Elizabeth over a fifteen-year period. He returned to New Zealand in 1967 to serve as Governor General and, on being made a life peer on his return to the UK in 1972, took the title Baron Porritt of Wanganui and Hampstead.

Shrubb's first Varsity Sports victory was followed in April 1920 by an eventful trip to the Penn Relays in the USA (covered fully in Chapter Twenty) and, in these early months of his incumbency, Shrubb experienced a good measure of success. Indeed, there was never a dull moment in 1920 and Shrubb often found himself witness to eccentric behaviour by the extrovert upper classes, who certainly knew how to enjoy themselves. For example, one day Lord Birkenhead, then the Lord High Chancellor, challenged one of Shrubb's athletes to a post-prandial race around one of the university quadrangles. The track was to be the footpath, which made it almost exactly 220 yards per lap. His Lordship bet he would complete four circuits before his more athletic opponent achieved eight (one mile). The challenge was accepted but His Lordship won.

In October 1920 Oxford took the step of admitting women for the first time to take full degree courses, but Shrubb's thoughts were more occupied by an upcoming event in December. The very first Varsity Relays contest had been arranged for Fenners in Cambridge, where, rather than passing a baton, each college provided a small flag in their colours to be passed from runner to runner. Hosts Cambridge won 4-1. This new event became a popular annual fixture, but later in Shrubb's era it was suspended after some Oxford high-jinks got out of hand. Rex Salisbury-Woods, a British international shot-putter, gave an account of what happened in his book *Cambridge Doctor*: 'The [relay] series was prohibited for good after the riotous return of an Oxford team in the 1920s. For some reason I have never discovered, Oxford men seem to take more readily to destruction in their celebrations and on this occasion they smashed the glass window of a dining car before leaving Cambridge and, on the way to Oxford, converted two compartments into one saloon, and nearly brained the Bletchley station master with a beer bottle. Having dealt with individual offenders, the Oxford proctors banned the Relays. This seemed a pity and most unfair to Cambridge men, so when the dust had settled I persuaded my opposite number in the OUAC, T D Weldon, the senior tutor of Magdalen, to intercede and … the ban was lifted.'

Laurence Chandy confirms that the OUAC calendar in Shrubb's era was very busy. Michaelmas (autumn) term included the Freshers versus Blues match early on, the Varsity Relays in December, and various College sports, each hosting one or two particular fixtures throughout the term. In Hilary (spring) term the focus was on the Varsity match, taking place just before term ended, and was preceded by the University Sports and the week's training for the Blues at Brighton. Trinity (summer) term was just as busy, with the annual fixture against London AC, the AAA versus OUAC match, in addition to contests against Harvard/Yale and Princeton/Cornell every other year from 1921. This era coincided with a noticeable shift in the way Oxford athletes approached their sport. Training was becoming more fashionable and the OUAC officials were seen to be encouraging the Blues to adopt a lifestyle compatible with an increased commitment to their club and athletics generally.

Chandy says that prior to Shrubb, what little serious coaching had taken place had come via the enthusiasm and commitment of Clement Jackson, a long-standing senior treasurer of the club. Jackson was closely involved in all aspects of OUAC, from his supervisory role on the club committee, to his organisation and running of matches, and the interest he took in the progress of individual members. From accounts of old Varsity matches, Jackson appears to have taken on a team manager's role for Oxford, leaving Shrubb to concentrate purely on coaching matters: 'Unlike Jackson, who was a fellow and tutor of Hertford College, Shrubb had no other affiliation with the university apart from his employment by OUAC. There is evidence in the minute books that Shrubb attended committee meetings, however … he might have been there to provide guidance on the best preparation for competition, this being one of his established areas of expertise.'

In 1921 Shrubb made news again when the International Amateur Athletics Federation (IAAF) published its first list of officially ratified world records. Shrubb, now 41, was declared the current holder of every record over the linear distances from two to ten miles, plus the one-hour record (see Appendix). Shrubb's record-breaking runs had been set almost twenty years earlier but there were few signs of many being bettered during the 1920s. Indeed some would last beyond the 1939-45 War. For example, the next British athlete to set a world record at a 'standard' distance would be Gordon Pirie at six miles in 1953 (28:19.4 at the AAA championships), 49 years after fellow South London Harrier Shrubb had set his mark (29:59.4 at Glasgow).

In August 1923 Finland's Paavo Nurmi finally cracked Shrubb's three-mile world record, which had been set at 14:17.04 at Stamford Bridge twenty years previously. Nurmi achieved 14:11.2 at Stockholm, during a 5,000 metres race. A year earlier he had recorded 14:08 but this was never recognised by the IAAF.

Oxbridge athletes were out in force for the 1924 Olympic Games in Paris and no fewer than six Oxford students, then coached by Shrubb, took part. Bill Stevenson (USA) won gold in the mile relay, Arthur Porritt took bronze at 100 metres and reached the 200 final, D M Johnson (Canada) was fourth in both the 400 and the mile relay, B M Norton (USA) was fifth in the 200, Aubrey Montague sixth in the steeplechase and C E Mackintosh competed in the high jump. In addition, several former Oxbridge students who had earlier worked with Shrubb also competed, including Bevil Rudd, Henry Stallard, William Milligan and Wilfred Tatham.

Athletes who came under Shrubb's influence also won many AAA titles during the 1920s. Rudd was 440 and 880 champion in 1920, Stevenson 440 champion in 1923, Stallard won the mile in 1923, the 880 winner in 1924 and the 440 in 1925, Tatham the 440 hurdles in 1924, Guy Butler the 220 in 1926 and the Achilles relay team won the 4 x 440 four times between 1927 and 1930, plus the medley relay in 1920. Shrubb also worked with Vernon Morgan, a talented three-miler who would later become sports editor at Reuters.

Over at Cambridge, perhaps noting Shrubb's influence at Oxford, the sprinter Harold Abrahams decided to hire a professional personal trainer, Sam Mussabini, to assist with his running. The Cambridge dons were outraged, feeling this was not in keeping with the amateur tradition of the Cambridge gentleman. Abrahams, a secular Jew, did not take kindly to their criticism, which he felt carried an undercurrent of anti-Semitism. It made him all the more determined to succeed on the track. This episode would be immortalised by the 1981 feature film *Chariots of Fire*, directed by Hugh Hudson, which focused on events surrounding Abrahams and fellow sprinter Eric Liddell and the 1924 Olympics. Also portrayed in the Oscar-winning film were two of Shrubb's charges, Aubrey Montague and Henry Stallard. In an interview given years after he retired from running,

Abrahams would recall the Oxbridge scene and his admiration of Shrubb: 'I remember in those days, Shrubb was still the holder of some ten world records.'

In 1925, Olympic hero Arthur Porritt was in his last year as OUAC President. The committee was also about to be replaced. It seems there were rumblings of discontent at how the club was being run. Shrubb was by now busy with his work as a city councillor and running his small tavern, and it seems his commitment to OUAC might have been questioned. After one OUAC committee meeting, a directive was issued and Shrubb was asked to attend the Iffley Road track on a daily basis in future, along with the 'rubber' (masseur) Jack Gorton.

Although it was by now nearly twenty years since he had left them, Shrubb retained affection for this first club, Horsham Blue Star Harriers. He decided to donate a trophy to them, to be put up for their three-mile club championship in July 1925. He put his proposal in writing to the club's secretary E H Gough and promised to attend a club dinner the night prior to the race. He subsequently arrived in Horsham accompanied by some of his Oxford runners, who attended the Blue Star dinner at the Town Hall and stayed overnight at the nearby Black Horse Hotel. The new Alf Shrubb Trophy was suitably engraved and, in addition to presenting it, Shrubb also offered his services to help train local runners.

Thousands of miles away, a runner Shrubb had never met was reaping the rewards of his coaching. In April 1926, Johnny Miles, aged only twenty, stormed to victory in the Boston Marathon, defeating the reigning Olympic champion Albin Steinroos. Miles won the race wearing discounted 98 cent sneakers, pared down with a knife to make them lighter. The youngster had initially trained as a boxer, but switched to running after a friend gave him a copy of Shrubb's 1909 coaching manual. He was fascinated by its contents and the book was elevated to the status of a second bible in the Miles household. The former mineworker trained like a demon, according to the strictures of the book, combining his running with his job as a delivery boy in Cape Breton, Nova Scotia. Miles would win Boston again in 1929 and also represented Canada at the Olympics and British Empire Games before retiring from athletics and embarking on a successful business career. He never forgot the part Shrubb's little book played in his famous victories.

CHAPTER TWENTY

Taking Pennsylvania by storm

The single event that gave Shrubb his finest hour and deepest satisfaction as a coach came soon after his arrival at Oxford, when he led a team of young Britons across the Atlantic to perform in the famous Penn Relays, normally the exclusive preserve of top American talent. Shrubb and his boys would bring the house down in Philadelphia – literally.

Shrubb's knowledge of the collegiate running scene in America meant he was a key man to have on board when the idea of sending a combined Oxford-Cambridge relay team was first mooted. Organisers of the annual event, at the University of Pennsylvania, had invited the British team to the 1920 races after fears that athletics talent in the States had been depleted by the 1914-18 war, requiring them to strengthen the field of competitors. Once the Varsity Sports were out of the way in England, the Oxford pair, Bevil Rudd and Colonel Arnold Strode-Jackson, put together a squad to represent the UK. Shrubb was seen as an essential man to have along, given his background as coach of Harvard, not to mention his experience at crossing the Atlantic.

Strode-Jackson appointed himself team manager, with Shrubb as coach and Rudd the team captain. Strode-Jackson was an Olympic gold medallist – he claimed the 1,500 metres at Stockholm in 1912 – and world record holder at that distance. He was also nephew of Clement Jackson, the Oxford tutor who had helped set up the AAA in 1880. In addition to Rudd, the squad comprised Aubrey Montague and H Jeppe from Oxford, and Wilfred Tatham, Henry Stallard and William Milligan from Cambridge. Rudd and the three Cambridge men would make up the four for the principal race, the 4 x 880 yards relay.

Relay running as an organised sport had effectively begun 27 years earlier at the University of Pennsylvania, when they took on Princeton. While earlier examples of relay races exist, nowhere else did the concept take hold and flourish. In 1893, the University's track committee, looking for ways to add interest to their spring handicap meeting, hit on the idea of four men each running a quarter mile. Interest in the first two years' races against big rivals Princeton was such that the committee sponsored a fully-fledged relay in 1895. The new Penn Relays served as the dedication for the Franklin Field stadium, built on the same ground it occupies today. The festive atmosphere provided by the tent camp – the primitive changing and refreshment area – was responsible for the term 'carnival' being adopted as part of the event's official name in 1910. Today, the carnival atmosphere still exists, extending to a surrounding Carnival Village, and outside on the nearby streets. A formal Relay Racing Code was adopted in 1910, allowing a twenty-foot zone in front of the starting line, in which a 'touch-off' could be performed. Beforehand, there had been neither batons nor zones. These ideas worked well and were soon introduced at the Olympics.

The Penn event grew in popularity and by 1915 had become a two-day meeting. Interest and crowds continued to grow, and the visit of Shrubb's British squad in 1920 smashed all previous records. Crowds of more than 25,000 turned out to see the action with an estimated 5,000 having to be turned away. The attraction of the ace runners from England literally brought the house down, for the ground had to be demolished soon afterwards to make way for a safer and more modern stadium. By the advent of the 21st century, the Penn Relays had been staged more than one hundred times. More athletes had run here than at any other single meeting in the world, and more spectators had witnessed the relays than any other in the world, bar the Olympics.

The Oxbridge party left England on April 7th, 1920, on the White Star liner *SS Adriatic*, with logistical arrangements made by Col Strode-Jackson, in consultation with Shrubb. The coach had sailed on this vessel before and knew that on its wide deck a route of ten laps to the mile could be marked out as a training track. Shrubb had run daily on his previous Atlantic crossings, but found the students were not quite so dedicated, particularly those who had never sailed long distance before, and they preferred to take things easy over the first few days. Eventually Shrubb had them walking briskly before breakfast and again between 11am and 1pm. Afternoons were used for rest and reading, and after a 7.30pm dinner the evening was spent strolling around deck, or doing a little running before bedtime at around 10.15pm.

The usual deck sports, including pillow fighting and potato races were tried, and once it had become known that some crack runners were on board, Shrubb was asked to set up an exhibition race to amuse the other passengers. He thought a one-miler would be an ideal workout in advance of the stiff task ahead of them in the States. Rudd, Milligan, Montague and Stallard put on their running kit, and, inevitably, Shrubb, twenty years their senior, could not resist joining in. Deckchairs were removed and passengers lined up around the course and great excitement heralded the 3pm start of the unofficial *SS Adriatic* one-mile championship.

Shrubb recalled: 'We lined up on the starboard side with the blue sea surrounding us and a splendid blue sky above – a strange but wonderful setting for a race. Aided by my experience I felt quite at home and took the lead and made the pace for six or seven laps until Stallard, Rudd and Montague passed me and finished in that order. Everyone was delighted with the exhibition and were mainly interested in Rudd, whose reputation as a great all-rounder was well known.'

Shrubb added this assessment: 'I have never seen a finer athlete than Rudd. I was quite satisfied in my own mind before we left England that given a good track, good weather and a sympathy with the American climate, Mr Rudd would put up one remarkable performance, if not more, before we sailed for home. None who were present at the Varsity Sports will readily forget his great running at Queen's Club in March 1920. That day he lost to Harold Abrahams of Cambridge in the 100 yards by a mere six inches in ten seconds dead. Half an hour later he dead-heated with Guy Butler of Cambridge in the quarter in 49.6 and then took part in the long jump. To cap it all he won the half-mile, the last event of the day, to give Oxford victory. It was a great race in which, showing wonderful judgement, Rudd beat Mountain of Cambridge in 1:57.4 − a truly remarkable all-round performance.'

Bevil Rudd was indeed a remarkable athlete. Born in Cornwall, he was the grandson of the co-founder of the De Beers Mining Company in South Africa. In the 1914-18 War, he served first with the Argyll and Sutherland Highlanders before joining the innovative Tank Corps of Winston Churchill, and received the Military Cross for bravery. Awarded a Rhodes Scholarship to Oxford, he played a leading role in revitalising the Oxford University Athletics Club, serving a term as President and also captaining the club. Following the Penn Relays trip he participated in the Antwerp Olympics and won gold in the 400 metres, bronze in the 800, and silver in the 4 x 400 relay. He also took the AAA quarter and half-mile titles and the Harvey Memorial Gold Challenge Cup in 1920. A year later he set a world record for the quarter mile. After leaving Oxford, Rudd would become a Master at Harrow, and then a private secretary to Lord Birkenhead before returning to his native South Africa. He worked as a sports writer for *The Cape Times*, but in 1930 returned to Britain to join *The Daily Telegraph* as athletics correspondent, subsequently dying suddenly aged only 53 in 1948.

As a coach, Shrubb had never worked with an athlete of Rudd's calibre before, and he was naturally keen not to over-burden his star performer with too heavy a training load. He combined a measure each of walking, running and light gym work, the latter in small doses as Shrubb wanted his men to feel the benefits of the fresh air up on deck. Early on the trip, the team suffered a major setback when Tatham slipped down some stairs and sprained his ankle. He was a valuable member of the squad and underwent intensive treatment for the rest of the six-day voyage. Shrubb massaged the swollen ankle twice a day and the ship's doctor was regularly consulted. Tatham had to be helped up and down stairs but improved as the ship neared New York. 'As we disembarked he needed sticks to walk but was very cheerful in spite of it and declared he would be fit by the time of the race,' Shrubb recalled.

'We were met by a delegation from the Pennsylvania university, among whom was Ted Meredith, one of the greatest half-milers, who held the world record of 1:52.4. We were escorted to the Pennsylvania Hotel in New York by the delegation and fixed up for the night. The next morning we left for Philadelphia where we were met by a second delegation from the university and taken to the Belle Vue Stratford hotel where we remained pending arrangements for proper training. As we'd come into port at New York quite an army of cameramen came aboard – 50 at least – and we were snapped by them on board in the dock, and our party submitted to the ordeal with a good grace. Again at the Belle Vue Stratford the photographers got busy, many snaps being taken on the roof of the hotel.'

Shrubb had two weeks in which to get his team ready for the big race. He imposed restrictions on their diet and issued precautions against the climate. 'Two weeks was none too long a time for the purpose as everyone with a knowledge of this subject must admit. The team didn't mind the dieting very much although one had to cut down their indulgence in ice cream, of which they were fond. For these, rice and tapioca puddings were generally substituted. The ice creams were only allowed occasionally as reward for good conduct.' Shrubb's words conjure up a quaint mental picture of this small, quietly spoken, working class man attempting to impose some sort of control on strapping, gregarious sportsmen with loud, upper class accents and an insatiable desire for vast quantitites of ice cream.

From the Belle Vue Stratford Hotel, Shrubb, Strode-Jackson and the runners strolled regularly down to the Philadelphia Cricket Club for training. 'At 7.30 in the morning we would go down there with baseball bats loaned to us by the university,' recalled the coach. 'Rudd was very handy with the cricket bat in England and quickly adapted to the baseball version. I served as pitcher and assure you he didn't miss many of the balls I sent down to him. The rest … joined us and we had some rare good fun. We breakfasted at 8, this consisting of American grapefruit, Corn Flakes, eggs on toast and coffee. Then an hour's rest and from 9 to 12 we played golf, and the team derived great benefit from this as it helped keep them fit and prevented their minds from dwelling too long upon the great event of the tour, the big relay race.

'Most of the walking was also on the golf course with Colonel Strode-Jackson as leader. On the second day of the stay we took the train to Franklin Field where the team had their first try-out. There was a great crowd present, most of the onlookers being anxious to find out what chance the team would have against the crack American Varsities. The track was very hard, differing largely from our English cinder tracks. In this respect the men were careful not to do too much fast work, for fear of stiffness in the muscles. The whole team, with the exception of Tatham, turned out and a half-mile was run at a steady pace and then several fast sprints of between 200 and 300 completed the work.

'Afterwards the team sat around in the sun and as usual there was an army of cameramen at work snapping them in every conceivable position. Dinner was at seven. The evenings were usually passed in reading and playing cards and we all turned in around 10-10.30. Occasionally in the evening we would go out upon the cricket ground in running things and do a bit of fast work. The weather throughout the two weeks was lovely, with the exception of one or two hot spells. Tatham's ankle was mending in response to constant treatment but his period of training was restricted and he did only around eight days in total. After several days work at the Franklin Field we discovered the Americans were puzzled because our team men did not indulge in faster work.'

Shrubb had to explain to reporters that he was anxious not to work his men too hard on an unfamiliar track, and pointed out they had all done plenty of intensive training before leaving England and only needed light exercise, varied by a few fast sprints, to stay sharp. Five days before the race, Shrubb despatched Milligan and Stallard on a half-mile time-trial which, to his satisfaction, saw Stallard clock 1:58.4 with Milligan a whisker behind. 'We felt satisfied after this that we had a chance of winning, provided Tatham's ankle could take the strain. He did only light work with his strapped ankle but was full of pluck and eager to do his best. His heart and soul were in the task and it was a big relief when one day he ran a half-mile with Milligan and stood the test well.'

On Friday, April 30th, the first of the two-day carnival, nearly 8,000 turned up for a programme that included an American Distance Medley in which the first man did three quarters of a mile, the second a half, the third three quarters and the fourth a full mile. The British visitors had been entered for this race, but an horrendous mix-up saw them fail to start. Due to heavy rain, the British, along with teams from Pennsylvania and Chicago, waited under cover, expecting to be called to their marks close to start time. When the call came it did not give sufficient notice, so that by the time they reached the start area the eager starter had already fired his gun. The race had already started. When race officials were told three teams had missed the start, there was great apologising all round, with the weather blamed for the mix-up. Shrubb hoped the fiasco was not an omen for the big race the following day. It was suggested the three inactive teams should run a Medley event between them, but this idea was abandoned due to the increasingly soggy nature of the track, the runners feeling they should be saving themselves for the main event.

Montague of Oxford competed in the international three-miler on the Friday and came second to Nightingale of New Hampshire State College, whose time was 14:56. Young Jeppe of Oxford ran a respectable heat in the 120 yards hurdles but found himself outclassed by more experienced opposition.

Shrubb knew the relay team was in with a chance, and felt the running order would be crucial. 'The day before the race we figured out our formation. Strode-Jackson, Rudd and I worked out every possible combination as this was an important factor. We more or less reached an agreement, but the actual order of running was not definitely settled until half an hour before the race. Tatham would cover the first half-mile because I was certain that owing to his ankle he would be bound to lose 20 yards or more; Stallard second, as I calculated that he would get most of this back and send Milligan away for the third section on pretty level terms, leaving Rudd to pull out his very best over the final stretch. My arguments were convincing and this was the order we decided upon.'

A noisy, record crowd in excess of 25,000 turned up at Franklin Field for the big showdown and the atmosphere was electric. Shrubb was as nervous as if he was running himself. The Oxbridge boys were up against strong-looking teams from Pennsylvania, Illinois, Ames, Cornell, Princeton, Massachusetts Institute of Technology, and Notre Dame.

Shrubb recalled how the dramatic race unfolded: 'Cornell set off and made a hot pace and Tatham as expected lost a lot of ground. Stallard collared the Cornell leader at three-quarters-of-a-mile and sped on with utmost determination and got a slight lead for Milligan, before collapsing. As fine a piece of plucky running as one could wish to see and Milligan with the utmost grit held on to the lead in spite of all efforts to pull him back. Rudd ran like a deer, increasing the gap until at the finish he beat Illinois by 35 yards, winning in a world record time of 7:50.4, the previous record being 7:51. Rudd's half-mile time was 1:54.6. Rudd passed the winning post amid a storm of applause and this was a very sporting crowd.'

What a superlative start to Shrubb's coaching stint with Oxford. He was perhaps lucky to have such a talented foursome under him in that early period, particularly team captain Rudd, but the fact that they had smashed the world record on their Penn Relays debut really was the icing on the cake. Shrubb reflected later that this victory had given him as much satisfaction as any other in his career.

The organisers were delighted at the huge crowd and the added interest that the British team had brought to their event. New friendships were forged and during post-meeting socialising it was agreed that a Princeton team would visit England later in the summer for a match against Oxford at Queen's Club in London. Although Shrubb and Strode-Jackson were involved in these talks, it seems the friendship struck up between Rudd and his Princeton opposite number, Charles R Erdman, had been pivotal in setting up this fixture. The event would prove to be such a success that it would lead to a series of meetings between Oxford-Cambridge and Princeton-Cornell teams in subsequent years.

Princeton triumphed in the inaugural contest but never won again during Shrubb's era at Oxford. The fixtures would be staged alternately in England and the United States and saw athletes from both teams living and training together in the build-up. At one post-meeting dinner, a speaker from the British Embassy said he could not tell the teams apart until, on that warm July evening, all present took off their coats. Then, he said, he recognised the Oxford and Cambridge men because they all wore braces. The American champion quarter-miler Bill Stevenson was the most equitable contributor to international amity during these meetings. After losing to Rudd in 1920, Stevenson beat him in 1921, but by 1925 he was able to switch sides as he had become a Rhodes Scholar at Oxford and had joined Shrubb's OUAC. He then promptly won his event for Oxford-Cambridge against both Princeton-Cornell and Harvard-Yale.

CHAPTER TWENTY-ONE

Farewell Iffley Road

For reasons that will probably never be fully explained, Shrubb's relationship with Oxford University Athletic Club soured during the final phases of his seven-year stint as coach.

Despite his wealth of experience and unprecedented success in the sport, the young men of influence within the OUAC declared Shrubb 'useless' in 1926 and demanded he be replaced. Whether this boiled down to a personality clash involving just a few students, or represented a more widely held view is hard to discern. Shrubb's daughter Norah insists that, as she understood it, the decision to part company with the university was Shrubb's alone, largely influenced by his wife's need to move to a drier climate because of poor health. Norah said the stories that blamed her father's departure on 'snobbery' and 'class differences' were wide of the mark.

At this author's request, early in 2003 the OUAC archivist John De'Ath pored over ancient OUAC committee minute books stored in the lofts of Jesus College. His findings included records of a meeting in June 1926 which saw the handover between old and new committees, with the Presidency moving from New Zealander and Olympian Arthur Porritt to Mr A C Newman of Christchurch College. The secretary of the time recorded: 'The question of Alfred Shrubb was then raised. It was shown that his agreement with the club terminated at the end of the season 1926-27, and it was suggested that the club should not renew his contract, but should find another trainer – several of those present giving it as their opinion that Alfred Shrubb is useless; the President, Mr Newman, and the captain of cross-country, Mr Hardy, being emphatic on this point.' Others at the meeting went along with this, it seems, and it was agreed a new trainer be sought.

Looking back at those stormy times, OUAC historian Laurence Chandy concludes: 'Here then, is the first clear indication that Shrubb's relationship with the club had become tenuous if not altogether sour. Later that winter [committee meeting, November 10th, 1926] we are told that the President had by now informed Mr Shrubb that his contract would not be renewed and by early in the new year [meeting on January 25th, 1927] Shrubb has been given official notice of his dismissal. What was particularly apparent to John De'Ath, when reading through the books, was the absence of any tribute or even an acknowledgment of

Shrubb's contribution. As Graham Tanner wrote in the OUAC history, 'Shrubb's involvement with the club does not always appear to have been a very happy one, certainly not in the final years of his employment.'

Chandy continues: 'It appears the club spent considerable time and care deciding on a suitable replacement for Shrubb. In the meeting of June 1926, when discussing the possibility of appointing E A Hunter, the then Honorary Secretary of both the Achilles club and the British Olympic Association, it was stated that, if appointed, Mr Hunter should receive no more than £150 per annum, which gives us a rough idea what Shrubb had been earning.'

Peter Lovesey, author of *The Official Centenary History of the AAA*, confirms that, despite his success in the Penn Relays with Oxford and in Varsity contests, Shrubb's coaching was not highly rated by everybody. Guy Butler, a Cambridge sprinter who participated in the 1920 Olympics and later became an IAAF photographer, told Lovesey that 'as a coach, Shrubb was a dead loss'. Further evidence can be gleaned via George Gretton, author of the 1968 book *Out In Front*. Gretton was at Oxford with Shrubb and reckons the great man only spoke to him once and that was to tell him not to run on the inside lane of the track because it had been raining and he did not want it damaged. Gretton was a promising distance runner and Lovesey believes his comments were borne out of annoyance that he did not receive more personal attention. Gretton even described Shrubb's 1908 coaching book as 'a very bad book' which is certainly not a widely shared view. The OUAC history concludes that Shrubb was a 'disappointment' and says that Oxford athletes of the period remember him starting a training session with the words: 'Now gentlemen, we'll just warm up with a few turns' and would then go 'scudding off round the track oblivious to who followed. He rarely said much.'

In October 1927, *The Times* reported how, after seven years as trainer, Shrubb has now left OUAC and E A Hunter, the Honorary Secretary of Achilles, and Secretary of the British Olympic Association (BOA), had become the new honorary trainer and general organiser. Shrubb effectively retired from athletics at this point, aged 47, apparently not good enough as a coach for the new OUAC president, Newman, even though such luminaries as Bevil Rudd and Arthur Porritt seemed quite happy with Shrubb earlier on. Perhaps the new president and committee felt it was high time they had 'one of their own' doing the job, not a working class outsider, and preferred someone who would not be distracted by pursuits outside of academic life. If not, then the reason for Shrubb's unpopularity at the Iffley Road running track remains a mystery. Elsewhere he appears to have been universally liked and respected.

The other major issue troubling Shrubb around this time was his wife Ada's health. She became confined to a wheelchair after suffering with rheumatoid arthritis and after visiting specialists in Europe was advised to move to a warmer and drier climate. This, coupled with events at Oxford, convinced Shrubb the time was right to hit the road again. Many might feel that Ontario's climate was not much of an improvement on Oxford's – Canadian winters are unimaginably cold – but nevertheless it was Canada the Shrubbs chose as a destination, influenced, no doubt, by the opportunities for Shrubb to exploit his former business connections. In order to make the return to Toronto, Shrubb even turned down an offer from William Morris, the famed head of the Morris car factory in Cowley, Oxford, who wanted to employ him.

This time the move west would be for good, the family decided, and emigration papers were completed and plans made to head back across the North Atlantic in April 1928. Many were sorry to see Shrubb go, particularly his colleagues at Oxford City Council. *The Oxford Times* reported that he was given 'a hearty send-off' at a local inn called The Chequers, where he was presented with a parting gift of a walking stick. Mr Frank Powell spoke in tribute and said Shrubb's main reason for departing was Ada's health. Referring to Shrubb's mighty collection of trophies, he said: 'Nothing in life he ever earned or won would carry with it richer sentiments from friends than this walking stick.' The company rose and sang 'For he's a jolly good fellow'. A letter was read out from Oxford's City Mayor, Alderman W M Gray, which praised Shrubb as a valued and capable member of the council. He was asked to take the letter and present it to the Mayor of Toronto, to help secure future employment. Shrubb stood up to respond, saying he had arrived in Oxford in 1920 to do his duty to the Empire and the citizens had been very kind to him. W Savage of Miranda FC thanked him for the support he had given that club and other local sports. A musical programme followed with singers accompanying the piano.

Daughter Norah recalled that in 1928 she and younger sister Nancy were at an age (fourteen and twelve, respectively) where such an upheaval was not particularly welcome. And she admitted in 2003 that she still felt the pull of England, some 75 years after leaving. The Shrubbs were not the typical family boarding the Cunard liner *SS Ascania* that spring, to head for a new life. They had done all this before, and in the case of dad, he had made the long journey many times.

For many fellow passengers, however, the whole experience could be nerve-racking and far from enjoyable. If the weather held, a fast ship could make the voyage over the Atlantic in a week. A slower ship might take up to two weeks. The constant rolling, even in good weather, could upset the healthiest of stomachs. The recorded tales of emigres show that those who could only afford a place in third class or steerage found the amenities very basic. Their food was often unappetising and even those who could keep a meal down tired of it. Plain biscuits, coffee, and tea were staples and, what little butter there was, could often be rancid. Sometimes salted herring or a piece of meat was offered, but too often this was in poor condition. Most travellers brought some food with them. Fresh laundry was rarely possible and washing facilities could be sparse, with many travellers sleeping in the clothes they travelled in. Privacy was limited. A third class cabin often meant sharing a room with three others if the ship was full. The Shrubbs were probably spared at least some of these inconveniences, for it should be remembered that Shrubb had become adept at getting to know the captain and senior officers on his many crossings and his international fame often led to his being offered certain privileges.

The Canadian immigration records reveal that 48-year-old Alfred and his wife Ada had boarded Cunard's *SS Ascania* at Liverpool on April 20th, 1928, arriving in Quebec nine days later. Shortly after their arrival, the family moved into 12 Liberty Place in Bowmanville, forty miles east of Toronto, close to the shores of Lake Ontario. Subsequently they would move to a farm on the north side of nearby Highway 2, where Strathaven retirement home now stands. Shrubb went to work at the Cream of Barley mill, linking up again with its owner, James Lake Morden, a business contact from years earlier. The mill produced one of North America's favourite breakfast treats, Cream of Barley cereal.

Before long, Shrubb was in charge of the tourist camp and zoo that had been developed alongside the handsome 96-year-old water-powered mill. Norah recalled: 'They had timber wolves and other creatures in cages at the little zoo, but dad released them as he didn't like to see this. He loved animals, and there were peacocks and deer and other species, none of which were caged in. Dad would also build a cinder running track, a nine-hole golf course, tennis courts, a swimming pool and around a dozen new summer cottages for the tourists. It became a very popular place and would be booked up well in advance by Torontonians.'

One newspaper reported that it was not long before Shrubb's zoo was alive with 'a whole caboodle of animals, which attracted adults and children by the hundreds. There were 23 ponies, 33 goats, foxes, a moose, Persian lambs, raccoons, a golden eagle, Arctic owl, peacocks, minks, turkeys and 13 deer, who were later freed, but would obediently come when Shrubb called them.' The article added: 'A nanny goat will kill any but her own offspring, so to be sure he had the right kids with the right mother, Shrubb invented the ingenious idea of tying similar coloured ribbons to the right families. The worry was finally too great and the goats had to go.'

His competitive running days were over, but Shrubb still made it into the local newspapers from time to time, despite the quiet, idyllic life he now led in rural Bowmanville. One article told how Shrubb had put a prize litter of timber wolves on display, big strong husky fellows of about two months old: 'Their manner is still polite, but Shrubb, the curator of the zoo, doesn't trust them and feeds them with a quick heave,' wrote the fascinated reporter. 'Watching the pups crunch big beef bones I am of the opinion that Mrs Shrubb senior didn't raise any foolish children.' Shrubb's work helped the zoo become hugely popular and, some 75 years after his arrival, it continued to thrive, claiming to be Canada's 'original children's zoo and home to many famous Hollywood celebrity animal actors'.

Norah recalls that her father used to run all over Bowmanville to keep himself in trim, and would run a pony to and from a village some nine miles away, to give it exercise, usually arriving home looking in better shape than the pony. Shrubb had always been good with horses, which suggests that with his light frame he might have made a fine jockey had he not been a gifted runner.

Almost every day he would stroll into Bowmanville town centre and always retained his love of fresh air and long walks. He enjoyed this new life and did not regret the move, not even when 1929 saw a big downturn in population growth and immigration to the Toronto area. 'Black Tuesday' hit the city's business world like a thunderbolt on October 29th, 1929, and this ushered in a decade of depression. The Wall Street Crash of November signalled the start of a worldwide economic slump.

Unexpectedly, Shrubb was tempted out of running retirement in August 1930 when the organisers of the Canadian National Exhibition in Toronto invited him to take part in a novelty race against old rival Tom Longboat. By now, Longboat's glory days were history. At the age of 43 he had been reduced to working for the local council as a refuse collector. Shrubb was by now fifty, but could not resist the temptation to pull on his track shoes once again for old times' sake.

The Toronto Star reported: 'Two veterans ran a mile after nearly ten years out of competition [and were given] a rousing reception as they posed with ex-mayor Sam McBride at the start. There was no semblance of the old-time bitter feeling between the two. Longboat broke to the front at the start but Shrubb caught him before they'd done 50 yards and the two ran neck and neck round the first bend of the half-mile circle. Shrubb then opened up a 15-yard lead to the completion of half-a-mile and seemed fresh while Longboat looked to be tiring. Coming down the final stretch Shrubb maintained his lead and although Longboat opened up and looked to be giving him a battle, Alfie stepped on the gas and won by 20 yards.' For one last time, Shrubb's running had made front page news around Canada. His winning time was 5:34, a remarkable achievement then for a man of fifty who had not raced in more than ten years.

As usual, Longboat did not say much – the Onondagan Indian had never been one for small-talk – but Shrubb enjoyed renewing acquaintance with his old rival. Longboat ran reasonably well that day, but did not look as fit as Shrubb, seven years his senior. The Indian was going through tough times. Unemployed after the 1914-18 War, he had travelled west to try and establish himself as a farmer. He found work as a farm hand but times turned so bleak in Alberta that he had to pawn his racing medals to make ends meet. Moe Lieberman, the Edmonton lawyer who bought the mementoes, kept them for a number of years, hoping someone would care enough to redeem them on Longboat's behalf. Nobody did and most were reported to have been melted down for their gold. Eventually, Longboat returned to Ontario, around the same time as Shrubb, and found permanent work with the City of Toronto. He drove horses and swept leaves, but for the most part collected garbage. He would do this for some twenty years and worked quietly, running his own car, providing for his family and building a circle of close friends. But in the eyes of the media he had hit 'rock bottom', as collecting garbage was seen as an ignominious fate for someone of his former fame. One writer described him as 'a rubbish man, a particularly nice rubbish man, an indian rubbish man' to whom young boys no longer looked up. Longboat would ultimately retire to the Six Nations Reserve, eventually dying of pneumonia aged 61. Shrubb was one of those quick to pay tribute, calling him 'the greatest of all the marathoners'.

Following the National Exhibition event, Shrubb returned to his animals and hung up his running shoes again for good, he presumed. He was curious to read in the newspapers at various point during the 1930s that some of his old track records were finally being broken. In the summer of 1933, for example, the Finn, Lauri Lehtinen won a three-mile race in England in 14:09.2 to topple Shrubb's world record of 14:17.6, set at Stamford Bridge thirty years earlier. This run earned Lehtinen the Harvey Memorial Gold Cup for best performance at the AAA championships. Another record, which fell a little earlier, was his two-mile mark of 9:09.6, beaten by the Swede Wide, who outran the great Paavo Nurmi in 9:01.4

in Berlin – 22 years after Shrubb had set his mark in Glasgow. Shrubb's ten-mile record fell in 1936 (32 years on) when William Eaton ran 50:30.8. Only nine days later Eaton was at it again, creating a new mark at six miles with 29:51.4.

In the summer of 1936, P H D Ward of Achilles also surpassed Shrubb's three-mile record at White City to become the English native record holder with a time of 14:15.8. Yet another Shrubb record of more than thirty years standing fell that summer, New Zealand Olympian Jack Lovelock beating Shrubb's allcomers record for two miles with 9:03.8 in the Waddilove Trophy at a Birchfield Harriers meeting. Shrubb would remain the top Englishman at two miles for 35 years until August 1938 when C A J Emery of Achilles ran 9:07.6 at Fallowfield, Manchester.

The Ontario press would occasionally visit Shrubb at his tourist park and reminisce. In one feature, *The Peterborough Examiner* wrote: 'His name will live forever in the annals of track and as long as men shall match their strength and speed against each other … some day if you are driving through Bowmanville and stop for gas at his camp, Alfie Shrubb will fill your tank and if you are old enough to remember the days of his greatness you'll jump from your car and pump his hand and tell him you are honoured …'

That article appeared in 1939. In the same year another newspaper observed: 'He's as lean and wiry today as he was at the height of his career thirty years ago. He's living an outdoor life, following his old training diet, keeping up the stringent rules of his old profession in every particular.' An advertisement appeared which featured Shrubb endorsing Cream of Barley as the best breakfast cereal: 'If you are figuring on going any great distance in this world, you should keep your pouch filled with this cereal. Look at Alf Shrubb. World champion marathon runner. He is superintendent of Cream of Barley zoo. Alf says that Cream of Barley will carry you farther than your reputation, particularly if you have a bad reputation.'

In 1946 Shrubb was hit by a double blow. In March his wife Ada died after years of suffering with rheumatoid arthritis. She had been wheelchair-bound for twenty years. Daughter Norah, by now married to H Lorne Allin, helped her sister Nancy support their father after he became a widower at the age of 66. Then, later the same year, Shrubb's business partner, the mill owner James Lake Morden, also passed away. He left his portion of their business to his nephew Jim Skinner, of Lockport, Manitoba. Shrubb decided the time was right to sell his share of the tourist camp and took over the mill itself in partnership with Morden's secretary-treasurer Beryl Percy.

Although he was now co-owner of the mill, Shrubb began to take life a little slower at this stage, according to a letter written by the local newspaper's sports editor. Shrubb had received a letter from track fan Thomas Leous in Buffalo seeking information about his running career, which Shrubb passed on to the sports editor for reply. Leous was duly told that Shrubb was now taking things easier and spent his time talking to service clubs and attending sporting events in Toronto and Hamilton. Shrubb intended to visit Buffalo the following summer, but in the meantime Leous was welcome to come to Bowmanville to learn more of Shrubb's career from his two huge scrapbooks.

Shrubb moved in with Norah, her husband, and his granddaughter Julia around this time. His second daughter Nancy had moved to the USA, first to Los Angeles, and later San Diego, to work for the Bank Of America, a position she obtained with the help of Shrubb's long-time associate Thomas Sinnott. Before long, having passed his seventieth birthday, Shrubb sold his interests in the mill to a Czech businessman, Leo Bierman, who transported the operation to Winnipeg. The zoo continued to flourish, but for a spell the mill stood empty. The Simpson Avenue premises would remain vacant until 1965, when the local Rotary Club turned it into a drop-in centre. Some years later the corporation took it over and converted it into an impressive visual arts facility.

His working days were now over, but Shrubb remained fit and active for his age. Norah recalls he always had an excellent appetite and retained his love of traditional English food. 'He loved everything from roast beef and Yorkshire puddings, vegetables, potatoes, fruit and spotted dick, and also ate lots of fish – kippers, Dover sole, salmon, mackerel and shrimps. He also loved lots of rice pudding, baked in the oven with lemon and nutmeg. I know this because I cooked all this for him many times, as my mother had done before her illness.'

He might have been an old man, but many of Shrubb's records were only just being eclipsed by the latest crop of athletes. Fred Wilt of the USA beat his Scottish allcomers record for two miles by running 9:05.4 at Hampden Park, 45 years after Shrubb's epic Glasgow run. And in 1951 Walter Hesketh (Manchester) chopped five seconds off the 24:33.4 national record for five miles set by Shrubb 47 years earlier. Hesketh achieved this on his way to a six-mile British allcomers record of 29:13 after a tremendous duel with Gordon Pirie in a Britain-versus-France match at White City.

In March 1952, Shrubb, at 72, was the oldest among a group of sports celebrities who guested at a gala dinner to aid disabled children at Toronto's Royal York Hotel. Twelve-year-old spina bifida victim Freddie

Atkinson of Woodstock, Ontario, represented the children and rubbed shoulders with 21 sports stars at this sell-out event. Young Freddie joined in the conversation as Shrubb mingled with the likes of boxing legends Rocky Marciano and Jack Dempsey.

Later in 1952, the Canada Sports Hall of Fame was inaugurated by the Canadian National Exhibition organisers in Toronto, to be officially opened in August. However, the initial list of candidates to be featured did not include Shrubb, an omission that his local paper, the *Statesman*, regarded with horror. 'We hereby nominate Shrubb,' cried the indignant paper. 'We were surprised and disappointed not to find the name of our fellow townsman and renowned champion Shrubb [on the list]. So that the committee will not overlook him we thought it advisable to give publicity to his remarkable record of winning 14 world championships, in which he won over a thousand first, second and third prizes in an amateur and professional career of 23 years … it is interesting to note that he has performed in the ten provinces of Canada, including Newfoundland.'

In the autumn of 1952 Shrubb indulged himself with a trip down Memory Lane, heading back to England to visit relatives and old friends. On October 16th he arrived back on the *SS Samaria*, and within a few days was installed as guest of honour at the South London Harriers annual dinner at the Horse Shoe, Tottenham Court Road. More than 100 guests and members flocked to see the old hero and the gathering was welcomed by club president Alick Pirie. *The Times* reported that Shrubb, still only 8st 6lbs at the age of 72, 'had a brief but astonishing career and was one of the outstanding sports personalities of his day. Had he been running in modern conditions and according to modern timetables, he would have been no less successful, if unable to kill [off] opponents by quite the same methods. No doubt the phenomenal Emil Zatopek would enter fully and effectively into the spirit of those Alfred Shrubb spurts.'

The Times' leader writer suggested: 'There is perhaps no amusement more essentially futile than that of comparing the athletes and games players of different generations and none that is more tempting. By one of sport's little ironies, two simultaneous events have made such a comparison more than ever irresistible. On Monday a dinner was given by SLH on his return from Canada for Alfred Shrubb, who is now 72, but it is to be hoped that his name still sounds stirring in other than elderly ears as unquestionably the greatest figure in British athletics in the early years of this century, the holder in his prime of world records from one-and-a-half miles to 10. Earlier in the same day it was announced that the incredible Emil Zatopek had just achieved three more world records at 15k, 25k and 30k.'

After toasting the newly crowned Queen Elizabeth II, the dinner guests mingled and greeted old friends, a queue building as they waited to shake Shrubb's hand. Songstress Victoria Cotton entertained on the piano, improvising the lyrics in order to 'pull the legs' of some guests. During the speeches, the club heard about the recent record breaking exploits of the President's son, Gordon Pirie, and his selection for the 1952 Olympics, along with hurdler Jack Parker. Olympians such as John Disley and Frank Sando were among the guests, but most of the attention focused on Shrubb. When he rose to speak he was greeted by a storm of cheering, which was led by some of his contemporaries. 'To those of us for whom Shrubb had been a respected name in the record books, or a 50-year-old photograph, it was exciting to see and hear him on this occasion; still seeming a frail eight-and-a-half-stones at 72, but very alert,' reported the SLH Gazette. 'He was moved by the warmth of his reception, expressed his appreciation and his pleasure at being back with the club if only for one night. He was glad to see some of his old records being beaten finally by Gordon Pirie. His advice to the present generation of distance runners was plenty of hard work and plain living.'

Other guests that night included Joe Binks, a rival of Shrubb's in mile races, who was there representing *The News of the World*, and J Densham, F Knott, H Watson and J George, who had all run in the 1908 Olympics. They posed in various combinations for the Press Association's photographer and the affection for Shrubb was plain to see.

Shrubb also took the opportunity to look up old friends in Birmingham. *The Sunday Mercury* reported: 'None of them had heard of him for years and all presumed he was dead.' Shrubb was photographed with old pals, including Olympian Joe Blewitt, and chuckled: 'I guess I have been lying low all these years but I was as shocked as anyone when we received a letter of sympathy from people who thought I had died … I thought I'm getting on so I'll come over while I could.' Old friends at Birchfield Harriers presented him with a silver spoon inscribed with the club crest and another group laid on a dinner and an inscribed silver cigar case.

The October 1952 edition of *Athletics World* proclaimed: 'The warrior returns!' and told how Shrubb had donated a trophy to his old club Horsham Blue Star Harriers, to be contested in future races. Shrubb naturally travelled down to the Horsham area and visited his brother Albert at his New Street home, and the one sister still living in the town, now Mrs Stringer of North Parade. Asked why he was not staying in the UK for a little longer, he explained that the coronation of the new Queen had meant 'you can't get bookings just when you want them'.

Shrubb spent a lively evening reminiscing in Horsham with old cronies Frank Farley, a well-known cyclist at the beginning of the century, Andrew Bryce, a fellow athlete, and personal friend Charlie King. The following day he went to see his birthplace at Slinfold, although Hayes Hill House had long since made way for more modern buildings. After a tour of other local villages he spent the evening with Blue Star members at their HQ in the Bishopric. He told *The West Sussex County Times*: 'There have been many changes since I was last here, West and Middle Street are much improved and I am most impressed by that fine railway station.'

Before departing, Shrubb told the WSCT he reckoned modern athletes needed more killer instinct and aggression. 'When I was running a long distance race I used to set out to kill the opposition, run them into the ground in the first three miles. I knew that if they were up with me they might beat me in a final sprint so I used to leave them trailing as early in the race as I could. I found out that if I tried to stride it out, bringing my knees up high, I wasted a tremendous amount of energy, so I used a short, economical stride and was able to quicken it up almost at will. I regarded my opponents as enemies. When I realised I had broken them it gave me a terrific kick and I was able to race on at an increased pace.' He added that he was optimistic about Great Britain's chances at the 1956 Melbourne Olympics: 'I've seen some of the youngsters of 20 or 21 we have now and they're magnificent material. If they keep at it they should just reach their peak at the Olympics. I think we'll be able to send a team of which everyone will be proud.'

Shrubb returned to Canada in mid-November, sailing from Liverpool to Halifax, Nova Scotia on the *SS Franconia*, and reflecting on an enjoyable trip during which he had been flattered by all the attention. Good news followed his return to Canada, for in May 1953, as a goodwill gesture, the AAA of England decided to restore his amateur status. The Southern Counties committee, whose predecessors had suspended him indefinitely 47 years earlier, formally reinstated him as an amateur, meaning he was now clear to rejoin South London Harriers and accede to their wish that he become a club vice-president. It was a development which pleased Shrubb greatly.

As 1952 drew to a close, the Shrubbs had something else to celebrate when Alf and the late Ada's nephew, Archer Martin, was among those to win the Nobel Prize for Chemistry for developing a process called partition chromatography. Born in North London, biochemist Martin was 42 when he won the prize and had just been appointed head of Physical Chemistry at the National Institute for Medical Research. He would later be made a CBE (Commander of the British Empire).

During this period Walter Hesketh and Gordon Pirie polished off the last of Shrubb's remaining native records, several of which had remained intact only a few months short of fifty years. Shrubb was prompted to acknowledge these feats in a letter from Canada, published in *Athletic Review*: 'These lads Hesketh and Pirie are just on the verge of world's records, and can and will break them when they reach maturity. If I may offer advice it is this. Take advantage of modern techniques, diet intelligently, train with gruelling diligence and compete with unflagging determination and on the home stretch make the final winning effort with one thought: This is for the prestige of Britain!'

It was only now, in the early 1950s, that distance running in Britain was beginning to shape up, following a long fallow period. Mel Watman, in his book *History of British Athletics*, writes: 'With the halcyon days of Alf Shrubb over, amateur distance running in Britain settled down to a rather undistinguished level which was to persist until after the Second World War. Capable runners there were, but for more than 40 years there was nobody worthy of being mentioned in the same breath as Shrubb.'

In 1953 the Essex marathon sensation Jim Peters made a bold attempt to crack Shrubb's 49-year-old one-hour record of eleven miles and 986 yards. Peters beat it by 54 yards to become the new English native record holder, but missed the GB allcomers mark set by Emil Zatopek by some 151 yards.

CHAPTER TWENTY-TWO

The Finish Line

Although his stride wasn't as brisk as it once had been, Shrubb was still in fine shape for a man in his late 70s. The last thing he expected, however, was to be invited to run in public once more. In the mid and late-1950s he spent most of his days pottering around the garden, reading and taking leisurely strolls into Bowmanville town centre from his daughter's home in Prince Street. Now they wanted the old master to dig out those dusty running shoes again and run to the Town Hall.

The idea was born in the summer of 1958 when the town's Centennial celebrations were being planned. A relay of runners was suggested as a means of transporting a ceremonial scroll from the Mayor of Oshawa, Lyman Gifford, some nine miles away, to the Mayor of Bowmanville, Nelson S Osborn. Members of the Bowmanville Track and Field Club would station themselves along the route, about one mile apart, to carry the scroll in Olympic torch style. Someone had the bright idea of asking Shrubb to run the final leg, which would be a mere 150 yards to the Town Hall steps.

Oshawa's *Daily Times-Gazette* announced that Shrubb's 'glory leg' would be the length of about two city blocks starting from Silver Street. Shrubb agreed to the idea, and told the paper: 'I thought my running days were over. Oh well, I guess one last little run won't do any harm! There's life in the old man yet. I think I shall be able to get my knees up a little bit, but I shall not be wearing a track-suit, just my ordinary clothes. It will be a great day for me and I really appreciate the honour the town has done me. I was a good 'un once you know. I raced about 50 world champions in my time and lost to only about two of them and I held approximately 12 world records. It will be great to be having a little trot again, even if it's my last race.'

So, at the age of 78, Shrubb donned running shoes, short dark socks, baggy dark shorts and a white T-shirt and trotted steadily with the scroll his 150 allotted yards. The sun shone and big crowds cheered the old champion heartily, with even the patrolling policemen applauding as he passed. It was a marvellous way for an old master to end sixty years of worldwide running. The Queen's representative in Ontario, the Lieutenant Governor Hon Keiller Mackay, was fascinated to meet Shrubb and made a special trip down from the VIP's platform to shake his hand and pose for pictures.

A few weeks prior to his eightieth birthday, the ever-restless old runner decided to make another trip to Britain. His Birmingham friends staged another dinner in his honour on Tuesday, September 8th, 1959, at the Rose Villa Tavern in Warstone Lane, with Mr and Mrs J Bartleet hosting and Colin Gibson, 'late of Aston Villa' entertaining on the piano. Shrubb tucked into his grilled halibut and roast leg of English lamb and they chatted once again about the good old days.

During this visit, writer Armour Milne took the chance to catch up with Shrubb, who had been one of his boyhood heroes. In an article in *Athletics Weekly*, Milne wrote: 'When I was a teenager I devoured, in addition to food, every sports record book I could lay my hands on. Without much difficulty, and without having to turn up the pages of the record books, I could tell anyone who was particularly anxious to know that … Alf Shrubb of South London Harriers was the holder of every English record from 1.5 miles to the hour, the records having been made in the years 1902-4. I did not meet [Shrubb] until this year, by which time he was well on his way to celebrating his 80th birthday. Alf told me that the basis of his stamina was in all probability laid in his boyhood in Sussex when he used to follow fox hunts on foot regularly. When at his peak he reckoned to do 15 miles of walking and running each day. Walking he considered to be just as important as running. At one time when he gave up work to concentrate on training for a big event, his daily routine consisted of a two miles walk before breakfast, another five miles of walking during the morning, a two-hour sleep after lunch, then anything from four to ten miles running in the late afternoon, followed by another walk of two miles before retiring to bed at ten.'

By the start of the 1960s and back home in Canada, Shrubb remained in fine fettle and, rather than any illness, it would take an accidental fall in his bathtub to lay him low. His nasty slip occurred on New Year's Eve 1960 and left him with four cracked ribs and a punctured lung. It would require a stay of several weeks in the local hospital, but Shrubb was still strong despite now being 81, and he bounced back from the setback.

Coincidentally, just days after Shrubb's accident, sportswriter Milt Dunnell of *The Toronto Daily Star* was contacted by an opposite number on *The New York Mirror*, Dan Parker, who wanted to know what had become of Shrubb. Parker had received a letter from Hannes 'Willie' Kohlemainen, the great Finnish runner, now retired and living in Boynton Beach, Florida. The 'Flying Finn' remembered the days of Shrubb and Longboat and demanded to know why the papers never recognised these forgotten heroes any more. Parker asked Dunnell to do some investigating and get back to him. Longboat, of course, had died in

1949, and Dunnell's phone call to Bowmanville revealed Shrubb's predicament in the local hospital.

'Sixty years ago the jaunty little fellow would have bounced right out [of the bath] again. Now, at 81, he has lost some of his resiliency,' wrote Dunnell. 'Today's fans would have idolised Alfie … although he never weighed more than 120 pounds, he was tougher than whalebone. Track experts of the day said Alfie had a heart as big as a bass fiddle – but that it was all granite when he was beating an opponent. He liked to punish runners who extended themselves beyond their capabilities. At any stage of a 10-mile grind he was liable to take off on a jaunt that would cover a quarter of a mile in 56 seconds. A rival whose tongue was hanging out was likely to feel discouraged. Off the track he was a warm and pleasant personality. [At Oxford] his pub provided a nightly battle between Alfie the coach and Alfie the host. Alfie the coach decreed that no athlete should consume more than one pint of bitter. Alfie the host was inclined to the belief that two pints might be permissible. It was strictly a matter of judgement then. Science hadn't come up with that fearsome gadget the breathalyser.'

Kohlemainen was wrong to think Shrubb had been completely forgotten. About a year after his slip in the bathtub, Shrubb was asked to go to Boston to be examined by the renowned heart specialist Dr Paul Dudley White. This was nothing to do with his recent accident, but part of a research project into how the heart and respiratory system of a top athlete was coping in old age. The research team were no doubt intrigued by those old stories about Shrubb finishing gruelling races with absolutely no distress and breathing normally. Someone had once written: 'No matter how hard may be the contest in which Shrubb has taken part, he never seems short of wind. Indeed, to get out of breath seems practically impossible for him.'

Dr Dudley White had been advised to use Shrubb as a 'guinea pig' following a tip-off from a medical colleague who had graduated from Oxford and remembered the Shrubb phenomenon. Tests were done on Shrubb and although the doctor's findings were not widely publicised, he was said to be amazed at Shrubb's lung capacity for a man of his build. The doctor was a world authority in his field and in 1931 had published the ground-breaking book *Heart Disease*. He had also been chief medical doctor to Dwight D Eisenhower. Dudley White might have been the so-called 'father of modern cardiology', but he had never seen anything quite like Alf Shrubb.

Asked about his legendary physical attributes, Shrubb told a correspondent he was now only three pounds over his running weight of forty years earlier. He believed people 'rusted out' if inactive. 'If only they'd get out and get more exercise they'd live longer. That's the reason I've lasted so long. You wear out quicker if you don't take care of yourself. I still try to walk a mile to a mile-and-a-half every day, weather permitting. Walking's fine exercise.' He added that nowadays he read a great deal, watched TV, followed the Maple Leafs ice hockey team, and was looking forward to a rise in fortunes for Canada's athletes following a recent five million dollar government grant for amateur sports. 'There's no doubt this [grant] will be a wonderful thing. It will give everyone better training and more opportunities. The pure amateur today can't afford to continue putting his hand in his own pocket. It's about time he had some help.'

Shrubb was always more than happy to pass on the benefit of his vast experience and was seen doing so to young runners when he was guest of honour at a track awards dinner in Toronto in early 1963. He received further unexpected publicity when a lengthy seven-verse poem, penned by one Ernie Sharpe, appeared in *Ontario Track Monthly*. The tribute included the lines:

At every meet – at every club
Wherever sporting men would meet
They spoke in awe of Alfie Shrubb
The man that no-one could defeat.
For when the people come to know
The pleasure that our sport can bring
The day may come – as long ago
When running reigned – and Shrubb was king.

Shortly after his 84th birthday in December 1963, Shrubb was made guest of honour at a civic reception for visiting athletes at the Toronto Telegram-Maple Leaf Indoor Games, where a new 425,000 dollar custom-built indoor track was inaugurated. Performing that night was the crack Georgetown University team, world record holders in the two-mile relay. Who could beat these boys? *The Telegram*'s Al Sokol mused: 'How about Alfie Shrubb, the guest of honour? In his prime he would have taken up the challenge ...'

Shrubb had indeed beaten top USA relay teams single-handedly in his time, but just now was not feeling quite as lively as he once had: 'I feel fine but the old legs aren't what they used to be. I get tired when I walk uptown for the mail.'

A month or two after this comment appeared in print, Alf Shrubb felt unwell and was taken into the Memorial Hospital, Bowmanville, just across the road from daughter Norah's house. Shortly afterwards the old champion passed away. He drew his final breath on Thursday, April 23rd, 1964, appropriately for such a patriot, St George's Day. Norah recalled that her father did not die of any specific illness, but a contributory factor may have been the bathtub accident, after which he had developed a bad cough. Typically, Shrubb had planned another Atlantic crossing to see England just before he died – it would have been his 21st since emigrating for good 36 years earlier.

By a quirk of fate, the very week Shrubb died, Essex runner Mel Batty was featured on the cover of *Athletics Weekly*, having followed in Shrubb's footsteps by breaking the ten-mile world record (47:26). And in the same issue, the editor P W Green bemoaned the fact that British athletics was suffering from a 'brain drain' to Canada, with leading coaches Lionel Pugh and Geoff Tyson having just headed off there. Apparently these days the Canadians placed far greater emphasis on coaching than we do, he observed.

Alfred Shrubb's funeral took place at the Morris Funeral Chapel, Bowmanville on Saturday, April 25th and he was buried in the local cemetery. Reverend K J Frampton of St John's Anglican Church officiated and the pallbearers included Shrubb's son-in-law H Lorne Allin, his grandson Eric and his granddaughter's husband Dan Cattran. A few days later his passing was announced thousands of miles away at the AGM of Horsham Blue Star Harriers and a flurry of lengthy obituaries appeared on both sides of the Atlantic.

Peter Lovesey wrote in *Athletics Weekly*: 'Occasionally in long distance running the predictable pattern of fractional record improvements is disturbed by a master-runner, who like some ocean breaker majestically forces the limit well beyond what had seemed possible. Walter George, Nurmi, Zatopek and Kuts were of such quality and so, undeniably was Alfred Shrubb. Shrubb's style was condemned by critics and coaches as ugly and unlikely to yield success, but he refused to alter his natural action, in which his feet, like Alain Mimoun's appeared to stroke the surface of the track in perpetually short, rapid strides while his trunk leaned well forward. The essence of his character is best expressed by his own observation on the many "miracle runners" who were nominated to achieve the overthrow of Shrubb: "Like deer they run for distance and keep me guessing. All of a sudden they would disappear and I, smilingly relieved, would trudge on alone".'

The SLH Gazette, edited by J Ward said: 'It is a measure of Shrubb's greatness that his records stood for so long and then fell only to athletes of similar stature, like Paavo Nurmi. Some of his English native records were still standing 50 years later and it was appropriate that his four miles record should be broken in 1952 by SLH's own Gordon Pirie who went on to emulate Shrubb in so many ways.' Club vice-president A W Clay-Thomas, who raced with Shrubb, added: 'I have nothing but praise for Shrubb's club spirit: in Yacht handicaps over the country when overtaking us, in spite of naturally wanting to win, he would ease his pace and offer words of encouragement with a happy smile on his face as he passed those he particularly knew which meant to much to myself and others. We had lots of plough in our courses and it was delight to see how lightly he skimmed it, while we were trudging heavily over it.'

Robbie Brightwell, European 400 metres champion, when performing the opening ceremony of new facilities at the Haslemere Border AC's HQ at Woolmer Hill playing fields in Surrey, reflected: 'It is from the ordinary club [like this one] that champions come, and this was never more true than of Alf Shrubb, produced by Horsham.'

In *The West Sussex County Times*, Horsham Blue Star Harriers' President George Etheridge said: 'The world is unlikely to see such a natural runner again. Without any of the modern-day aids he completely dominated distance running shortly after the turn of the century and the silver cups, canteens of cutlery and medals he collected would fill a small room.' The paper noted that his greatest test had been at the age of 82 when falling into his bath and puncturing a lung. 'But the great little fighter came back and shortly before his death was walking a mile-and-a-half per day just to keep in trim.'

In Bowmanville, *The Statesman* columnist Ed Youngman wrote: 'I'd idolised him since boyhood as one of the all time greats in athletics. I often wished I could meet him … but one day it happened … I shook hands with my boyhood hero and stood tongue tied. I just couldn't believe it …'

At the time of Shrubb's death, and throughout the 1960s, the man to beat at distances of between two miles and 20,000 metres was Ron Clarke of Australia. Clarke set a total of 21 world records (one unratified, three indoors), including eleven in a spell of sixteen races in 1965. It was an achievement that recalled Shrubb's dominance of sixty years earlier. And, in common with Shrubb, Clarke was a bold, front-running type who never achieved Olympic glory despite being clearly the fastest man at his distances.

In the years following his death, Shrubb would occasionally be remembered in the media via nostalgia shows and flashback articles. One example came when a Toronto radio station invited daughter Norah and Canadian's best-known middle-distance runner Dr Bruce Kidd into their studio. The presenter played an old audio tape of Shrubb, recorded shortly before his death, talking about how athletics had changed. Kidd told the presenter he had met Shrubb but admitted that at the time he had not realised the full extent of the modest old champion's achievements. On another occasion, Norah visited England and met old friends of her father and donated another of his cups to the Blue Star club, to be contested annually in a road race.

In 1989, Steve Payne of *The West Sussex County Times* began researching Shrubb's past. His articles prompted letters from elderly readers who remembered him. Horsham decided to honour its local hero by naming an indoor sprint track after him. Norah flew back to England in 1990 to perform the opening ceremony and the sixty-metre indoor track at Broadbridge Heath sports centre – often referred to as 'The Tube' – was named after Shrubb. Norah unveiled a special plaque beside the track, mounted adjacent to a huge mural of legendary runners, including her father. The plaque read:

THE ALFRED SHRUBB INDOOR SPRINT TRACK
Dedicated to Alfred Shrubb, born in Slinfold on December 12 1879, who held every world record for running from 2,000 yards to 11 miles. Died on St George's Day 1964 aged 84 years. His running was consistent and altogether was a performance that will never be forgotten by those who were privileged to witness it.

Ewan Shinton, sports centre manager, described Shrubb as a phenomenal athlete, as unique as the facility that now carried his name. The track, with an Olymprene surface, manufactured from a rubber crumb-type material, was and is a popular venue, with the likes of Kriss Akabusi, Mark Rowland and Sally Gunnell among the well-known names to have trained on it. After the unveiling of the plaque, the Alf Shrubb Two-Mile race was staged on the centre's outdoor track nearby, and was won by Graham Saker of the GEC club in 9:21.

Back in Canada, Shrubb's adopted home town of Bowmanville recognised its most famous sportsman with displays in the town's museum: his bowler hat and golf clubs were put on permanent display, in addition to occasional displays of other trophies and memorabilia. In 1993 a short-lived Bowmanville Museum Fun Run was staged, using Shrubb's name, though it did not really catch on.

A few years later, the former British runner Don Taylor was holidaying in Toronto with his wife when, by chance, he got chatting to a local woman in City Hall. Finding Taylor to be English, the woman told him she was seeking information on another Englishman – a famous runner by the name of Shrubb, who had once part-owned her workplace, the former Bowmanville mill. Astonished by the coincidence, Taylor was able to reveal that between 1963 and 1965 he had been British 10,000 metres record holder, a record once held by Shrubb, the very man she was interested in. On his return to England, Taylor carried out research on Shrubb and was able to send over the information the woman had needed for an exhibition she was setting up. From this chance meeting, Shrubb's name was beginning to come alive again.

Then, in the winter of 2002-03, Bowmanville running enthusiast Al Storie chanced upon the Shrubb legend and became eager to discover more. Inspired by the fascinating snippets he had picked up, Storie visited Shrubb's daughter and subsequently became determined to set up a major annual road race in Shrubb's name. His aim was to attract hundreds of runners from across Canada and establish the event as one of the biggest and best. With the help of friend Don Air and the support of Canada's huge Running Room organisation, Storie began setting things up, coincidentally, just as work on this book began on the other side of the Atlantic. This happy coincidence has helped the development of both projects.

The first Annual Alfie Shrubb 8k race took place on Sunday, June 1st, 2003 and was a huge success. Nearly 300 runners, far more than expected for a debut staging, turned out. Three generations of Shrubbs were present – daughter Norah, who fired the starting pistol, granddaughter Julia, and great grandson Scott, who took part in the race. Bowmanville Museum put on a special display of Shrubb memorabilia and a replica of one of Shrubb's 100-year-old medals was produced as a memento for all finishers. Appropriately, Longboat Runners, a Toronto club named in tribute to Shrubb's great rival, sent a team. Their spokesman John G Lyng praised the historical tone of the event and the replica medal, and said the race had a great deal of potential, with its organisers clearly committed for the long term. The race was won by Badza Shingirai, a South African who had recently won the Buffalo Marathon, and who beat the Longboat club's Charles Bedley into second place.

Interest in Shrubb and his achievements began to snowball in 2003 and the Mayor of Bowmanville, John Mutton, declared that a new street in the town would be named after Shrubb. Al Storie also announced plans to start a running club called Shrubb Striders. Later that year Shrubb was inducted into the regional Clarington Hall of Fame. Some of his many trophies were put on display and a plaque in his honour mounted at the Garnet B Rickard Recreation Complex in Bowmanville.

Norah said her father would have been delighted and proud at all the renewed interest in him, forty years after his death. Now, for certain, new generations of sports fans will hear or see his name and will marvel over this exiled Englishman who ran an estimated 1,800 races, and only lost a handful.

He may have died thousands of miles from where it all began, but no longer is Alfred Shrubb the forgotten hero of athletics.

Alf Shrubb's Official and Unofficial World Records

(* = ratified in 1921 by the IAAF)
(§ = passed by the AAA records committee)

2,000 yards
5:07.2 Stamford Bridge, September 26th, 1903

1¼ miles
5:40.2 Stamford Bridge, September 26th, 1903
5:37.0 Glasgow, June 11th, 1904

1½ miles
(i) 6:50.0 Ilford, May 30th, 1903 (On grass)
(ii) 6:47.6 § Stamford Bridge, September 26th, 1903
(Beat 3-year-old existing record by 3.4 secs)

1¾ miles
8:21.0 Glasgow, June 11th, 1904

2 miles
(i) 9:17.0 § Kennington Oval, September 12th, 1903
(Beat 7-year-old existing record by 0.4 secs)
(ii) 9:11.0 Ilford, May 30th, 1903 (On grass)
(iii) 9:09.6 *§ Glasgow, June 11th, 1904
(Lasted 22 years as world record and 32 years as GB record)

4,000 yards:
10:57.6 Stamford Bridge, September 27th, 1902
(Beat 9-year-old existing record by 0.6 secs).

3 miles
(i) 14:25.0 Chelmsford, July 19th, 1902
(On grass; beat 13-year-old record by 9 secs)
(ii) 14:22.4 Horsham, August 3rd, 1903 (On grass)
(iii) 14:17.6 *§ Stamford Bridge, May 21st, 1903

(Lasted 29 years as world record and 33 years as GB record)
(iv) 14:17.2 Abergavenny, August 27th, 1904 (On grass)

5,000 METRES
(i) 15:03.0 (estimated) Glasgow, June 15th, 1903
(ii) 14:59.0 (estimated) Glasgow, June 13th, 1904

4 MILES
(i) 19:31.6 § Brighton, October 25th, 1902
(ii) 19:26.8 Reigate, September 20th, 1902
(On grass; beat 15-year-old existing record by 18 secs)
(iii) 19:23.4 § Glasgow, June 13th, 1904
(Lasted 20 years as world record)

5 MILES
24:33.4 § Stamford Bridge, May 12th, 1904
(Beat 12-year-old record by 20 secs; lasted 48 years as GB record)

6 MILES
29:59.4 *§ Glasgow, November 5th, 1904
(Beat 12-year-old existing record by 18.4 secs; lasted 26 years as world
record and 32 years as GB record)

10,000 METRES
31:02.4 Glasgow, November 5th, 1904
(Lasted 7 years as world record and 32 years as GB record)

7 MILES
35:04.6 Glasgow, November 5th, 1904
(Beat existing record by 34.2 secs)

8 MILES
40:16.0 Glasgow, November 5th, 1904

9 MILES
45:27.6 Glasgow, November 5th, 1904

10 MILES
50:40.6 *§ Glasgow, November 5th, 1904
(Beat 20-year-old existing record by 39.4 secs; lasted 24 years as a world
record and 31 years as a GB record)

11 MILES
56:23.4 Glasgow, November 5th, 1904

ONE HOUR
11 miles, 1,137 yards (18,738 metres) *§ Glasgow, November 5th, 1904
(Beat existing record by 205 yards; lasted 9 years as a world record and
49 years as a British record)

NOTES ON THE RECORDS

In Shrubb's era, records set in the UK would be considered by the AAA at an end-of-year meeting and only 'passed' if the conditions of the race met their criteria. Some of Shrubb's finest runs were on grass, as opposed to cinder tracks, meaning he held a number of records not regarded as 'official', although widely publicised as such in the press. A further complication for statisticians of the time was the existence of records for both amateur and professional runners – although, again, only the amateur marks, with AAA approval, were considered 'official'. In 1921, the International Amateur Athletics Federation (IAAF) decided to tidy up the whole situation by issuing a list of ratified world records at standard distances. From that day, their figures would be the only 'official' world records.

In Shrubb's day, timing was by hand. Seconds were broken down into fifths. For the purposes of this book, one-fifth is always denoted as 0.2, two-fifths as 0.4, etc.

Shrubb's tally of official and unofficial world records set on British soil is thought to be higher than that of any other runner, before or since.

Even though Shrubb left the amateur ranks in 1905, the IAAF's new ratified records list of 1921 still featured his name at a number of distances. Many of these records finally fell in the 1930s, but some of his English native records lasted into the early 1950s.

After Shrubb in 1904, the next UK runner to set a world record at a standard distance was Gordon Pirie, some 49 years later, with his 28:19.4 for six miles in the 1953 AAA championships.

A remarkable fact about Shrubb's records is that none was set with the help of pacemakers. Moreover, most were achieved at events where there were no other runners of comparable ability to push him. However, in some handicap races, he did sometimes have opponents to chase.

Although he was twice English mile champion, Shrubb never broke one-mile records. His best time was 4.22 (July 2nd, 1904) at Rochdale.

Shrubb's three-mile world record, set in London on May 21st, 1903 was beaten on September 12th, 1922 by Paavo Nurmi, who clocked 14:08.4. As the IAAF did not recognise Nurmi's performance, Shrubb's mark stood until June 19th, 1932, when Lauri Lehtinen ran 13:50.6; Shrubb's time was not beaten by a Briton for 33 years until Peter Ward on July 11th, 1936, who ran 14:15.8.

Shrubb's three-mile performance on May 21st, 1903 was the last time a world record would be set at this distance on British soil for 51 years, until Vladimir Kuts achieved the feat in 1954.

In August 1973, Brendan Foster became the first British world record holder at two miles since Shrubb, some 69 years earlier. Foster clocked 8:13.8 to beat Lasse Viren's mark by 0.2 secs.

Shrubb's six-mile world record at Glasgow on November 5th, 1904 was beaten on November 16th, 1911 by Jean Bouin of France (29:51.6), but this was not recognised by the IAAF, so Shrubb's mark stood for nearly 26 years until Paavo Nurmi ran 29:36.4 on June 9th, 1930. No Briton beat Shrubb's time until William Eaton ran 29:51.4 nearly 32 years later on April 13th, 1936.

Shrubb was declared 'world indoor record holder at three miles' by the press after he clocked 14:27, then 14:23.4, then 14:19 – all during February 1906 in professional races at London's Olympia.

Shrubb's ten-mile time at Glasgow on November 5th, 1904 (50:40.6) would only be bettered once by an Englishman during the next half-century (i.e. between 1904 and 1954).

Shrubb ran fifteen miles in 80:15.0 at Stamford Bridge on July 21st, 1902, which was fully two minutes inside the existing ten-year-old world record. Unfortunately for Shrubb, Fred Appleby ran even quicker in the same event to become the new record holder.

SHRUBB'S AAA TITLES

ONE MILE
(i)   1903, 4:24.0   Northampton
(ii) 1904, 4:22.0   Rochdale

FOUR MILES
(i)   1901, 20:01.8 Huddersfield
(ii)   1902, 20:01.4 Stamford Bridge
(iii) 1903, 20:06.0 Northampton
(iv)   1904, 19:56.8 Rochdale

TEN MILES

(i)   1901, 53:32.0 Crewe
(ii)   1902, 52:25.6 Stamford Bridge
(iii)   1903, 51:55.8 Northampton
(iv)   1904, 54:30.4 Rochdale

(These ten AAA titles, achieved by Shrubb in only four track seasons, equalled the career record set by Walter 'W G' George)

SHRUBB'S MAJOR CROSS-COUNTRY TITLES

International XC championships (latterly the World Championships):
Winner 1903, 46:23 at Hamilton (inaugural event)
Winner 1904, 47:59 at St Helens

English National XC:
Winner 1901, Leicester
Winner 1902, Lingfield Park
Winner 1903, Haydock Park
Winner 1904, Wolverhampton
(4 successive wins equalled Percy Stenning's record)

Southern XC:
Winner 1901, Wembley Park
Winner 1902, Lingfield Park
Winner 1903, Haydock Park
Winner 1904, Lingfield Park

SHRUBB'S FOUR-WEEK TRAINING PROGRAMME, PRIOR TO HIS NOVEMBER 1904 WORLD RECORD ATTEMPT AT GLASGOW (M = MILES)

DATE	MORNING	AFTERNOON	WEIGHT STRIPPED
October 6th	3m fairly slow	6m decent pace	122lbs
October 7th	4m good pace	5m good pace	120lbs
October 8th	4m good pace	Wet – no run	120lbs
October 9th	Rest day		122lbs
October 10th	3m fairly fast	3m slow	121lbs
October 11th	2m fast	6m slow	120½lbs
October 12th	No run	6m medium pace	120lbs
October 13th	3m good pace	4m medium pace	119¾lbs
October 14th	5m steady	No run	120lbs

October 15th	Brisk walk	3m fast	119½lbs
October 16th	Rest day		121lbs
October 17th	8m steady	2m fast bursts	120¾lbs
October 18th	4m good pace	2m time-trial (9:18)	120lbs
October 19th	No run	10m time-trial (51:10)	119lbs
October 20th	5m steady	No run	118½lbs
October 21st	No run	2m bursts	119¾lbs
October 22nd	6m goodish pace	8m slow	118¾lbs
October 23rd	Rest day		119¾lbs
October 24th	4m steady	2m time-trial (9:17.8)	119lbs
October 25th	No run	10m time-trial (51:02)	118¼lbs
October 26th	4m steady	2m time-trial (9:18.6)	119lbs
October 27th	8m steady	No run	118lbs
October 28th	Rest day		119¾lbs
October 29th	4m steady	8m slow	118¼lbs
October 30th	Rest day		119¾lbs
November 1st	3m steady	10m time-trial (50:55)	118lbs
November 2nd	2m fast	5m steady	119lbs
November 3rd	8m steady	4m fairly fast	119¼lbs
November 4th	Rest day		119lbs
November 5th	Race day, Ibrox Park, Glasgow (See below)		

Shrubb devised the above schedule himself, with the aim of getting himself in sufficiently good shape to break the ten-mile world record on November 5th, 1904. Unlike modern-day distance runners, he did no 'over-distance' training at all, but the volume of mileage was still higher than anything undertaken at that time. Training twice a day was almost unheard of before Shrubb came along. Even 100 years later, his schedule looks a good mixture of pace and distance, and clearly brought him to a 'peak' perfectly (note the steady improvement in the three ten-mile time-trials).

SHRUBB'S 'NORMAL' DAILY TRAINING REGIME

1. Rise 7am
2. Ten minutes free exercise
3. Brisk walk of 2 miles
4. Breakfast
5. Short rest
6. 4-8 mile run
7. Lunch 1pm

8. 3pm run: (3 miles in Week 1; 8-10 miles in Week 2; 2 miles fast in Week 3; 2-8 miles fast or 10 miles steady in Week 4.
9. Early evening: Dinner
10. Retire to bed: 10-10.30pm
    (Most pre-run warm-ups involved 880 yards jog in weighted boots.)
    (The above routine would be adjusted to allow for races. Sundays were normally a rest day.)

DETAILS OF SPLIT TIMES FROM VARIOUS RACES

(1)   Ibrox Park, Glasgow, November 5th, 1904:
(As certified by A G Rennie & J W Brownrigg; records passed by AAA on January 11th, 1905)

LAP	LAP TIME	DISTANCE	OVERALL TIME
1	64.8		
2	69.8		
3	73.8		
4	75.8	1 mile	4:44.2
5	74.0		
6	74.2		
7	76.0		
8	75.6	2 miles	9:44.2
9	75.0		
10	75.4		
11	75.8		
12	76.4	3 miles	14:45.8
13	75.8		
14	76.4		
15	76.6		
16	77.4	4 miles	19:50.6
17	76.6		
18	76.0		
19	76.2		
20	76.4	5 miles	4:55.8
21	76.0		
22	75.4		
23	76.0		
24	76.2	6 miles	9:59.4
25	75.4		
26	76.0		

27	77.2		
28	76.6	7 miles	35:04.6
29	77.6		
30	77.4		
31	78.0		
32	78.4	8 miles	40:16.0
33	78.4		
34	77.4		
35	76.8		
36	79.0	9 miles	45:27.6
37	80.8		
38	77.4		
39	79.6		
40	75.2	10 miles	50:40.6
41	85.0		
42	85.0		
43	86.0		
44	86.8	11 miles	56:23.4
45	85.2		
46	82.2		
47 (part of)	49.2	11 miles, 1,137 yards	60:00.0

(The six, seven, eight, nine, ten, eleven, and one-hour marks above were all World (amateur) Record times; all times for five miles and over were Scottish allcomers records. The times for eight, nine, ten, and eleven miles improved on the existing world professional records.)

(2)   AAA 10, Stamford Bridge, London, April 5th, 1902. Mile splits: 4.46, 5.06, 5.07, 5.09, 5.16, 5.23, 5.19, 5.27, 5.33, and 5.20.

(3)   Ibrox Park, Glasgow, June 11th 1904. Two-mile world record. 440-yard lap splits: 1.00, 2.06, 3.15, 4.27, 5.37, 6.49, 8.02, and 9:09.6.

(4)   Horsham Bank Holiday Sports, Five-Mile challenge v A Aldridge, August 7th, 1905. Mile splits: 4:36.0, 5:01.4, 5:03.8, 5:05.2, and 5:04.8.

(5)   'Head-to-head' versus Henri St Yves, Fifteen Miles, New York Baseball Grounds, April 24th 1909. Mile splits (Shrubb led throughout): 4:54, 10:14, 15:32, 20:36, 26:23, 31:56 37:29, 43:19, 49:23, 55:39, 61:32, 68:03, 73:15, 80:17, and 86:12.

(6)   Progressive AC Games, Revere, Massachusetts, September 4th, 1911. Ten-Mile challenge v T Longboat. Mile splits: (Shrubb leading, unless stated): 4:50.0, 10:03.6, 15:22.6 (Longboat), 20:43.4, 26:12.4, 31:46.4, 37:21.6, 42:55.8 (Longboat), 48:11.0, and 53:28.4.

Research Sources and Acknowledgements

BOOKS:

Amateurism in Sport: An Analysis and Defence (Lincoln Allison)

An Athletics Compendium: An Annotated Guide to the Literature of Track & Field (McNab, Lovesey & Huxtable)

Boston Marathon (Tom Derderian)

Cambridge Doctor (Rex Salisbury-Woods)

Champions: Great Figures In Canadian Sport (Jack Batten)

Death at the Excelsior (P G Wodehouse)

Five Kings of Distance (Peter Lovesey)

First Four Minutes (Roger Bannister)

Front Runners: The First Athletic Track Champions (Warren Roe)

Gertrude Bell (H V F Winstone)

Ghosts of Haileybury (Various)

History of British Athletics (Mel Watman)

The Impossible Hero (Dick Booth)

The Longboat story: The Man Who Ran Faster Than Everyone (Jack Batten)

Long Distance Running and Training (Alfred Shrubb)

Lore of Running (Tim Noakes)

The Lost World (Arthur Conan Doyle)

Marathon Kings (Norman Giller)

The Official Centenary History of the AAA (Peter Lovesey)

The Olympians (Sebastian Coe)

Olympic Facts and Feats (Stan Greenberg)

Out In Front (George Gretton)

Oxford Companion to Sports and Games

Running and Cross-Country Running (Alfred Shrubb)

Running Through The Ages (Edward S Sears)

Today's Athlete (Brian Mitchell – edited)

A World History of Long Distance Running (1880-2002) Track Events (Roberto L Quercetani)

World Record Breakers In Track and Field Athletics (Gerald Lawson)

NEWSPAPERS

UNITED KINGDOM: *Abergavenny Chronicle, Athletic News and Cyclists Journal, Daily Telegraph, Daily Mail, Essex Weekly News, Glasgow Herald, Mid-*

Sussex Times, Morning Leader, Oxford Times, The People, Sporting Life, Sunday Mercury, Sussex Daily News, The Times, West Sussex County Times

United States: *The American, Boston Post, New York Mirror, New York Post, The World*

Canada: *Bowmanville Statesman, Manitoba Free Press, Montreal Free Press, Montreal Star, Oshawa Daily Times-Gazette, Peterborough Examiner, St John's Daily News, St John's Evening Herald. St John's Evening Telegram, Toronto Daily Star, Toronto Globe & Mail, Toronto Evening Telegram, Winnipeg Morning Telegram*

Australasia: *Southland Times (NZ), Sydney Daily Telegraph, Sydney Morning Herald*

Magazines and Periodicals

All Sports Weekly, Athletic Field & Swimming News, Athletics Arena, Athletics Weekly, Bell's Life In London, The Belvedere (Bowmanville Museum), C.B. Fry's Magazine, Harper's Weekly, Health & Strength, Illustrated Sporting & Dramatic News, Ontario Track Monthly, Running Times, Runners World, South London Harriers Gazette, Sport and Play, Sporting Sketches, The Sportsman, Track & Field News, Truth, W G's Athletic Weekly, World Sports

Articles and Academic Papers etc:

Developments in Amateurism and Professionalism in Early 20th Century Canadian Sport (Kevin G Jones of York University, Toronto);
The Gertrude Bell Project – University of Newcastle Upon Tyne;
Run for Acoose, by Barbara Zieman, from 'Saskatchewan Indian';
A Day at the Races, by Brian Dobbs from 'Ghosts of Haileybury';
UK census of 1901.

Internet Sites (selection)

abc.net.au
gbrathletics.com
trackfield.brinkster.net
www.sportsfacts.net
airsports.fai.org
gordonpirie.com
davidblaikie.com
trackandfieldnews.com
athsvic.org.au
mattoleriver.com
aafla.org
jonentine.com

ceiu-seic.ca
eh.net
pennathletics.ocsn.com
lps-athletics.co.uk
galaxy.bedfordshire.gov.uk

MY THANKS FOR ASSISTANCE TO:
Norah Allin (Alf Shrubb's daughter), Al Storie (Race Director, 'Shrubb 8k'), Peter Lovesey (author & athletics historian), John Stanton and Mike Mendzat (Running Room, Canada), British Library (Newspaper Library) Colindale, Keith May (Horsham Blue Star Harriers), Charles Taws and colleagues (Bowmanville Museum), Laurence Chandy, Michael Rush, Graham Tanner, Peter Thompson and John De'ath (Oxford University Athletics Club), Ron Clarke (Olympic medallist and multi-world record holder), Trevor Vincent (Commonwealth Games gold medallist 1962), Brian Comber (distant relative of Alf Shrubb), Gary Bott (distant relative of Alf Shrubb), Tom and Val Worrell (Melbourne-based athletes), Broadbridge Leisure Centre, Horsham, Prof Lincoln Allison (Warwick University), Horsham Museum, Horsham Pubic Library, Don Taylor (former GB 10,000 metre record holder), Stan Greenberg (athletics statistician), Ferdie Gilson (historian, South London Harriers), Kevin Kelly (historian, Herne Hill Harriers), Warren Roe (athletics historian & author), Steve Chilton (Barnet & District AC), Richard (Visual Arts Centre of Clarington), Julia Cattran (Alf Shrubb's granddaughter), Scott Cattran (Alf Shrubb's great-grandson), John G Lyng (Longboat Runners, Toronto), Bob Phillips (National Union of Track Statisticians), Penny Joyce (Athletics Canada), Metro Toronto Reference Library, Clarington Public Library, Rhona Mitchell & Tracy Butler (Christ's Hospital School, Sussex), Charmaine Sommerfeldt (Archives of Ontario), Duncan Thorn (Ontario Road Runners), Mary Lou Naccarato (Bowmanville), Jennifer Rupp (Harvard University), Barrie Shepley (Canadian performance coach), Stephanie Jenkins (Oxford historian), Matthew Scholtz (Tillsonburg Public Library), Peter Williams (OWLS AC), Colchester Evening Gazette, BBC Essex, BBC Look East, Christopher W Osland (Haileybury Heritage Museum), P N Heidenstrom (New Zealand athletics historian), Martin Rix (athletics statistician), Ian Tempest (athletics statistician). And, not forgetting my wife Katie (checking, encouragement and advice), plus John, Bev, and Arcos, all in Sydney, Australia.

APPENDIX 3

References

INTRODUCTION

p.19   'Nelson Smith had' *West Sussex County Times*, 1919

CHAPTER 1

p.21   'The 1870s was' *Britain 1783-1918*, (ed) Murphy

p.21   'The arrival of' Copy of Birth Certif., via B Comber

p.22   'Horsham was a' T Lambert article, website: geocities.com

p.22   'Although an older' 1901 Census/B Comber.

p.22   'As well as learning' Shrubb's notes/*All Sports Weekly*, 1920

p.22   'It could be hazardous' *West Sussex County Times*, 1899

p.23   'Shrubb felt at home' *C.B. Fry's Magazine*, 1904

p.23   'And Shrubb himself' *Running & Cross-Country Running*, Shrubb

p.23   'Shrubb's fondness' Shrubb's notes/*All Sports Weekly*, 1920

p.24   'The warm evening in' Shrubb's notes/*All Sports Weekly*, 1920

p.25   'It was soon damped' *West Sussex County Times*, 1900

p.25   'Tonight's haystack fire' *West Sussex County Times*, 1899

p.25   'Spencer realised' 1901 Census

p.26   'Shrubb recalled' Shrubb's notes/*All Sports Weekly*, 1920

p.26   'His new pals' *West Sussex County Times*, 1899

p.27   'With the coming' *West Sussex County Times*, 1899

p.28   'After his systematic' *West Sussex County Times*, 1900

p.30   'Equally excited' *Athletic Field & Swimming News*, 1910

p.30   'Three days after' *West Sussex County Times*, 1900

CHAPTER 2

p.31   'With the approach' *Olympic Facts and Feats*, Stan Greenberg

p.32   'Shrubb was content' Shrubb's notes/*All Sports Weekly*, 1920

p.32   'It now dawned' Shrubb's notes/*All Sports Weekly*, 1920

p.32   'A number of' *Sporting Life*, 1900/*Athletic News*, 1900

p.33   'Leading was the' Shrubb's notes/*All Sports Weekly*, 1920

p.34   'He felt privileged' *Dickens Dictionary of London*, 1879

p.34   'In their sights' *Essex Weekly News*, 1900/*West Sussex County Times*, 1900/*Athletic News*, 1900

p.36   'Shrubb's new trophy' *The Times*, 1919

p.36   'Upon his return' *West Sussex County Times*, 1900

p.38   'In early September' *Athletic News*, 1900

p.70 'Albert Aldridge was' *West Sussex County Times*, 1902

p.71 'This slip-up was' *Sporting Life*, 1905

p.72 'This wasn't the only' Shrubb's notes/*All Sports Weekly*, 1920

p.74 'The 27th National was' *Athletic News*, 1902/*West Sussex County Times*, 1903/*Sport and Play*, 1903

p.74 'His coach, Harry' *Atheltic Field and Swimming News*, 1910

p.74 'The Magazine' *Sport and Play*, 1903

p.75 'Shrubb's impeccable unbeaten' *Athletic News*, 1903/article on web site: mattoleriver.com

CHAPTER 7

p.79 'Shrubb's plans received' *Sporting Life*, 1903/Warren Roe's notes

p.83 'Hordes of day-trippers' *West Sussex County Times*, 1903

p.84 'At Villa Park' *West Sussex County Times*, 1903/*The Sportsman*, 1903

p.84 'Raging storms on' *The Times*, 1903

p.85 'In late September' *The Times*, 1903

p.86 'Shrubb enjoyed trouncing' *West Sussex County Times*, 1903

p.86 '1904 began for Shrubb' *Athletic News*, 1904

p.87 'Spectators and runners' *Athletic News*, 1904

p.87 'A record entry' *West Sussex County Times*, 1904, *Athletic News* 1904

p.87 'The Midlands AAA' *Athletic News*, 1904/*The Times* 1904

p.90 'Shrubb's utter dominance' *Athletic News*, 1904

CHAPTER 8

p.92 'After an evening' Shrubb's notes/*All Sports Weekly*, 1920

p.93 'Around the same' *Athletic News*, 1904

p.94 'At the end of May' P Lovesey's notes/*The Times*, 1904

p.95 'On race day, Shrubb was seen' *Athletic News*, 1904

p.97 'Rochdale also coincided' *W.G.'s Athletic Weekly*, 1904

p.99 'The crowd enveloped ' *Athletic Field and Swimming News*, 1910

p.99 'A week after his' *W.G.'s Athletic Weekly*, 1904

p.101 'The Inter-Town Sports' *Abergavenney Chronicle*, 1904

p.101 'Abel was a diminutive' Shrubb's notes/*All Sports Weekly*, 1920 /*Athletic News*, 1904

p.101 'Although it seems' Shrubb's notes/*All Sports Weekly*, 1920

CHAPTER 9

p.105 'Even Doctor Badger' *W.G.'s Athletics Weekly, 1904*

p.106 'Grim-faced' *Five Kings of Distance*, Peter Lovesey

p.106 'Shrubb drew' *Running & Cross-Country Running*, Shrubb p.107 'For his attempt' Shrubb's notes/*All Sports Weekly*, 1920

p.107 'On race day' *Five Kings of Distance,* Peter Lovesey, 1968

p.108 'The track was' *Athletic News*, 1904

p.108 'Admission to' J Keddie & P Lovesey's notes

p.109 'Starter Cameron' *Athletic News*, 1904

p.109 'He opened up' J Keddie & P Lovesey's notes

p.111 'Just a hint' *Five Kings of Distance*, Peter Lovesey

p.111 'Into the last' Shrubb's notes/*All Sports Weekly*, 1920

p.111 'To a deafening roar' Shrubb's notes/*All Sports Weekly*, 1920

p.112 'As he made' Shrubb's notes/*All Sports Weekly*, 1920

p.113 'During the evening' *West Sussex County Times*, 1904

p.113 'With his 20-year-old' *W.G.'s Athletic Weekly*, 1904

p.113 'George wasn't the' Copy of letter via P Lovesey

p.114 'At the station' Shrubb's notes/*All Sports Weekly*, 1920

CHAPTER 10

p.116 'The Amateur Athletic' Shrubb's notes/*All Sports Weekly*, 1920

p.116 'Thursday December 29' *West Sussex County Times*, 1905

p.116 'Fowler-Dixon, the' Original letter, Mrs N Allin's collection

p.117 'After lunch the' Shrubb's notes/*All Sports Weekly*, 1920

p.117 'Duffey pranced like' *Athletic News*, 1903

p.118 'On Friday January 6' The Gertrude Bell Project, University of Newcastle-upon-Tyne/*Desert Queen,* Janet Wallach

p.119 'A degree of colour' *Peeps at Great Steamship Lines,* G E Mitton

p.119 'Although Australia was' The Gertrude Bell Project, University of Newcastle-upon-Tyne

p.120 'The Mayor was among' *Sydney Morning Herald*, 1905

p.121 'The championships commenced' *Sydney Morning Herald,* 1905/website: athsvic.org.au

p.121 'Still in buoyant mood' SLH Gazette/P Lovesey's notes

p.121 'In mid-week Shrubb' *Sydney Morning Herald*, 1905/*The Times*, 1905 /Unidentified cuttings, Mrs N Allin's collection

p.122 'The ship' Websites: home.plant.nl/worldwar1.co.uk/etext.lib.vir ginia.edu/blaxland.com

p.123 Six hours out' Shrubb's notes/*All Sports Weekly*, 1920 /Unidentified cutting, Mrs N Allin's collection

p.124 'Various correspondents were' *NZ Southland Times*, 1905

p.125 'The following day' *Sydney Morning Herald*, 1905

p.126 'Also at Auckland' *NZ Herald*, 1905

p.126 'On April 12' Original invitation, Mrs N Allin's collection

p.126 'He was also a guest' Mrs N Allin/Mrs A Southam

p.127 'NSW's mile championship' *Sydney Morning Herald*, 1905

p.127 'The following day' *West Sussex County Times*, 1905

p.128 'On Saturday, April 22nd' *Sydney Morning Herald*, 1905

p.129 'Taking a retrospective' P Heidenstrom's notes

p.130 'Shrubb was certainly' Shrubb's notes/*All Sports Weekly*, 1920

p.130 'The ship steamed' *West Sussex County Times*, 1905

p.131 'Because of the train timetables' *West Sussex County Times*, 1905

CHAPTER 11

p.132 'The incident occurred' *The Morning Leader*, 1905/*The Times*, 1905 /*C.B. Fry's Magazine*, 1905/*West Sussex County Times*, 1905

p.133 'Shrubb was glad' *West Sussex County Times*, 1905/Original invitation, Mrs N Allin's collection.

p.134 'While mulling these' *West Sussex County Times*, 1905

p.135 'Their decision was not' Shrubb's notes/*All Sports Weekly*, 1920

p.136 'Matters came to' Shrubb's notes/*All Sports Weekly*, 1920

p.138 'Writing under his' *The People*, 1905

p.139 'On Saturday, October 21st' *West Sussex County Times*, 1905

p.139 'By November it had' *Sporting Life*, 1905

p.141 '£40 5s 11d, converted' Website: eh.net

p.144 'An anonymous letter in the' *Sporting Life*, 1905

p.146 'On Saturday, January 20th' *West Sussex County Times*, 1906

CHAPTER 12

p.180 'A handful of relatives' *Sporting Life*, 1906/*Mid-Sussex Times*, 1906 /Unidentified cuttings, Mrs N Allin's collection

p.181 'The couple were clearly' Shrubb's notes/*All Sports Weekly*, 1920

p.181 'Certainly the twenty-year-old' Website: eco.co.uk

p.183 'Although his days in' SLH Gazette 1906/*Sporting Life* 1906

p.184 'The local press told' *West Sussex County Times*, 1906

CHAPTER 13

p.186 'Little would change' Phillip article, *Weekly Telegraph*, 2003

p.186 'In the modern age' *The Olympians*, S Coe & N Mason

p.186 'Today the main problem' Website: airsports.fai.org

p.186 'One man with answers' Website: abc.net.au

p.188 'In 1949, at the' Website: abc.net.au

p.189 'He was philosophical' Shrubb's notes/*All Sports Weekly*, 1920

p.189 'It is curious' *The Primrose Path*, Sir Derek Birley, via website: umist.ac.uk

p.190 'This surreal world' Website: users.moscow.com/ronrobb/life p.190 'One such character' Southwark Borough Council. Websites: Southwark.gov.uk/bbc.co.uk

p.191 'The Soviet was' Phillip article, *Weekly Telegraph*, 2003

p.191 'Paula Radcliffe' bbc.co.uk/sport gives a figure of £630,000

p.192 'The five Olympiads' *Olympic Facts and Feats,* Stan Greenberg

CHAPTER 14

p.195 'The cable came' Shrubb's notes/*All Sports Weekly*, 1920

p.197 'Shrubb, meanwhile, threw' Shrubb's notes/*All Sports Weekly*, 1920

p.197 'Duffey was nowhere' Shrubb's notes/*All Sports Weekly*, 1920

p.201 'Race-fixing and betting' Original 1968 letter, P Lovesey

p.202 'In the mean time' Shrubb's notes/*All Sports Weekly*, 1920

p.204 'On Thursday, July 4th' *Boston Post*, 1907

p.204 'Shrubb may have beaten' Shrubb's notes/*All Sports Weekly*, 1920

p.205 'While Shrubb was staying' *Boston Post*, 1907

p.205 'On Saturday, August 10th' *The World*, 1907

p.205 'Meanwhile, in Canada' *Montreal Free Press*, 1907

p.205 'The head-to-head with' Shrubb's notes/*All Sports Weekly*, 1920

p.206 'Back in England' *West Sussex County Times*, 1907

p.207 'A big crowd turned' *Toronto Telegram*, 1907/Shrubb's notes/*All Sports Weekly*, 1920.

CHAPTER 15

p.209 'Flanagan was deeply immersed' *The Man Who Ran Faster Than Everyone*, Jack Batten, 2002

p.211 'Many years later' *Belvedere Magazine*, Bowmanville, 1995

p.212 'He recalled later' Shrubb's notes/*All Sports Weekly*, 1920

p.212 'Staying at the Avenue' Shrubb's notes/*All Sports Weekly*, 1920

p.212 'In the autumn' *Manitoba Free Press*, 1907

p.214 'One Shrubb fan who' *Winnipeg Telegram*, 1907

p.215 'On his arrival, the' *West Sussex County Times*, 1908

p.215 'Meanwhile, returning' *West Sussex County Times*, 1908

p.215 'A correspondent from' *Sussex Daily News*, 1908

p.217 'The ship docked' Shrubb's notes/*All Sports Weekly*, 1920

p.218 'To put these figures' Website: eh.net

p.219 'The only aspect' Various, incl. *Olympic Babylon,* Pat Shiel, 1998

p.220 'A group of expats' Shrubb's notes/*All Sports Weekly*, 1920

p.221 'On Thursday, November 26th' *Toronto Telegram*, 1908

CHAPTER 16

p.223 'In the mean time' *West Sussex County Times*, 1909

p.223 'Promoter Pat Powers was delighted' *The Man Who Ran Faster Than Everyone,* Jack Batten

p.223 'Three days prior' *Toronto Telegram,* 1909

p.224 'Around 12,000' Various, incl: Shrubb's notes/*All Sports Weekly,* 1920/*Toronto Telegram*/Website: davidblaikiecom

p.229 'I'd slipped away' Shrubb's notes/*All Sports Weekly,* 1920

p.230 'Before leaving' *Toronto Telegram* 1909/Mrs N Allin's collection

p.231 'Shrubb forged' *Toronto Telegram,* 1909

p.232 'The bubbly Pietri' *Track and Field News,* 1959

p.233 'Despite glowering skies' Various, incl. *Toronto Telegram,* 1909

p.235 'One spectator at' *West Sussex County Times,* 1909

CHAPTER 17

p.238 'The occasion was' *Manitoba Free Press,* 1909/Shrubb's notes/*All Sports Weekly,* 1920

p.242 'Instead of breaking' *Manitoba Free Press,* 1909/Zieman article, *Saskatchewan Indian,* 1982.

p.243 'Fulfilling his coaching' Shrubb's notes/*All Sports Weekly,* 1920

p.244 'This was in May' *Boston Daily Globe,* 1910

p.244 'One English paper' *The Times,* 1910

p.244 'Later Shrubb penned' Harvard University magazine, 1910

p.244 'Local historian' Dobbs article, *Ghosts of Haileybury*

p.246 'Shrubb and Longboat' Shrubb's notes/*All Sports Weekly,* 1920 /*West Sussex County Times,* 1911

p.246 'Sportswriters called it' *Boston Post,* 1911

p.247 'Both authors acknowledged' *Death At The Excelsior,* P G Wodehouse,/*The Lost World,* Arthur Conan Doyle

p.248 'Whatever vestiges of professional racing' *The Man Who Ran Faster Than Everyone,* Jack Batten

p.248 'This was the year' *Canadian Statesman,* 1945

CHAPTER 18

p.250 'Skippered by Captain' *Evening Herald,* St John's, 1919/*Evening Telegram,* St John's, 1919/*St John's Daily News,* 1919

p.252 'After going ashore' 1919 telegram, Mrs N Allin's collection

p.254 'Shortly before the' 1919 letter, Mrs N Allin's collection

p.254 'As they steamed' *West Sussex County Times,* 1919

CHAPTER 19

p.256 'Chandy, Tanner and Rush' *Oxford University Athletics Club History*

p.256 'While working at his' Shrubb's notes/*All Sports Weekly* p.258 'Once he had begun' *First Four Minutes,* Rover Bannister

p.260 'Shrubb's first months as' *Oxford University Athletics Club History*

p.263 'Over at Cambridge' Website: movie-reviews.collosus.net

p.264 'Although it was' 1925 letter, Mrs N Allin's collection

p.264 'Thousands of miles' *Boston: The Canadian Story,* David Blaikie/
Johnny Miles: *Nova Scotia's Marathon King,* Floyd Williston

CHAPTER 20

p.265 'Organisers of the annual' *Oxford University Athletics Club History*

p.265 'Relay running as' Website: pennathletics.ocsm.com

p.266 'The Oxbridge party left' Shrubb's notes/*All Sports Weekly,* 1920/
Oxford University Athletics Club History

p.267 'Bevil Rudd was' *The Times,* 1953/Website: bdb.co.za/kimberley

p.268 'We were met by' Shrubb's notes/*All Sports Weekly,* 1920

p.271 'Princeton triumphed' *Oxford University Athletics Club History*

CHAPTER 21

p.272 'His findings included' Oxford University Athletics Club minute
books, 1920-28

p.273 'Peter Lovesey, author' P Lovesey's notes

p.273 'In October 1927' *The Times,* 1927

p.274 'The other major issue' Mrs N Allin

p.274 'Many were sorry' *Oxford Times,* 1928

p.274 'Daughter Norah recalled' Mrs N Allin

p.274 'For many fellow' Website: geocities.com/kouhi_world/atlantic

p.275 'Canadian immigration' Canadian Archive immigration records

p.275 'Shortly after their' Mrs N Allin/Clarington Visual Arts centre

p.276 'Unexpectedly, Shrubb was' *Toronto Daily Star,* 1930

p.278 'The Ontario press' *Peterborough Examiner* (Ontario), 1939

p.279 'Although he was' 1945 letter, Mrs N Allin collection

p.279 'In March 1952' *Canadian Statesman,* 1952

p.280 'More than 100 guests' *The Times,* 1952

p.281 'After toasting the' SLH Gazette, winter 1952-53

p.281 'The October 1952' *Athletics World,* 1952

p.282 'Shrubb spent a lively' *West Sussex County Times,* 1952

p.282 'As 1952 drew' Mrs N Allin/*The Guardian,* 2002

CHAPTER 22

p.284 'The idea was born' *Oshawa Daily Times-Gazette,* 1958/*Belvedere
Magazine,* Bowmanville, 1995

p.285 'During this visit' *Athletics Weekly,* 1959

p.285 'By the start of the 1960s' Mrs N Allin

p.285 'Coincidentally, just days' *Toronto Daily Star*, 1961

p.286 'About a year after' *Canadian Statesman*, 1990/Mrs N Allin
/Website: clinical.chestpaincentres.org

p.286 'Asked about his' *Toronto Daily Star*, 1962

p.287 'He received further unexpected publicity' *Ontario Track Monthly/Canadian Statesman*, 1963

p.287 'Shortly after his 84th' *Toronto Telegram*, 1963

p.287 'Shrubb had indeed beaten' *Toronto Telegram*, 1964

p.288 'Peter Lovesey wrote' *Athletics Weekly*, 1964

p.288 'The SLH Gazette, edited' SLH Gazette, 1964

p.289 'Robbie Brightwell' *Athletics Weekly*, 1964

p.289 'In the West Sussex' *West Sussex County Times*, 1964

p.289 'In Bowmanville' *Canadian Statesman*, 1964

p.290 'Ewan Shinton, sports' *West Sussex County Times*, 1990

p.291 'A few years later the former' Don G Taylor